W9-COX-353

Historical Dictionaries of Literature and the Arts
Jon Woronoff, Series Editor

Historical Dictionary of Architecture

Allison Lee Palmer

Historical Dictionaries of
Literature and the Arts, No. 29

The Scarecrow Press, Inc.
Lanham, Maryland • Toronto • Plymouth, UK
2008

SCARECROW PRESS, INC.

Published in the United States of America
by Scarecrow Press, Inc.
A wholly owned subsidiary of
The Rowman & Littlefield Publishing Group, Inc.
4501 Forbes Boulevard, Suite 200, Lanham, Maryland 20706
www.scarecrowpress.com

Estover Road
Plymouth PL6 7PY
United Kingdom

British Library Cataloguing in Publication Information Available

Library of Congress Cataloging-in-Publication Data

Palmer, Allison Lee, 1963–
   Historical dictionary of architecture / Allison Lee Palmer.
      p. cm. — (Historical dictionaries of literature and the arts ; no. 29)
   Includes bibliographical references.
   ISBN-13: 978-0-8108-5821-3 (cloth : alk. paper)
   ISBN-10: 0-8108-5821-5 (cloth : alk. paper)
   eISBN-13: 978-0-8108-6283-8
   eISBN-10: 0-8108-6283-2
   1. Architecture—History—Dictionaries. I. Title.
   NA200.P35 2008
   720.9—dc22   008013926

∞™ The paper used in this publication meets the minimum requirements of
American National Standard for Information Sciences—Permanence of Paper
for Printed Library Materials, ANSI/NISO Z39.48-1992.
Manufactured in the United States of America.

To my father, Melvin Delmar Palmer

Contents

Illustrations

Note: Photographs appear in the center of the book.

Editor's Foreword

Architecture is unquestionably one of the arts, and certainly not a lesser one, but dealing with it purely as an art would be very incomplete. For, more than other arts, it depends heavily on technology as concerns materials used, construction techniques, and new technological possibilities in other fields. There is also a commercial aspect, as cost matters in many—if not quite all—cases. Meanwhile, broader trends in society and politics impinge on just what will be built, while aesthetic currents and even fads determine what style will be adopted. Thus a multifaceted approach is essential, one that is applied here and makes this historical dictionary particularly useful. This being said, it starts at the beginning, with Ancient Egyptian, Near Eastern, Greek and Roman architecture, and others, does not forget the middle with the Gothic, Renaissance, Baroque, and Rococo, and again others, and goes right up to Post-Modernist and High-Tech architecture and, yet again, others. While much of the coverage is "western," other areas are not forgotten, such as China, India, Japan, or Mesoamerica and, for the last time, others. So it covers all the historical periods from the oldest to the most recent and all the major regions of the world.

This makes the *Historical Dictionary of Architecture* a welcome addition to the pool of information on the subject even in this age of the Internet when so much can be found on the Web. However, unlike the Web, this is all written by one person who has gone out of her way to integrate the material, so that one dictionary entry relates to another, and there are few gaps and little duplication. This is most obvious from the extensive dictionary section, which covers the periods and styles mentioned above, and the various regions, and also has entries on notable architects, landmark buildings, technical terms, and various building materials. The progression over time and to some extent geographically can be traced in the chronology, which also refers readers to specific entries. Meanwhile, the introduction puts architecture in its broader context, and is worthwhile reading in its own right but also as a preliminary to looking up dictionary entries. The bibliography then directs readers to other sources of literature on the topic and even to some websites where further information can be found.

This book was written by Allison Lee Palmer, who is an associate professor of art history at the University of Oklahoma, a place where architecture is particularly appreciated. There she teaches in the School of Art, giving courses on Renaissance art through the art of the 18th century. Obviously she has a specialization, which is Renaissance and Baroque art, on which she has written extensively. This is quite normal for an academic. What is less so is that she has such a broad view of architecture that in this book she can cover the whole field competently, a less common achievement in this age of academic specialization. There is no doubt that an awful lot of work went into writing this historical dictionary, and there is also no doubt that it fills an important gap in this series on Literature and the Arts. It will serve as an unusually helpful and handy guide to many students, teachers, and the general public with an interest in one of the more unique arts.

Jon Woronoff
Series Editor

Preface

The entries in this encyclopedia include architectural developments, major structures, primary materials, and noted architects. By developments, I mean historical eras like the Renaissance, for example, or movements such as Art Deco. Structures include not only major achievements such as the Alhambra, but also diverse architectural inventions including the arch and the skyscraper. Materials discussed range from concrete to stone, and glass to wood. Noted architects include theorists from the Ancient Roman engineer Vitruvius to many current architects like Zaha Hadid and Santiago Calatrava. Nevertheless, this volume is neither a history of architecture nor a comprehensive cataloging of movements, architects, and their creations. Like other encyclopedias, the organization here is alphabetical. However, unlike encyclopedias that aim to include more comprehensive but less detailed information, I have tried to provide more substantial commentary in fewer entries. I have especially aimed to make the historical entries capable of standing alone and, if taken all together, of providing a sufficient history of architecture for the general reader. I realize that my method overlooks a number of extremely gifted artists and outstanding structures. In lieu of comprehensiveness, however, I trust that the contexts provided in this book will enable the reader not only to identify and examine those aspects of architecture that lie outside this volume but also to find a richer appreciation of the basic human urge to build both functional and beautiful structures.

Acknowledgments

I would like to thank my father, Melvin Delmar Palmer, for his work in editing my manuscript through several stages of its writing. His careful reading took most of the summer of 2007, and his personal knowledge of these sites ensured a careful and critical reading of the architectural descriptions presented in this volume. My series editor, Jon Woronoff, also provided excellent suggestions for additional buildings and entries that improved my text. In addition, I am very grateful to both my parents for giving me the opportunity to travel so extensively throughout my childhood. Having seen the majority of these buildings firsthand certainly influenced my decision to focus my studies on the history of architecture. I would also like to thank my mother, Nancy Lee Palmer, for supplying some of the photographs published in this volume. Dawn St. Clare, who received her M.A. in art history at the University of Oklahoma, also provided me with photographs from her collection of images, and her work in assembling the photographs for this publication has been invaluable.

Chronology

While the dictionary itself provides an alphabetized presentation of entries, this chronology gives a framework of architectural developments over time. Under each heading, the dictionary's references to architects, buildings, and relevant styles are listed in historical order. The concluding topic, Structures and Materials, lists architects and buildings that illustrate the use of common architectural materials. (Bold italic type indicates that the item has its own entry in the dictionary.)

ANCIENT ARCHITECTURE (EUROPE, NEAR EAST, NORTH AFRICA) (15,000 BC–AD 400s)

Prehistoric Architecture (Paleolithic and Neolithic)

c. 15,000 BC	Mammoth-bone house, Mezhirich, Ukraine (Paleolithic)
c. 6500 BC	Çatal Hüyük, village, Turkey (Neolithic)
c. 3100 BC	Skara Brae, village, Orkney Islands, Scotland (Neolithic)
c. 3100–1500 BC	*Stonehenge*, Salisbury Plain, Wiltshire, England (Neolithic)
c. 3000–2500 BC	Newgrange, tombs, Ireland (Neolithic)

Ancient Near Eastern Architecture (Sumerian, Mari, Babylonian, Assyrian, Persian)

c. 7200 BC	Ain Ghazal, Jordan (Neolithic)
c. 7000 BC	Jericho, walls of the city (Neolithic)
c. 6500 BC	Çatal Hüyük, Turkey (Neolithic)

c. 2100 BC	Nanna Ziggurat, Ur, Iraq (Sumerian)
2000s BC	Palace of Zimrilim, Syria (Mari)
late 900s BC–AD 70	*Temple of Solomon*, Jerusalem (Jewish)
c. 720 BC	Citadel of Sargon II, modern-day Khorsabad, Iraq (Assyrian)
c. 575 BC	Ishtar Gate and throne room (Neo-Babylonian)
c. 518–460 BC	Palace of Darius at Persepolis, Iran (Persian)

Ancient Egyptian Architecture

c. 2665 BC	King Djoser's funerary complex, Saqqara
c. 2589–2503 BC	*Pyramids of Giza, Egypt*
c. 2100 BC	Model from Tomb of Meketra, Thebes
1473–1458 BC	Temple of Queen Hatshepsut, Deir el-Bahri
c. 1295–1186 BC	Great Temple of Amun, Karnak
c. 1279 BC	Temple of Amun, Mut and Khonsu, Luxor
c. 1279 BC	Temple of Rameses II and Temple of Nefertari, Abu Simbel

Ancient Aegean Architecture (Minoan and Mycenaean)

c. 1900–1400 BC	Palace at Knossos, Crete (Minoan)
c. 1600–1200 BC	Citadel at Mycenae, Greece (Mycenaean)
c. 1300 BC	Citadel at Tiryns, Greece (Mycenaean)

Ancient Greek Architecture

c. 550 BC	Temple of Hera I, Paestum, Italy
c. 530 BC	Treasury of the Siphnians, Delphi
500s BC	Sanctuary of Apollo, Delphi
mid-400s BC	*Acropolis, Athens*
c. 400 BC	Athenian Agora, Athens
c. 400 BC	Temple of Athena Pronaia, Delphi
300s BC	Miletos, city plan, modern-day Turkey
c. 200 BC	Theater at Epidauros
AD 132	Temple of the Olympian Zeus, Athens

Etruscan Architecture

480 BC	Tomb of the Lioness, Tarquinia
200s BC	Tomb of the Reliefs, Cerveteri
c. 100s BC	Porta Augusta, Perugia

Ancient Roman Architecture

late 100s BC	Pont du Gard, Nîmes, France
late 100s BC	Temple of Portunus, Rome
13 BC	Ara Pacis, Rome
AD 72–80	*Colosseum, Rome*
AD 79	Pompeii, city plan
AD 81	Arch of Titus, Rome
AD 100s	Timgad, Algeria
AD 113	Basilica Ulpia, Rome
AD 113	Column of Trajan, Rome
c. AD 125	Hadrian's Villa, Tivoli
AD 118–125	*Pantheon, Rome*
AD 200s	Hadrian's Wall, Great Britain
AD 211	Baths of Caracalla, Rome
AD 300s	Roman Forum, Rome
AD 310	Basilica of Maxentius and Constantine, Rome
AD 315	Arch of Constantine, Rome

Vitruvius Pollio, Marcus (c. 80–25 BC)

Early Semitic and Christian Architecture

AD 240s	House-Church, Dura-Europos, Syria
AD 320s	*Saint Peter's Church, Rome*
AD 350s	Santa Costanza, Rome

AD 420s   Santa Sabina, Rome
AD 425   Mausoleum of Galla Placidia, Ravenna

ARCHITECTURE OF ASIA

Indian Architecture (and Pakistan,
Afghanistan, Nepal, Bangladesh, Sri Lanka)

c. 2600 BC   Mohenjo-Daro
200s BC   Ajanta Caves, Deccan
200s–100s BC   Great Stupa, Sanchi
100s BC   Rock-Cut Hall of Karla
c. AD 530   Vishnu Temple at Deogarh
c. 1000   Kandariya Mahadeva Temple, Khajuraho,
                   Madhya Pradesh, India
c. 1000   Rajarajeshvara Temple to Shiva, Thanjavur,
                   Tamil Nadu, India
1057–1287   Bagan, temple complex, Myanmar
1632–1648   *Taj Mahal, Agra*, Mughal Empire

Chinese Architecture

AD 618–907   Chang'an, Capital of Tang Dynasty
AD 645   Great Wild Goose Pagoda at Ci'en Temple,
                   Xi'an, Shanxi Province, Tang Dynasty (rebuilt
                   700s)
AD 782   Nanchan Temple, Wutaishan, Shanxi Province.
                   Tang Dynasty
1368–1644   *Forbidden City, Beijing*, Ming Dynasty

Foster, Norman (1935–): 1986, Hongkong and Shanghai Bank, Hong
   Kong
Pei, I. M. (1917–): 1980s, Bank of China, Hong Kong
Skidmore, Owings & Merrill: 1998, Jin Mao Building, Shanghai

Japanese Architecture

early AD 100s   Ise, Inner Shrine, Mie Prefecture, Yayoi Period
                   (rebuilt 1993)

600s	Horyu-ji, Main Compound, Nara Prefecture, Asuka Period
c. 1053	Byodo-in, Uji, Kyoto Prefecture, Heian Period
early 1600s	*Katsura Palace, Kyoto*, by Kobori Enshu
1600s	Himeji Castle, Hyogo, near Osaka, Momoyama Period

Tange, Kenzo (1913–2005): 1964, Yoyogi Gymnasium, Tokyo Olympics
Ando, Tadao (1941–): 1976, Azuma House, Osaka; 1988, Church on the Water, Tomamu; 1989, Church of the Light, Ibaraki-shi, Osaka
Ito, Toyo (1941–): 1984, Silver Hut, Tokyo

Southeast Asian Architecture (Myanmar [Burma], Malaysia, Singapore, Indonesia, Thailand, Taiwan, Laos, Cambodia, Vietnam, etc.). See Indian Architecture

| 1100s | *Angkor, Cambodia*, begun |

PRE-COLUMBIAN ARCHITECTURE OF THE AMERICAS (900s BC–AD 1500s)

Mesoamerican Architecture (Aztec, Inca, Maya, Olmec, Teotihuacan, Zapotec)

c. 900–600 BC	La Venta, Great Pyramid and Ballcourt, Mexico (Olmec)
c. 500 BC	Teotihuacan, ceremonial center, Mexico
AD 400s–700s	Tikal ceremonial center, Guatemala (Maya)
800s–1200s	Chichen Itza, Yucatan, Mexico (Maya)
1200s–1500s	Tenochtitlan, Great Pyramid, Mexico City (Aztec)
1450–1530	*Machu Picchu, Peru*

Native American Architecture (North and South America)

| 900s–1400s | Anasazi "Great Houses," New Mexico, Utah, Arizona, and Colorado |
| 900s–1400s | Chaco Canyon, New Mexico |

c. 1150   Cahokia, East St. Louis, Missouri
1450s   Pueblos at Taos, New Mexico

MEDIEVAL ARCHITECTURE (400s–1300s)

Byzantine Architecture

530s   Hagia Sophia, by Anthemius of Tralles and
                          Isidorus of Miletus, Istanbul
AD 546   San Vitale, Ravenna, Italy
early 1000s   Monastery of Hosios Loukas, near Stiris,
                          Greece
c. 1017   Cathedral of Santa Sophia, Kiev, Ukraine
1063   Cathedral of San Marco, Venice, Italy

Islamic Architecture (Moorish, Mughal, Ottoman, Seljuk)

692   Dome of the Rock, Jerusalem, begun
740s   Mshatta Palace, Jordan, begun
785   Great Mosque, Cordoba, Spain
847   Great Mosque, Samarra
1350s   *Alhambra, Granada*, Spain
1570s   Sinan, Selimiye Mosque, Edirne, Turkey
1632–1648   *Taj Mahal, Agra*, India (Mughal Empire)
1980s   King Faisal Mosque, Islamabad, Pakistan
1986–1993   King Hassan II Mosque, Casablanca, Morocco

Sinan, Mimar Koca Agha (1489–1588): 1550s, Süleyman Mosque,
Istanbul

Early Medieval Architecture (Carolingian and Ottonian)

529   *Monastery* of Montecassino, Italy
late 600s   Santa Maria de Quintanilla de las Viñas, Bur-
                          gos, Spain
792–805   Palace Complex of Charlemagne, Aachen, Ger-
                          many (Carolingian)

799	Abbey Church of St. Riquier, Monastery of Centula, France (Carolingian), dedicated
c. 817	Saint Gall Monastery (Carolingian)
961	Church of Saint Cyriakus, Gernrode, Germany (Ottonian), begun
1001–1032	Church of Saint Michael, Hildesheim, Germany (Ottonian)

Romanesque Architecture; see also Castle

1030s	Krak des Chevaliers, Syria, begun
1060s	*Pisa Cathedral Complex, Italy*
c. 1060s	Saint-Étienne, Caen, Normandy, France
c. 1075–1100s	*Durham Castle and Cathedral*, England
1078	Tower of London, London, begun
1078–1122	Cathedral of Saint James, Santiago de Compostela, Spain
1080	Sant'Ambrogio, Milan
1130s	Saint-Lazare, Autun
1130s	Cathedral of Saint-Lazare, Autun, begun
1240s	Castel del Monte, region of Puglia

Gothic Architecture

c. 1130s	Chartres Cathedral, Chartres, France
1160s	*Notre Dame, Paris*
1211	Reims Cathedral, Reims, France, begun
1240s	Sainte-Chapelle, Paris, France
1240s	Cologne Cathedral, Cologne, Germany
1250s	Amiens Cathedral, Amiens, France
1300s	Milan Cathedral, Milan, Italy

PRE-MODERN ARCHITECTURE IN EUROPE (1400s–1700s)

Renaissance Architecture

| 1290s | *Florence Cathedral, Italy*, begun |
| 1290s | Palazzo della Signoria, Florence, 1290s |

1505	*Saint Peter's Church, Rome*, begun
1520s	*Fontainebleau, France*, begun
1530s–2000s	*Louvre, Paris*
1559	*Escorial, Madrid*, begun

Brunelleschi, Filippo (c. 1377–1446): 1420s, Florence Cathedral Dome, Italy; 1420s, Ospedale degli Innocenti (Foundling Hospital), Florence; 1420s, San Lorenzo, Florence; 1430s, Santo Spirito, Florence; 1430s, Pazzi Chapel, Florence

Michelozzo di Bartolomeo (1391– c. 1472): 1440s, Medici Palace, Florence

Alberti, Leon Battista (1404–1472): 1450s, Tempio Malatestiano, Rimini; 1470, Sant'Andrea, Mantua

Sangallo, Giuliano da (c. 1443–1516): 1480s, Villa Medici at Poggio a Caiano, outside Florence; 1485, Santa Maria delle Carceri, Prato, Italy

Bramante, Donato (1444–1514): 1501, Tempietto; 1505–1513, *Saint Peter's Church, Rome*

Serlio, Sebastiano (1475–1554)

Michelangelo Buonarroti (1475–1564): 1520s, façade, San Lorenzo, Florence; 1530s–1540s, Capitoline Hill, Rome; 1530s–1560s, *Saint Peter's Church, Rome*

Raphael Sanzio (1483–1520): 1510s, Villa Madama, Rome

Sangallo, Antonio da the Younger (1484–1546): 1530s, Farnese Palace, Rome

Sansovino, Jacopo (1486–1570): 1520s, Library, Venice

Palladio, Andrea (1508–1580): 1560s, Villa Rotunda; Vicenza, Italy; 1560s–1570s, San Giorgio Maggiore, Venice, 1560s–1570s; 1580–1585, Teatro Olimpico (with Vincenzo Scamozzi), Vicenza

Mannerism

Michelangelo Buonarroti (1475–1564): 1520s, Laurentian Stairs, Florence; 1520s, New Sacristy, San Lorenzo, Florence

Peruzzi, Baldassare (1481–1537): 1534, Palazzo Massimo alle Colonne, Rome

Romano, Giulio (c. 1499–1546): 1520s, Palazzo del Tè, Mantua

Tudor Style

early 1500s	Arden House, Stratford-Upon-Avon
1515–1521	Hampton Court Palace, London

Baroque Architecture

1505–1650s	**Saint Peter's Church, Rome**
1620s–1650s	Piazza Navona papal enclave, Rome, 1620s–1650s
1660s	**Versailles Palace, France**, by François Mansart (1598–1666), Louis Le Vau (1612–1670), and Jules Hardouin-Mansart, Versailles, France

Jones, Inigo (1573–1652): 1620s, Banqueting House, Whitehall Palace, London

Campen, Jacob van (1595–1657): 1633 (with Pieter Post), The Maurit-shuis, The Hague; 1648–1655, Town Hall, Amsterdam

Cortona, Pietro da (1596–1669): 1650s, Santa Maria della Pace, Rome

Bernini, Gian Lorenzo (1598–1680): 1650s, Sant'Andrea al Quirinale, Rome

Borromini, Francesco (1599–1667): 1630s–1665, San Carlo alle Quattro Fontane, Rome: 1640s, Sant'Ivo alla Sapienza, Rome

Rainaldi, Carlo (1611–1691): 1660s, Twin Churches at Piazza del Popolo, Rome

Wren, Christopher (1632–1723): 1675–1710, St. Paul's Cathedral, London

Vanbrugh, John (1664–1726): 1705, Blenheim Palace, Woodstock, England

Rococo Architecture

Fischer von Erlach, Johann Bernhard (1656–1723): 1696, Schönbrunn Palace, Vienna

Prandtauer, Jakob (1660–1726): 1702–1736, Benedictine Monastery Church, Melk, Austria

Boffrand, Germain (1667–1754): 1732, Salon de la Princesse, Hôtel de Soubise, Paris

Ribera, Pedro de (c. 1681–1742): 1720s, Hospicio de San Fernando, Madrid

Neumann, Johann Balthasar (1687–1753): 1719–1744, Residenz, Würzburg, Bavaria, Germany; 1743, Vierzehnheiligen, Staffelstein, Germany

Cuvilliés, François (1695–1768): 1730s, Amalienburg Pavilion, Munich

Rastrelli, Francesco Bartolomeo (1700–1771): 1749–1754, Church of Saint Andrew, Kiev; 1752–1756, Catherine Palace, Tsarskoye Selo, outside St. Petersburg; 1754–1762, Winter Palace, St. Petersburg

Neo-Classical Architecture; also see below
under Architecture of the United States

Gibbs, James (1682–1754): 1722–1726, Saint Martin-in-the-Fields, London; 1739–1749, Radcliffe Camera, Oxford

Boyle, Richard (Lord Burlington) (1695–1753): 1720s, Chiswick House, West London

Wood, John the Elder (c. 1704–1754): 1750s, The Circus, Bath, England

Soufflot, Jacques-Germain (1713–1780): 1755–1792, Sainte-Geneviève (Panthéon), Paris

Adam, Robert (1728–1792): 1759, Kedelston Hall, Derbyshire, commissioned; 1760s, Syon House, Middlesex, England; 1770s, Osterley Park, Middlesex, England

Ledoux, Claude-Nicolas (1736–1806): 1770s, Chaux city plan, France

Boullée, Étienne-Louis (1728–1799): 1780s, funerary monument for Isaac Newton

Schinkel, Karl Friedrich (1781–1841): 1822, Altes Museum, Berlin

19th-CENTURY ARCHITECTURE IN EUROPE

Gothic Revival Architecture; see also *Romantic Architecture;*
also see below under Architecture of the United States

Walpole, Horace (1717–1797): 1749, Strawberry Hill, Twickenham, England

Barry, Charles (1795–1860): 1830–1860s, Houses of Parliament, London

Scott, George Gilbert (1811–1878): 1865, Saint Pancras Railway Station, London

Pugin, Augustus Welby Northmore (1812–1852): 1830s, Houses of Parliament, London

Romantic Architecture; see also *Gothic Revival Architecture;*
also see below under Architecture of the United States

1890s–1940s   Cotswold Cottage; *see Tudor Revival Style*

Nash, John (1752–1835): 1815–1832, Royal Pavilion, Brighton, England

Beaux-Arts Architecture; **also see below**
under Architecture of the United States

Garnier, Charles (1825–1898): 1860s, Opéra, Paris

Art Nouveau

Gaudí, Antoni (1852–1926): 1880s, Palau Güell, Barcelona; 1880s, Sagrada Familia, Barcelona; 1905, Casa Mila, Barcelona

Horta, Victor (1861–1947): 1892, Tassel House, Brussels

Olbrich, Joseph Maria (1867–1908): 1896, Secession House, Vienna

Guimard, Hector (1867–1942): 1899–1905, Paris Metropolitan stations

Hoffmann, Josef (1870–1956): 1904, Purkersdorf Sanatorium, Vienna; 1904–1911, Stoclet Palace, Brussels

Arts and Crafts; **also** *see below* **under**
Architecture of the United States

Mackintosh, Charles Rennie (1868–1928): 1893–1895, Glasgow Herald Building, Glasgow, Scotland; 1897–1909, Glasgow School of Art, Glasgow, Scotland; 1902–1904, Hill House, Helensburgh, Scotland

EARLY-20th-CENTURY ARCHITECTURE
IN EUROPE, ASIA, AND SOUTH AMERICA

Expressionism; also see below under
Architecture of the United States

Taut, Bruno (1880–1938): 1912, Falkenberg Housing Estate, Berlin; 1914, Glass Pavilion, Cologne Werkbund Exhibition
Mendelsohn, Erich (1887–1953): 1917, Einstein Tower, Potsdam
Corbusier, Le (1887–1965): 1950s, Notre Dame du Haut, Ronchamp

Bauhaus Architecture; see also International Style

Gropius, Walter (1883–1969): 1925, Bauhaus Building, Dessau, Germany
Mies van der Rohe, Ludwig (1886–1969): 1929, German Pavilion, Barcelona

Futurist Architecture; see also Constructivist Architecture

Sant'Elia, Antonio (1888–1916): 1914, *Città Nuova*

International Style; also see below under
Architecture of the United States

Berlage, Hendrick Petrus (1856–1934): 1896–1903, Amsterdam Stock Exchange, Amsterdam
Behrens, Peter (1868–1940): 1909, AEG Turbine Factory, Berlin
Loos, Adolf (1870–1933): 1910, Steiner House, Vienna; 1926, Tristan Tzara House, Paris; 1927, Moller House, Vienna; 1928–1930, Villa Müller, Prague
Gropius, Walter (1883–1969), and Adolf Meyer: 1911, Fagus Shoe Factory, Alfeld an der Leine, Germany
Asplund, Erik Gunnar (1885–1940): 1915, Woodland Cemetery, Stockholm, Sweden; 1920s, City Library, Stockholm, Sweden
Corbusier, Le (1887–1965): 1929, Villa Savoye, Poissy-sur-Seine, France; 1946–1952, Unité d'Habitation, Marseilles, France; 1950s, Chandigarh, India, city layout

Aalto, Alvar (1898–1976): 1935, Viipuir Library, Vyborg, Finland; 1938–1939, Villa Mairea, Noormarkku, Finland
Breuer, Marcel (1902–1981): 1953, UNESCO World Headquarters, Paris
Tange, Kenzo (1913–2005): 1949, Hiroshima Peace Memorial Park and Museum; 1964 (Olympics) National Gymnasium Complex, Yoyogi Park, Tokyo
Niemeyer, Oscar (1907–): 1960s, Palace of the National Congress and Cathedral, Brasilia

Constructivist Architecture; see also Futurist Architecture

Golosov, Ilya (1883–1945): 1926–1928, Zuev Worker's Club, Moscow
Tatlin, Vladimir (1885–1953): 1919, design for "Tatlin's Tower" (never built)
Melnikov, Konstantin Stepanovich (1890–1974): 1925, Soviet Pavilion, World's Exposition, Paris; 1927–1929, Architect's House, Moscow; 1927–1929, Kauchuk Factory Club, Moscow; 1927–1929, Rusakov Worker's Club, Moscow
Ginsburg, Moisei (1892–1946): 1928–1932, Narkomfin Building, Moscow

Rationalism (and Neo-Rationalism)

Rietveld, Gerrit (1888–1964): 1924, Schroeder House, Utrecht, Netherlands
Terragni, Giuseppe (1904–1943): 1932–1936, Casa di Fascio, Como, Italy
Rossi, Aldo (1931–1997): 1980s, New Town Hall, Borgoricco, Italy

Brutalism; also see below under Post-Modernism and Beyond

Perret, Auguste (1874–1954): 1903–1904, 25 bis Rue Franklin apartments, Paris; 1922–1924, Church of Notre Dame du Raincy
Corbusier, Le (1887–1965): 1946–1952, Unité d'Habitation, Marseilles

ARCHITECTURE OF THE UNITED STATES (1600s–1960s)

Colonial Architecture (1620–1820s)

1680s	Paul Revere House, Boston, Massachusetts
1683	Parson Capen House, Topsfield, Massachusetts
1700s	Turner-Ingersall House, Salem, Massachusetts

Georgian Style (1690–1790)

Neo-Classical Architecture (1720s–1860s)

1803   *United States Capitol, Washington, D.C.*, begun

Jefferson, Thomas (1743–1826): 1770s, Monticello, Charlottesville, Virginia
Bulfinch, Charles (1763–1844): 1796, Old State House, Hartford, Connecticut
Latrobe, Benjamin Henry (1764–1820): 1801, Bank of Pennsylvania

Gothic Revival Architecture (1760s–1840s)

Upjohn, Richard (1802–1878): 1840s, Trinity Church, New York

Federal Style (1783–1830)

Bulfinch, Charles (1763–1844): 1796, Old State House, Hartford, Connecticut; 1798, Massachusetts State House, Boston, begun

Greek Revival Style (1820–1870); see Romantic Architecture

Romantic Architecture (1830s–1870s); see also Gothic Revival Architecture

Hunt, Richard Morris (1827–1895): 1890s, Vanderbilt Mansion, Newport, Rhode Island

Italianate Style (1840–1890s); *see Romantic Architecture*

Second Empire Style (1855–1885); *see Victorian Architecture*

Stick Style (1860–1890); *see Victorian Architecture*

Victorian Architecture (1860–1900)

Richardson, Henry Hobson (1838–1886): 1880s, Stoughton House, Cambridge, Massachusetts

Eastlake Style (1870–1890); *see Victorian Architecture*

Richardsonian Romanesque (1870s–1900)

Richardson, Henry Hobson (1838–1886): 1870s, Trinity Church, Boston; 1885–1887, Marshall Field Warehouse, Chicago

Shingle Style (1870s–1900); *see Victorian Architecture*

Queen Anne Style (1870s–1910); *see Victorian Architecture*

Mission Style (1890–1915); *see Arts and Crafts*

Beaux-Arts Architecture (1890s–1920s)

Hunt, Richard Morris (1827–1895): 1890s, Biltmore Estate, Asheville, North Carolina; 1890s, Vanderbilt Mansion, "The Breakers," Newport, Rhode Island; 1893, World's Columbian Exposition, Chicago; 1895, Metropolitan Museum of Art, New York

McKim, Charles Follen (1847–1909), William Rutherford Mead (1846–1928), and Stanford White (1853–1906): 1887–1895, Boston Public Library; 1895–1903, Rhode Island State Capitol, Providence;

1906, Morgan Library, New York; 1910, Pennsylvania Station, New York
Carrère, John (1858–1911) and Thomas Hastings (1860–1929): 1897–1911, New York Public Library, New York
Wetmore, Charles (1866–1941) and Whitney Warren (1864–1943): 1903, Grand Central Station, New York

Arts and Crafts (Bungalow, Craftsman) (1890s–1930s)

Greene, Charles Sumner (1868–1957) and Henry Mather Greene (1870–1954): 1908, Gamble House, Pasadena, California

Tudor Style (1890–1940)

Colonial Revival (1890s–2000s); see Colonial Architecture

American Foursquare (1895–1930s)

Prairie Style (1900–1920s)

Wright, Frank Lloyd (1867–1959) and Marion Mahony Griffin (1871–1961): 1906–1909, Frederick C. Robie House, Chicago

Expressionism (and Blobitecture) (1910s–1950s)

Aalto, Alvar (1898–1976): 1947–1949, Baker House, MIT, Boston; 1959, Opera House, Essen, Germany
Goff, Bruce (1904–1982): 1947, Ledbetter House, Norman, Oklahoma; 1950s, Bavinger House, Norman, Oklahoma
Wright, Frank Lloyd (1867–1959): 1940s–1950s, Solomon Guggenheim Museum, New York
Saarinen, Eero (1910–1961): 1956–1962, Trans World Airport Terminal, New York

Art Deco (1920s–1930s)

Hood, Raymond (1881–1934) and John Mead Howells (1868–1959): 1924, Chicago Tribune Tower, Chicago

Hood, Raymond (1881–1934): 1929, New York Daily News Building, New York; 1930s, Radio City Music Hall, Rockefeller Center, New York

Alen, William Van (1883–1954): 1930, Chrysler Building, New York

Shreve, Lamb and Harmon: 1931, Empire State Building, New York

International Style (and Modernism) (1920s–1960s)

Saarinen, Eliel (1873–1950): 1942, First Christian Church, Columbus, Indiana

Gropius, Walter (1883–1969): 1937, Architect's House, Lincoln, Massachusetts

Howe, George (1886–1955) and William Lescaze (1896–1969): 1931, Philadelphia Savings Fund Society Building (PSFS), Philadelphia

Breuer, Marcel (1902–1981): 1938, Breuer House I, Lincoln, Massachusetts; 1945, Geller House, Lawrence, Long Island; 1948, Breuer House II, New Canaan, Connecticut

Mies van der Rohe, Ludwig (1886–1969): 1946, Farnsworth House, Plano, Illinois; 1951, 860–880 Lake Shore Drive, Chicago; 1954, with *Philip Johnson*, Seagram Building, New York

Neutra, Richard (1892–1970): 1946, Kaufman House, Palm Springs, California

Johnson, Philip (1906–2005): 1949, "Glass House," New Canaan, Connecticut; 1978–1983, AT&T Corporate Headquarters, New York

Kahn, Louis (1901–1974): 1950s, Yale University Art Gallery, New Haven, Connecticut; 1967–1972, Kimbell Art Museum, Fort Worth, Texas

Niemeyer, Oscar (1907–): 1952, with *Le Corbusier*, United Nations Headquarters, New York; 1960s

Saarinen, Eero (1910–1961): 1954, Irwin Union Bank, Columbus, Indiana

Pei, I. M. (1917–): 1968–1974, Christian Science Center, Boston; 1977, Hancock Tower, Boston

Skidmore, Owings & Merrill (Gordon Bunshaft): 1952, Lever House, New York

Ranch Style (1930–1970s)

Neutra, Richard (1892–1970): 1946, Kaufman House, Palm Springs, California

Usonian House (1930s–1960s)

Wright, Frank Lloyd (1867–1959): 1937, Edgar Kaufmann House, Mill Run, Pennsylvania

Tudor Revival Style (1950s–1970s)

POST-MODERNISM AND BEYOND (1960s–2000s)

Post-Modern Architecture (1960s–1990s)

Johnson, Philip (1906–2005) and John Burgee: 1978–1983, AT&T Headquarters, New York

Pei, I. M. (1917–): 2006, Suzhou Museum, Suzhou, China

Utzon, Jørn (1918–): 1959, Sydney Opera House, Sydney, Australia

Moore, Charles Willard (1925–1993): 1978, Piazza d'Italia, New Orleans

Venturi, Robert (1925–) and Denise Scott Brown (1931–): 1960s, Vanna Venturi House, Chestnut Hill, Pennsylvania; 1963, Guild House, Philadelphia; 1991, Seattle Art Museum, Seattle

Pelli, Cesar (1926–): 1977–1984, World Trade Center Financial Center, New York; 1986–1988, Wells Fargo Center, Minneapolis; 1990, Bank of America Corporate Headquarters, Charlotte, North Carolina; 1998, Petronas Twin Towers, Kuala Lumpur, Malaysia

Rossi, Aldo (1931–1997): 1980s, New Town Hall, Borgoricco, Italy

Graves, Michael (1934–): 1982, Portland Public Service Building, Portland, Oregon; 1990s, Dolphin Resort, Orlando, Florida

Safdie, Moshe (1938–): 1967, Habitat '67, 1967 World Exposition, Montreal

Brutalism (1960s–1980s)

Pei, I. M. (1917–): 1961–1967, National Center for Atmospheric Research, Boulder, Colorado; 1974–1978, East Wing of the National Gallery of Art, Washington, D.C.

Bunshaft, Gordon (1909–1990): 1974, Hirshhorn Museum, Washington, D.C.

Ando, Tadao (1941–): 1989, Church of the Light, Ibaraki-shi, Osaka

Neo-Rationalism (1980s–1990s): *See Rationalism*

Meier, Richard (1934–): 1995, Barcelona Museum of Contemporary Art; 1997, Getty Center, Los Angeles

Botta, Mario (1943–): 1999–2003, Kyobo Tower, Seoul, South Korea; 2003–2006, Church of Santo Volto, Turin

Deconstructivism (1980s–2000s)

Gehry, Frank (1929–): 1991–2003, Walt Disney Concert Hall, Los Angeles; 1993–1997, Guggenheim Museum, Bilbao, Spain

Eisenman, Peter (1932–): 1989, Wexner Center for the Arts, Ohio State University, Columbus, Ohio

Koolhaus, Rem (1944–): 2001–2005, Casa di Musica, Porto; 2004, Seattle Central Library

Tschumi, Bernard (1944–): 1999, Alfred Lerner Hall, Columbia University, New York

Libeskind, Daniel (1946–): 1999, Jewish Museum, Berlin; 2006, Frederic C. Hamilton Addition, Denver Art Museum, Denver, Colorado

Hadid, Zaha (1950–): 1989, Vitra Fire Station, Weil-am-Rhein, Germany

Coop Himmelb(l)au: 1993–1998, UFA-Palast, Dresden

Herzog and De Meuron Architekten: 2005, Walker Art Center Expansion, Minneapolis; 2005, M. H. de Young Museum, San Francisco

Critical Regionalism (1980s–2000s)

Barragán, Luis (1902–1988): 1934, Chapel in Tlalpan, outside Mexico City; 1958, with Mathias Goeritz, Ciudad Satélite, Mexico City

Ando, Tadao (1941–): 1976, Azuma House, Osaka; 1988, Church on the Water, Tomamu; 1989, Church of the Light, Ibaraki-shi, Osaka; 2002, Modern Art Museum, Fort Worth, Texas

El-Wakil, Abdul (1943–): 1975, Halawa House, Agami, Egypt

High-Tech Architecture (1980s–2000s)

Tange, Kenzo (1913–2005): 1980s, Akasaka Prince Hotel, Tokyo; 1996, Fuji Television Building, Tokyo

Erskine, Ralph (1914–2005): 1992, London Ark, London

Foster, Norman (1935–): 1986, Hongkong and Shanghai Bank, Hong Kong

Piano, Renzo (1937–) and Richard Rogers (1933–): 1970s, Pompidou Center, Paris

Libeskind, Daniel (1946–): 2002–2003, design for *World Trade Center, New York*

Calatrava, Santiago (1951–): 1992, Montjuic Communications Towers, Olympic Games, Barcelona; 2001, Quadracci Pavilion, Milwaukee Art Museum, Milwaukee, Wisconsin; 2001–2005, "Twisting Torso," Malmö, Sweden; 2007 (planning), Transportation Hub, World Trade Center, New York

Skidmore, Owings & Merrill: Fazlur Khan, 1969, John Hancock Center, Chicago; Fazlur Khan and Bruce Graham, 1970–1973, Sears Tower, Chicago; Adrian Smith, 2009, Burj Dubai, United Arab Emirates

Herzog and De Meuron Architekten: 2000, Tate Modern Art Museum renovation, London; 2002–2005, Allianz Arena, Munich, Germany

Green Architecture (1980s–2000s)

Wright, Frank Lloyd (1867–1959): 1935–1939, Fallingwater, Bear Run, Pennsylvania

Jones, E. Fay (1921–2004): 1980, Thorncrown Chapel, Eureka Springs, Arkansas

Piano, Renzo (1937–): 1991, Tjibaou Cultural Center, Nouméa, New Caledonia

Nouvel, Jean (1945–): 1994, Foundation Cartier, Paris

STRUCTURES AND MATERIALS

Brick

c. 7000 BC	Jericho (Ancient Near Eastern Architecture)
c. 6500 BC	Çatal Hüyük, western Turkey (Ancient Near Eastern Architecture)
c. 2600 BC	Mohenjo Daro, Indus Valley Civilization (Indian Architecture)
c. 2000 BC	Ziggurats, Sumerian (Ancient Near Eastern Architecture)
c. 575 BC	Ishtar Gate, Neo-Babylonian (Ancient Near Eastern Architecture)
AD 211	Baths of Caracalla, Rome (Ancient Roman)
AD 425	Galla Placidia Mausoleum, Ravenna (Early Christian Architecture)
AD 546	San Vitale, Ravenna (Byzantine)
1200s	Great Mosque of Djenné, Mali (Islamic Architecture)
1450s	Taos Pueblo, New Mexico (Native American Architecture)

Vitruvius Pollio, Marcus (c. 80–c. 25 BC) (Ancient Roman Architecture)
Brunelleschi, Filippo (c. 1377–1446): 1420s, Florence Cathedral dome (Renaissance Architecture)
Sullivan, Louis (1856–1924): 1891, Wainwright Building, St. Louis
Berlage, Hendrick Petrus (1856–1934): 1903, Amsterdam Stock Exchange
Wright, Frank Lloyd (1867–1959): 1906–1909, Frederick C. Robie House, Chicago
Gropius, Walter (1883–1969) and Adolf Meyer: 1911, Fagus Shoe Factory, Alfeld an der Leine, Germany
Aalto, Alvar (1898–1976): 1947–1949, Baker House, MIT, Boston
Venturi, Robert (1925–): 1963, Guild House, Philadelphia

Stone

c. 3100 BC	Skara Brae, village, Orkney Islands, Scotland (Prehistoric Architecture)

3100–1500 BC   *Stonehenge, England* (Prehistoric Architecture)

Post-and-Lintel

3100–1500 BC   *Stonehenge, England* (Prehistoric Architecture)

Column

c. 2665 BC   Funerary Complex of Djoser, Saqqara (Ancient Egyptian Architecture)

1295–1186 BC   Great Temple of Amun, Karnak (Ancient Egyptian Architecture)

c. 518–460 BC   Palace of Darius at Persepolis, Iran (Ancient Near Eastern Architecture)

447–438 BC   Parthenon, *Acropolis, Athens* (Ancient Greek Architecture)

c. 425 BC   Temple of Athena Nike, Acropolis, Athens (Ancient Greek Architecture)

Vitruvius Pollio, Marcus (c. 80–c. 25 BC)
Palladio, Andrea (1508–1580): 1560s, Villa Rotonda, Vicenza (Renaissance Architecture)
Bernini, Gian Lorenzo (1598–1680): 1650s, Saint Peter's piazza, Rome (Baroque Architecture)
Soufflot, Jacques-Germain (1713–1780): 1755–1792, Church of Sainte-Geneviève, Paris (Neo-Classical Architecture)
Latrobe, Benjamin (1764–1820): 1803–1820s, *United States Capitol, Washington, D.C.* (Neo-Classical Architecture)

Arch

c. 3100 BC   Skara Brae, village, Orkney Islands, Scotland (Prehistoric Architecture)

1250 BC   Lion Gate, Mycenae, Greece (Ancient Aegean Architecture)

late 100s BC   Pont du Gard, Nîmes, France (Ancient Roman Architecture)

AD 100s	Market of Trajan, Rome (Ancient Roman Architecture)
AD 211	Baths of Caracalla, Rome (Ancient Roman Architecture)
AD 310	Basilica of Maxentius and Constantine, Rome (Ancient Roman Architecture)
late 600s	Santa Maria de Quintanilla de las Viñas, Burgos, Spain (Early Medieval Architecture)
785	Great Mosque at Cordoba, Spain (Islamic Architecture)

Gaudí, Antoni (1852–1926): 1884, Cathedral of Sagrada Familia, Barcelona
Strauss, Joseph (1870–1938): 1937, Golden Gate Bridge, San Francisco
Saarinen, Eero (1910–1961): 1960s, St. Louis Gateway Arch, Missouri

Marble

mid-400s BC	*Acropolis, Athens* (Ancient Greek Architecture)
AD 118–125	*Pantheon, Rome* (Ancient Roman Architecture)
1200s	Abbey at Montecassino, Italy (Romanesque Architecture)
1632–1648	*Taj Mahal, Agra* (Indian Architecture)

Hunt, Richard Morris (1827–1895): 1888–1892, "Marble House," Newport, Rhode Island (Beaux-Arts Architecture)

Dome

AD 118–125	*Pantheon, Rome* (Ancient Roman Architecture)
1505–1650s	*Saint Peter's Church, Rome* (Renaissance Architecture)
2002	Oklahoma State Capitol, Oklahoma City

Brunelleschi, Filippo (c. 1377–1446): 1420s, Florence Cathedral dome (Renaissance Architecture)

Palladio, Andrea (1508–1580): 1560s, Villa Rotonda, Vicenza (Renaissance Architecture)
Boyle, Richard (1695–1753): 1720s, Chiswick House, West London (Neo-Classical Architecture)
Jefferson, Thomas (1743–1826): 1770s, Monticello, Charlottesville, Virginia (Neo-Classical Architecture)
Latrobe, Benjamin Henry (1764–1820): 1803, *United States Capitol, Washington, D.C.* begun (Neo-Classical Architecture)
Nervi, Pier Luigi (1891–1979): 1959, Palazzetto dello Sport, Rome
Fuller, Richard Buckminster (1895–1983): 1945, Dymaxion House, Henry Ford Museum, Dearborn, Michigan; 1960s, Geodesic Dome, Expo '67, Montreal
Rogers, Richard (1933–): 2000, Millennium Dome, London

Concrete

AD 118–125   *Pantheon, Rome* (Ancient Roman Architecture)

Wright, Frank Lloyd (1867–1959): 1930s, Kaufmann House, Mill Run, Pennsylvania
Perret, Auguste (1874–1954): 1903, Apartment at 25 bis Rue Franklin, Paris
Nervi, Pier Luigi (1891–1979): 1931, Stadio Artemia Franchi, Florence; 1959, Palazzetto dello Sport, Rome
Candela, Felix (1910–1997): 1958, Xochimilco Restaurant, Mexico City
Utzon, Jørn (1918–): 1973, Sydney Opera House, Sydney
Rogers, Richard (1933–) and Buro Happold: 2000, Millennium Dome, London

Wood

AD 711   Buddhist Shrine, Horyu-ji, Japan
1125–1150   Borgund Stave Church, Sogn, Norway
1368–1644   *Forbidden City* Complex, Beijing

Cast Iron

Darby, Abraham III (1750–1791): 1779, Severn River Bridge, Coalbrookdale, England
Paxton, Joseph (1801–1865): 1851, Crystal Palace, London Exhibition
Labrouste, Henri (1801–1875): 1840s, Reading Room, Bibliothèque Sainte-Geneviève, Paris
Garnier, Charles (1825–1898): 1860s, Opéra, Paris (Beaux-Arts Architecture)
Eiffel, Gustav (1832–1923): 1889, Eiffel Tower, Paris
Richardson, Henry Hobson (1838–1886): 1880s, Marshall Field Warehouse, Chicago

Glass

Paxton, Joseph (1801–1865): 1851, Crystal Palace, London Exhibition
Gropius, Walter (1883–1969): 1938, Architect's House, Lincoln, Massachusetts
Johnson, Philip (1906–2005): 1949, Glass House, New Canaan, Connecticut

Steel

Roebling, John Augustus (1806–1869) and Washington Augustus Roebling (1837–1926): 1860s–1880s, Brooklyn Bridge, New York
Burnham, Daniel (1846–1912): 1902, Flatiron Building, New York
Fuller, Richard Buckminster (1895–1983): 1967, Geodesic Dome, Expo '67, Montreal
Gehry, Frank (1929–): 1990s, Guggenheim Museum, Bilbao, Spain

Skyscraper

Jenney, William Le Baron (1832–1907): 1891, Leiter II Building, Chicago; 1891, Manhattan Building, Chicago
Richardson, Henry Hobson (1838–1886): 1880s, Marshall Field Warehouse, Chicago

Sullivan, Louis (1856–1924): 1891, Wainwright Building, St. Louis; 1899, Carson Pirie Scott Department Store, Chicago

Gilbert, Cass (1859–1934): early 1900s, Woolworth Building, New York

Wright, Frank Lloyd (1867–1959): 1952–1956, Price Tower, Bartlesville, Oklahoma

Alen, William van (1883–1954): 1930, Chrysler Building, New York

Howe, George (1886–1955) and William Lescaze (1896–1969): 1931, Philadelphia Savings Fund Society Building, Philadelphia

Johnson, Philip (1906–2005) and *Ludwig Mies van der Rohe* (1886–1969): 1950s, Seagram Building, New York

Yamasaki, Minoru (1912–1986): 1973, *World Trade Center, New York*

Pelli, Cesar (1926–): 1996, Petronas Twin Towers

Foster, Norman (1935–): 1986, Hongkong and Shanghai Bank, Hong Kong

Shreve, Lamb and Harmon: 1931, Empire State Building, New York

Skidmore, Owings & Merrill: 2009, Burj Dubai, United Arab Emirates

Introduction

Architecture, which can be understood in its most basic sense as a form of enclosure created with an aesthetic intent, first made its appearance in prehistoric times. From its earliest developments, architecture changed over time and in different cultures in response to changing cultural needs, aesthetic interests, materials, and techniques. The historical study of these structures, however, is a quite modern concept and results from a more reflective age. The earliest Paleolithic constructions were simple dwellings that could offer shelter from the elements of nature and from animals, and these structures soon came to define the family or community unit, its belief system, and its unique cultural characteristics. These structures were for domestic purposes and consisted of a type of circular hut centered on a fire pit and covered with branches or animal hides.

While the Upper Paleolithic era, which dates from 40,000 BC to around 8000 BC, has not been fully studied, excavations reveal relatively complex architectural structures from that early time. Interior spaces were divided into different functions sectioned off by multiple fire pits, and aesthetic intentions included decoratively carved bones for support and floors that were colored. Thus architecture, in its very origins, can be understood as both a functional and creative pursuit. Given the fact that glaciers covered much of Europe during this time, this cold region was populated by mammoths, reindeer, bison, wild goats, and bears, the bones and hides of which, together with wood, stone, and other materials found in nature, came to be used as building materials by these Cro-Magnon humans. Small-scale carved figures of humans and animals, as well as the famous cave paintings of southern France and northern Spain, are testament to the broad-based aesthetic culture that developed at this time.

As agriculture developed and animals were domesticated during the transition to Neolithic times, architecture began to reflect a less nomadic lifestyle. Architectural functions thus came to include storage space, pens for animals, and the cultivation of farmland and pastures surrounding the domestic structures. This era also reveals an increasingly sophisticated social structure demonstrated architecturally by the development of fortified villages. With the retreat of the ice across much of Europe, wood became more abundant as a building material for homes, and funerary and other types of ritualistic buildings began to appear. Domestic dwellings of this age are characterized either by a post-and-lintel structure with thatched roofs and walls made of woven branches covered with clay or mud, or by an early masonry construction.

The most famous domestic masonry structures from this time are found in the village of Skara Brae on the Orkney Islands in Scotland (around 3100 BC); they reveal some of the earliest corbelled walls, with stone hearth, bed, and storage enclosures filling the interiors. Corbelling is also found in the extremely sophisticated burial mounds from this era, which developed from the relatively simple dolmens to the megalithic tombs entered via a passageway of standing stones rising up into a corbel vault. The passage graves found in Newgrange, Ireland, from around 3000 BC are some of the best-known evidence of this type of ritualized funerary structure, while spirals, circles, and other carved images reveal both a symbolic and aesthetic intent. Solar alignments leading toward the inner burial shrines at Newgrange suggest that the ritualized religion seen in this funerary context, together with the civic identity implied in the organized construction practices of these complexes, were likely both conflated and well-defined by the Neolithic era. Although a full understanding of the belief systems of Neolithic people remains to be developed, menhir alignments and circles, carved and arranged with some degree of consistency, can be found across much of Europe at this time. Certainly these structures attest to a geographically broad populace that used architecture not only for protection against nature and animals, but also to demarcate cultural identity through the assertion of dominance over other peoples and with the commemoration of their deceased—that is, through both exclusion and inclusion.

It was not until the establishment of the Sumerian city-states, however, that architecture developed its monumental format, as shown by the famous description in the Epic of Gilgamesh of the city Uruk, located along the banks of the Euphrates River in ancient Mesopotamia. The Anu Ziggurat at Uruk (modern-day Warka, Iraq) dates to about 3100 BC and stands today as testament to the sophisticated social hierarchy and codified governmental and religious practices, along with the wealth and general stability that characterized Sumerian society. This stepped-pyramid, possibly dedicated to the sky god Anu, is symbolic of the sacred mountain of the gods and was topped by a temple and covered by painted clay mosaics. Built from the rubble of earlier structures, these massive pyramids were constructed on a rectangular ground plan with their corners oriented to the compass points. While some ziggurats could be entered at ground level to arrive at the altar rooms, storage spaces, and courtyards, other ziggurats were entered by sets of broad stairways that led directly to the roof temple.

Subsequent Mari, Babylonian, Assyrian, and Persian peoples in Mesopotamia continued to construct increasingly complex temples, palaces, fortresses, and monumental entryways, decorated with painted murals, painted and glazed clay mosaics, and limestone relief sculptures. Excavations along the Indus River Valley, most notably at Mohenjo Daro and Harappa in Pakistan, also reveal that around 2600 BC, well-organized city plans included straight streets, multistory housing made of some of the earliest fired brick, and sophisticated drainage systems. A palace complex at Mari in modern-day Syria, built for the Amorite king Zimrilim (ruled 1779–1757 BC), demonstrates the increased importance given to political structures that incorporated temples and ziggurats into larger urban complexes. Located about 250 miles north of Babylon, the city of Mari is described in ancient documents as containing noble private homes, paved roads lined with alabaster, a good sanitation system, and buildings created for an increasingly large number of complex, large-scale industries, including bronze foundries and shops. The palace, destroyed by Hammurabi, appears today only in fragments of wall murals located in the Louvre Museum in Paris; these fragments reveal scenes of the palace's famous gardens and courtyards. The main architectural compound of the Persian Empire was built in Persepolis by Darius and Xerxes in the sixth century BC. At its height, the Persian Empire not only absorbed most of the Mesopotamian world, but included parts of Anatolia and some of the Aegean islands. Anticipating the more famous Roman imperial organization, the Persian Empire under Darius I was characterized by an able and efficient organization of twenty regions maintained with a tribute system and with a general economic prosperity characterized by the monumental architectural structures that continually drove home the message of Achaemenidian superiority.

Ancient Egypt is best known for its monumental architecture, which symbolized the ideas of both power and permanence. From the great pyramids at Giza, outside Cairo, to the massive temple compounds located along the banks of the Nile River, this regional architecture consists of a complex religious structure focused on the preservation of the soul, called the "ka," after physical death. Permanent architectural structures, together with mummification and ancestor worship, ensured this form of immortality. Egyptians were described by the Ancient Greek historian Herodotus as extremely religious, and he further stated that no other country "possesses so many wonders, nor . . . has such a number of works which defy description" as Egypt does. Annual flooding along the Nile River provided a fertile soil that allowed for irrigation and agricultural prosperity, and in prehistoric times a large population began to settle into permanent communities along the river. Around 3000 BC these communities were forcefully unified under the ruler Menes, whose authority was unquestioned, divine, and therefore permanent.

Architecture symbolized this idea of permanence and stability through a consistency of design and a monumental form. The stepped-pyramid of the Third Dynastic ruler King Djoser, located in Saqqara and dated c. 2665 BC, is the earliest large-scale royal tomb in Egypt. While Mesopotamian ziggurats functioned as elevated tombs, this pyramid was a funerary monument that held the body and possessions of the deceased deep within the solid stone structure. A burial shaft leads through the pyramid down into the burial chamber, while a separate chapel and worship chamber could be accessed via a secret doorway into the pyramid wall. Enclosed by a tall limestone wall, the pyramid, temple, and royal pavilion are further enclosed with a series of fictive building fronts, courtyards, and false walls, while the pyramid itself has a false doorway, all in order to protect both the body and the rich possessions carried by the deceased into the afterlife. These are the complex funerary rituals that have fueled an interest in Egyptian architectural culture, from the era of Herodotus through the military campaign of Napoleon, when Egyptology became a widespread fascination that has endured to this day.

In the Aegean world, modern excavations carried out by Heinrich Schliemann and Arthur Evans brought to life via tangible architectural discoveries the legendary stories of Agamemnon, Achilles, and Theseus, as well as ancient cities such as Troy, Mycenae, Tiryns, and Knossos. The Palace at Knossos on the island of Crete dates to around 2000–1400 BC. Its complex plan, with multiple stories, courtyards, and underground storage areas, all within a very large square footage, is certainly consistent in its complexity with the labyrinth-like design created by the mythical architect Daedalus to prevent the escape of the minotaur kept by King Minos. The Citadel at Mycenae in Greece dates to around 1600–1200 BC and consists of a heavily fortified complex located on a hilltop, consistent with Homer's descriptions of Agamemnon's burial site. The 20-foot-thick stone walls of the city of Tiryns, located 10 miles away from Mycenae, certainly reveal in their defensive design the celebration of great strength, consistent with the city's most famous mythical inhabitant, Hercules.

These early Helladic peoples then came together with nomadic Indo-European peoples to form one of the greatest ancient civilizations in history, that of classical Greece. Ancient Greek architects established a new standard of architectural aesthetics, one that mimicked the proportions of the human body to create highly sculptural, freestanding structures of timeless beauty. The Parthenon, built around 448–432 BC on the Acropolis in Athens, epitomizes these principles. Constructed by Iktinos and Kallikrates, this elevated rectangular temple with a continuous colonnade of Doric columns, a gabled roof now collapsed inward, and the remains of an inner shrine, reveals in its clear, simple design a form of logic and order invented by the Ancient Greeks. In this building, measured with a degree of mathematical exactitude not found in earlier structures, we find the earliest design principles that codify with precision different column orders, capital types, height and width requirements, and appropriateness of external decoration. These principles are embedded in Greek philosophical thought and have created a timeless, universal concept of beauty that has been revived countless times through history.

The Ancient Romans were, in fact, the first people to appreciate and emulate classical Greek architecture, which they could find on the Italic Peninsula, and these buildings, together with the architectural knowledge gained through trade, travel, and conquest, certainly influenced early Roman architecture. Romans used architecture not only for religious inspiration, but also to cultivate an image of political power and superiority. While Ancient Roman roads connected all parts of the far-flung empire and water was brought to the people via carefully engineered aqueducts, architects blended regional materials with stone to create large, uniformly designed structures that stood as monuments of Roman superiority. The domed Pantheon (AD 118–125) and the Basilica of Constantine (AD 310–320) in Rome were both overwhelming in scale, with the largest unencumbered interior spaces ever built. This overwhelming scale necessitated new technical innovations such as the dome, the barrel vault, and the cross-vault, as well as the invention of stronger materials such as concrete, made from the nearby volcanic rock. Broad avenues separated market areas from religious zones, while neighborhoods were separated by social class. One important aspect of Roman society was an increased emphasis on leisure activities, which resulted in the development of such building types as the bathhouse and the arena. Vitruvius, a Roman architect and engineer who lived in the first century BC, wrote the earliest known treatise on architecture, called *De architectura*; it discusses in separate chapters both technical and aesthetic principles of ancient Roman architecture, as well as different building types. This tremendously influential treatise was rediscovered in the early years of the Renaissance and was central to the revival of classicism in that era.

Religion remained the main source of inspiration for architecture, however, and in the West this is even more evident in subsequent centuries with the establishment of both Christianity and Islam. With the help of the far-reaching Roman Empire, Christianity quickly spread and was accepted in the early 300s by the Emperor Constantine. Thus, through the next several hundred years, private worship in the house church grew into public gatherings held in large basilica-plan churches built across western Europe. Modeled on ancient Roman government buildings, these large structures became potent symbols of Christianity. The Early Christian church of St. Peter, built in Rome around AD 333, was the most important church because it marked the site where the Apostle Peter was buried. By the early 1500s its old age and disrepair necessitated a completely new structure, which was begun during the papacy of Julius II by the architect Bramante. Many subsequent architects, including Michelangelo and Bernini, worked on the massive structure over the next several hundred years. While the western church was typically formed as a longitudinal, or basilica-plan, church, the eastern churches were more often centrally planned. The church of Hagia Sophia, built in Constantinople (modern-day Istanbul) by Anthemius of Tralles and Isidorus of Miletus in the 500s, transcends Imperial Roman buildings in scale, with a massive dome resting on pendentives that link the round dome to the square plan of the floor. The square base then opens up into a massive unencumbered interior, while windows around the base of the dome and along the walls of the church bathe the golden mosaic interior with light.

After the Ottoman conquest of 1453, Hagia Sophia was transformed into a mosque with minarets built at the exterior corners of the structure. By that time, mosques could be found across all of Asia, Europe, and into Africa as well. Muslim rulers followed Roman principles of scale in their construction. The Great Mosque of Samarra, Iraq, built in the mid-800s, was the largest mosque in the world, covering ten acres, half of which consisted of an open courtyard, while the rest was covered by a wooden roof supported by closely set piers. The *quibla* wall faces Mecca; in its center is a niche called the *mihrab*, which likely symbolizes where the Prophet Mohammed would have stood in his house at Medina to lead prayers. On the other side of the Muslim world, the Great Mosque of Cordoba, Spain, from around AD 785, reveals an interior that epitomizes the beauty and richness of Islamic architecture: stripped, horseshoe-shaped arches, multi-lobed arches, and gilded mosaic dome over the *mihrab*. As Islam spread into Africa via extensive trade routes established across the continent, mosques began to appear in the native adobe material. The Great Friday Mosque built in the flourishing trade town of Djenné in Mali in the 1200s and rebuilt in 1907 is the oldest structure in the world made entirely of adobe, or dried clay and straw bricks. *Torons*, or wooden beams that project out from the walls, reveal the internal wood reinforcement of the stucco-covered adobe walls. The wooden beams create a rhythmic design to the exterior wall that is otherwise punctuated with relatively few windows. The façade of the rectangular mosque has three stepped towers with a *mihrab* in the center.

Throughout the Middle Ages, architecture continued to be used to carve out identity and establish areas of authority. Charlemagne, the Frankish ruler who sought to unify Europe under the banner of

Christianity, chose to construct large stone buildings in the midst of the dominant northern European timber structures in order to cultivate this association with Ancient Roman imperial rule. The Palatine Chapel in Charlemagne's palace complex in Aachen, Germany, built around 800, perhaps emulates such imperial structures as the Church of San Vitale in Ravenna. The Ottonian rulers, who drove out Viking invaders and shifted the authority of the Holy Roman Empire to the regions around modern-day Germany, continued this tradition of monumental masonry construction. It was also during the early Middle Ages that monasteries became architecturally prominent, epitomized around 819 by the plan of the Monastery of St. Gall in Switzerland; it shows a grid-like layout of buildings surrounding a basilica-plan church, cloister, refectory, and dormitories. These self-sufficient compounds often provided hospitals, schools, and a local industry for the general populace, often creating, despite the more reclusive qualities of monastic life, the beginnings of late medieval urban settlements.

By the 11th century, feudalism emerged as the dominant power structure and provided some degree of regional stability across Europe via a complex system of personal relationships and social obligations. Because power was increased through land ownership, the Romanesque period was also plagued by battle. Thus it was during this time that the castle emerged as a potent symbol of rural rule. The Castel del Monte in southern Italy, from the 1240s, was built for the Emperor Frederick II as a hunting lodge. For that reason, it has no moat or drawbridge, but it was beautifully designed as an octagonal structure with octagonal bastions at each corner and an eight-sided *bailey*, or courtyard, inside. The thick outer walls have a walkway around the top, accessible via one of the eight guard towers. This tall structure stands on a hill as testament of Frederick's authority. Crusader castles, such as the Krak des Chevaliers in Syria, from the 1030s, were used in battle regularly, while Durham Castle in England, from the 1100s, was fully occupied with a church and palace. Romanesque churches, often built as great pilgrimage sites, are characterized by the use of columns and rounded arches that hark back to antiquity, while the heavy masonry and large scale of such churches provide a symbol of religious solidarity and political authority. The Pisa Cathedral complex, built to commemorate the Pisan victory over the Muslims in the 1060s, is a good example of this style. These buildings, increasingly complex in design, reveal an increase in travel and trade during the Romanesque era as feudalism, monasticism, and a new urbanism continued to take hold across the continent. With the continued growth of Christianity, architectural construction reached a high point during the Gothic era. With the goal of creating larger and lighter churches, stonemasons of the next century developed a series of innovative structural features, including a more complex column and vaulting system, a more sophisticated measuring system, and the use of flying buttresses and pinnacles to support walls that were even more fenestrated than before. Thus, Gothic edifices such as Chartres Cathedral, begun in the 1140s, are typically characterized in their interiors by a more clearly measured structure, where the nave colonnade is made of a series of engaged half- and quarter-columns. These continue into the upper registers with ribs from the colonnade that separate each bay unit and travel into the ceiling, where they define the ribbing of the vaults and then move down into the opposing colonnade. Pointed arches are used in the nave to add more height to the church than the prior Romanesque rounded arch could achieve, and this pointed effect also created a visual directional pull upward toward the heavens. Gothic church elevations were taller than Romanesque, while larger clerestory windows had stained glass that allowed for colored light to filter into the church and symbolize the presence of the divine. The exterior of the Gothic church was increasingly ornate, with a complex grouping of figures and designs around each portal, rose windows, and enough carved pinnacles and niches above to provide an almost encyclopedic presentation of biblical figures and symbols. The architectural complexity of Gothic buildings continues to provide ample interest in and research about this highly prolific time of European architectural construction.

At the same time, in fact, highly significant constructions could be found around the world. The region around India, which includes modern-day Pakistan, Afghanistan, Nepal, Bangladesh, and Sri Lanka, reveals some of the earliest civilizations in the world that merit further study. The Kandariya Mahadeva Temple, in Khajuraho, Madhya Pradesh, in central India, from around AD 1000, is in the form of a stupa. It is dedicated to Shiva and reveals the growing importance of providing architectural shape to Hindu beliefs. This highly ornate stone structure is built on a platform to demarcate the sacred space of the structure. A post-and-lintel structural system results in an exterior sculptural massing, with small interior rooms and few windows. Exactitude in measuring and designing the building is required in order for the structure to be worthy for use as a divine residence. Thus, important considerations include the selection of a proper site, building orientation, and construction on a symbolic plan called the *mandala*. Seen as a series of squares, the building is formed around a windowless inner sanctum called the *garbhagriha*, which symbolizes Brahman. Other square sections represent a variety of gods, with the protector gods represented along the perimeter. While the *garbhagriha* houses an image of the god on its inside, its exterior is articulated with a *shikhara* that rises like a mast above the *garbhagriha* to demarcate the *axis mundi*. A series of smaller hallways, called *mandapas*, lead to the inner sanctum and are formed on the exterior as smaller, mountain-like massings.

Hinduism and Buddhism spread first across Southeast Asia and then into China and eventually Japan. Angkor Wat, in Cambodia, dates to the 1100s and was originally dedicated to Vishnu. It grew from a Hindu temple into a massive Buddhist complex to symbolize in physical form the Hindu cosmology. Thus, it is designed with five central towers that symbolize Mount Meru, where the Hindu gods live. The square outer walls and moat, located outside the walls, represent the edges of the world. The overall complex is aligned to the cardinal points and thus likely refers to an astrological calendar. Much like Gothic cathedrals, the entire exteriors of these temples are intricately carved to reveal in encyclopedic form many legends and stories of Hindu gods and legendary figures.

In China, Taoism and Confucianism played a pivotal role in the early culture of this vast area in the center of Asia. Buddhism was introduced into China from India very early, and Buddhist architecture is characterized there by the pagoda, a temple format that grew out of the Indian stupa design. The Great Wild Goose Pagoda at Ci'en Temple in the Shanxi Province, which dates to around AD 645, is a multistory masonry building modeled on the early Han watchtowers, but with projecting tile roofs at each of the seven levels and with the entire structure topped by a finial to demarcate the *axis mundi*.

The simple, graceful proportions of these buildings carried over into the intricately bracketed wooden pagodas of Japan. Japanese architecture in particular is linked to surrounding nature, and Japanese Buddhism, built upon earlier Shinto beliefs, celebrates this harmony between humans and nature in its nature-based architectural aesthetics. The Byodo-in, in the Kyoto Prefecture, was built around AD 1053 as a secular palace to symbolize the home of Amida Buddha in paradise. It was later transformed into a temple, but its palace structure, modeled on the movement of a phoenix, remained. The roof tips upward in a graceful curve, while the side wings of the palace are elevated on slender columns to suggest weightlessness. Open porticoes connect the interior to the exterior, where a pond shimmers in front of the beautiful red-painted wooden building. The intricate roof bracketing of Japanese architecture, as well as its graceful, natural simplicity, has attracted many architects through time; it is seen most notably in the 20th century in the domestic structures of American architects such as Frank Lloyd Wright.

These developments in Asia correspond in time to the European medieval period, when far-reaching trade routes were established, resulting in an awareness of and material influences on architectural developments among various cultures. These trade routes were expanded in the 1400s to nearly the whole world, and in Europe this period of discovery was called the Renaissance. During the Renaissance a profound cultural shift occurred, which resulted in a self-conscious study of architecture whereby the philosophical and theoretical discipline of architectural history began to take shape. "Historical" architecture was cultivated in the Renaissance in part to champion the intellectual culture of ancient Rome and to shape Renaissance authority through Imperial Roman precedents. While stylistic referencing was not new in the Renaissance, this sustained reverence for classical antiquity was directly pertinent to many Renaissance cultural goals and created a lasting frame of reference to which all subsequent architectural styles responded. The canon of architecture formed along this stylistic duality of "classical" and "non-classical" buildings continued into the next centuries.

Brunelleschi's dome, built for the Cathedral of Florence in the 1420s, is considered the first true Renaissance structure due to its technical advances mingled with classical sources. Through the next century, monumental classicizing buildings were constructed using the architectural principles laid out by Vitruvius in the first century BC. Bramante's Tempietto, built in Rome in 1502, is considered the best example of Vitruvian ideals, but Palladio's buildings in northern Italy became the most popular in subsequent centuries. His Villa Rotonda, built on a hill outside Vicenza in the 1560s, signified a specific interest in the classical villa type, now built for the new class of country "gentlemen" farmers in the Veneto. The villa is designed as a perfectly symmetrical, centrally planned Roman temple. With a six-columned portico on each of the sides of the square building, elevated aboveground by a basement level, the visitor is provided a grand entry into the building from each of its four doors. The entire structure is capped by a dome over its center, thus recalling the ancient use of the *domus* on an imperial home rather than the more common subsequent use of the dome on a church. Palladio's influential style was disseminated through the publication in 1570 of his treatise on architecture called *I quattro libri dell'architettura*, which formed the guiding principles of 18th-century Neo-Classicism.

This classicism carried first into the Mannerist style and then into the Baroque. Mannerism, a short-lived, highly intellectual movement, was championed by such architects as Michelangelo, Giulio Romano, and Baldassare Peruzzi, who sought to elaborate upon classicism by questioning its basic principles. We see this in such elegant homes as the Palazzo del Tè in Mantua, built by Giulio Romano in the 1530s. This villa displays in its irregular proportions and unorthodox use of classical architectural elements a questioning of the strictly Vitruvian understanding of Ancient Roman architecture, which had until then dominated classical style. Having recovered from the Sack of Rome of 1527, papal rulers then turned their attention to the rejuvenation of Catholicism in response to the growing threat of Protestantism. This Counter-Reformation, as it is called, was marked by large-scale architectural construction, which was used to provide a firm visual symbol of papal authority across Europe. Saint Peter's Church in Rome and Versailles Palace outside of Paris are the most famous examples of Baroque architecture. Saint Peter's was begun by Bramante in the early 1500s, continued by Michelangelo and Carlo Maderno, and completed by Bernini in the 1650s to include a wide *piazza*, or square, in front of the complex façade with an oval shape that symbolizes the protection of the Church. The massive size of the building was enough to overwhelm visitors, who could also enter the church to see the broad, short nave filled with marble sculpture, the huge bronze baldachin built by Bernini in the 1620s to cover the crossing altar, and the intricate gilded bronze high altar sculptural program built by Bernini in the 1660s to commemorate the church's dedication to Peter, Christ's first apostle. Louis XIV used this same highly propagandistic style to assert his authority at Versailles in the 1660s. This classicizing Baroque complex is dynamic and theatrical, with a broad vista that dominates the surrounding countryside. It was during this era that most Catholic missions were established across the New World. European explorers had "discovered" the Americas during the Renaissance, and by the Baroque era, Europeans had settled into newly constructed colonial port cities across North and South America and were bringing incredible wealth back to Europe. While this wealth helped to fund architectural construction across Europe and to transform society into a consumer culture, its impact on the Americas was most dramatic and changed the course of history. When Hernán Cortés's army first saw the Aztec city of Tenochtitlan in 1519, they were amazed at this vast city of monumental stone architecture and the straight thoroughfares built on islands in the center of Lake Texcoco outside modern-day Mexico City. The earlier architectural cultures of the Olmec and Maya were soon discovered to reveal similar monumental stone axially-oriented platform pyramids, temple compounds, and urban palaces. Temples were constructed as sacred mountains with shrines located on the top, arrived at via a steeply ascending stairway accessible only to the highest priest-kings and their sacrificial victims.

In time, these native Americans were converted to Christianity, and the Spanish invaders built their own colonial city over Tenochtitlan, leaving few remains of this enormously interesting culture. Although the Inca Empire in South America suffered the same fate as these Mesoamerican peoples, the Inca city of Machu Picchu is better preserved due to its isolated location atop a high mountain outside Cuzco in Peru. By the 1500s, the Incas ruled a territory as vast as the Ancient Roman Empire. With an excellent road system, their far-flung cities were united under an efficient government system that focused on close communication and frequent travel. By the 1530s, native cities like Machu Picchu were abandoned, leaving their stone buildings, broad avenues, open squares, and elaborate mountain terraces shrouded in mystery. In North America, Spiro Mounds, located in eastern Oklahoma, and Cahokia, in East St. Louis, Missouri, both suffered the same fate.

Meanwhile, in Europe the newfound wealth drove the economy to even higher levels of architectural luxury, and a new architectural style called the Rococo developed in the early years of the 18th century. The Rococo took many of the large-scale Baroque principles and shaped them into a more intimate, organic form suited to the aristocratic lifestyle in Paris, Munich, and Vienna. Schönbrunn Palace, begun in Vienna in 1696 by Johann Bernhard Fischer von Erlach, epitomizes this opulence. The undulating exterior details lead the visitor into the richly designed interior, created with marble, gold, and a profusion of fresco painting and sculptural detail that blends painting, sculpture, and architecture into a whole. While the Rococo style celebrated courtly culture and advanced the arts to a new level of luxury and playfulness, the growing middle class in France became increasingly disillusioned with this rigid social structure and began a series of protests that ultimately led to the French Revolution.

The architectural style that best represented this new moralizing approach to the arts, based on current philosophical principles espoused by Voltaire, Rousseau, and others, was classicism. Thus, by the mid-18th century, the revival of classical ideals in architecture was formed through a thriving travel industry centered in Rome and guided by the architectural treatises of Vitruvius and Palladio. Richard Boyle's Chiswick House, built in West London in 1720, is one of the best-known examples of Neo-Classicism. Modeled on Palladio's Villa Rotonda, Chiswick House has a simple symmetrical arrangement that is divided into three parts and centered by a six-columned portico topped by a triangular pediment and a dome. Neo-Classicism, seen as reflecting a stylistic purity and honesty, was increasingly used to reflect enlightened ideals of the era. These ideals formed the basis for the earliest official architecture of the United States, which was decidedly Neo-Classical, as seen in Thomas Jefferson's house, Monticello, built in Charlottesville, Virginia, beginning in the 1770s, and the United States Capitol, constructed mainly by Benjamin Latrobe in the early 1800s. This monumental white building has a massive colonnaded portico at the elevated entrance and a tall dome that rises from its center. Meant to suggest Ancient Greek and Roman ideals, this Neo-Classical style quickly became the official style of the United States government.

Revivalist styles are always Romantic in nature, given that they reflect idealized notions of past cultures and movements, and are therefore based in part on a selective nostalgia. Romantic architecture of the 19th century included a revival of the Gothic style, seen most famously in the Houses of Parliament in London, built in the 1830s by Augustus Welby Northmore Pugin, and the later Colonial and Tudor Revival styles found in the United States. The Federal, Georgian, and Greek Revival structures in the United States all follow this same notion, while the Beaux-Arts style is best understood as an amalgam of the Renaissance, Baroque, and Rococo in order to infuse architecture with an opulent historical grandeur. Richard Morris Hunt's Metropolitan Museum of Art in New York City, built in 1895, conforms to these principles.

By the early 20th century, a new architectural style was introduced, based upon a sparer aesthetic influenced by the factory designs of the increasingly industrialized European society. While the Art Nouveau, Art Deco, and Arts and Crafts movements sought to bring a more handcrafted aesthetic to the increasingly mechanized designs of the modern world, the Bauhaus and International styles were instead defined mainly by Walter Gropius on more uniform, universal, and enduring design principles that celebrated function over decoration. Thus, Le Corbusier's Villa Savoye, built outside Paris in 1929, consists of a geometrically ordered white concrete building, designed as a square elevated upon slender piers, with no applied ornamentation. The materials themselves—concrete, glass, and steel—are the aesthetic focus. New materials and technical advances were increasingly sought after through the 20th century, while Ludwig Mies van der Rohe's motto "less is more" became the battle cry for modern architecture. This strictly geometric formula of the International style was balanced by a concurrent trend toward a more expressionist approach to architecture, seen in the work of Bruno Taut, Erich Mendelsohn, and Eero Saarinen. Saarinen's Trans World Airport Terminal in New York City, built of concrete in the 1950s, provides a flowing, organic design to symbolize the aerodynamic, fast-paced movement of modern travel.

Many European modernist architects settled in the United States after World War II and inspired the creation of a uniquely American form of modern design, exemplified in both urban skyscrapers and domestic architecture. Mies van der Rohe and Philip Johnson's Seagram Building in New York City was constructed in the 1950s as a glass tower that celebrates corporate power through its spare, impersonal design. On the other hand, Frank Lloyd Wright's Prairie style and Usonian homes brought about a more organic approach to domestic architecture and reflected the less formal lifestyle of modern families. The Robie House, built in Chicago in 1907, is a one-story brick structure with a strongly horizontal design and an open interior formed around the kitchen and family room. Overhanging roofs, strip windows, large glass sliding doors, porches, and patios were all adapted from Wright's designs in the ever-popular American Ranch style home of the 1950s.

Post-Modern architecture developed in the 1970s as a reaction to the overly spare aesthetic of the International style. Structures such as Michael Graves' Portland Public Service Building in Portland, Oregon (1982), reveal a playful and eclectic mix of historical references, while Deconstructivist buildings, such as Frank Gehry's Guggenheim Museum in Bilbao, Spain, from the 1990s, are inspired by the writings of Jacques Derrida and are meant to question the structural and aesthetic notions of architecture. Bulbous forms flow together in a structure that appears to defy its structural foundations, refuses to harmonize with its surroundings, and does not favor any one particular historical style. Covered in titanium rather than steel, this structure also reveals an increased emphasis on highly technical materials, which when given primary focus in a structure constitutes High-Tech architecture. Richard Rogers and Renzo Piano's Pompidou Center in Paris, built in the 1970s, appears to be a building turned inside out to expose the "inner functionality" of the building on its exterior. Thus, this six-story building is formed from color-coded tubes, pipes, and framing elements that cover its exterior. Jørn Utzon's Sydney Opera House (1959) also reveals a highly technical use of reinforced concrete in thin, curving shells to create the effect of sails blowing across the harbor.

The creation of buildings that suit their environment and are formed from their existing cultural aesthetic has become a more recent concern of current architects. Critical Regionalism is the name given to architecture that draws inspiration from not only its surrounding environment, but also from the use of regional materials and the work of local, not necessarily internationally known, architects who are tuned into the symbolism and values of their own culture. As these styles continue to blend and overlap, architects have also become increasingly concerned with creating so-called green buildings, which allow for a more efficient use of lighting, heating, and cooling. As architects continue to challenge cultural assumptions about buildings, question preconceived notions of construction, and seek out new architectural modes that respond to our changing cultural needs, building design in the 21st century will certainly change in ways hard to imagine.

Architectural history will also change. Initially framed within a discourse similar to that of painting and sculpture, which early on were allied with literature, music, and drama, the study of architecture was also initially driven by the need to define "historic" structures that could be identified through the use of guidebooks and confirmed via the travel industry, for which such buildings became tourist destinations. This industry was fully formed by the mid-18th century, when tourism and consumerism merged to create a vibrant new intellectual pursuit in Europe. Architectural history, then, is the historical examination of a selection of tangible, three-dimensional spaces. In this regard, since it is not possible to understand the totality of world architecture, historians have, over time, developed a narrative format to help organize this study in a linear fashion. This linear mode often uses style as a way of grouping structures together, and therefore the organizational system is based on a coherence that is both selective and exclusive. Although exclusive, stylistic considerations nonetheless remain a vital way of identifying and organizing aesthetic patterns found in structures. The scholar can create a description of a structure that coordinates with a particular style and with this stylistic category be able to understand some of the cultural decisions made during the coordinating historical era in which the building was constructed. Of course, the physical context of buildings changes through time, as does the cultural context in which buildings exist in subsequent eras. Therefore, as a cultural artifact, architecture is subjective and constantly changing. It has more recently become clear to scholars that a richer examination of architecture can result when the narrative direction changes and moves along multiple lines of inquiry.

While creating a facile organizational system, the focus on a sole *capomaestro* and on buildings that conform to the dominant styles presents only part of the story of architecture. Gone are the more modest structures that did not survive due to their temporal building materials, their less valued construction style that did not merit preservation, or their destruction in the ever-shifting power struggles through history. Gone are the names of the architects who did not involve themselves in such theoretical discourse. Nonetheless, although authorship must now be questioned, it remains a vital component to the construction of the discourse on history, and it can be used as a platform upon which further methodological issues, such as power, class, and gender, can be examined.

The impact of current methodological approaches on architecture is evident to the visitors of Stonehenge today. We still struggle to understand the significance of these massive stones, arranged in a circle on a rural plain in a relatively deforested region of England. Before Stonehenge was constructed, this part of Europe was heavily forested. Mesolithic postholes that date to around 8000 BC have been found under the modern-day parking lot. These pine posts were set into the ground in an east-west alignment. By around 4000 BC, the land had been cleared for cultivation and pastures, and long barrow tombs have been excavated nearby. Certainly, the megalithic structures of Stonehenge must be understood as the integral center of a vibrant Neolithic culture rather than as a cultural oddity. Similarly, the dry desert areas that now surround Giza, in Egypt, and surround the Sumerian ziggurats at Ur, in modern-day Iraq, do not provide us with a full picture of these once-thriving, fertile zones populated with people highly motivated to construct large-scale architecture.

Machu Picchu also fascinates us today due to its seemingly remote and inaccessible location, but a quick glance around the area reveals an extensive amount of similarly terraced land in the surrounding mountains. Hiram Bingham "found" the "lost" city of Machu Picchu in 1911, but this well-known center of Inca civilization, linked to other Inca cities by an intricate series of roads that rival those of ancient Rome, was never really considered lost by local Peruvians. Angkor and Tikal share a similar history. They are both now surrounded by jungle, but at one time each of these architectural complexes functioned as the religious and political center of their culture. Currently, less than 10 percent of the area of Tikal has been excavated, but it is clear that the original city of over 200,000 people lived in thatched huts and more elaborate homes surrounding the ceremonial center. Angkor was equally large during its historical high point. The historical fate of Cahokia Mounds State Historic Site, located near East St. Louis, is slightly different. It is instead the victim of urban encroachment, which must be curtailed if this platform mound city is to be preserved. The common problem shared by all of these examples, however, is the lack of resources needed to address the problems of preservation and restoration, which in turn prevents these cultures from receiving the scholarly attention they deserve.

Elitism and issues of power continue to obscure the study of architecture through the exclusion of certain cultures and structures from the canon. The study of architecture, however, is increasingly understood to be not just the examination of isolated buildings, but an interdisciplinary inquiry into the entire built environment, with its varied building types, qualitative issues, social concerns, and power struggles. With this fuller methodological approach to architecture, we can move forward in enlarging the canon of architecture to include a much richer array of three-dimensional structures. We will, then, in the future be able to better understand how buildings reveal the aesthetic inclinations of their original cultures as well as to demonstrate in a more sophisticated way why these buildings remain worthy of examination today.

The Dictionary

– A –

AALTO, ALVAR HUGO HENRIK (1898–1976). Alvar Aalto is credited with establishing modern architecture in his native Finland. After completing his studies at Helsinki Polytechnic in 1921 and an initial foray in the **Neo-Classical architecture** that was prevalent in Finland at the time, Aalto began to employ natural materials of **wood** and **brick** rather than **concrete** to develop a more modern style that can be characterized as simple and functional yet elegant. It is this style that has come to be described as a quintessentially Scandinavian form of modernism.

Aalto was inspired by **Le Corbusier** and the **International style**, as seen initially in his commission for the Viipuri Library, now called the Municipal Aalto Library of the City of Vyborg, completed in 1935. This beautiful spare, white building with rows of unadorned windows was groundbreaking in design. Inside, round wooden chairs and plain round tables echoed the rows of round windows built into the ceiling to emit a diffused light into the central reading room. After World War II, parts of eastern Finland, including the city of Viipuri, were ceded to Russia. Although the city had been bombed during the war, the library suffered little damage. However, years of neglect followed. The building was exposed to the elements through breaks in the roof and it lost all of its original furnishings. By 1991, a full restoration project was begun, organized by both the Finnish and Russian governments, and this project has become a model in modern architectural restoration.

The Villa Mairea, built in 1938–1939 in Noormarkku, Finland, is another example of Aalto's soft, more expressive form of modernism; the simple white exterior achieves warmth through the use of beautiful stained wood window and door frames. A year later, Aalto came to the United States to teach at Massachusetts Institute of Technology in Boston, and in 1947–1949, he built the Baker House on the MIT campus. This six-story brick dormitory facing the Charles River rests on a white **stone** basement level and features a distinctive undulating exterior façade that results in wedge-shaped interior rooms unique to campus architectural design. This expressive organic shape is echoed in Aalto's designs for furniture and **glass** arts as well, and in these multiple venues his modernist aesthetic came to be found across Europe and in the United States. *See also* CRITICAL REGIONALISM; EXPRESSIONISM.

ACROPOLIS, ATHENS. The city of Athens was home to some of the most aesthetically sophisticated architecture of the ancient world. In particular, the Acropolis, a sanctuary of religious structures, has been extensively excavated to reveal the superior place its wonders occupy in classical architectural history. Located on a hill in the center of Athens, these buildings celebrate the origins of Athenian culture through the veneration of the goddess Athena. After the first Acropolis complex was destroyed by Persian troops in 480 BC, a new complex was commissioned by the Athenian ruler Pericles and directed by the architectural sculptor Pheidias. This new complex was much criticized by surrounding communities because their payments to the Delian League's treasury, kept in Athens to provide military support across the region, was instead used for Pericles's reconstruction of the Acropolis. In Athens, however, the Acropolis became a symbol of Athenian supremacy across the region, demonstrative of Athenian pride and cultural values.

Marble was brought from quarries outside the city to construct a complex of seven major buildings, including the Propylaia, or grand portico entrance into the walled complex accessible by the "Sacred Way"; the Pinakotheke, or picture gallery on the left of the Propylaia; the little Temple of Athena Nike on the edge of the hill to the right of the entrance; the courtyard sanctuary of Artemis Brauronia (protector of animals); and the armory, called the Chalkotheke, which finally directs the visitor to the Erechtheion on the left, and on its right, to the famous Parthenon, located on the most elevated site of the Acropolis. Many votive statues, such as the colossal bronze of Athena the Defender located just through the Propylaia, filled the rooms, court-yards, and open areas.

The Parthenon, dedicated to Athena Parthenos, to whom votive of-ferings were brought, housed a monumental statue of Athena made of ivory and gold. Construction began in 480 BC by the architect Kallikrates but was halted for about 30 years and then expanded upon by the architect Iktinos. This white marble rectangular temple is ele-vated by several marble steps, called the *stereobate*, that surround the entire building and lead up to a continuous portico lined in a *peristyle* on all four sides with a single row of **columns**. Additionally, because the temple has a single *peristyle* rather than double columns, it is called a *peripteral* temple. At the Parthenon, a *pronaos*, or smaller porch, provides an entrance from the eastern platform, or *stylobate*, into the internal sanctuary, called the *cella*. A separate, unconnected portico then faces west, providing symmetry to the building. The columns that surround the building are of the most austere order, the Doric. Above the Doric capitals is a smooth architrave, and above this begins the frieze of *triglyphs*, or three-part glyph patterns, and *metopes*, or square panels carved with relief sculptures of various battle scenes. Rising above this frieze is a triangular pediment sur-rounded by a cornice filled with sculptures of gods and goddesses. Triangular pediments occupy the west and east façades of the slightly gabled roof, which is made of marble and not the usual wood or ter-racotta. Although most of the building remains today, the roof was destroyed and most of the architectural sculpture was placed in the British Museum in London.

Greek architects are best known for their graceful columns, and here the Doric columns are *fluted*, or carved with vertical lines, and calculated mathematically to rise to an increasingly more slender width from the drum, through the shaft, and to the necking right be-neath the capital. It is this attention to mathematical detail, focused on symmetry, harmony, and proportionality, that provides the Parthenon with an enduring beauty called the "classical" aesthetic. Many **Renaissance** and later **Neo-Classical** buildings found across the western world have been modeled on the Parthenon, not only for its aesthetics, but also because its architecture came to symbolize general prosperity, democratic principles, and honest leadership. *See also* ANCIENT GREEK ARCHITECTURE.

ADAM, ROBERT (1728–1792). Robert Adam, perhaps the best-known 18th-century Scottish architect, developed an opulent form of **Neo-Classical** architectural and interior design. Coming from a prominent family of builders, Adam trained with his father and brothers and studied in Italy, where he focused on the examination of **Ancient Roman** domestic interiors. He then settled in London in 1758, where he became instrumental in leading the classical revival in England.

Kedelston Hall, located in Derbyshire, England, was one of Adam's first architectural commissions. Originally hired to help design the gardens, Adam was commissioned in 1759 to build the country estate begun by Matthew Brettingham. Adam designed the main façade of the villa with a dramatic, protruding classical portico of six Corinthian **columns** set in the center of a tripartite façade, while he designed the garden façade with an arched central bay and a shallow **dome** in emulation of **Andrea Palladio**'s **Renaissance** villa designs.

The Syon House, built outside London, is an elegant country estate renovated by Adam in 1762–1769 for the Duke of Northumberland. This building displays Adam's more ornate interiors of colored **marble**, gilded reliefs, and intricate moldings, which are clearly inherited from the **Rococo style** but are tempered by a strong classicizing organizational design. Adam's interiors for the estate of Osterley Park, Middlesex, England, from 1761 to 1780, are perhaps his most innovative interior designs. Here, the **Etruscan** dressing room displays an arrangement of motifs that reveal not just a fanciful rendition of the Etruscan style but a creative use of carefully studied examples from antiquity that Adam would have seen outside Rome. These are the commissions that sealed Adam's fame as an architect known for his unique blend of classical models embellished with his own creative interpretations.

In 1761, Adam was appointed by King George III as Architect of the King's Works. Although classical purists never approved of Adam's style and therefore never elected him to the Royal Academy, he remained very popular with the English aristocracy, who preferred his more opulent version of classicism to the spare examples prevalent during this time.

ALBERTI, LEON BATTISTA (1404–1472). Leon Battista Alberti, the leading theorist in **Renaissance** Italy, was born into a noble Florentine family expelled to Venice. It was in Padua that Alberti first studied classical humanism, and in Bologna that he received a law degree in 1428. Able to return to Florence the following year, he began his career as an author, writing books on upper-middle-class family life, painting, sculpture, and architecture. His architectural treatise, finished in 1452 and titled *De re aedificatura*, is dedicated to his patron in Rome, Pope Nicholas V. This treatise is the first since antiquity and was modeled on the Roman treatise by **Vitruvius**. Like Vitruvius, Alberti defined ideal architecture as that which demonstrates strength, utility, and beauty. He also updated Vitruvius's classical orders by canonizing the Composite order of **columns**, which Vitruvius considered merely a late variant of the Corinthian. Alberti's treatise is less of a practical manual, however, and more of a theoretical discussion of the aesthetics of classical architecture, considered the ideal style in the Renaissance.

Alberti put his ideals into practice with his Tempio Malatestiano, built in the 1450s as a funerary church for the ruler of Rimini, Sigismondo Malatesta. Despite the fact that it lacks its originally planned **dome** over the crossing of the nave, this **stone** building recalls a classical temple in its façade, which is made to recall the design of a Roman triumphal **arch**, and in its basilica interior, which has piers lightly carved with Roman motifs. His later church of Sant'Andrea in Mantua, from 1472, is Alberti's most fully formed classical building. Here, a colossal arch rises up over the central door, flanked by side wings with separate entrances. Thus, the façade is divided into three parts separated by smooth colossal Corinthian pilasters that rise up to the entablature, creating an elevated porch entrance into the church. The façade is further divided into three parts vertically, by the placement of two arches over each side entrance to create three stories. Finally, a frieze separates the lower levels from the triangular pediment that caps the sloping, unfinished roofline. Entering the building under the coffered portico, the visitor immediately recognizes that the interior of the church matches the exterior in height, proportion, and design. The vast coffered barrel vault provides an expansive Latin-cross plan, with a nave flanked by side aisles. It was the Latin-cross church plan that Alberti used here, which was the most practical in organization and size. Thus, with these churches one can see how Alberti sought to infuse a rational approach to his ideal architecture by providing not only overt classical references but also a visual harmony and order that suited Renaissance aesthetics.

ALEN, WILLIAM VAN (1883–1954). *See* SKYSCRAPER.

ALHAMBRA, GRANADA. While the Great Mosque of Cordoba, begun in 785, signals the advent of Muslim power on the Iberian Peninsula, the Alhambra Palace complex, built in Granada from 1354 to 1391, was the seat of the last great Moorish dynasty in Spain. Muslim traders had settled in southern Spain in the early 700s, after the Berber ruler Tarik conquered the Visigoths on the Iberian Peninsula. A few years later, in 750, the early Umayyad Dynasty, centered in Damascus, Syria, was overthrown by the Abbasids, and the last remaining members of the Umayyad royal family fled their capital and found refuge among Syrian expatriates living in southern Spain, which they had named Al-Andalus. While the Abbasid *caliphs* went on to establish their empire in Baghdad and Samarra and extended Islamic authority across the eastern world, the Umayyad family created a western empire, where Abd-al-Rahman I ruled as a local *emir* beginning in 756. This shift in dynastic power ultimately resulted in the dramatic expansion of Islam in western Europe, where the powerful Umayyad Dynasty of Cordoba ruled most of the Iberian Peninsula until 1031.

Afterward, internal conflicts abetted Christian advances so that the Moors had to enlist the aid of the Almoravids from Marrakesh, who sailed across the Strait of Gibraltar and helped to stabilize Islamic rule for the next several hundred years. Despite this external aid, the Moors' economic power never fully recovered and was dealt a severe blow in 1063 when they lost control of the trade routes of the Mediterranean Sea to the Pisans of Italy. The definitive battle, incidentally, was celebrated in Pisa with the construction of the **Pisa Cathedral Complex** begun the following year. Nonetheless, the final Moorish Dynasty, the Nasrids, who governed from their capital in Granada from 1232 to 1492, carved out a rich culture that is seen today in the Alhambra, a palace complex built in Granada beginning in 1238 and adapted through the next several hundred years. The complex as it appears today is the result of a construction campaign that dates to the mid-1300s, and although subsequent Christian rulers either altered or destroyed several of the buildings, much of the complex was left intact, probably as a symbol of the vanquished Islamic rule.

The Alhambra is a fortified complex of buildings surrounded by walls and towers. Located on a hilltop outside of Granada, it was largely self-sufficient. It included a fortified royal complex of six palaces, government buildings, mosques, barracks, servants' quarters, a mint, workshops, stables, bathhouses, and fountains, all set amid beautiful enclosed gardens that were meant to look like paradise on earth. The Palace of the Lions was the royal retreat of Muhammad V, who ruled from 1362 to 1391. It reveals a spectacular courtyard with a central fountain that has a basin elevated on the backs of a cluster of lions, all of whom face outward around the courtyard. The courtyard would originally have been used as a garden and planted with citrus trees and flowers. Above the courtyard, projecting balconies, called *miradors*, have open windows that overlook both the gardens and the valley below. Large rooms with pavilions that open onto the courtyard at the ground floor were used for entertainment, with music and selected poetry. One of the two-storied rooms, the Hall of the Abencerrajes, has a richly carved, star-shaped vaulted ceiling set on squinches rather than pendentives, which is **Byzantine** in origin. The entire **dome** is made up of a series of tiny niche arches called *muqarnas* that give the effect of a cave ceiling covered with stalactites, yet the ceiling appears to float up above the square room, weightless in appearance. The original Moorish walls reveal a complex surface decoration of richly colored stone intarsia and wood in arabesque patterns of densely interlinked geometric shapes and organic lines. The Palacio de Generalife has been altered, but its garden setting is thought to resemble its original Moorish format. The large pool in the Court of the Myrtles provided a sparkling reflective surface as well as a cool respite from the intense summer heat. The complex, with its sophisticated irrigation system that allowed for incredibly lush gardens, was repeatedly described with a mixture of admiration and wonder by visitors.

The Moorish empire ended in 1492 when Isabella of Castile and Fernando II of Aragon unified much of the Iberian Peninsula with the Christian world. That same year, Christopher Columbus visited the king and queen in Granada and was received personally in the throne room at the Alhambra, where the queen agreed to fund his exploration. Subsequent Christian rulers continued to use the Alhambra, although some destroyed parts of the Moorish complex. Charles V in the 1500s tore down the winter palace to build his own **Renaissance** structure, while in the 1700s, Philip V updated many of the interiors and built his own palace in the complex. It was saved from Napoleon's attempted destruction in the early 1800s and has subsequently received the protection so long deserved as one of the most important travel destinations in all of Spain. *See also* ISLAMIC ARCHITECTURE.

AMERICAN FOURSQUARE. American Foursquare houses date from 1895 to the 1930s and are so named for their boxy shape and four-part floor plan. These houses were typically simpler and more economical than the Victorian homes of previous years. They were normally of a wood frame and clapboard construction, but brick foursquare homes were also sometimes built, and more elegant versions were constructed with rich interior woodwork and other **Arts and Crafts** features. By the early 1900s, for the first time in history, cheaper land and construction materials offered most Americans the opportunity to own their own home. The square houses had two-and-a-half stories, a hipped roof with a central dormer, and a front porch. Inside, the floor plan was divided into four smaller squares; the typical ground floor consisted of an entrance foyer and stairwell, which moves clockwise to a living room, then the dining room, separated by an arched entry, and a kitchen behind the entrance foyer. The second story was similarly divided to include three bedrooms and a bathroom.

The most interesting feature of the foursquare homes is the fact that they could be purchased through mail-order catalogues such as Sears Roebuck or the Aladdin Company of Bay City, Michigan, and all precut parts and an instruction booklet would arrive on a boxcar to be assembled by local carpenters. Foursquare homes were therefore popular in suburban settings that featured small, square lots and were located near the railways. The *Aladdin "Built in a Day" House Catalog* from 1917 features over 60 homes costing from $300 to around $2,000, each named and detailed with floor plans, drawings, and interior and exterior photographs. The simple "Herford" foursquare house cost $836.00, while the "Suburban," which cost $1,075.40, was four feet wider than the Herford and featured a more sharply gabled, shingled roof, exposed rafters, and cornice brackets. The mass production of these popular homes ultimately transformed the urban landscape of the United States in the first two decades of the 20th century.

ANCIENT AEGEAN ARCHITECTURE. Before the dawn of Ancient Greece, a vibrant Neolithic and then Bronze Age society thrived in several different cultures found along the Aegean Sea. The Aegean is home to many clusters of islands, and the earliest known Aegean culture, established around 6000 BC, was centered on several of the Cycladic Islands off the southeast coast of Greece. Today these islands appear to be quite barren, rocky outposts with few trees, but by around 3000 BC they were home to a thriving culture of farmers and seafaring traders, and their inhabitants began to use local **stone** to create not only the famous Cycladic figurines of musicians, but also fortified towns and burial mounds. Several of these islands have quarries of the beautiful white **marble** that later became the preferred building material in Ancient Greece. To date, however, no habitations have been excavated on these islands.

Also from around 3000 BC, another Bronze Age culture thrived on the much larger island of Crete, located in the southern area of the Aegean, and this island culture developed into what was later called the Minoan civilization. Minoan peoples are named after their legendary ruler, King Minos, who is described in Homer's epic tales as ruling from his labyrinth-like palace in the ancient city of Knossos. This palace, dating from 1900 BC to around 1100 BC, was discovered by the archaeologists Heinrich Schliemann, who located the site, and then Arthur Evans, who subsequently discovered and excavated the area. Both scholars argued that Homer's tales were not entirely fictional, but could be used to unearth pre-Homeric cities such as the ancient site of Troy in Turkey and the Peloponnesian city of the ancient ruling family of Atreus, known as Mycenae.

Minoan peoples farmed and maintained herds of animals, but they also fished for food and established vast trade routes across the Aegean and the Mediterranean. This thriving culture is also known for its own system of writing, which was needed in order to keep sophisticated trade account books, while music, dance, and other high levels of aesthetic culture appear in murals painted on the walls of vast palace complexes. The most famous palace, the Palace of Knossos, had beautiful walls made of mud **brick** and rubble shaped within a wooden framework that was then covered in a veneer of local stone. Certainly the marble constructions of the Cycladic peoples or the alabaster walls of the Mesopotamians must have inspired the use of this new material, called dressed stone. After an earthquake destroyed several parts of the palace around 1700 BC, it was rebuilt and extensively enlarged. This newer palace was multistoried, which was a newer architectural feature made possible by the relatively light materials of **wood** framing and stone veneer used in construction. Not only did many windowed openings allow light and air into the internal courtyards, but many stairs, open porticoes, and columned rooms set at different levels also allowed light and air to circulate in an unprecedented manner. Organized around a large rectangular central courtyard, the palace complex was divided into quadrants loosely organized into suites of royal apartments, administrative wings, areas for various social entertainments and religious rituals, workshops, and vast storage areas that clearly reveal an extremely centralized urban unit. Wall murals and the various artifacts found on the island attest to a beautiful maritime aesthetic and prosperous culture.

Although not obviously fortified, the palace enjoyed an island location that was logistically difficult to breach by foreigners and a complexity of design that defied entry by outsiders not familiar with the layout of the palace. These are the two features of the palace that helped to shape the legend of the Minotaur, who lived beneath the palace and was paid an annual tribute of 14 young girls and boys brought from the city of Athens, ruled by King Aegeus at the time but dominated by King Minos of Knossos. One of these sacrificial victims was Theseus, who went on to free his people from this punishing tribute by navigating the underground labyrinth of the palace to slay the Minotaur, all the while untwining a ball of silk thread so that he could then find the exit. Even better known is the legend of the architect of the palace, Daedalus. Because Daedalus had designed the palace, he was not allowed to leave the island of Crete so as not to divulge the secret layout of the palace to foreigners. It was for this reason that Daedalus and his son, Icarus, fashioned wings of bird feathers and wax in order to flee the island, a venture that was not successful because Icarus did not heed his father's warning and flew too close to the sun.

Ultimately, this Minoan culture did not survive; it was usurped in regional importance by the Mycenaean peoples from the northern Peloponnese. These Bronze Age people, whose earlier origins remain unknown, anticipated many of the great advances of the Ancient Greeks. They spoke a proto-Greek language and came into the Peloponnese around 3000 BC, overthrowing the preexisting Neolithic culture and establishing a more sophisticated culture evident in their expert metalwork and architecture. The citadel at Mycenae, home to the legendary Agamemnon, king of Mycenae and conqueror of Troy, as well as the smaller citadel at Tiryns, where Hercules is reputed to have been born, form the core of what remains of this culture. Unlike the Minoans, the Mycenaean peoples earned a reputation as fierce warriors, given that their territory was centrally located along a major migratory route and was therefore more vulnerable to outside invaders. The citadel at Mycenae, begun around 1350 BC, was built atop a hill and reflects this need for protection, with its huge stone ring walls and an entry that restricts the visitor to a narrow path through the famous Lion Gate of Mycenae, and then into the walled compound.

The Lion Gate, dated around 1250 BC, is built with megalithic stones that rise up in a **post-and-lintel** system and are then capped with a keystone, an inverted triangular stone that helps direct the weight of the heavy materials as well as the weight of gravity down through the posts rather than over the center of the weaker lintel. This feature reflects a more sophisticated structural system than previously employed in architecture. Although the use of the keystone here is conflated with the more traditional post-and-lintel system, which is formed with a slight arch to relieve more of the weight, it set the stage for later structural developments found in Ancient Rome. Two lions are carved into the keystone and flank a column, resting their front legs on its base. The use of guardian lions flanking palace entrances was widespread in **Ancient Near Eastern architecture**, while the elaborate burial rituals seen in Mycenaean tombs attest to **Ancient Egyptian** influences. Inside the citadel, beehive tombs, formed in a conical shape, housed hammered gold face masks, bronze swords, pottery, and carved figurines. These beehive tombs, made with massive rocks, recall **Prehistoric** passage graves in Newgrange, Ireland, but have a more fully developed corbel vault, in which the stone layers rise up and gradually close inward to a keystone that anchors the pointed arched roof. Over the entrance, one triangular window allowed a ray of light to enter the dark tomb.

The citadel at Tiryns, built several hundred years later, reveals more extensive corbelling in hallways that run through the center of the ring walls. Inside the citadel an audience hall, called a *megaron*, was located in the center of the city. The *megaron* was fronted by a courtyard and entered through a two-columned porch. The center of the room had a raised roof with open windows, set above a ritual hearth that was surrounded by four supporting columns. This *megaron* plan anticipated the arrangement of many subsequent Ancient Greek temples.

ANCIENT EGYPTIAN ARCHITECTURE. The architecture of the Ancient Egyptians is traditionally considered only in relation to their elaborate burial rituals and what is called the "cult of the dead." This somewhat narrow understanding of Egyptian culture is largely the result of the fact that monumental religious structures such as the great **Pyramids of Giza**, the large funerary complex of Queen Hatshepsut, or the Great Temple of Amun in Karnak, were built on a large scale and with materials far more permanent than the materials used for private dwellings. Despite this, funerary chambers were stocked with furnishings, pottery, and other artifacts, as well as decorated with murals inscribed with hieroglyphics that show a lifestyle rich with song and dance, good food, and strong family ties. Small **wood** models of houses and gardens were also placed in tombs to remind the soul, called the *ka*, of the life the deceased has left behind to journey into the permanent afterlife. A model from the tomb of Meketra in Thebes, from around 2100 BC, during the Middle Kingdom, reveals a portico of painted **columns** that opens up into a lush walled garden with a central pool of water. Egyptian columns were used for both support and decoration. Often painted, these columns consisted of a base, shaft, and then a capital carved to recall a lotus flower, papyrus, or a palm leaf. Thus, the vertical reed or tree is the aesthetic source for these earliest columns.

It was the Ancient Greek historian Herodotus who in the fifth century BC first described Ancient Egypt and divided its chronological development into the Early, Middle, and Late Kingdoms, with further dynastic divisions. Most early cities lined the banks of the Nile River and ultimately stretched from the Mediterranean Sea all the way down to Nubia in central Africa. As the rich delta was extremely conducive to agriculture, human habitation first appeared along the Nile around 8000 BC, with towns developing around 5500 BC during the Neolithic period, and then a cluster of city-states appearing in the northern part of the Nile, called the Lower Nile, around 3500 BC.

The social cohesion of Old Kingdom Egypt (c. 2700–2100 BC) created a climate in which large-scale public architecture could be built. The *mastaba*, which looks like a flat-topped pyramid made of mud **brick**, was the earliest tomb structure found in Egypt. Inside the *mastaba* was a small internal room called a *serdab* that housed a statue of the *ka*, the worldly possessions of the deceased, and a shrine used for the worship of ancestors. Deep beneath the *mastaba* was a sealed burial chamber housing the mummified body of the deceased. A small shaft descended from the top of the *mastaba* into the burial chamber, creating the unintended entry point for grave robbers, who through history made a living looting these tombs. King Djoser's funerary compex at Saqqara, from around 2600 BC, is one of the earliest of these monumental structures that also included sham shrines around the temple to better foil thieves, and the earliest monumental **stone** structure in Egypt. Imhotep, King Djoser's prime minister and personal physician, was the designer of this complex and the first architect known by name. Completely loyal to the king, Imhotep could be trusted to keep secret the location of the vast funerary treasures of Djoser's reign. It was this high level of trust and secrecy required of the earliest architectural designers that explains their highly respected and almost cultish personae. Still debated are what measures might have been taken to maintain such secrecy among the manual laborers who completed construction of these chambers.

Subsequent funerary monuments were larger and therefore more difficult to breach. An entire funerary complex, called a necropolis or "city of the dead," can be found in Giza outside modern-day Cairo, where the great Pyramids of Giza are located. Traveling from Cairo, one can begin to see three huge pyramids rising up from an entire complex of structures that were built for three pharaohs from Dynasty 4. The largest of these pyramids, made for the pharaoh Khufu (ruled 2589–2566 BC), covers 13 acres with solid rubble that rises up along four slanted faces to a height of about 480 feet at the central point. Granite and smooth limestone originally covered each pyramid, some of which remains on the top of the pyramid of Khafra (?–2532 BC). The smallest pyramid, dedicated to King Menkaura (2532–2503 BC), still has some of the original red granite along its base. These pyramids were made of solid **stone**, except for the internal burial chamber beneath the pyramid and the various sham chambers, false passageways, corridors, and escape routes that descended diagonally into the pyramid either toward or away from the burial chamber. The original entry, sealed after burial, might well be several stories up on one face of the pyramid, making subsequent entry almost impossible except for the most dedicated tomb robbers.

By the Middle Kingdom, tombs were cut into the mountains along the bank of the Nile, and by the New Kingdom the rulers of Dynasty 18 had regained control of the entire stretch of the Nile and ushered in a time of vast architectural construction unrivaled in history. Great temple complexes began to appear, including the Temple of Queen Hatshepsut, from around 1470 BC; the Great Temple of Amun in Karnak, begun around 1295 BC; the Temple of Amun, Mut, and Khonsu in Luxor, from around 1279 BC; and finally, the Temple of Rameses II and the adjacent Temple of Nefertari, both in Abu Simbel, from around 1279 BC. The temple in Karnak, north of the capital city of Thebes, reveals a walled complex reached by an avenue lined with monumental sculptures. The thick entrance, called a pylon, was flanked by colossal stiffly seated or standing figures, or obelisks. Beyond the pylon was an internal courtyard that led the visitor into an enclosed courtyard filled with colossal columns that supported a tall stone roof.

This enclosed courtyard is called a *hypostyle hall*. Invented in Egypt, the hypostyle hall is characterized by the use of a taller central section to the roof that allowed windows to run along the upper registers of the outer walls and bring some light and cooler air into an otherwise very dark and hot interior space. Called clerestory windows, these were later employed in church design. The massive columns were made by stacking huge stones, cut into thick disks, one atop another. They were then carved in low relief from top to bottom. The hall led into the inner sanctuary, accessible only to kings and priests. Subsequent rulers added additional pylons, hypostyle halls, and shrines, always in an axial direction, which ultimately covered about 60 acres. These temples, along with the murals, sculpture, and Books of the Dead, attest not only to the cohesive and organized power of these family dynasties, but also to the complex funerary traditions that necessitated such complex burial rituals and systems of worship. Although Egyptian religion was based on a polytheistic belief system, the rule of Amenhotep IV, who reigned around 1352 BC, anticipated for a brief time the monotheistic beliefs of subsequent religions through the king's dedication to one god, the sun deity Aten. As can therefore be seen, Ancient Egyptian culture was innovative in its own right, yet it anticipated many of the innovations of subsequent cultures.

ANCIENT GREEK ARCHITECTURE. Ancient Greek architecture is widely revered for its formal elements that have come to be called "classical." These include a canon of proportion based on the human body, symmetry and harmony in terms of the relationship between all parts and the whole, and a standardized design created for a variety of building types. Greek buildings, made of **stone**, were highly sculptural, free-standing monuments of enduring appeal.

Greek civilization developed out of a mix of new migrants and the former Minoan and Mycenaean peoples who lost dominance over the region of the Aegean Islands and the Peloponnese. Interestingly, although these peoples lived in different city-states around 900 BC and had differing backgrounds, they all spoke variants of the same language and considered themselves to have a similar Helladic heritage. The mainland cities of Athens, Sparta, and Corinth supplanted the Aegean Islands in power. In addition to their military strength, these cities developed literature, music, theater, and philosophical ideals that still inform western culture today. While Greek religious beliefs were polytheistic, philosophers maintained that humans were superior on earth and had a great responsibility in upholding the ideals of truth and beauty. Thus humanism, which focuses on cultivating and celebrating human achievements on earth, was born in Greece. Naturally, high aesthetic standards in the flourishing venues of art and

architecture characterize this time in history. As in earlier civilizations, architecture continued to be used to assert economic power and
confirm political and religious authority; therefore large market areas, administrative buildings, and monumental temples dominate the
typological development of architecture in Ancient Greece. However,
the broad-based social and cultural achievements of Greek society
necessitated the introduction of such varied civic structures as amphitheaters, libraries, and museums.

The religious temple—of clear proportions, a rational design, symmetry, and balance—epitomizes the Greek aesthetic ideal. Following
the traditional focus on the sky gods in earlier Egyptian and
Mesopotamian cultures, the religious beliefs of Ancient Greeks focused on the sky gods and deemphasized the female deities so important to Neolithic and Early Bronze Age peoples and their agricultural concerns. Greek religious buildings were therefore elevated.
Several important sanctuary complexes are located in the mountainous areas of Greece; Mount Olympus, in the northeastern region of
Greece, is where the pantheon of Greek gods and goddesses was believed to have lived. The Sanctuary of Apollo, high up in Delphi near
Mount Parnassus, marked the sacred birthplace of Apollo, who would
communicate to humans through an oracle in the sanctuary's main
temple, built in the 500s BC. Pilgrims would trek upward to get there
through a ceremonial gate and the "Sacred Way."

The complex also has athletic and performance areas, since the
Pythian Games, which featured athletic events as well as music and
theatrical performances, were hosted there annually. The rest of the
complex consists of treasuries and memorials. The Temple of Apollo,
now destroyed, was a rectangular building made of stone and was elevated from the ground by several steps that led to a continuous portico supported by a colonnade wrapped around the entire exterior. Although the vast majority of these temples were rectangular, smaller
round temples were also built. Called a *tholos*, the round temple often had a funerary context. The beautiful round temple of Athena
Pronaia in Delphi, dated around 400 BC, is a good example of this
format. The **Acropolis**, located in Athens, is the most famous of these
elevated sanctuaries.

This profusion of **columns** and clear, geometric order became
characteristic of Greek architecture in general. In the Archaic Period,

temples featured simple Doric columns with wide, unadorned capitals. The Ionic order developed next, and featured scrolls in the capitals as well as more slender columns. Often, the shaft of the column would be ridged with vertical lines, called fluting. The Corinthian order, with taller columns and capitals carved with acanthus leaves and other organic decoration, was the most ornate of the supporting orders. The Temple of Hera I in Paestum, Italy, dated c. 550 BC, is a good example of a Doric ordered temple, while the Erechtheion as well as the small temple of Athena Nike, both on the Acropolis in Athens, feature the scroll-like Ionic order, and date to around 430 BC. The Temple of the Olympian Zeus in Athens was completed around AD 132, with the floral Corinthian order. All of these temples featured a **post-and-lintel** structural system, but with a raking, or slanted roof, which provided for the use of triangular pediments on either short end of the rectangular structure.

In addition, architectural sculpture was integral to these buildings, and high relief carvings found in the frieze, located above the columns, and in the triangular pediments, depicted complex narratives related to the temple dedications. In the reconstructed Treasury of the Siphnians at Delphi, from around 530 BC, carved female figures called caryatids act as columnar supports to the front portico of this small one-room temple, called a temple "in antis," which has a front porch of two columns and no colonnade. Votive statues filled the rooms and courtyards on the Acropolis, while caryatids support the porch of the Erechtheion and gods and goddesses filled the triangular pediments of the Parthenon.

The agora, or marketplace, was the center of civic life in Ancient Greece, and the Athenian Agora, located at the foot of the Acropolis and built around 400 BC, featured *stoas*, or covered walkways, that opened up into shops. Over time, agoras grew in size and importance to include temples, public and administrative buildings, and modest stucco-faced private dwellings, although private dwellings rarely revealed the degree of grandeur that is found in later Roman homes. Entertainment was very important to these people, and their theaters reflect this interest. All outdoors, the earliest theaters were small, with a dirt floor stage and a simple mat floor for spectators. Later, theaters grew into permanent structures built with tiered seating formed in a semicircle around an elevated stage of stone. The theater at Epidauros, from the 200s BC, is set against a hilly backdrop, and the stage, called an orchestra, originally had an elaborate set made of **wood**.

Finally, the cities of Ancient Greece also often featured a symmetrical, regularized plan. While early Greek cities expanded out from a central citadel, later classical cities were more often built on a grid pattern, anticipating the organized urban plans of **Ancient Roman architecture**. The Ancient Greek city plan of Miletos in modern-day Turkey, from the 300s BC, shows this orthogonal plan. Because the southern region of Italy had been settled by the Ancient Greeks, who ultimately expanded their empire from Italy all the way to Persepolis in Iran, many architectural innovations of the Ancient Greeks were then expanded upon by the Romans. Thus, the classical aesthetic of these Greek buildings continued to be used by many subsequent cultures, and it is still seen today as the most enduring architectural style ever to have been developed. *See also* ANCIENT AEGEAN ARCHITECTURE.

ANCIENT NEAR EASTERN ARCHITECTURE. The various cultures of the Ancient Near East were extremely important in the development of architecture and the civic aspects of urban space. From the Sumerians, who developed the pyramidal religious structure called the *ziggurat*, to the Hebrews and the great **Temple of Solomon** known today only in written descriptions, to the legendary palace of Sargon I in a still undiscovered site near Akkad, to Nebuchadnezzar's "Hanging Gardens of Babylon" known as one of the classical "Seven Wonders of the Ancient World," the people of the Ancient Near East were some of the first to use architecture to organize society and affirm power. Much is known today of the ancient cultures found in the grassy western plains of Anatolia in modern-day Turkey, modern-day Syria, Iraq, Iran, and Israel and covering entirely the fertile area around the Tigris and Euphrates rivers, but continuing excavations and historic preservation in this war-torn region are important to our increased understanding of the area known to us today as the cradle of civilization.

Remains of Neolithic culture date to around 9000 BC and are evident from north to south, as seen in the reconstructed site of Çatal Hüyük in western Turkey, the large Neolithic city of Jericho, and the even larger town of Ain Ghazal, or "Spring of the Gazelles," in Jordan. Begun around 7200 BC, Ain Ghazal came to consist of about 30 acres of mud-**brick** houses built on slightly elevated terraces reinforced with **stone** retaining walls. Jericho's Neolithic city was about six acres in size, and by 7000 BC its population was around 2,000. Çatal Hüyük, from around 6500 BC, was discovered in the 1950s when an earth mound was uncovered. This town housed about 5,000 people, who lived in one-story, mud-brick structures with shared courtyards and walls. Unlike the earlier Paleolithic peoples, these Neolithic peoples produced an abundance of food that needed to be stored and defended, and they also traded black obsidian used to make tools. As a result of their size and economic activity, their dwellings became increasingly complex, revealing a stratification of society with designated positions and a social hierarchy. A room at Çatal Hüyük also reveals one of the earliest religious shrines known, with an interior space divided into three parts, with molding and columnar structures attached to walls decorated with images of animal skulls, horns, and women giving birth. In particular, the image of the bull and the focus on fertility, so central to these ancient peoples, carried through into later cultures and times.

The earliest city-state to develop along the Euphrates River was Sumer, dating to around 3500–2300 BC. Sumerian peoples are thought to have migrated to this southern area of Mesopotamia from the north and built some of the earliest monumental architecture. With the invention of the wagon wheel, they were able to transport building materials far more easily than previous cultures. The invention of the plow allowed them greater control over their agriculture and produced an agricultural surplus that needed to be stored and protected. What separates Sumer from previous prehistoric cultures, however, is the invention of writing, which in Sumer consisted of what was called cuneiform blocks (while hieroglyphic writing developed almost simultaneously in Egypt). Thus, through the earliest stories ever written, such as the *Epic of Gilgamesh*, one learns of the city of Uruk, built by this legendary ruler.

Uruk, in modern-day Warka, Iraq, was about 1,000 acres large, and had two monumental stepped pyramids, or ziggurats. Ziggurats were the largest of Sumerian structures, built over the generations with surrounding rubble to create a mountain-like structure with a shrine on top. Ziggurats were often decorated with painted clay mosaics, sometimes shaped like a cone, which would be pressed into wet plaster to create a beautifully colored and decorated exterior that would have shimmered in the distant sun. The Nanna Ziggurat at Ur, also in Iraq, is the best-preserved of these structures, having been partially reconstructed in recent years. Dated to around 2100 BC and dedicated to the moon goddess Nanna, it was built of mud brick in a huge rectangle that measures 190 by 130 feet. Three external stairways leading through three platforms create a grand entrance up to the shrine. The rectangular shape was oriented to the points of the compass, suggesting its use as an agricultural calendar. Its large scale was certainly meant to overwhelm the viewer and clarify the power structure within the region. Access to the uppermost shrine was restricted to the ruling elite, also known as the priest-kings. There, votive figures would be offered to the gods and storage space provided for the clay tablets that detailed stories of the gods and goddesses, as well as mathematical accounts of tributes paid to the ruler in exchange for protection throughout the region.

The legendary Temple of Solomon, built by the son of David in the late 900s BC, was destroyed first by the Babylonians and then by the Romans. However, a description of construction found in the book of 1 Kings speaks of how timber was supplied by Chiram of Zor. Stone from Jerusalem was used for the walls, while timber from Lebanon was used for the floor and ceiling of this three-storied building. Two **columns** supported a porch over the entrance that led into a courtyard, and pillars lit with fire might have topped the porch, which was elevated a number of steps.

In addition to these religious structures, people of the Ancient Near East also built palace complexes. The palace of Zimrilim, the Amorite King of Mari, currently being excavated in Syria, reveals some of the earliest murals of political ceremonies set amid beautiful gardens. The palace, with courtyards lined in alabaster, had superior plumbing that brought water to its many fountains. However, the water was not enough to prevent Hammurabi from burning Zimrilim's palace to the ground in 1757 BC. Later palaces were more heavily fortified, as seen in reconstructions of the Assyrian citadel and palace of Sargon II, from 721 BC. This northern Mesopotamian stronghold rose to power around 1400 BC and dominated the entire area all the way to

Egypt. Assyrian citadels housed huge palaces built on top of a huge rectangular platform. The entire walled complex consisted of over 30 courtyards set in a labyrinth-like organization of over 200 rooms in buildings flanking the central palace. The palace could be entered only via a ramp that passed through a towered gate and then a large courtyard. Attached to the left side of the palace was a ziggurat. Low-relief carvings done on alabaster attest to the power of the king, seen dominating ceremonial lion hunts. Here the use of architecture as propaganda was fully realized.

The use of painted glazed brick to decorate the exterior of these buildings can best be seen on the Neo-Babylonian Ishtar Gate, dated to around 575 BC and reconstructed today in the State Museum of Berlin. Nebuchadnezzar II, known in the book of Daniel, was a great patron of architecture, building the city of Babylon across the Euphrates River so that the city was joined by a monumental bridge. This gate is one small section of a city reputed to shine with brilliantly glazed bricks of blue, orange, yellow, white, red, and green that depicted images of lions, dragons, birds, and bulls sacred to the Babylonian god Marduk.

Finally, the Persian Empire rose to power in the 500s BC to dominate the entire Near East, all the way to the Aegean Islands. Darius I (ruler from 521 to 486 BC) brought to his lands a standardized monetary system, an effective system of communication, and tolerance for diversity. He commissioned the construction of a palace complex first at Susa and then at Parsa, or Persepolis, in the highlands of Iran. The Apadana, or audience hall, is preserved in part today. It is arrived at via a monumental double stair that leads to a raised rectangular platform of tall columns that support open porches on three sides of a square hall large enough to hold thousands of people. The architectural sculpture of the palace is more complex than in previous Mesopotamian structures, given that artisans were brought from as far away as Egypt to work on this construction, thereby enriching the local visual repertoire. Across the front of the stairwell appears a low-relief image of people and animals paying tribute to Darius and then his son Xerxes I, in a potent symbol of regional prosperity and propaganda. It was not until 334 BC that the Ancient Greeks, led by Alexander the Great, swept across Mesopotamia, defeated Darius III, and destroyed Persepolis.

ANCIENT ROMAN ARCHITECTURE. Ancient Romans are traditionally known for the creation of an architectural style founded on
Greek models, but it had to accommodate a larger population and
denser urban society as well as a much larger empire. As a result, Roman architecture was both practical and propagandistic. That is, Roman engineers are famous for their aqueducts that brought water hundreds of miles to the center of the cities, for their lined streets, for
their well-organized towns, and also for their monumental architecture that stands today as testament to their far-reaching power.

The Roman Republic was formed in 509 BC, and by the 300s BC,
Romans had asserted total control over the Etruscan-dominated Italic
Peninsula of modern-day Italy. By the second century AD, the Romans ruled over territory as far north as modern-day Scotland, down
to northern Africa, across to the Near East, and down into Egypt.
Thus, ruins of Ancient Roman construction, first seen in the capital
city of Rome, can be found across all of Europe, as far north as northern England, where Hadrian's Wall had been built in the second century AD to provide a 73-mile-long **stone** divide between the Roman
territories and the land of the Scots, and as far south as Mediterranean
Africa and the Near East.

Given that Rome was the capital of the Roman Empire, Roman
Republic and Imperial architecture there is the most lavish. The roads
were first paved by Augustus, who also built the first Imperial forum
and claimed to have transformed the entire city from mud-**brick**
structures to **marble**. The forum is laid out from the *Via Sacra*, or Sacred Way, through numerous temples, **arches**, and large open courtyards with colonnade-lined storefronts and an open market area. Two
large basilicas anchor the forum. The Basilica Ulpia, from AD 113, is
a massive rectangular building with several entrances into a huge, unencumbered interior space, called a nave. Clerestory windows allow
light in through a colonnade on the upper story of the nave, while
shorter side aisles were lined with colonnades running along the sides
of the nave on the ground floor. Administrative rooms were located
off both side aisles, while each short end of the basilica had an apse,
used for the court of law. While this building had a massive timber
roof, the later Basilica of Constantine maintained a larger interior,
made possible by the use of a groin, or ribbed, vault. Above the forum, on the Palatine Hill, Imperial homes were built with a grand

view of the city. In addition to the forum, Rome had the Circus Maximus, used for chariot races, a gigantic bathhouse built under the reign of Caracalla, and the **Colosseum**.

The Baths of Caracalla, built around AD 212, were built as a public bathhouse with a swimming pool, a gymnasium, a library, saunas, and hot, warm, and cold baths that were heated and cooled from an elaborate system of temperature controls maintained in a series of subterranean rooms. The difficulty of this feat of engineering remains staggeringly impressive today. With vast interior spaces and massive walls, this entire building complex covered over 50 acres. Of course, the ability to bring water into the city of Rome was central to its survival. The Pont du Gard, in Nîmes, France, survives today and demonstrates how water was brought from a spring about 30 miles away into the Ancient Roman town of Nîmes. The bridge was constructed with an imperceptibly gradual slant over the 30 miles so that water would flow toward the city gradually, across an uneven terrain. Three levels of arches would bring water in different quantities that averaged about 100 gallons a day for each person.

Temples filled the forum and could also be found all across the city of Rome. The small rectangular temple possibly dedicated to Portunus, from the late second century BC, reveals the blending of **Etruscan architecture**, in that it is an axially planned structure with one entrance into one room elevated onto a **column**-lined portico, with Greek temple design, in its suggestion of the continuation of columns around all four sides of the building. Instead of free-standing columns, as found in Greek temples, here they appear as half-columns engaged, or attached to a wall. The **Pantheon** is equally significant in Rome, boasting one of the largest **domes** in all of antiquity, a feat of engineering not to be fully understood again until the **Renaissance**.

Romans also used architectural monuments such as triumphal arches and monumental freestanding columns to glorify their accomplishments. The Ara Pacis, or Altar of Peace, built around 13 BC to commemorate the peaceful reign of Augustus; the Column of Trajan, built after AD 113 to commemorate Trajan's victory over the Dacians in northern Europe; and the Arch of Titus, built in AD 81 when Titus returned triumphantly from Jerusalem after having looted and burned the **Temple of Solomon**, all exemplify this idea. The Arch of

Constantine, built in AD 313 by Constantine to commemorate victory over his rival Maxentius, is perhaps the best known of this monument type; it later came to symbolize the triumph of Christianity and was therefore a popular classical model in the Renaissance.

Provincial towns were built with a grid-like plan, like the Roman military encampments, which were called *castra*. Timgad in Algeria is an excellent example of this Roman frontier military city. Built around AD 100 under the reign of the Roman Emperor Trajan, Timgad was built as a square town and covers over 30 acres, with broad paved streets laid out on a north-south, east-west axis that provided housing for over 15,000 people, a central market area with administrative buildings, a theater, a library, and a public bathhouse. Because of its remote location today, Timgad is in an excellent state of preservation and has been designated a World Heritage Site by UNESCO. However, further research remains to be done here.

Pompeii has also survived in good condition, given its odd circumstance of being covered in volcanic ash in the first century AD and then excavated gradually after being rediscovered in 1594. In the year AD 79 Pompeii, located south of Rome, was a thriving town home to over 20,000 people, when nearby Mount Vesuvius erupted and immediately covered the entire area with a thick layer of volcanic ash, instantly killing thousands of people and ending all city life. Pompeii today reveals cobblestone streets with shop fronts that open onto the street and a central administrative, religious, and market area, called a *forum*. For entertainment, the town had a bathhouse, gymnasium, theater, and amphitheater.

Houses in Pompeii reveal the layout of a Roman villa with simple exteriors but with one or two open courtyards in the central part of the house. Courtyards were used to bring light and air into the center of the home; the first courtyard, with a shallow pool to store water, functioned as an entrance atrium while a second courtyard, lined with columns and thus called a peristyle court, might have a garden. The atrium of the House of the Silver Wedding is excellently preserved, while the House of the Vetii reveals a peristyle court. The walls of these homes were lavishly painted with murals that depict landscapes, urban scenes, and still lifes, as well as faux niches and other architectural elements, like columns, that cover the entire wall surface. Just outside Rome in Tivoli, Hadrian's Villa, from around AD

130, is a model of Roman interest in rural life, with an open villa design that is integrated into a setting of beautiful formal gardens, pools, grottoes, and garden sculpture.

The Roman engineer **Vitruvius**, in his first-century BC treatise called *The Ten Books on Architecture*, discussed in detail these building types and classical rules, and it was his treatise that had the most impact on subsequent generations of classicizing architects. Thus, the appeal of Ancient Roman architecture is based not only on its enduring aesthetics, borrowed from the Greeks, but also on its expansion of civic structures to include more varied types with a more sophisticated engineering. One could argue that the vast Roman Empire was successful due in part to its incredible architectural feats, which stood as powerful propagandistic tools of a highly sophisticated culture. *See also* ANCIENT GREEK ARCHITECTURE.

ANDO, TADAO (1941–). Born in Osaka, the contemporary Japanese architect Tadao Ando traveled widely and worked in a variety of diverse jobs before, with no formal training in architecture, he opened his firm Tadao Ando Architects and Associates in 1970. Since then, Ando has cultivated a style of construction using unfinished **concrete** to create highly abstract, geometric spaces. One of his earliest buildings, the Azuma House, built in Osaka in 1976, reveals a concrete slab façade with a door centered in the front of the spare, narrow structure. Inside, a courtyard connects the front building to a back structure, thereby integrating the courtyard into the living space of the house.

Culturally responsive to the smaller, more enclosed spaces of traditional **Japanese architecture**, Ando's design for the Church of the Light in Ibaraki-shi, Osaka, built in 1989, also uses simple square spaces, but in this church a cross shape cut into the reinforced concrete wall allows two slits of light to enter the room, one horizontal and one diagonal. With no other decorative elements, the visitor must focus on these lines of light, which refer to the more universal religious symbolism of enlightenment and the divine presence. Zen philosophy informs Ando's contrast between the solidity of the concrete and the immaterial nature of the light, and visitors have noticed that his spare rooms provide a sense of peacefulness and serenity. Simple benches, made from scaffolding timber, are the only furnishings found in the chapel. Ando soon became known for his detailed crafts-manship and his focus on the natural surroundings of his buildings, together with a unique use of light and a weaving of geometrically arranged interior and exterior spaces to create a unified whole. In 1995, Ando won the Pritzer Architecture Prize.

Ando's design for the Modern Art Museum in Fort Worth, Texas, which opened in 2002, demonstrates his ability to match his con-structions to the surrounding nature. Here, this expansive public art museum responds to the flat, wide geography of this region of Texas with a broad, low building that has large tinted windows and a flat roof. The roof's wide, cantilevered concrete cornice deflects the bright sun off the sides of the building and conforms to the strong horizontality of the Midwestern land. Reflecting pools allow light to play off the building and provide a cool surface in this hot southern climate. Ando's very prolific career is proof that culturally sensitive concerns can be translated on an international level, while his meld-ing of global and regional architecture continues to occupy the design principles of current architects who seek to integrate ever-changing aesthetic issues into their work. *See also* BRUTALISM; CRITICAL REGIONALISM.

ANGKOR, CAMBODIA. In the early ninth century, the powerful Khmer rulers began the construction of a massive ceremonial and ad-ministrative center in Angkor, Cambodia, located near the Siem Reap River and dedicated to the Hindu god Vishnu. This center was real-ized with over 100 temples and other buildings, originally sur-rounded by **wood** housing and other timber structures long gone to-day. The Khmer rulers (AD 802–1220) governed a vast and powerful area that stretched from Vietnam to China to the Bay of Bengal, and Angkor itself was originally located in an agriculturally productive, militarily appropriate crossroads of their territory.

Begun in the ninth century by Jayavarman II, the main structures date from the 12th century during the reign of the Khmer King Suryavaram II. Many scholars have argued that the selection of this particular site for such a vast complex was dictated by Hindu cos-mology. Certainly, the buildings and intricate sculptural decoration confirm its astrological significance. Additionally, the main temple complex, Angkor Wat (*wat*, meaning temple), is oriented west, which could mean that it was built as a funerary temple for Suryavaram II. Unlike the larger and more highly visible complex of *stupas* built in Bagan, located on a vast plain in Myanmar (Burma) and completed in the 11th through the 13th centuries, Angkor was swallowed up by jungle, used intermittently over the years by Buddhist monks, and rediscovered by the western world only in the 19th century.

Angkor Wat consists of a series of structures meant to symbolize the mythic Mount Meru and is surrounded by walls that recall parts of a chain of mountains. A square moat symbolizing the cosmic ocean surrounds the entire temple complex. The complex is arrived at via an earthen bridge at the eastern, or back, entrance, or a **stone** bridge across the moat at the western, or front, entrance. The temple consists of a series of covered galleries that link five lotus-shaped towers arranged in a domino pattern, with the central tower rising up above the rest of the complex. The galleries reveal Hindu narratives in the form of the longest continuous bas-reliefs in the world. Hindu temples at this time were either built to recall mountains or else were in the form of galleries, and Angkor Wat demonstrates both types. Aligned on a north-south axis, the east-west coordinates are set 0.75 degrees south of a correct alignment, giving a three-day warning of the spring equinox. A cross-shaped platform is located in front of this main temple and confirms these coordinates.

Most of the structures are made from sandstone with an unidentified mortar, and remains of gilded stucco have been found on some of the towers. Other structures include the Phnom Bakheng Temple, which is surrounded by 108 towers, a number sacred to Hindu and then Buddhist beliefs. The equally impressive and larger Angkor Thom Temple was constructed to the south of the Angkor Wat complex by Suryavaram's successor, Jayavarman VII, and this temple remained the main administrative seat of Angkor until the city was abandoned after it was sacked by the indigenous Thailandese in 1431. While much of Angkor was renovated in the 20th century, the Temple of Ta Prohm was left covered by thick tree trunks and intertwined jungle branches, the way Angkor appeared when it was rediscovered in 1860 by the French explorer Henri Mouhot. *See also* INDIAN ARCHITECTURE.

ARCH. The arch was invented around 2500 BC in the Indus Valley of ancient India. It is a curved structure that rests on posts or walls and allows for the spanning of an architectural space. Prior to the use of the arch, the **post-and-lintel** structure provided for such spatial enclosures. The arch is technically superior to the post-and-lintel because its curvature directs the weight of the structural materials, usually **stone**, as well as gravity, more forcefully toward the posts or walls rather than upon a straight lintel.

The arch gradually developed from simple corbelling to corbelling that culminated in a keystone. Corbelling is found in the **Prehistoric** era around 3000 BC in such buildings as those in the Neolithic village of Skara Brae on the Orkney Islands off the coast of Scotland. Here the walls are made of layers of flat stones stacked up and gradually sloped inward to a small opening that would probably have been covered with thatching or left open above the interior hearth. The most famous use of the keystone is found in the Mycenaean Lion Gate (1250 BC) located in the **Ancient Aegean** citadel of Mycenae in the Peloponnese of Greece. Here an inverted triangular-shaped stone carved with two lions is located above a slightly curved lintel over the entranceway. This keystone encourages the dispersal of weight into the side walls rather than over the entrance void.

Although prototypes of the arch were widespread, appearing in the **Ancient Near Eastern**, **Ancient Egyptian**, and **Etruscan** cultures, it was not until **Ancient Rome** that its use became fully developed in the repetition of an arch to create a barrel vault, in the intersection of two barrel vaults at a 90-degree angle to create a cross vault, and finally, in spinning an arch on its axis to create the **dome**. Roman arches were semicircular and built with special arch **bricks** called *voussoirs* that were capped by a keystone. Typical are the arches found on the Ancient Roman aqueduct called the Pont du Gard in Nîmes, France, from the late first century BC, in which three registers of such arches traverse 30 miles over uneven terrain to reach its destination, bringing water at three different levels to the city of Nîmes. Arched bridges were not only stronger than a masonry wall, but also more economical.

Furthermore, by repeating an arch to span not just the width but also the length of a structure, the Ancient Romans were able to create vast interior halls with tall arched ceilings. Trajan's market in Rome, from the second century AD, demonstrates the use of a **concrete** barrel vault to cover a building and provide for a long interior

hallway uncluttered with supporting columns. The Basilica of Maxentius and Constantine, built in Rome in the fourth century AD, reveals the use of two intersecting barrel vaults to create a cross-vault,
also called a groin vault because of the groin-like angles. Sometimes
the groin vault is articulated with ribbing and thus is often called a
ribbed vault. The vast ceiling of the basilica is covered by three massive groined vaults. More intricate vaulting systems can be found in
the Baths of Caracalla, built in Rome in the early third century AD.
The vaulting system of Ancient Roman bathhouses may have been
based on even earlier vast underground water storage and drainage
systems.

The semicircular arch continued to be used in **Early Medieval**,
Romanesque, and then **Gothic architecture**, when the pointed arch
was introduced. The pointed arch allows for an increase in height and
was usually employed in the clerestory windows of a Gothic church
to increase the dimensions of the fenestration and therefore the
amount of light that enters the building. Because **glass** windows are
inherently weaker than a masonry wall, the flying buttress support
system was then introduced on the exterior of the Gothic cathedral to
provide the additional support needed for the tall walls. The pointed
arch also assumed an important symbolic meaning, as it more ex-
plicitly draws the eye upward toward the heavens.

The pointed arch may have originated in Assyrian architecture,
and certainly variations such as the horseshoe arch were widespread
prior to the Gothic period. The horseshoe arch, which appears to be
pinched inward at the impost blocks, has traditionally been considered an Islamic invention, but it first appeared in ancient **Indian architecture**. Then in western Europe—in Burgos, Spain, for example—the horseshoe arch is found in Visigothic buildings such as in
the entrance doorway of the Church of Santa Maria de Quintanilla
de las Viñas, built by Visigothic Arian Christians in the late seventh
century. The double arch is another way in which the height of a
wall can be increased. Double arches are found in the 780s in **Islamic architecture**, as in the Great Mosque at Cordoba, Spain.
Here, the arch is not used to span a large, unencumbered space, but
rather, as double arches, they link together a densely colonnaded interior courtyard and allow for a greater circulation of air in this hot-
ter climate.

Parabolic, or catenary, arches are structurally superior, and were not introduced until the modern age of architecture. The Catalonian architect **Antoni Gaudí** is credited with creating the catenary arch, a more steeply curved form that directs all horizontal thrust down into the posts or walls and therefore does not need additional systems of support. Constructing the arch from *voussoirs* or other individual materials attached together perpendicular to the curvature of the arch minimizes the shear stress at the joints, and therefore the thrust is more effectively directed into the ground, following the line of the arch. In his Cathedral of Sagrada Familia, begun in Barcelona in 1884 and not yet finished, are a series of catenary arches that recall the pointed Gothic arch but provide a superior support system. The St. Louis Gateway Arch, built by **Eero Saarinen** in the 1960s, is perhaps the most famous catenary arch. Here, the 630-feet tall arch is shaped into equilateral triangles, and made of stainless **steel** over reinforced concrete.

Finally, the inverted parabolic arch is also employed in the suspension bridge, where the catenary arch is attached at intervals to create a parabola. Simple suspension bridges can be found as early as AD 100 and can be seen in the ancient Inca rope bridges, but modern suspension bridges developed out of the truss arch bridge to span several miles. Perhaps the most famous suspension bridge is the Golden Gate Bridge in San Francisco, built in 1937 based on the original idea by Joseph Strauss; it was at the time the longest bridge in the world. New materials and more sophisticated mathematical calculations will continue to provide more functional and aesthetic possibilities for the use of the arch in architectural construction. *See also* PANTHEON, ROME.

ARNOLFO DI CAMBIO (c. 1245–1302). *See* FLORENCE CATHEDRAL, ITALY.

ART DECO. Art Deco is a uniquely urban style of architecture that celebrated modernity. In some respects it was modeled on the sleek, streamlined modern architecture found in Europe, such as the **Bauhaus** or the **International style**; but rather than these structural forms devoid of any applied ornamentation, Art Deco buildings reveal applied, machine-like patterns such as repetitive stamp-like images of machine gears, wheels, or automobile imagery, or zigzag patterns of more exotic images. For example, the discovery of Tutankhamen's tomb in 1922 fueled an interest in things Egyptian, and so Egyptian-styled patterns found their way onto Art Deco buildings. The high point of Art Deco occurred between the two world wars, from the 1920s through the 1930s, but its major source of inspiration came after the 1925 Exposition Internationale des Arts Décoratifs et Industriels Modernes in Paris; it then spread across to the United States and remained popular through the 1950s.

In the United States, Art Deco made its first appearance in New York City and became the preferred style during this era that found a confluence of prosperity, an interest in travel, and the arts. Thus, the rhythm of jazz music, the growth of the American automobile industry, and the drive to create the tallest building in the country are all part of the cultural heritage of Art Deco. Raymond Hood was one of the earlier architects to work in the Art Deco style in the United States. His Chicago Tribune Tower, built in 1924 with John Mead Howells, exhibits a **Gothic Revival** style that was typical of the earliest **skyscrapers**, but then Hood sought to modernize and streamline this style with a new machine aesthetic. His Radio City Music Hall auditorium at Rockefeller Center in New York City (1930s) and the New York Daily News Building (1929) reflect this new style.

When Walter Chrysler commissioned William Van Alen to construct the Chrysler Building in New York City in 1930, it was meant to be the tallest building in the world. Constructed with a stainless steel frame, the building features decorative elements in the Art Deco style, such as eagles, car imagery, zigzags, a stepped-cone top, and a spire to increase the height of the building. At the same time, John Jacob Raskob of General Motors was planning the Empire State Building, begun in New York City by Shreve, Lamb, and Harmon in 1931 and finished just over one year later. This skyscraper measured 1,250 feet tall and was built with a **steel** skeleton and **bricks**. In the top third of the building, tiered sections allude to a stepped-pyramid format, like a Mesopotamian ziggurat. A spire was then added, making the Empire State Building the tallest building in New York, until it was surpassed by the **World Trade Center** in 1972. After the World Trade Center was destroyed in 2001, the Empire State Building again became the tallest building in New York City.

Art Deco came to symbolize all of the modern-age technical ingenuity that allowed for the great advances in the steel industry, the automobile industry, and the new "machine age" that brought great
prosperity and optimism to the United States. This style remained
popular through the next several decades. It spread across the country and can be found in Midwestern railroad stations, business office
headquarters, and local civic buildings. *See also* ANCIENT NEAR
EASTERN ARCHITECTURE.

ART NOUVEAU. Art Nouveau, translated simply as the "New Art,"
originated in Belgium and then France in the 1880s as highly stylized
and ornate, with floral shapes and patterns applied to buildings that
feature curved walls and other organic forms. Recalling natural rather
than man-made objects, Art Nouveau provided a contrast to the mass
production characteristic of the increasingly industrialized urban society found at the turn of the century. Popular through the first two
decades of the 20th century, Art Nouveau then became popular in
Spain, where it was called *modernisme* and is seen in the work of **Antoni Gaudí**; then in Munich and Berlin, where it was called the *Ju-
gendstil*; and also in Vienna, where it influenced the establishment of
the Vienna Secession, or *Sezessionsstil*, which in turn shared traits
with the **Arts and Crafts** style that had just been introduced in
Britain.

The first "true" Art Nouveau building is the Tassel House in Brussels, built by the Belgian architect Victor Horta in 1892 for science
professor Emile Tassel. Here Horta creates a rich environment that
blends curved wall surfaces, stained glass windows, mosaics, and
even stairwells with uniquely organic iron railings sweeping upward.
Both Horta and the Belgian artist Henry van de Velde can be seen as
the founders of the Art Nouveau style. Van de Velde, also influenced
by the English Arts and Crafts movement, was active in the German
Werkbund, where he argued for individuality in design over standardization.

In 1895 the French architect Hector Guimard went to Belgium and
saw the Tassel House. He then returned to Paris to begin working in
the Art Nouveau style. Guimard is best known for his Paris metro stations, built between 1899 and 1905. The Porte Dauphine, with a
glazed canopy that covers the underground entrance like a bonnet,

was built in 1899 and is today the only surviving Art Nouveau closed-roof metro station entrance. The entrances featured green-tinted cast iron railings, light figures, and sign posts that appear to grow out of the ground like bean stalks sprouting upward and twining around the stairwell. These "Metropolitain" entrances created a dramatic contrast to the prevailing classical style found in Paris at this time.

In 1897 in Vienna, 19 artists who had become increasingly disillusioned by the historical conservatism of the Vienna Kunstlerhaus formed their own organization called the Vienna Secession and elected the painter Gustav Klimt as their first president. In the same year in Vienna, Joseph Maria Olbrich constructed the Secession Building to house the group's art exhibitions. The exterior is painted a shining white with a very modern, streamlined version of classical articulation to give the impression of a temple. The angular aspects of the building are diminished by an overlay of applied organic patterns done in thin black lines to give the impression of vines growing across the exterior. A golden dome rests on top of the building, with no drum, but styled like a ball of intricately intertwined flowers held together by a gilded **iron** sphere.

Josef Hoffmann was also a member of the Vienna Secession, yet his more angular style relates less to the organic qualities of the Art Nouveau and more to the Arts and Crafts movement. His Palais Stoctlet, built in Brussels in 1905–1911 for a wealthy banker, reveals a smooth masonry exterior with strongly linear black and white outlines that run vertically and horizontally across the surface of the building. The rectangular windows echo the geometric shapes used to create this modern version of classicism. As architects sought a more varied approach to modern construction, the application or denial of applied decoration and presence or lack of historical references became a recurring discourse through the 20th century.

ARTS AND CRAFTS. The English Arts and Crafts movement was first introduced in the 1860s by the English artist, writer, and socialist William Morris. With a particular focus on higher standards of handcrafted work that was more accessible to the growing middle class, the Arts and Crafts Movement came as a reaction to both the impersonal mechanization of the Industrial Revolution and the overly ornate, upper-class Victorian style of previous generations. Inspired by the writings of John Ruskin, the style reached its high point in Great Britain from the 1880s to the 1910s and sometimes shared design elements with the French **Art Nouveau** style, the Austrian *Sezessionsstil*, and the accompanying *Wiener Werkstatte*, which focused on arts and crafts made for a select market.

Charles Rennie Mackintosh, a Scottish architect who worked mainly in Glasgow, is one of the best known Arts and Crafts architects. Mackintosh, in his building for the Glasgow School of Art, constructed from 1897 to 1909, blends the curving, organic design elements of Art Nouveau with a more modern angularity characteristic of the Arts and Crafts style. He designed the interior as well, with rich **wood** paneling, wood light fixtures, and beautiful hand-crafted, yet modern, furnishings. It is the Hill House, built on a hill overlooking the small town of Helensburgh, Scotland, that reveals Mackintosh's most famous use of the Arts and Crafts style. Built in 1902–1904 for the publisher Walter Blackie, this modern version of a baronial country house features exterior walls made of smooth local **stone**, a mix of organic shapes and straight lines with 90-degree angles, and his characteristic windows filled with 30 or so small panes of **glass**. Inside, Mackintosh designed the interior space to include his famous tall ladder-back Mackintosh chairs, as well as a beautiful set of garden furniture.

The American Bungalow, or the Craftsman style, as the Arts and Crafts style came to be called in the United States, was first introduced in the 1890s when an interest in new forms of domestic architecture spread across the country, lasting through the 1920s. In 1897 a group of architects and designers in Boston organized an exhibition of contemporary crafts at Copley Hall with a focus on Arts and Crafts designs that were incorporated into bungalow interiors. Shortly thereafter, in the early 1900s, the designer Gustav Stickley introduced his publication *The Craftsman*, which featured furniture based on the Mission style to match these homes.

Arts and Crafts bungalows, built across the United States until around 1920, are characterized by low-pitched roofs with steep gables, deeply overhanging eaves, exposed rafters, and brackets beneath the eaves. A front porch with square piers that support the roof, other architectural motifs based on the buildings of **Frank Lloyd**

Wright, and a handcrafted mixture of wood and stone lent elegance to these popular homes. Inside, the bungalows had features appropriate to the middle-class home buyer. For example, the "breakfast nook" began to appear in houses around this time, and the Victorian butler's pantry was replaced by built-in wood shelving in the kitchen and dining room. Unlike the **Victorian** kitchen, which was used by servants and therefore separated from the main living areas of the family, the Craftsman house featured a kitchen that was gradually becoming central to family life. Because the servants ate in the Victorian kitchen, it was never considered appropriate for family members to eat there, but the Craftsman breakfast nook, often placed in a bay window in the kitchen, allowed a place mainly for children to eat informal meals during the daytime.

Some of the most elegant Craftsman houses were built in California by the brothers Charles Sumner Greene and Henry Mather Greene, who established their architectural firm in Pasadena in 1894. Their most famous house is the Gamble House, built in Pasadena in 1908–1909 as a winter home for the family of David B. Gamble. This elegant bungalow, one of the best examples of domestic architecture in the United States, reveals the Greenes' desire to create a custom-built domestic structure that is both informal and elegant. The teak, maple, oak, and mahogany structure features wide overhanging roofs with timber brackets, a strongly horizontal design, side porches, and a wooden exterior that reflects **Japanese architecture**, while the more rustic appearance recalls an English country house. Sleeping porches and a garden setting provide a connection to nature and reflect current ideas on the need for sunlight and air circulation within a home. Although in some respects this home resembles the Japanese-influenced houses of Frank Lloyd Wright, the bungalow did not feature a new floor plan, as did Wright's homes. In addition, although the bungalow's dark-stained wood exterior recalls the look of a shingle home, it features a consistent custom interior that sets it apart from this other house type. In California, this Arts and Crafts style was also called the Mission style because it sometimes included Spanish Mission design elements.

Like the more simple **American Foursquare** houses, bungalows allowed children to be monitored from the kitchen because of the more open ground plan and large kitchen windows that looked out into the backyard. These houses reflect many transformations found in early-20th-century American family life, and ultimately bungalows and foursquare homes became the most popular house types purchased from pattern books. Bungalows, however, retained the regional characteristics and handcrafted features that gave middle-class domestic architecture a new elegance in the early decades of the 20th century.

ASPLUND, ERIK GUNNAR (1885–1940). Sweden's leading modern architect, Gunnar Asplund studied at the Royal Institute of Technology in Stockholm, completed his degree there in 1909, and went on to create an austere form of modernism that reveals a stripped-down version of classicism. Asplund's most famous building is his huge City Library in Stockholm, constructed in the 1920s. This monumental **brick** structure, consisting of three stories of library space, reveals a classical layout whereby a massive round drum surrounded by clerestory windows sits atop a giant square base. This symmetrical building, with a colossal door located at the center of each of its sides, recalls the ideal **Renaissance** centrally planned church. However, although the overall symmetrical design recalls **Andrea Palladio**'s Villa Rotonda, here Asplund's drum is not topped by a **dome**, but is flat, which creates a strikingly original silhouette in this urban setting.

Asplund's Woodland Cemetery, built into a beautiful park-like setting, was begun in Stockholm in 1915, with a crematorium added in the 1930s, and is one of the few 20th-century building complexes listed on UNESCO's World Heritage Sites. Here the wooded landscape and slopping fields create a pleasing contrast to Asplund's sharply angular and somber buildings. A small, modern chapel, one of several built in the surrounding woods in 1918–1920, was constructed as a simple white structure with a sharply hipped black roof and timber **columns** organized in a classicizing style. In contrast, the crematorium (1934–1940) includes three chapels, with the imposing Monument Hall located on a grassy lawn in front of the Chapel of the Holy Cross. This **stone** structure has a sharply angular rhythm of pillars supporting a thin flat roof that creates a subtle contrast to the landscape. Rather than dominating the land, however, these structures reveal the architect's desire to organize the surrounding space in order to provide places of contemplation and rest. Asplund's modernism ultimately brought Swedish aesthetics into the forefront of 20th-century architecture. *See also* INTERNATIONAL STYLE.

ASSYRIAN ARCHITECTURE. *See* ANCIENT NEAR EASTERN ARCHITECTURE.

AZTEC ARCHITECTURE. *See* MESOAMERICAN ARCHITECTURE.

– B –

BABYLONIAN ARCHITECTURE. *See* ANCIENT NEAR EASTERN ARCHITECTURE.

BAROQUE ARCHITECTURE. The 17th century in Europe is traditionally called the Baroque era. Although the origins of this term remain obscure, this century was incredibly important in the sciences, the arts, religion, and politics. Thus, architecture thrived during this age. By now, artists routinely modeled their imagery upon close observations of nature, thereby linking the sciences and the arts. In the 1500s, Copernicus had argued that the Earth revolves around the sun, and in the Baroque era Johannes Kepler first observed the elliptical orbits of the planets and Galileo developed a telescope to better observe the surface of the moon. People also learned more about their world through increased trade and travel, and it was during this era that many European countries created a flourishing economy by seeking to establish both economic and religious control over the Americas, Africa, and Asia. Protestantism had gradually taken hold in northern Europe, while southern Europe remained strongly Roman Catholic, which spurred on the Counter-Reformation. Counter-Reformatory leaders sponsored some of the most elaborate architectural construction of the century, while the newly wealthy middle class as well as the entrenched aristocracy sought to match this construction with their own government buildings and lavish homes.

Stylistically, Baroque architecture elaborates on **Renaissance** aesthetics by expanding classical references beyond **Vitruvius** to reveal a more eclectic form of classicism, one that is more sculptural and ornate. Baroque architecture is also considered to be more massive in size and more theatrical in its design and placement. It makes clear reference to its surrounding environment, which is why many people consider Baroque architects to exhibit some of the first ideas on urban planning. It came about at a time of extensive architectural construction, as seen in the monumental projects for **Saint Peter's Church in Rome** and **Versailles Palace** outside Paris.

One could argue that the Counter-Reformation was largely an architectural campaign, in which massive construction projects not only affirmed the power of the Roman Catholic Church but also inspired believers to remain loyal to this age-old faith. This was very different from the Protestant focus on a simplified church hierarchy, with its more restrained approach to artistic display in church architecture. The more lavish Baroque style is considered to have first appeared in Rome, where the Counter-Reformation's newly established Catholic religious orders sought to establish themselves with the construction of new churches at the same time that the papacy embarked on a massive campaign of architectural renewal. The leader of this movement in Rome was the architect **Gian Lorenzo Bernini**, who worked in a style that blended Renaissance classicism and a dynamic interaction with the surrounding environment. This style is seen in his famous church of Sant'Andrea al Quirinale, built in Rome in the 1650s, in which the façade curves back in a concave shape while a rounded portico pushes outward in the opposite direction. Inside, the oval ground plan provides a more varied and more sculptural effect than the Renaissance use of the square and circle to define church interior space. **Francesco Borromini** also worked in Rome during this time, and his church of Sant'Ivo alla Sapienza, built in the 1640s, reflects similar ideas. Here the façade rises up from a Renaissance courtyard to reveal a **dome** and lantern with fanciful spirals and sculptural elements that refer to its papal patronage. Considered eclectic and unique, Borromini's work reveals the new architectural freedom found in the Baroque era.

Neighborhood complexes were also constructed at this time, exemplified by the Piazza Navona, built in downtown Rome over an Ancient Roman stadium to house the family of Pope Innocent X. In the 1640s, the Pamphili Palace, which fronts onto the long, oval-shaped piazza, was enlarged, and then in the next decade Pope Innocent X commissioned the construction of a large church next to his palace, in emulation of Saint Peter's Church on the other side of town. This church, dedicated to Sant'Agnese, replaced a smaller church marking the spot where this early Christian saint was martyred. The original commission was given to Girolamo Rainaldi, who had been in charge of constructing the Pamphili Palace, and to his son Carlo Rainaldi. Borromini is credited with the undulating design of the façade, which curves outward from the center toward the tall, flanking towers. A dome then rests upon a tall drum that rises up to provide broad visibility across the city and to create a visual link with the dome of Saint Peter's Church. The highly sculptural façade as well as its monumentality are typical of Baroque architecture.

Gian Lorenzo Bernini was also commissioned during this same time to complete a large fountain sculpture called the Fountain of Four Rivers to symbolize the unification of the four parts of the world under the Catholic Empire. This fountain, located directly in front of Sant'Agnese, was designed with powerful water spouts to spray water over the travertine rock and provide a visual link to the church. It is also an auditory experience consistent with the Baroque interest in theatricality and the unification of the arts. This papal interest in neighborhood revitalization found favor on a smaller scale across the city. For example, Pietro da Cortona's church of Santa Maria della Pace, built in Rome in the 1660s, included carving out a small piazza in front of the church to accommodate carriage traffic, and renovating the façades of several of the surrounding apartment buildings to provide a visual regularity to the square.

Finally, the large Piazza del Popolo, which was particularly important as the northernmost entrance into the city of Rome, also received a thorough renovation in the 1660s to include the paving of the square, the addition of a large obelisk to anchor what was designated as the middle of this trapezoid-shaped square, and finally, the addition of matching churches built by Carlo Rainaldi at the ends of the trident-shaped streets that come together in the piazza. These churches, called Santa Maria dei Miracoli and Santa Maria in Montesanto, give the impression of perfect symmetry, but this symmetry is just an illusion because one church is oval and the other is circular in plan. Rainaldi adjusted the shapes of these churches in this ingenious way because the circular church was seen at a slightly raking angle from the piazza entrance, and thus, when viewed from across the piazza, it appears to match the oval church. It is this interest in theatricality and a more sophisticated understanding of optics and visual illusions that provide a dramatic and powerful first impression of the city of Rome so characteristic of the Baroque age.

Baroque-style architecture spread across Europe, and can be seen at Versailles Palace, built by François Mansart and Louis Le Vau beginning in the 1660s for King Louis XIV. This massive complex consists of a central core of royal apartments flanked by extensive administrative wings, a huge chapel, and various theaters and concert halls, some of which appear as separate buildings constructed throughout the extensive formal gardens of the palace. It is evident here how Roman Catholic Counter-Reformatory religious propaganda was adapted for use by the aristocracy across Europe to assert their dominance. In this case, the massive architectural complex of Versailles and its extensive surrounding gardens provided a powerful visual reminder of the king's far-reaching political influence. In the Netherlands, the Dutch "Golden Age" of Baroque architecture followed the classical principles of the Italian architects **Andrea Palladio** and Vincenzo Scamozzi, and classical buildings constructed by architects such as Hendrick de Keyser and **Jacob van Campen** in Haarlem and Amsterdam sought to legitimize rule through such historical precedent. In England, this aristocratic Baroque style was adapted for use by the court architects **Inigo Jones** and **Christopher Wren**, who constructed palaces and churches around London, while **John Vanbrugh**'s Blenheim Palace, located north of London and begun in 1705, recalls Versailles in its vast plan, symmetrical arrangement, and extensive surrounding gardens. This emphasis on theatricality and ornamentation set the stage for the architectural style of the next century, called the **Rococo**.

BARRAGÁN, LUIS (1902–1988). The modernist Mexican architect Luis Barragán is best known for his infusion of vernacular color and regional elements into an **International style** formula. Born in Guadalajara, Barragán traveled through Europe after receiving an engineering degree in his hometown. Deeply influenced by the Moorish gardens of southern Spain as well as the spare geometric architecture of **Le Corbusier**, Barragán returned to Mexico to develop a unique modern idiom that incorporated a deep interest in nature, spiritual elements, and regional characteristics such as thick walls and bright colors. Barragán was also influenced by the theoretical architect Frederick Kiesler, who worked in theater design and promoted a more organic, surrealist style, as well as by Mathias Goeritz, who trained in the **Arts and Crafts** movement in Berlin before accepting a position at the School of Architecture in Guadalajara in 1949. Goeritz's manifesto on emotional architecture from 1952 infused art and urban planning with an expressive and spiritual context that he found lacking in the prevailing International style.

Barragán returned to Mexico the same year as Goeritz's manifesto, and in 1954 he received a commission for the renovation of a convent and construction of an adjoining chapel in Tlalpan, outside Mexico City. The chapel is built from **concrete** as a yellow rectangular room with two light sources. One window at the back of the chapel directs a stream of light into the congregational space, while a hidden second window illuminates a slim orange crucifix located at the altar's right side. The crucifix then casts a shadow directly on the altar, providing a subtle spiritual message. A **wood** floor warms the stark interior, while the roughly textured walls create a rich quality to the otherwise spare interior. The enclosed space of the Tlalpan Chapel provides an emotional environment formed from light and color that is both universal and regional. In 1958, Barragán and Goeritz collaborated on their best-known work, the Ciudad Satélite (Satellite City), which consists of five triangular concrete towers that recall Ancient Egyptian temple pylons. These brightly colored monuments are built at a busy intersection in Mexico City and provide an unusual and dramatic focal point to an otherwise crowded and monochromatic urban context. Barragán's work is limited to a region of Mexico, and therefore he did not initially receive much international acclaim, but in 1980 he was awarded the prestigious Pritzker Architecture Prize. Certainly future scholars will better understand Barragán's work and the role he played in anticipating the regional focus found in the current architectural style called **Critical Regionalism**.

BARRY, CHARLES (1795–1860). *See* GOTHIC REVIVAL ARCHITECTURE.

BAUHAUS ARCHITECTURE. Bauhaus architecture is intricately linked to the **International style**, which sought to redirect architectural aesthetics toward less opulent, more streamlined construction. The word Bauhaus ("House of Building") was the name of a design school that, despite its initial lack of an architectural curriculum, was fundamental in shaping modern German architecture. The German architect and designer **Walter Gropius** founded the school in Weimar in 1919 after convincing local authorities to allow him to bring together the city's art and craft schools into one curriculum so that he could reconcile the differing tracks of art and industry into one aesthetic unit. In 1925, the Bauhaus moved to Dessau. An architectural curriculum was added there in 1927.

Only after students studied craft art with Johannes Itten (1888–1967) could they then focus their studies on architecture, but because Itten's artistic interests were more in line with the individualized **Arts and Crafts** movement than Gropius's emphasis on industrial design, he was eventually replaced by Laszlo Moholy-Nagy (1895–1946) and a focus on the mass production of his own crafts. The fundamental philosophical tension between the unique and the mass produced in art was magnified in architecture, which suffered from a more complex economic reality, and therefore the architects rarely were able to satisfy their dreams in Germany. Both Gropius and Moholy-Nagy left the Bauhaus in 1928, and Gropius went on to introduce the modern Bauhaus style of architecture in the United States. In 1932, the school was moved to Berlin, and its last director, **Ludwig Mies van der Rohe**, joined Gropius in the United States just before Adolf Hitler closed the school a year later. In the United States, both architects were instrumental in the establishment of the succeeding **International style**.

BEAUX-ARTS ARCHITECTURE. The Beaux-Arts style of architecture first appeared in Europe in the mid-19th century and can be characterized as a blending of classical, **Renaissance**, **Baroque**, and **Rococo** elements to create a new type of bold, large-scale, and noble construction. The epicenter of this new stylistic development was the École des Beaux-Arts in Paris, where this type of historicism formed the core of the architecture curriculum. The style is best exemplified in Paris by the Opéra, built by **Charles Garnier** in the 1860s, and it became popular in the United States after it was introduced in the "White City" of the World's Columbian Exposition, held in Chicago in 1893. Here, the idea of the "City Beautiful," with its grand Neo-Baroque boulevards, clean streets, and opulent **marble** architecture, cultivated a new interest in beautifying the crowded, dirty industrial cities of the United States.

Money was not lacking during the "gilded age" of the 1880s through the 1920s, when wealthy philanthropists in the United States sought to carve out their fame through the construction of opera houses, libraries, museums, government buildings, and massive private mansions. These clients favored the Beaux-Arts style of **Richard Morris Hunt** and **Charles Follen McKim**, both of whom trained at the École in Paris. McKim, Mead, and White's completion of the Boston Public Library in 1895, done in the Beaux-Arts style, coincided with Hunt's commission for the construction of the Beaux-Arts Metropolitan Museum of Art in New York City. Not to be outdone by construction in Boston, however, New York City officials campaigned for donations to build the New York Public Library, which was begun in 1902 by the little-known architects John Carrère and Thomas Hastings, both of whom had studied at the École des Beaux-Arts in Paris. At the time of its completion, the New York Public Library was the largest marble building in the United States.

Finally, Grand Central Terminal, from 1903, was built in this same style by the architectural firm of Whitney Warren and Charles Wetmore. Thus, not 10 years after the introduction of the ideal Beaux-Arts city at the Chicago Exposition, New York City was well on its way to transforming itself into this model. By the 1920s, however, European modern architecture, with its sparer appearance and clean lines, was beginning to filter into the United States; it created a sharp aesthetic contrast to the Beaux-Arts style, which was increasingly seen as too opulent and overblown. Finally, the Wall Street crash of 1929 signaled the end of the Beaux-Arts tradition, and post–World War I architecture came to be oriented toward entirely different concerns. *See also* INTERNATIONAL STYLE.

BEHRENS, PETER (1868–1940). Peter Behrens was instrumental in the architectural reform in Germany at the turn of the 20th century that led to a more modern form of architecture called the **International**

style. In 1907, Behrens, together with 11 other architects and designers, formed the *Deutscher Werkbund* (German Work Federation) to cultivate a link between the traditional **Arts and Crafts** Movement and modern mass production so that Germany could compete economically with England and the United States yet still champion the artistic ideal of individuality in design over standardization. Other architects of this movement included Henry van de Velde and **Josef Hoffmann**, both of whom worked in the **Art Nouveau** style.

Known mainly for his construction of factories and office buildings, Behrens's most famous building is the AEG Turbine Factory, built in Berlin in 1910. Constructed of **brick**, **glass**, and **steel**, this spare building anticipates in its functional "factory" aesthetic the future work of Behrens's students and assistants, **Ludwig Mies van der Rohe**, **Le Corbusier**, and **Walter Gropius.** Behrens had initially been hired as the artistic director for the company, responsible for crafting its "corporate identity." With this important building, however, he brought the "factory" aesthetic into the forefront of modern architecture.

BERLAGE, HENDRIK PETRUS (1856–1934). One of Holland's first modernist architects, Hendrik Berlage studied with the historically oriented architect Gottfried Semper, but gradually Berlage began to experiment with a more geometric, spare, rational approach to architecture. His most famous building is the Amsterdam Stock Exchange, known as the Beurs van Berlage, built in the center of the city from 1896 to 1903. The style of this monumental **brick** building can be characterized as a stripped-down **Richardsonian Romanesque**, and it features a tripartite entrance façade with a triple-arched entrance portico flanked by a clock tower. The long exterior side walls are visually organized by groupings of windows that provide a rhythm to the exterior and demonstrate Berlage's interest in proportion. The building contained three exchange halls, the chamber of commerce, a post office, and a cafeteria, and is today used as a museum and community center. To Berlage, a successful building will achieve the idea of *riposo*, or repose, through carefully proportioned spaces that are organized so as to reveal the idea of "unity in plurality." To him, it is only through this unity that true beauty can be achieved in architecture. Berlage was influential in the establishment of modernism in the Netherlands, seen mainly in the subsequent work of the *de Stijl* architects. *See also* RATIONALISM.

BERNINI, GIAN LORENZO (1598–1680). Gian Lorenzo Bernini, the best-known Italian architect of the **Baroque** era, was born during the time of the Counter-Reformation and became the major architect in the revitalization of the city of Rome after the establishment of Protestantism in northern Europe. During the 17th century, church patrons in Rome embarked on an architectural renewal of the city to "counter" the influence of Protestantism and to showcase the city's worldwide importance as the seat of Roman Catholicism. Bernini, who came from a family of sculptors attached to the papal court in Rome, was exposed from an early age to aristocratic culture and the art community. His earliest work was in sculpture; he gained a reputation for imitating classical models so closely that his works could be mistaken for antique.

From this experience, Bernini moved on to architecture, working at **Saint Peter's Church in Rome** in the 1620s to construct a huge bronze baldachin over the crossing of the nave and in the 1660s to create a bronze altar in the choir of the church. In the 1650s, Pope Innocent X commissioned Bernini to create an enclosed piazza for Saint Peter's, and here Bernini designed a huge oval-shaped piazza connected to the smaller, existing trapezoidal square located in front of the church. Meant to symbolize the comforting "arms" of the church, the oval piazza allowed for the much larger open congregational space needed during annual celebrations and especially jubilee years. The colonnade that defines the oval was designed by Bernini as a continuous loggia topped by rows of statuary along the roofline. In the center of the piazza, a huge **Egyptian** obelisk anchors the symmetry of the design and is flanked by matching fountains on either side that bring water to the piazza. **Marble** lines located on the pavement of the piazza reinforce this oval plan and recall the intricate pattern found on the pavement of the Capitoline Hill piazza, designed by Michelangelo a hundred years earlier.

Bernini's most famous building is his church of Sant'Andrea al Quirinale, built in Rome beginning in 1658 and paid for by the papal nephew Camillo Pamphili. This church, located on the Quirinale Hill, was limited in size by site restrictions and an awkwardly narrow space. Issues of space became highly pronounced in the Baroque period, when hundreds of new Catholic religious orders were established in Rome and needed their own churches. Sant'Andrea was constructed for the newly established Jesuit order. Although the site is small, Bernini set the church back off the street, thereby sacrificing interior congregational space, to provide for a small curved piazza that would give the building a stronger presence on its crowded street. He then gave the façade a semicircular set of steps leading up to a small portico with a curved roof that matches the curvature of the porch steps. Two large **columns** support the porch roof, and the corners of the façade are flanked by colossal pilasters that rise to a triangular pediment. The front is built as one tall bay unit, creating what is called an aedicular façade. Baroque churches differ from Renaissance buildings in that they tend to be larger, more monumental, and with a greater emphasis on sculptural details and a theatrical interest in the space surrounding the building. Despite its small size, Bernini was able to monumentalize the church of Sant'Andrea al Quirinale. The oval interior of the church is richly decorated with colored marble and sculptured figures that interact across the congregational space of the room. For example, a painting of Saint Andrew, located over the high altar, appears again in sculpted form above the altar pediment. Here the saint is perched on a curved ledge that supports his body, pausing on his way up to heaven via the gilded **dome** of the church. It is this type of dynamic and theatrical approach to architecture that best epitomizes the Baroque style of Bernini in Rome.

BLOBITECTURE. *See* EXPRESSIONISM.

BOFFRAND, GERMAIN (1667–1754). *See* ROCOCO ARCHITECTURE.

BOFILL, RICARDO (1939–). *See* POST-MODERN ARCHITECTURE.

BORROMINI, FRANCESCO (1599–1667). Francesco Borromini has traditionally been considered the great rival of **Gian Lorenzo Bernini** in **Baroque** Rome, but more recent research has shown that they collaborated on a number of commissions through their coinciding careers. Borromini initially came to Rome from northern Italy when he was 20 years old to work as an apprentice in the architectural workshop of his uncle, Carlo Maderno. During the 1620s, Maderno was working on the façade of Saint Peter's Church, and there Borromini probably first met Bernini, who was at the time working inside the church on a series of sculptures. Borromini's architectural style can be characterized as more dynamic and perhaps more eclectic than Bernini's, whose Baroque style is tempered with a classicizing organization.

Borromini's best-known building is his small church of San Carlo alle Quattro Fontane, located just down the street from Bernini's church of Sant'Andrea al Quirinale. San Carlo, begun in the 1630s, is located at the corner of an intersection between two major Counter-Reformatory streets where a wall fountain had been installed in each of the four corners; thus the church received its name both from this location and from its dedication to San Carlo Borrommeo, one of the leaders of the Counter-Reformation. The church was commissioned by the newly established Catholic Order of the Trinitarians as their mother church in Rome, and its interior was beautifully decorated to reflect this significance. The façade of the church, completed in 1665, has a dramatically undulating curvature that creates a break from the straight line of the street. The center of the façade bulges outward together with the central stairs that spill out into the street, while the flanking bays of the tripartite front curve inward. A carved figure of San Carlo appears over the central doorway, while the entablature above separates the first story from the second with a strong, undulating movement. The highly sculptural second story features in the center of the façade a giant cartouche held by angels. The interior congregational space, built in the 1630s, reveals an oval shape that seems to be pinched inward slightly to form four curved "corners" of large **columns**. This effect provides an axial direction to the curved ground plan, allowing the visitor to focus on the high altar. The **dome** is also shaped into an oval, with pendentives that connect the dome to the "corner" columns of the room. It is this type of highly sculptural church interior that gives the appearance of being modeled out of clay.

Borromini's Church of Sant'Ivo alla Sapienza, built in Rome in the 1640s, is even more audacious in the way the architect mixes the three basic shapes of circle, square, and triangle in very plastic ways to create star patterns, ovals, and other forms. It is this architectural complexity that earned Borromini the reputation as an architect truly unique in his profession, eclectic and unusual, but who in this regard also demonstrated the Baroque architect's freedom from the rigid rules of **Vitruvius** and **Renaissance architecture**.

BOTTA, MARIO (1943–). The Swiss architect Mario Botta studied art and architecture first in Milan and then in Venice. During his education at the Istituto Universitario di Architettura in Venice, he was an assistant to **Le Corbusier** and then to **Louis Kahn**. Combining the geometric aesthetic of Le Corbusier's version of the **International style** with his own urban interests, Botta's architecture is often called Neo-Rationalist, the style also favored by the Italian architects Carlo Scarpa and **Aldo Rossi**. Neo-Rationalist tendencies include a very precise geometric organization of space into crisply delineated straight lines that reveal a clear symmetry and overall order. Botta's Kyobo Tower in Seoul, South Korea (1999–2003), is a good example of this style. The monumental structure, built as a pair of matching **brick** towers connected in the middle with an upper-story **glass** skywalk, has a thin strip of square windows running down the center of the front of each tower. The central entranceway steps up in height to create a tiered opening at ground level that echoes the square shape of the towers and windows. On the opposite side of the building, a *brise-soleil* filters light inside the building through a grid-like pattern of openings.

In addition to the creation of this very ordered style, Botta is also interested in giving an urban focus to his monumental structures. His Church of Santo Volto, built in Turin in 2001–2006, was constructed in an abandoned industrial area of the city with the hope of revitalizing this neighborhood through new architectural construction. This structure is designed with a central brick tower cleaved very precisely into eight parts that are loosely joined together at their base, which is then surrounded by paired *exedra*, or chapels, that curve up and then outward from the central core of the building as if rotated on an axis from their traditional semicircular orientation. While *exedra* often help buttress the domed center of a church, in this case, these external side chapels split off from the fragmented central core and point outward, creating a strongly regular rhythm to both the exterior and the interior congregational space. A good example of Post–Vatican II architectural design, the circular format of the building seems at first to minimize the axial direction of the church interior, but the carefully aligned rows of pews in the congregational space provide a clear direction toward the altar.

Mario Botta's strongly geometric structures provide a modern take on the traditional classical idiom so historically prevalent in Italy. While Botta's buildings are more rational than organic, he remains interested in the symbolic qualities of light and space in his structures and considers the relationship between his buildings and their surrounding urban context central to an understanding of their function and meaning. *See also* RATIONALISM.

BOULLÉE, ÉTIENNE-LOUIS (1728–1799). *See* NEO-CLASSICAL ARCHITECTURE.

BOYLE, RICHARD (LORD BURLINGTON) (1695–1753). Richard Boyle, Third Earl of Burlington, was one of the English "gentlemen architects" of the 18th century who worked in the **Neo-Classical** style. This era is characterized by a widespread yet serious openness to all of the arts and sciences, hence its designation as the "Age of Enlightenment." Fields of inquiry included the new "social" sciences, alongside the traditional sciences and arts, while the ideals of Ancient Rome were taken as models. Therefore, it became popular for wealthy students to complete their university education with a grand tour of Europe, thereby establishing the origins of the modern tourist industry. Richard Boyle was one of these "tourists" who went on to become an amateur architect. He argued that the prevailing **Rococo** style was too decadent and immoral and instead advocated a return to classical ideals to bring architecture back to its "pure" form.

Boyle went to Italy to study the **Renaissance** work of **Andrea Palladio**, which epitomizes this classical style. Palladio was famous for his villas constructed in the region around Venice, and it was this domestic type that was the model for Chiswick House, designed in the 1720s by Richard Boyle as his private home in West London. English country homes were very popular among wealthy clients, who used these villas to display the collections of art they acquired while traveling. Thus, Chiswick House recalls in its overall design Palladio's Villa Rotonda, also called the Villa Belvedere, which was built in the 1560s outside the town of Vicenza in the Veneto. While the Villa Belvedere is a square building with a columned portico on each of the four sides, Chiswick House has one main entrance portico and thus a more axially directed interior. Additional rows of stairs lead up on either side of the portico, which is designed with fluted, Corinthian **columns** that support a triangular pediment. The rectangular windows and octagonal **dome** update Palladio's Renaissance structure while the interior, designed by William Kent, is more ornate than Palladio's building. Kent also designed around the villa a picturesque English garden that is characterized by a less formal and more relaxed setting than the popular French gardens, such as those at **Versailles** and Rococo palaces. In the second half of the 18th century, Boyle's version of Neo-Classicism became very popular across Europe, and it ultimately supplanted the Rococo style to endure for the next two centuries.

BRAMANTE, DONATO (1444–1514). Donato Bramante is considered the first High **Renaissance** architect in Rome because his classical style shifted from the more general use of classical references characteristic of the Early Renaissance to a more specific and sustained use of classical vocabulary. Originally trained as a painter in the court of Urbino, in central Italy, Bramante first worked for the Sforza family of Milan, where he probably met Leonardo da Vinci and became interested in architecture.

In 1502, Bramante settled in Rome and received a commission from King Ferdinand and Queen Isabella of Spain to complete a small shrine located on the supposed site of Saint Peter's crucifixion. This small round church came to be called "The Tempietto," or "Little Temple," in recognition of the fact that it most closely recalls buildings from classical antiquity that followed the principles of architecture first defined in Ancient Rome by **Vitruvius**. Given that this small church is a memorial to Saint Peter, it therefore does not have a large congregational space but instead is meant to be a *martyrium*, that is, a building that demarcates the site of the martyrdom or burial of a person. This centrally planned church features a base that leads up to the colonnaded portico via three steps. Although most churches in the Renaissance and subsequent **Baroque** eras were longitudinal in plan, this circular plan was considered the more perfect shape for a church. A circle is completely symmetrical, with no beginning and no end, and in the Renaissance it came to symbolize infinity, and therefore, God himself. It follows that the round Tempietto is therefore the most nearly perfect, or ideal, ground plan. Its portico is supported with Doric **columns**, the simplest capital design, favored by Vitruvius for the commemoration of male gods and consequently also used in the Renaissance to commemorate male saints. Above the columns of the Tempietto, triglyphs separate the square metopes, which are carved with symbols of Saint Peter, including his keys and papal tiara. A balustrade, or porch balcony, caps the portico, while a graceful drum behind the balustrade supports a **dome** capped by a lantern with a cross on top.

After the election of Julius II to the papacy in 1503, Bramante was given the most prestigious commission in all of Rome, that of rebuilding the ancient church of **Saint Peter**. The original church was over one thousand years old but it had been reinforced over the centuries so that it still functioned as the main church of Roman Catholicism, built over the site where Saint Peter was buried. Given the historical importance of this building, earlier popes had hesitated to tear it down, but Julius II considered the rebuilding of the church an important step in revitalizing the city of Rome. Bramante devised a Greek-cross-plan church with a massive dome that would rise over the Roman skyline. Pope Julius II and Bramante both died before the work was completed, but subsequent popes continued the massive project into the next century and achieved Pope Julius's dream of building the largest church in the entire Christian world. With these buildings epitomizing the High Renaissance architectural style, Bramante's short-lived architectural career received lasting recognition.

BRETON, GILLES LE (c. 1506–1558). *See* FONTAINEBLEAU, FRANCE.

BREUER, MARCEL (1902–1981). Born in Hungary, Marcel Breuer first trained at the famous **Bauhaus** School of Design in Germany and worked with the German modernist architect **Walter Gropius**. Known as one of the founders of modernism in both architecture and furniture design, Breuer was initially interested in creating simple, geometric forms and modular shapes, while later in life he began to experiment with a softer, more expressive form of construction. In addition, this modernism characterizes his furniture, as seen in his famous 1925 Wassily Chair made with a curved tubular **steel** frame. Breuer also experimented with bent and formed plywood furniture.

Breuer left Germany in the 1930s to flee Nazi persecution and settled first in London and then in Boston, where he taught students such as **Philip Johnson** at Harvard University. In Boston Breuer was reunited with his colleague Gropius, and together they built a few homes in the Boston area, thereby helping to establish modernist domestic architecture in the United States. In 1941, Breuer opened his own firm in New York City. His Breuer House II in New Canaan, Connecticut, built in 1948, is very daring in that its hillside construction integrates a stark white geometric structure made of cantilevered **concrete** and large **glass** windows into a more structurally sophisticated version of **Le Corbusier**'s villa designs. Breuer's Geller House, built in Lawrence, Long Island, in 1945, is perhaps his most important home. Here he introduced what he called a "binuclear" house, in which an entrance foyer and hallway separate the living areas from the sleeping areas, a format used in most subsequent **ranch** houses built in the United States. Working with the famous Italian structural architect Pier Luigi Nervi, Breuer was finally able, through his commission for the UNESCO World Headquarters built in Paris in 1953, to translate his experimental concrete designs and structural sophistication into a large-scale public monument. Despite this large-scale commission, Breuer remains best known for his modernist domestic architecture. *See also* INTERNATIONAL STYLE.

BRICK. Brick is a form of man-made masonry that can be layered to enclose a space or held together with a mortar binder to create a structural support. Brick is made of a mixture of clay and sand, while the mortar is made of sand and a paste. The earliest mud bricks were pressed into molds and sun-dried. This technique was first used around 7500 BC in **Prehistoric architecture** found in the Neolithic towns of Çatal Hüyük in western Turkey and in Jericho. Sun-dried bricks are less stable than fired bricks and typically last about 30 years, which is why **Ancient Near Eastern** monuments such as the

Sumerian ziggurats (2000 BC) were continually rebuilt upon mounds made from the rubble of prior monuments.

The largest sun-dried mud brick building that exists today is the Great Mosque of Djenné, in the western African country of Mali, which is one of the most unusual examples of **Islamic architecture**. The town of Djenné was settled by merchants around 800 and is the oldest sub-Saharan city, historically important as one of the major crossroads of African trade. Built for the first time in the 13th century, this mosque symbolizes the 26th king of Djenné's conversion to Islam. The current building dates to 1907, and great care was taken to reconstruct it according to its original design. The people of Djenné have continued to place a great emphasis on the preservation of the historical design of this mosque, which is why it is now listed as a UNESCO World Heritage Site. The mosque is a wide, brown, mud plaster–covered building with conical minarets that give it a highly sculptural appearance. It has one entrance and no windows or external decoration, but the upper portion of the walls is constructed with palm **wood** timbers that jut out of the wall surface and provide exterior scaffolding needed for access to the roof. The entire structure is built up on a platform to protect it from flooding, while the mud plaster helps to seal the porous mud bricks. Despite these precautions, the mud brick must be attended to regularly, so each year, the Djenné community participates in maintenance on the building that includes repairing the cracks and other damage created from rain, heat, and erosion.

Although less stable than other materials, this type of mud brick is a sustainable material found in all cultures and is therefore very versatile. In the western United States, a form of mud brick called *adobe* by Spanish settlers was used in **Native American** dwellings that can still be seen today, for example, in the Pueblo of Taos in New Mexico. Constructed around 1000–1450, this original settlement is located about one mile away from the modern city of Taos. The form of mud brick used here is a mud mixed with straw or dung to increase its durability. Fired bricks are more durable than sun-dried mud bricks, and therefore they allow for the construction of larger, more long-standing structures. Some of the earliest fired mud bricks can be found in the ancient **Indian** settlements along the Indus Valley, such as at Mohenjo-Daro, which dates to around 3000 BC. In later

Mesopotamian structures, fired ceramic tiles were colored, glazed, and used as a decorative covering for brick, as seen in the Neo-Babylonian Ishtar Gate, which dates to 575 BC and is now located in the State Museum in Berlin. Though fired bricks are more stable than sun-dried bricks, they are more difficult to make in climates that lack adequate timber resources for fire.

The Ancient Greeks had adequate supplies of **stone** to use for their buildings, but the **Ancient Romans** often used a stone veneer over **concrete** or brick. Therefore, the Roman brick industry became widespread, as discussed by **Vitruvius** in his treatise *The Ten Books on Architecture*, written in the first century BC. Roman bricks were used for construction across the varied geography of the Roman Empire, and, in keeping with the Roman cultivation of architectural propaganda, their bricks were stamped with a Roman insignia. Roman bricks were used for both support and for cladding. Brick was laid into intricate patterns, such as the herringbone pattern that first appeared in Mesopotamia and became famous in the Roman Empire, and both brick patterns and different brick shapes allowed for greater flexibility in the use of brick in load-bearing construction. For example, the vaulting in the Baths of Caracalla, built in Rome in AD 211, consists of a layer of brick laid flat alternating with brick laid on its edges and bonded with quick-set mortar to give the vault its curved shape.

By the Middle Ages, the wedge-shaped bricks used in Ancient Roman construction disappeared, and over time, the recipe for concrete was lost. Medieval brick developed out of many localized industries and had distinct regional characteristics. **Early Christian** brickwork in Ravenna is best seen in the Mausoleum of Galla Placidia, Ravenna, from AD 425. This small building was constructed with rectangular bricks of all different sizes, while the larger, **domed Byzantine** church of San Vitale in Ravenna, built in AD 546, reveals an intricate use of octagonal bricks in the drum of the dome. By the **Renaissance**, stone or stucco-covered brick found favor, given the desire to emulate Ancient Roman buildings. However, **Filippo Brunelleschi** studied Ancient Roman brickwork intently, and used the famous Roman herringbone pattern in the interior shell of his dome for the **Florence Cathedral**; constructed in the 1420s, it was the largest dome built since the concrete dome of the **Pantheon**.

In the modern era, the desire to construct taller buildings with larger unencumbered interiors encouraged the development of more sophisticated construction materials such as modern concrete and **steel**. Thus, brick was not often used for support in high-rise buildings, although **Louis Sullivan** alluded to its supportive function in his Wainwright Building in St. Louis (1891), which he covered with brick on the exterior to mimic the internal steel framing. Gradually, modern architects began to distrust the structural capabilities of brick, preferring to use it more sparingly as cladding. Brick continued to be used, however, to cultivate a modest, natural, or regional aesthetic. This can be seen in **Hendrick Petrus Berlage**'s Amsterdam Stock Exchange, completed in 1903 with a spare brick cladding that creates a humble, unadorned surface, in keeping with the modernist desire to strip away excessive ornamentation. **Walter Gropius** and Adolf Meyer's Fagus Shoe Factory, in Alfeld an der Leine, Germany (1911), has a brick-clad exterior with large **glass** curtain windows in keeping with the "factory" aesthetic of early-20th-century modernism. Through the 20th century, however, brick is most consistently used in domestic architecture. Famous examples include **Frank Lloyd Wright**'s Robie House, built in Chicago in 1906–1909, **Alvar Aalto**'s Baker House Dormitory at MIT, Boston, in 1947–1949, and **Robert Venturi**'s Guild House in Philadelphia, from 1963. Despite the great variety of architectural materials available today, brick continues to be extremely versatile and low in cost, and therefore it remains an important building material, with about one-half of all domestic architecture worldwide still constructed of brick or mud brick.

BRUNELLESCHI, FILIPPO (c. 1377–1446). Filippo Brunelleschi, traditionally considered the founder of early **Renaissance architecture** in Italy, trained as a goldsmith in Florence and gained an understanding of architecture while studying classical buildings in Rome. Many Renaissance architects were interested in antiquity, but Brunelleschi's desire to examine the proportions and engineering of Roman buildings with mathematical precision enabled him to more fully understand Roman structural innovations. In order to facilitate his more accurate system of measurement, Brunelleschi invented an optical device whereby he created a pinhole at the center of a painted image of the Baptistry of Florence and then angled a mirror toward the front of the image. By looking through the pinhole from the back of the painting, one could see the mirror reflection of the painting, and when the mirror was removed, the actual baptistery, identical in scale, would appear to the viewer. After this experiment was described by Brunelleschi's biographer and friend Antonio Manetti, in his *Vita di Filippo Brunelleschi* (c. 1480), one-point perspective came to be used by many early Renaissance sculptors and painters, including Donatello and Masaccio.

Around 1407, Brunelleschi returned to Florence from Rome and received the very prestigious commission to complete the **dome** of the **Florence Cathedral**, a church dedicated to Santa Maria del Fiore. This project had languished for more than 40 years because earlier architects did not know how to cover the massive crossing of the existing church with such a large dome. No dome this size had been built since antiquity, and because the knowledge of **concrete**, seen in the **Pantheon** dome, remained lost in the Renaissance, Brunelleschi designed a dome that featured the use of **bricks** to create an interior shell, while **wood** was used to build an outer shell. Brunelleschi's plan involved the construction of a tall drum covered by a double-shell dome featuring **Gothic** ribs and a Roman oculus window topped by a classical lantern. Since the 138-foot (42 meter) diameter was too large for any type of a centering device and too tall for any ground scaffolding, each layer of the dome was self-supporting and reinforced between the two shells with interior **arches** and Roman herringbone-patterned brickwork. The lantern was completed by Brunelleschi's student Michelozzo di Bartolommeo in 1461, and the Cathedral of Florence came to be called the "Duomo" because of its imposing silhouette. Brunelleschi's almost immediate fame rested on the ingenious solutions he proposed to the logistical challenges of such a monumental construction, and he parlayed that fame into a secondary career in theatrical machinery.

Brunelleschi's subsequent buildings provide a more fully addressed aesthetic system that blends mathematical ratios with classical philosophy and Christian symbolism. In 1419, he was hired to complete the Ospedale degli Innocenti, or Foundling Hospital, in Florence, one of the first public orphanages built since antiquity.

Civic buildings traditionally had a loggia, or open portico, across the front, and here Brunelleschi's loggia creates a classically harmonious design of nine round arches set in bay units of 10 *braccia*, or about 20 feet each unit. Because the diameter of each arch is equal to the depth of the porch and the height of each **column**, the effect is a perfect cube. A green-gray **stone**, called *pietra serena*, separates the Composite Corinthian columns and classical arches from the white wall background, while blue terracotta medallions featuring standing swaddled infants appear above each column. A clear relationship between all parts can be found in this building, which is a trait that became the hallmark of Renaissance design.

Brunelleschi's churches of San Lorenzo and Santo Spirito, both of which were conceived in the 1420s and completed after his death, also demonstrate a classical aesthetic as well as an interest in geometry, but his architectural philosophy is most fully realized in his small Pazzi Chapel, a freestanding building located next to the Gothic church of Santa Croce in Florence that was mainly built in the 1430s. The exterior of the chapel was constructed with an arched, tripartite portico that might have been completed after Brunelleschi's death. The design recalls the Arch of Constantine (built in AD 312–315 to commemorate Constantine's victory over Maxentius) and was subsequently used as a general façade design in the Renaissance to symbolize the triumph of Christianity. The portico ceiling of the Pazzi Chapel, decorated with classicizing shells and coffers, directs the visitor into a spare room articulated with wall molding and **marble** floor patterning that divides the rectangular room into ratios of 1:2, 1:3, and 1:4 from the crossing square, with an altar square across from the entrance. These divisions continue with explicit number symbolism and religious meaning. For example, the four corner pendentives feature medallions of the four Evangelists, and the 12 wall pilasters divide the room into vertical sections featuring medallions of the 12 apostles located just beneath the entablature. This symbolism is further reinforced in the 12 ribs of the small umbrella dome above the crossing square.

In these ways, the Pazzi Chapel most fully and clearly realized the Renaissance reverence for the circle, the triangle, and the square, as well as the meaning of these shapes and their numerical equivalents in both classical philosophy and Christian symbolism. Thus, while the dome of the Florence Cathedral displays Brunelleschi's understanding of Roman structural innovations, the Pazzi Chapel, in its simple harmony, best represents Brunelleschi's classical aesthetic.

BRUTALISM. The term "Brutalism" was introduced by the architectural critic Reyner Banham in his 1966 publication *The New Brutalism: Ethic or Aesthetic?* This movement was meant to redirect modern architecture toward a more monumental and heroic form and away from what was increasingly perceived as a frivolous, less utilitarian modern mode of architecture. Although the origins of Brutalism are found in **Le Corbusier**'s later work, the style was further established in London by Peter and Alison Smithson, and it flourished through the 1960s and 70s in the **concrete** buildings of many internationally known architects such as Gordon Bunshaft, **I. M. Pei**, and **Tadao Ando**, all three of whom have received the prestigious Pritzker Architecture Prize. One of the earliest buildings in the Brutalist style is Le Corbusier's Unité d'Habitation, built in Marseilles, France, in 1946–1952. This 12-story apartment building consists of a rectangular structure elevated on piers. Made from reinforced concrete, the grid design allowed for precast apartment modules to be set into the building frame. Le Corbusier's *béton brut*, or "raw concrete," became the most popular style of material for Brutalist buildings, and is characterized by the appearance of seams and imprints left in the concrete after being processed. Although Brutalism was initially meant to restore honesty to modern architecture, it quickly became synonymous with the more severe and ugly concrete buildings constructed across Europe after World War II.

The need for inexpensive housing probably initiated the use of this highly functional, although somewhat severe, architectural style, but Brutalism was later used in many other types of structures such as offices, churches, government buildings, and museums. Gordon Bunshaft's Hirshhorn Museum and Sculpture Garden, built in Washington, D.C., in 1974, typifies this style. Built as a large, concrete cylinder elevated on four wide piers, the building dominates the Mall with a modern grandeur that is in sharp contrast to what was increasingly considered an overly pompous **Beaux-Arts** architectural surrounding. I. M. Pei's National Center for Atmospheric Research, built in Boulder, Colorado, in 1961–1967, is made from massive rough-cut, block-like concrete rectangles set at 90-degree angles to each other. A complex interweaving of solids and voids provides a visual interest to the building that Pei capitalizes upon further in his design for the East Wing of the National Gallery of Art in Washington, D.C., built in 1974–1978. Here he integrates triangles and pyramids into these concrete block-like shapes to create a building of striking spatial complexity.

Finally, **Tadao Ando**'s use of concrete in his Church of the Light in Ibaraki-shi, Osaka, from 1989 can be characterized as Brutalist in its forceful presence, interrupted only by a thin cross shape cut into the concrete wall that emits two slivers of light into the otherwise unfenestrated room. Here the solidity of the concrete is contrasted with light in order to set up a comparison between the material and the immaterial, and thus to provide a spare, spiritual ambience within the church. Therefore, Brutalism, despite its sometimes negative connotations, has not lost its usefulness today but endures in a great variety of contemporary work. *See also* INTERNATIONAL STYLE.

BULFINCH, CHARLES (1763–1844). Born in Boston, Massachusetts, Charles Bulfinch is thought to be the first native-born North American architect. After studying at Harvard, he traveled across Europe, where he was introduced to the classical architecture of **Christopher Wren** and **Robert Adam**, among others. In the United States, Bulfinch was inspired by the architecture of **Thomas Jefferson**. Hired as the Commissioner of Public Buildings in Washington, D.C., Bulfinch divided his time between there and Boston.

The Old State House in Hartford, Connecticut (1796), is considered Bulfinch's first public building commission. This **Federal style** building is a uniquely American adaptation of European classical architecture. His most famous work, however, is the Massachusetts State House, located on Beacon Hill overlooking the Boston Commons. Begun in 1798, this huge red-**brick** building is accentuated with a white-**columned** portico that rests on top of an **arched** portico at ground level, arrived at by a wide row of steps. The entire central portico is flanked by symmetrical wings that divide the building into three parts, and its most unusual feature is its gilded copper **dome** that shimmers in the sun. Originally the wooden dome, topped with a lantern, was covered in copper, but in 1874 the entire dome was covered in gold leaf, giving it a rich appearance without parallel in American public government buildings. *See also* NEO-CLASSICAL ARCHITECTURE.

BUNGALOW ARTS AND CRAFTS (CRAFTSMAN). *See* ARTS AND CRAFTS.

BUNSHAFT, GORDON (1909–1990). *See* BRUTALISM; SKIDMORE, OWINGS & MERRILL.

BURGEE, JOHN. *See* JOHNSON, PHILIP.

BURNHAM, DANIEL HUDSON (1846–1912). *See* STEEL.

BYZANTINE ARCHITECTURE. Byzantine culture produced an architectural style that spans over a thousand years and can be found mainly in eastern Europe and the eastern Mediterranean. It originated in modern-day Istanbul when the Roman Emperor Constantine established his Eastern Empire there and named the city Constantinople. The city's earlier name, Byzantion, continued as the name of this culture and denotes an architectural style that, although widely adopted in western Europe from the 400s onward, was originally an eastern form of construction that predated the establishment of Constantinople and was instead influenced by **Ancient Greek** and **Ancient Near Eastern** sources. Byzantine architecture is divided into three broadly defined periods. Early Byzantine style begins with the era of Constantine, the fall of Rome and its reestablishment in Ravenna, and ends with the Iconoclastic Controversy of the 700s and early 800s. The Middle Byzantine starts with the reign of the Empress Theodora, who reinvigorated the iconic culture, and ends with the occupation of Constantinople by the Christian Crusaders in 1204. Late Byzantine style developed with the reestablishment of the Byzantine Empire; after the fall of Constantinople in 1453, it spread across Europe and can be found employed even today in Greek Orthodox churches across the world.

After the fall of Rome, for the next several hundred years much of western Europe struggled with political and economic crises and religious controversy. In contrast, during this time Constantinople flourished economically under a strong political system and enjoyed a thriving art culture. During the reign of Justinian I and Empress Theodora, architects were hired to complete a building campaign larger than the vast Roman constructions orchestrated by Constantine over 200 years earlier. It was during this time, from AD 532 to 537, that the famous church of Hagia Sophia was built in the center of Constantinople. Constructed by Anthemius of Tralles and Isidorus of Miletus, this massive church is characterized by a centralized plan covered by a huge **dome**, while smaller domes and *exedrae*, or attached chapels with half-domes, surround the structure and provide additional support to the monumental dome. Because Anthemius was a geometrician and Isidorus was known for his vault designs, together they were able to construct a vast dome surrounded by windows in the drum and a painted gold interior. Thus, when the light shone in, the dome seemed to hover weightlessly, high above the interior processional space.

This drum fenestration was made possible by pendentives, which are the four triangular shapes created by the integration of the circular dome on its square base to provide additional support to the dome. Although the origin of pendentives is obscure, their appearance at Hagia Sophia marks their earliest use on such a vast scale. Two half-domes then flank the main dome, while four smaller half-domes located at the four corners of the square nave offer additional support. The smaller domes cover *exedrae*, which act as internal chapel space surrounding the main core. What makes the dome of Hagia Sophia so innovative is the row of windows along the drum of the dome, a daring feature that weakens the wall structure and was therefore never attempted in such Ancient Roman buildings as the **Pantheon**. After the first dome fell in 558, a newer, steeper dome with additional buttressing was built; it continues to be stable today. Lacking the strongly axial direction of a western-designed church, this multidomed, centrally planned structure directed the visitor's attention upward to the heavens and thus came to typify Byzantine style and religious symbolism.

Ravenna, Italy, was established as a Byzantine base by Emperor Justinian I in AD 540, and from there the Byzantine style spread across the peninsula and endured until the beginning of the **Renaissance**. In Ravenna, the Church of San Vitale best reflects the Byzantine style. Commissioned by the Bishop of Ravenna in 526, this centrally planned church was dedicated to an Early Christian martyr venerated in Ravenna, and the interior of the church is decorated with mosaics honoring the saint and Christ. After Justinian established control over the city in 540, a processional mosaic featuring Justinian and Theodora was created at the high altar. San Vitale is similar to Hagia Sophia in its centrally planned space with an octagonal dome supported by surrounding *exedrae*. An ambulatory allows for the free flow of visitors around the processional area. A narthex demarcates the entrance into the church, while the opposing wall features the rectangular sanctuary. Therefore, although the structure lacks a strong axial direction, the visitor is still provided with visual cues to the layout of the church.

From Ravenna, in the Middle Byzantine period the style spread to the northeastern port city of Venice, where the famous Cathedral of San Marco, begun in 1063, features the same proliferation of domes and a centralized gilded, mosaic-covered interior. During this time, Byzantine Christianity was adopted by the rulers of Russia and the Ukraine, descendants of Vikings who had been Christianized in the ninth century. The Cathedral of Santa Sophia, built in Kiev around 1017, offers a well-preserved regional variant to the Byzantine style. Greece was also a Byzantine outpost during this time, and the **Monastery** of Hosios Loukas, near Stiris, is a good example of the Middle Byzantine style. It reveals a more compact ground-plan than found at Hagia Sophia. Byzantine influences continued to expand in the Late Byzantine era but increasingly featured more and more diversity and regional variants. Today, the Byzantine style endures in the context of the Greek Orthodox Church.

– C –

CALATRAVA, SANTIAGO (1951–). The Spanish modernist architect Santiago Calatrava is best known for his ability to imbue his **concrete** structures with an organic plasticity that is both highly technical and beautiful. After receiving a degree in civil engineering from the Swiss Federal Institute of Technology in Zurich, Switzerland, Calatrava established an architectural firm in Zurich that has expanded to include firms in Paris and New York City. His earliest commissions consisted of bridges and train stations, but in 1991 his Montjuic Communications Tower, built in Barcelona for the 1992 Olympic Games, catapulted Calatrava to international fame and provided him with a prodigious number of commissions. The Communications Tower is characterized by a thin concrete pier that rises up from the ground at a slight angle and turns to join a U-shaped connection from which a separate concrete mast points upward to the sky.

Calatrava's new exhibition space for the Milwaukee Art Museum, built in 2001 and called the Quadracci Pavilion, is a beautifully complex design of thin horizontal registers built up to enclose an exhibition space topped by a giant movable set of wings supported by steel cables. Called a *brise soleil*, this device can open and close to regulate the amount of sunlight emitted into the long, slanted roof windows. The overall appearance of the building is that of a large sailboat, befitting its location near Lake Michigan. Calatrava's "Turning Torso," a 54-story **marble** skyscraper built in Malmö, Sweden, in 2001–2005, is a highly technical structure modeled on the serpentine twist of the human torso. It is designed as nine five-story cubes that each twist slightly to arrive at a 90-degree turn from the bottom cube to the top. Sets of square windows create a grid pattern on each of the exterior wall sections, and the entire structure is supported by an internal **steel** frame and white external steel bars. Calatrava continues to meld technical solutions with expressive aesthetics by crafting very organic, thin-shelled concrete shapes in his buildings. Currently, Calatrava is applying these design principles to his **World Trade Center** Transportation Hub in New York City. *See also* HIGH-TECH ARCHITECTURE.

CAMPEN, JACOB VAN (1595–1657). Jacob van Campen is credited with introducing **Baroque** classicism to the Netherlands in a style that reached its high point during the 1630s–1660s, primarily in the prosperous cities of Haarlem and Amsterdam. Hendrick de Keyser had laid the foundation for this Dutch "Golden Age" with his **Renaissance**-style buildings constructed in Amsterdam, and van Campen, together with the architects Pieter Post and Philip Vingboons, then sought to bring Dutch architecture further into the international arena with an even more overtly classical style. Van Campen was born into a wealthy Haarlem family, and he initially trained as a painter in the shop of Frans de Grebber. What set van Campen apart from other architects of the day, however, was his extended stay in Italy, which lasted from 1616 to 1624 and resulted in his thorough examination of the ancient classical and Renaissance architectural ideals of **Vitruvius**, **Andrea Palladio**, and Vincenzo Scamozzi. Thus, van Campen's introduction of classicism into the Netherlands allowed Dutch architecture to become part of the more theoretical and international architectural discourse of the Baroque age and to further legitimize rule through the idea of historical precedent.

One of van Campen's first buildings, constructed with Pieter Post, is the Mauritshuis in The Hague, completed in 1633. This two-story **brick** building follows classical proportions in its division of the façade into five parts to include a wide three-part central bay covered in **stone** and topped by a triangular pediment, flanked by two pairs of side bays divided by stone Ionic **columns** that run through both stories to separate the clearly delineated fenestration found at both levels. Classical molding, a classical entablature, and swags around the windows and central door complete the Palladian-inspired building. In 1638, van Campen constructed the first theater in the Netherlands, the Stadsschouwburg in Amsterdam, based on the classical interest in drama, and in 1645 his brick Nieuwe Kerk in Haarlem was constructed in the style of the English Baroque architect **Christopher Wren**.

Jacob van Campen's best-known building is the Town Hall in Amsterdam (1648–1655). This wide, classically proportioned five-story sandstone building is again divided into five parts, with a protruding central portal unit of seven bays topped by a triangular pediment that is flanked on either side by a five-bay unit, which is then flanked by a slightly protruding three-bay wing at either end. Each bay is separated by equally spaced Corinthian columns, while swags further decorate the exterior. The center of the roof supports a tall drum and **dome** topped by a cogship, the symbol of Amsterdam's wealth. These imposing structures served to link Dutch architecture with the classical past and thus allowed Dutch architects to work on a more theoretical and historical level and to elevate Dutch architecture into the realm of international discourse.

CANDELA, FELIX (1910–1997). *See* CONCRETE.

CAROLINGIAN ARCHITECTURE. *See* EARLY MEDIEVAL ARCHITECTURE.

CARRÈRE, JOHN (1858–1911). *See* BEAUX-ARTS ARCHITECTURE.

CAST IRON. Wrought iron began to appear in India around 1800 BC, and iron smelting is first found in the Nok culture on the African continent by 1200 BC. Iron had gradually replaced bronze, probably after a tin shortage and the higher cost of copper required people to find a new material. Cast iron was then invented in AD 31 by a man named Du Shi, who worked in the **Chinese** Han Dynasty and created molds to mass-produce figurines, cannons, and pots. It was not until the advent of the Industrial Revolution, however, that superior production methods reduced the cost of cast iron, thus dramatically increasing its use as a major building material.

Cast iron first appeared as the main structural component in the Severn River Bridge, built by Abraham Darby III in Coalbrookdale, England, in 1779. In this bridge, five parallel cast-iron **arches** supporting the roadway replaced the heavy **stone** voussoirs that would otherwise have formed the arch of the bridge. Iron provided a lighter, more flexible material that became widely popular and created its own aesthetic qualities. When Darby manufactured thinner iron pots at the Coalbrookdale Furnace, the iron industry grew dramatically, quickly filling the surrounding valley with worker housing and necessitating the increasing infrastructure. Thus, cast iron immediately moved from the construction of bridges to use for massive buildings, such as train stations, factories, and then schools and libraries.

Interest in new materials and technological progress formed the impetus for the London Great Exhibition of 1851 held in the Crystal Palace, built by Joseph Paxton. Paxton, a gardener known for his greenhouse designs, used cast iron, **glass**, and **wood** to create in just six months a giant fusion between a greenhouse structure and a railway building. It was unprecedented in scale. The building featured a rectangular hall with side aisles and a barrel vault made of iron-framed glass planes that were almost 30 by 50 inches in size. Cast iron was used to create a structural skeleton into which the iron-framed glass panels could be fitted. Wooden ribs were used to reinforce the glass panes in the curvature of the vault. This building, even with the predominance of glass, provided the largest enclosed interior in its day, with over 18 acres of exhibition space.

Although cast iron was widely used in internal architectural supports that were then sheathed in more traditional stone or other materials, its bare aesthetic qualities became more highly valued through the 19th century, as it appeared much more visibly in such buildings as the reading room of the Bibliothèque Sainte-Geneviève, built in Paris in the 1840s by Henri Labrouste. The exterior of the building is constructed of masonry, and the entrance foyer has stone columns with cast-iron decoration. In the reading room, thin cast-iron columns with Corinthian capitals and tall concrete pedestals run down the middle of the room to support two flanking parallel barrel vaults. The vault then features curved cast-iron ribs decorated with a classical rosette design.

It was the Eiffel Tower, built in 1887–1889 along the Seine River in Paris by Gustav Eiffel that really demonstrated to the broader public the incredible technical possibilities of cast iron. At first built only as a temporary structure and denigrated in the local newspapers as an iron monstrosity, the Eiffel Tower came to symbolize modern progress and human achievement. Today, as an observation tower with several restaurants, it is one of the most visited tourist sites in the world, and it also functions as a radio tower. Built for the 1889 Universal Exposition, the 984-foot-tall tower (now 1,063 feet with its radio spire) was the tallest structure in the world until New York's 1,047-foot-tall Chrysler Building was constructed in 1930. The innovative structural design of the Eiffel Tower, with its broad base curving upward gently into a pinnacle, allows it to sway slightly in the wind to withstand the effects of severe weather and time.

Since cast iron was also used to reinforce **concrete**, it remained an important material in other major structures as well, in which its own aesthetic qualities were not so glorified. For example, the **Beaux-Arts** architect **Charles Garnier** used iron beneath the more traditional stone materials of his opera house in Paris, built in the 1860s. Iron was also used in the United States by architects such as **Henry**

Hobson Richardson, who trained at the École des Beaux-Arts in Paris and worked in a modern historically inspired style, as seen in his Marshall Field Warehouse, built in Chicago in the 1880s. Soon thereafter, **steel** was introduced as a superior structural material and was subsequently used mainly in **skyscraper** buildings in the United States.

CASTLE. Because of the increasingly complex political environment of **Romanesque** Europe in the 1000s and 1100s, fortified castles, which still dot the countryside across Europe, came to share political authority with the powerful monasteries of the Middle Ages. Similar to the urban development around a **monastery**, a town often grew around the castle; thus castles were found not only in the countryside, but in either the downtown or periphery of a late medieval or **Renaissance** urban community. While some castles are small, abandoned, crumbling structures, others have either been rebuilt or remain well preserved. The origin of the term "castle" is unknown, but it refers to many types of fortified structures, and therefore castles are not unique to Europe, although the European castle-type became the best-known example.

The earliest **stone** fortifications were constructed by Germanic tribes soon after the fall of Rome, and these tribes oversaw castle construction through the Carolingian era of the ninth century. The end of the Carolingian Empire and the subsequent Viking expansion across Europe resulted in a castle-building boom through the next several centuries. This period coincided with the emerging feudal society, in which the landed gentry increasingly used the castle as a potent symbol of its authority. By the time William the Conqueror from Normandy invaded England in 1066, the Norman-style castle was the most popular among the landed gentry. Unlike Ancient Roman forts, medieval castles never followed a standardized plan but rather were built on hilltops, near rivers, or even in marshland, and their structure adapted to this varied geography. In general, however, they followed the fortified residential tower plan or the moat-and-bailey defensive garrison design. Castles continued to be constructed through the Middle Ages, becoming obsolete only in the early 1600s when more effective gunpowder and artillery could easily breach the thick stone walls.

While earlier castles were not often built for the comfort of the ruling family, who might not even live there year-round, the Romanesque castle came to be seen as the seat of aristocratic life as well as the site of great battles. Castles grew out of Frankish military structures adapted for use by the Normans, who first built castles from **wood**, and only later began to construct larger compounds from *ashlar*, or cut stone. Initially, castles were of the quickly built *mound-and-bailey* type, which featured a round ditch dug out to create a moat. The loose earth was piled into the center and used to create a wall, which was in turn surrounded by a wooden wall called a *palisade*, adjacent to the outer courtyard, called the *bailey*, where the garrison and livestock were located. Stone castles became popular during the Crusades, when Christian soldiers were able to see firsthand some of the massive stone **Byzantine** castles of Eastern Europe.

Later, stone castles were constructed as permanent homes for feudal lords. These castles were constructed around a central hall with a hearth. The hall served as the main gathering room for the landlord, his family, and his staff. The earliest hall plan was modeled on the church interior, with a broad center separating the side aisles by a row of stone or wooden pillars that helped to support the timber roof. The hall was often on the ground floor, but in larger castles the hall was built on an upper floor with an external entry stairway. Windows were initially small, shuttered, and secured with iron bars, and only later in the 14th century was **glass** used in them. The earliest castles had bedrooms for the landlord's family at the upper end of the hall, while the simplest castles did not have room divisions but curtains to separate the sleeping areas. During the Saxon era, the guards might sleep next to the great hall hearth during the winter and in the towers or basements in the summer, but with the invention of the fireplace, heating was decentralized so that the landlord's bedrooms were located in separate wings and full garrisons were built for the guards. The larger castles maintained separate kitchens and mess halls for the military. They also had a small chapel for the family and an interior courtyard. The inner stronghold, or keep, of the castle was also often called the *donjon*. The entire complex was surrounded by a stone curtain wall that was punctuated by *bastions*, or smaller towers that were located either in the side walls or at the corners of the complex, and might also have *turrets* protruding outward for additional lookout windows. The outer wall might feature an elaborately gated entrance set forward from the external wall, called a *barbican*, and also a drawbridge over a moat. The only windows on these fortified walls would be arrow loop windows—that is, thin slits cut into the stone walls to allow arrows to be shot out from the castle. In addition, the outer wall was often topped by *crenellations*, square stone sections of the roofline that projected upward in a dentile pattern. A wall walk, also called an *allure*, provided an upper-level passage between the *parapet,* which is the inner part of the outer wall, and the battlement, which is the external-facing outer wall. Over the years, all types of castles have stirred the imagination of many people, who romanticize this era for its chivalric codes and ideas on courtly love. Examples of castles can still be found across most of Europe today. *See also* DURHAM CASTLE AND CATHEDRAL.

CHARTRES CATHEDRAL. *See* GOTHIC ARCHITECTURE.

CHILDS, DAVID (1941–). *See* SKIDMORE, OWINGS & MERRILL.

CHINESE ARCHITECTURE. Ancient Chinese architecture is modeled on basic principles of order and balance; **wood** was the first material used, supplemented later with **brick**. The earliest buildings were laid on foundations of packed earth; in the areas of China where wood was sparse, a lightweight architectural structure was devised whereby the fewest number of pillars, spaced far apart, would support lightweight rectangular roofs. Plaster walls, made thinner with the inclusion of latticework and other decorative elements, filled the areas between the pillars. It was the roof that ultimately received the most attention, however, with an ingenious system of brackets supporting a hipped roof that featured corners tilted upward, giving the effect of weightlessness.

China, located in the center of Asia, can be traced back 8,000 years; it is one of the oldest continuous cultures in the world. Most of its inhabitants live along rivers: the Yellow River to the north, the Yangzi River in the middle, the Xi River in the south. While the northern part of China has a more forbidding climate along the Gobi Desert, the south is green and fertile, with a lively maritime trade along the coast. By the Neolithic period, small but relatively advanced communities appeared throughout the center of China, where structural foundations have been excavated. More recent excavations have shown a larger number of Neolithic settlements spread more widely across China, and these ongoing excavations are transforming our understanding of early Chinese history.

During the Bronze Age, China was ruled by three successive dynasties, each of which constructed vast palace complexes and ceremonial centers surrounded by walls that are currently being excavated. The Qin Dynasty, dated to the third century BC, is credited with uniting China under one centralized rule, while dividing the country into administrative regions linked by roads and building the Great Wall along the northern frontier. It was during the next dynasty, called the Han, that the great Silk Road, the longest road in the world, was completed, leading from the Han capital of Honan (now Luoyang) all the way to Rome. This route stretched from the western gate of the Great Wall across Central Asia, through modern-day Iran, Iraq, and then to Antioch, Syria, where boats left for Venice. Taoism and Confucianism were also both established during the Han Dynasty, Taoism focusing on the relationship between humans and nature and Confucianism on a moral system of behavior among people.

The earliest written records of feng shui, or *kan-yu*, as it was originally called, also date to the Han Dynasty. Feng shui, which translates as "wind-water," refers to the arrangement of space to create a balanced and harmonious environment. It is rooted in the *I Ching*, the "Book of Change," which was gradually written down from the Bronze Age onward; it became increasingly popular during the Zhou Dynasty (770–476 BC), together with the growing influence of Taoism, Confucianism, and Buddhism. Feng shui is based on the flow of energy, or *chi*, through the universe and how it affects our lives. *Yin* and *yang*, the mutually dependent balanced opposites, refer to the idea of continual change that is central to the philosophy of feng shui, while the five elements (fire, water, metal, earth, and wood) form its aesthetics. Feng shui was first used to help establish proper housing and burial sites and has expanded in complexity since then to become a fully formed, nature-based aesthetic philosophy. When the People's Republic of China was established in 1949, feng shui was banned, but since then it has enjoyed an increase in popularity.

From this rich cultural background was built the Han capital of Honan, now largely destroyed but described in ancient literature and pictured in painted ceramic models of houses made for tombs. These models, from the first century AD, reveal multileveled homes with wide, overhanging tiled roofs at each level. A watchtower at the top register faces a walled courtyard. A double doorway is located in the center of the model, which features innovative brackets that support the eaves, as well as elaborately painted exterior walls. This bracketing is essentially a **post-and-lintel** support system, but it is specific to Chinese construction, later adapted in Japan as well. Although no domestic buildings from this early period survive, the Nanchan Temple, built on Mount Wutai in central China in the 780s during the Tang Dynasty, must recall earlier domestic buildings. It is a small, three-bay building elevated on a platform that features a broadly overhanging tile roof supported by brackets. Here, the gray tiled hipped roof curves upward slightly, and in the center are two sculpted shapes of curled owl tails. This temple is the earliest surviving wood-framed structure in China, and the square or rectangular bay modules seen here were widely used in Chinese architecture to define the size and space of a building.

Buddhism and therefore Indian influences came to China very early via the Silk Road. Reflecting this Indian influence is the Great Wild Goose Pagoda, built in the Ci'en Temple Complex in the Tang capital of Shanxi in 645 by a monk who had spent several decades studying Buddhism in India. Here the shape of the *pagoda* is modified from an ancient Indian *stupa* into a stepped tower. The *stupa* shape, symbolizing the ancient burial mound of the Buddha, was blended with the stepped registers of the Chinese watchtower to create this new form of the *pagoda*. Similar to Indian structures, this pagoda was built of **stone** to resemble wood, although in general Chinese architecture is not overly sculptural. The Great Wild Goose Pagoda epitomizes a graceful simplicity in its seven stories. It is devoid of sculptural detail except for the finial on top, which serves the same function as the *stupa* mast or spire—that is, to symbolize the *axis mundi*, or axis of the world. *Pagodas* are the best-known architectural form found in East Asia. The early Chinese stone *pagodas* were often solid structures with niches carved out for altars; later, more elaborate versions, such as the wooden *pagodas* found in

Japanese architecture, might have a small ground-floor room and even accessible rooms above. A good example of this larger type is the Liuhe Pagoda, in Hangzhou, China, built during the southern Song Dynasty in 1165. This impressive pagoda is made of 13 square stepped registers with wooden eaves that tilt upward in their corners. It served as a light tower to guide boats traveling along the Qiantang River.

During the Tang Dynasty (618–907), most political positions were held by the intellectuals, who achieved a high level of respect and maintained important positions in courtly life. Unique to China, this powerful class of scholars helped to shape an architectural culture that combined aesthetic beauty and beautiful garden retreats that asserted their superiority over other peoples. The standard dimensions of these structures were predicated on the length of the timber used for their construction, and the intricate bracketing systems were seen as modules of this initial unit of measure. In 1103, the *Ying tsao fa shih*, or *Methods and Designs of Architecture*, written by Li Chieh, codified this module system of construction. In addition, he discusses the type of applied decoration appropriate for structures, as well as the latticework and ceiling panels. Later dynasties altered this ratio system slightly over time and added correctives to various optical illusions such as the width and lean of internal pillars and corner pillars.

The Mongol invasions of the 1200s, led by Genghis Khan, changed the course of Chinese history. His grandson Kublai Khan founded the Yuan Dynasty (1280–1368) and built the Mongol capital in Beijing, which was laid out in the traditional format of an ancient Chinese walled city with streets organized on a grid pattern. During the Ming Dynasty, which lasted from 1368 to 1644, the famous **Forbidden City** palace complex was completed in Beijing. Today, Shanghai is the largest city in China. Its modern history began in the 19th century, when rapid growth necessitated the construction of entire neighborhoods of narrow streets lined with walled houses called *shikumen* homes. These are two- or three-story stone structures with tall walls surrounding lush gardens that provided an oasis within the increasingly urbanized city. Today, the *shikumen* are dwarfed by the **skyscrapers** built to accommodate the rapid growth in population, yet recent attempts to protect the *shikumen* have successfully transformed some of these neighborhoods into elegant restaurant districts.

Chinese skyscrapers require the structural innovations first utilized in early skyscraper design that originated in Chicago, and accordingly, many of these 20th-century buildings in China were constructed by western architects. The thoroughly modern **High-Tech architecture** of the Hongkong and Shanghai Bank, built in Hong Kong by the English architect Norman Foster in 1986, celebrates the advent of international modern structural advances in China, while at the same time the laws of the ancient Chinese philosophy of feng shui were employed to ensure the selection of an appropriate site for the building. Similar principles can be found in the 30-story apartment building constructed about the same time in the high-priced area of Repulse Bay, Hong Kong, which features an eight-story-high hole in the middle of the building that allows a dragon's access from the mountains behind the building to the water in front. Traditional Chinese architectural features are also found in the Jin Mao Building, currently ranked the fifth largest in the world, which is an 88-story building constructed in Shanghai by the Chicago firm of **Skidmore, Owings & Merrill** in 1998. This building, with its stepped registers leading up to a pyramidal cap topped by a tall mast, recalls the ancient Chinese *pagoda* and reflects in this way its Chinese heritage. Certainly, China, together with its neighboring Tibet, Bhutan, and Nepal, each face a challenging future that will require a careful balance between the preservation of their architectural history and the accommodation of modern construction needs. *See also* INDIAN ARCHITECTURE.

CHURCH. *See* DURHAM CASTLE AND CATHEDRAL; EARLY CHRISTIAN ARCHITECTURE; FLORENCE CATHEDRAL; GOTHIC ARCHITECTURE; PISA CATHEDRAL COMPLEX; RENAISSANCE ARCHITECTURE; ROMANESQUE ARCHITECTURE; SAINT PETER'S CHURCH.

CHURRIGUERESQUE STYLE. *See* COLONIAL ARCHITECTURE; ROCOCO ARCHITECTURE.

COLONIAL ARCHITECTURE. Colonial architecture is the term used for the style and type of building imported by colonizers in a "foreign" land. Thus, it can refer to the English styles of architecture that were first introduced on the East Coast of the United States, called the **Georgian** and **Federal styles**, or the Dutch Colonial homes of German immigrants also found in the United States; yet it can refer more broadly to the Spanish Colonial styles found across the south and southwestern United States and in Mexico and South America. Colonial architecture was also introduced into India by the English and Portuguese, into South Africa by the Dutch, into parts of Togo and Cameron by the Germans, and into Libya by the Italians, while French Colonial style is found in many places, including New Orleans.

Because most of these imperialistic tendencies, excluding those from antiquity, emanated from Europe in the **Renaissance** and **Baroque** eras, Colonial architecture is typically a European-styled construction with classical motifs, yet with strong regional variations. American Colonial architecture began, then, when the Pilgrims first arrived in North America and settled in Plymouth, Massachusetts, in the winter of 1620. The earliest settlers quickly built **wood** homes with limestone walls and thatched roofs that were simple variations on European models, but were reinforced against the cold weather with wattle and daub—that is, thatch and woven branches held together with clay and packed between the timber walls. Houses were then covered with clapboards on the exterior. Large fireplaces, small windows with glass panes, and steeply gabled wood-shingled roofs were all used in northeastern dwellings. Strikingly different from **Native American** dwellings, these homes were instead modeled on rural English homes.

One well-preserved house from this time is the Parson Capen House in Topsfield, Massachusetts, from 1683. This house is unusual in that it is a two-story home with a central room at both levels where the fireplace was located, and then two flanking rooms on either side of the main living areas. Other good examples of the Colonial style of architecture include the Turner-Ingersoll House, also called the House of the Seven Gables, in Salem, Massachusetts, and the Paul Revere House in Boston, both of which were also built before 1700. The Turner-Ingersoll House, made famous by Nathaniel Hawthorne's 1851 publication of *The House of the Seven Gables*, was originally a two-story, two-room house built with cross gables. Built in 1668 by Captain John Turner, it faced the Salem

Harbor and was added to over the generations, culminating in the Georgian style that Hawthorne knew. The Paul Revere House, a U.S. National Landmark, was built in the 1680s but also subsequently remodeled in the Georgian style; it was inhabited by the Revere family from 1770 to 1800.

Colonial architecture also included French, Dutch, and Spanish architectural elements to the original English Colonial style found in the United States, bringing an increased diversity to North American architecture. Spanish Colonial architecture is seen in the San Xavier del Bac Mission outside Tucson, Arizona, which was built in the 1780s by Franciscans on the site of an earlier Jesuit church. The huge white church rises up from its spare desert surroundings to create a powerful image of Catholic authority. The three-part façade consists of two bell towers that flank a central portal aedicule that is not painted white but is instead carved in an intricate, Spanish *Churrigueresque* style. This richly organic sculptural style, which recalls Gothic and Moorish influences, can be found across Spain in the Baroque and Rococo eras and is most notably seen on the portal of the Hospicio de San Fernando in Madrid, built by Pedro de Ribera in 1722.

The continued popularity of these Colonial styles can also be seen in the Colonial Revival style, which began on the East Coast in the 1890s, and the Spanish Colonial Revival and Mission styles found during the same time in California, all of which continued through the next several decades of the 20th century.

COLONIAL REVIVAL STYLE. *See* COLONIAL ARCHITECTURE.

COLOSSEUM, ROME. The Colosseum in Rome is one of the largest arenas built in antiquity. This huge monument to Roman sporting events and other public spectacles could seat over 55,000 people in tiered rows of **stone** benches that rise over 150 feet into the air. The oval shape of the arena is a colossal expansion upon the earlier semicircular amphitheaters built in Ancient Greece and used to host theatrical performances. It was begun under Vespasian in AD 72 and completed under the rule of Titus, and was widely copied across the Roman Empire.

The four-story exterior of the Colosseum consists of three levels of open **arched** colonnades called arcades, topped by an attic level articulated by flat pilasters that are in turn topped by a cornice. The arched colonnades alternate round arches with **columns** attached to the wall, called engaged columns. The ground floor columns are Doric, followed by Ionic columns above and then by Corinthian columns. This hierarchy of order originated in classical Greek architecture and was described in detail by the Roman architect **Vitruvius** in his manual written in the first century BC titled *The Ten Books on Architecture*. Once the visitor enters through any of the arched porticoes on the ground floor, stairwells connect to different sections of seating on all three levels via barrel-vaulted hallways. Sectioning the seating indicates the organizational skill of the Romans, as seats and specific seating areas could be numbered and located easily, and thousands could exit at about the same time.

Inside the arena, an oval stage about 280 feet long was covered with sand and elevated on a platform above a series of basement service rooms and tunnels. These subterranean rooms were used for storage of equipment and to house performers, who were often slaves brought from the far-flung regions of the Roman Empire. Lions and other animals used in various events were kept in cages beneath the stage, ready to burst into the arena on cue. Known for brutal gladiator battles and subsequent early Christian persecutions, the Colosseum, one of the largest public buildings from antiquity, came to symbolize Roman authority, civic ideals, and public policy. *See also* ANCIENT GREEK ARCHITECTURE; ANCIENT ROMAN ARCHITECTURE.

COLUMN. Columns developed as ornate, cylindrical posts that functioned as part of the **post-and-lintel** structural system. These pillars were originally modeled after trees or other forms of upright vegetation. A column is typically divided into three sections, with a base that supports a shaft, which is then topped by a capital. Columns are most often disengaged and support a roof, but columns may also be engaged to a wall, where they are more decorative than supportive. Engaged columns are often half-columns, but they may appear in different ratios as well. Columns rarely appear alone but rather form a colonnade that supports an exterior porch or portico or on the inside of a building holds up the ceiling.

Columns first appear in **Ancient Egypt**, where they can be found engaged to the walls of the North Palace of the Old Kingdom Funerary Complex of Djoser at Saqqara, which dates from 2667 to 2648 BC. Here, the columns do not have bases, but the shafts are capped by capitals in the abstract shape of papyrus blossoms. By the New Kingdom, vast temple complexes featured courtyards and hypostyle halls filled with massive columns that supported heavy **stone** roofs. The Great Temple of Amun in Karnak, which dates around 1295 BC, has a hypostyle hall of 134 thick columns, closely spaced and made of disks individually carved and stacked one atop another, without mortar. The tops of the columns reveal lotus flowers in the center and lotus buds along the sides. In the **Ancient Near East**, tall slender columns were used to support the ceiling of the broad audience hall of the Persian Palace of Darius at Persepolis, built around 520–460 BC. Although the roof of the palace is now long gone, the columns remain standing today above the entry stairs. Running up the shaft of these columns are vertical ridges called fluting. Fluting helps to accentuate the verticality of the column and recalls the shape of a reed, such as the bamboo, or even wheat, which originated in this region of Iran.

The **Ancient Greek**s are best known for their use of highly sculptural columns. The Greek orders consist of a column that supports an entablature, and thus conforms to the post-and-lintel structural system. All four sides of Ancient Greek temples very often feature a continuous colonnade that gives the effect of a free-standing sculptural monument. The Greeks originated the three main classical orders of columns, called the Doric, Ionic, and Corinthian. The Doric order, the earliest and most severe, is considered a masculine order and developed sometime before 600 BC. It features a fluted shaft, necking, and then a capital that looks like a simple curved impost block. The shaft rises up with a decreasing diameter, allowing the bottom of the shaft, called the drum, to assume the role of a structural foundation. The capital then acts as a transitional feature from the shaft to the entablature, which is articulated with an architrave topped by a register of triglyphs and metopes that support a gabled roof, called a pediment. The Parthenon, built by Kallikrates and Iktinos on the **Acropolis** in Athens from 447 to 438 BC, is the most famous example of a Doric temple. The Ionic order, named after Ionia, developed next; it certainly existed around 600 BC and consists of a base, a shaft, and a capital carved with a volute. This more sculptural capital is thinner; it supports an entablature that features an architrave divided into three horizontal registers and then a continuous frieze of narrative relief carvings. The roof pediment is equally ornate, with a carved cornice of dentil molding. The small Temple of Athena Nike on the Acropolis, dated to c. 425 BC, epitomizes the Ionic order. Finally, the Corinthian order, the most ornate, began to appear around 450 BC in Ancient Greek interiors. Slightly thinner than the Ionic order, the Corinthian shaft is capped by an intricately carved capital of acanthus leaves, rosettes, and an embedded volute. Because columns were based on the ideal proportions of the human body, they were therefore codified into a rigid system of interdependent parts that could not be altered without repercussions to the entire order as defined by the *Canon* of Polykleitos of Argos (c. 450 BC). Therefore, as sculptures of the human body began to appear taller and thinner, so did the Greeks' corresponding architectural columns.

This system was further codified by the Roman architect **Vitruvius** in his treatise *Ten Books on Architecture*, written in the first century BC. Picking up on Etruscan changes, which included the addition of a base to the Doric order, the Romans added the Tuscan order, a thinner, more elegant Doric column, and the Composite order, a variation on the Corinthian. Later stylistic variations of the column, as well as its more diverse building materials, continued to influence architecture through the **Renaissance** and **Baroque** era, and into the **Neo-Classical** era. **Andrea Palladio** placed a row of six Ionic columns across the front of each of the four porticoes on his Villa Rotonda, built in the Veneto in the 1560s. With a clear visual link to both Vitruvius and the **Pantheon** in Rome, Palladio sought to highlight the use of columns as an important structural and aesthetic element in his classicizing architecture. Baroque columns, seen in the vast oval Doric loggia in front of **Saint Peter's Church** designed by **Gian Lorenzo Bernini** in the 1650s, reveal the more theatrical and urban interests of the Baroque age. In the mid-18th century, Corinthian columns appear on the colossal façade of the Church of Sainte-Geneviève in Paris, designed by **Jacques-Germain Soufflot** in the 1750s, while freestanding columns encircle the drum of its **dome**. By now, the use of columns had come to be seen as synonymous with classicism. Thus, when **Benjamin Henry Latrobe** built the **United**

States Capitol in Washington, D.C., in the early 1800s, his overt use of columns (in the form of pilasters, engaged and disengaged columns, and pairs of columns along the façade and in the dome of the building) was immediately understood to recall the original form of democracy as established in Ancient Greece.

CONCRETE. Concrete is a compound made from sand, gravel, and cement, while cement is a mixture of minerals that become hard when water is added, binding the sand and gravel into a solid mass. Although concrete is traditionally considered an **Ancient Roman** invention, earlier forms have been found, such as in eastern European floors that date to around 5000 BC and in some **ancient Indian** *stupas*. The first civilization to use concrete extensively, however, was the **Ancient Egyptian**, where concrete has been found and dated as early as 2500 BC. However, it was the Romans who around 100 BC found that a far stronger material resulted from mixing a volcanic ash obtained from Pozzuoli with their normal lime-based concretes. This type of concrete came to be called *pozzolana,* which is any siliceous (or siliceous and aluminous) material containing little or no cement in itself but if finely divided and mixed with water will react with calcium hydroxide to form a cement-like material. In fact, it is from the Latin *caementum*, which refers to the materials, and *concretus,* which refers to the process of binding the materials together, that the modern-day names for these two materials are derived.

The Romans also experimented with lightweight aggregates and used them in concrete in the cast **dome** of the **Pantheon** around AD 120. The Pantheon dome features coffering, or square sections carved out of the concrete to reduce the dome's weight but not its strength. Coffering became a widely used classical feature that later on assumed a more decorative function in such ceilings as flat timber roofs and small barrel vaults. Concrete was mainly used for Roman foundations, however, in which workers framed the concrete wall with a diagonal **brick** or **stone** setting called an *opus reticulatum*. Onto this pattern, the Romans then put a stone or stucco veneer to protect the concrete from moisture. The *opus reticulatum* was beneath the veneer and allowed it to adhere better, but when this design was rediscovered in the **Renaissance** revival of classicism, it was reused merely as a decorative pattern on the outside of Renaissance palace walls.

Searching for even more inventive architectural forms, the Romans began to experiment with the use of bronze bars embedded in concrete, thereby creating the first reinforced concrete. But since the differing thermal expansion of the two materials often caused a problem in concrete breakage, its use never became widespread. The Romans had already begun to add horsehair to concrete to make it less likely to shrink when dried. They also added animal blood to make the concrete more frost-resistant.

The rediscovery of concrete had to wait until 1756, however, when the British engineer John Smeaton created the first Portland cement. Then, in 1892, François Hennebique patented a ferro-cement, or reinforced concrete, which was threaded with **steel** to create not only a stronger material, but also to solve the problem of how to join the separate building materials together. Thus, with the integration of the binding material into the building material, the problem of the *monolithic joint* was solved. This innovation paved the way for larger unencumbered interior spaces and more highly technical structures. Reinforced concrete was first used in industrial buildings, but in 1903 **Auguste Perret** first introduced its use in domestic architecture in Paris with his eight-story apartment building constructed at 25 bis Rue Franklin.

In the 20th century, Pier Luigi Nervi is best known for his aesthetic concrete designs that reflect his ideas on the integration of math and nature in order to create stronger yet more aesthetically pleasing feats of engineering. This Italian architect, after concluding his studies at the University of Bologna, began to experiment with wide-spanning construction in the 1920s on a series of airplane hangar commissions. He then went on to construct in Florence in 1931 a soccer stadium made entirely of reinforced concrete, called the Stadio Artemia Franchi. Using simple geometry and prefabricated concrete pieces, Nervi's structural ideas were very accessible and economical and therefore were widely adapted in the reconstruction of Europe after World War II. In 1959, Nervi built his famous Palazzetto dello Sport in Rome for the 1960 Olympics. Here he created a round concrete building with a concrete roof that resembles from the outside a tent-like canopy with its corners "staked" into the ground by flying buttresses. Made of precast concrete, this compressive form–active dome is one of the best-known unencumbered interior spaces.

Marcel Breuer, **Eero Saarinen**, and Felix Candela began in the 1950s to experiment with a "softer," more expressive aesthetic for their concrete designs. Candela, a Spanish-born Mexican architect, is best known for his creation of a thin-shelled dome, which is a more efficient use of concrete and has minimal tensile forces. Clearly influenced by the hyperboloid structures of **Antoni Gaudí** in Barcelona, Candela, called the "shell builder," maintained that basic geometry, not complex math, was the key to successful lightweight construction in concrete, and that thicker concrete did not necessarily make the material any stronger. The Xochimilco Restaurant (Los Manantiales), built in Mexico City in 1958, demonstrates Candela's interest in modeling concrete into organic forms. With its corners appearing to balloon upward, propelled by wind, this thin-shelled concrete hyperbolic building resembles a giant ocean shell. Candela's aesthetic was further developed by Jørn Utzon in his Sydney Opera House, completed in 1973. These thin-shelled, organic-styled concrete roof coverings were more recently the source of inspiration for the Millennium Dome, a massive, mast-supported dome built in southeast London for the year-long millennium celebrations held there in 2000. Constructed by Richard Rogers and the structural engineer Buro Happold, this massive building is currently an indoor sports arena.

Innovative modern uses for concrete also include the earlier daring types of cantilevering. In the 1940s, architects working in the United States, such as **Walter Gropius** and **Marcel Breuer**, continued the domestic use of cantilevered concrete, first seen in the work of **Le Corbusier** in France. This use of concrete could provide strong, horizontal lines and a crisp geometric framework consistent with the prevalent **International style**. It was **Frank Lloyd Wright**, however, who became best known for his use of cantilevered concrete in the American home, where porch terraces and widely overhanging rooflines formed the prairie-style aesthetic that Wright is so famous for. Wright's Fallingwater, built as a vacation home in rural Mill Run, Pennsylvania, in the 1930s, reveals the most daring use of cantilevered concrete. The Kaufmann family initially wanted a home that would overlook a waterfall, but instead Wright designed the house directly on top of the waterfall, with a strongly horizontal tiered appearance that mimicked the rocky levels of the waterfall.

The house is therefore constructed with two 15-foot-wide rectangular cantilevers that form a stepped terrace directly over the water and a 6-foot-wide concrete slab cantilevered out from a bedroom to create a porch. Although reinforced with steel and supported by parapets, the walls began to crack over the years and were not fully repaired and reinforced until 2002. Since these 20th-century innovations, architects continue to fuse the structural and aesthetic application of reinforced concrete in new ways.

CONSTRUCTIVIST ARCHITECTURE. Constructivist art and architecture, found in the Soviet Union in the 1920s and 1930s, grew out of the geometric, dynamic, and kinetic styles of both Cubism and **Futurist architecture**. Russian Constructivism, as it is also called, was then overlaid with Communist ideals to form a new, modernist aesthetic that symbolized the "New Economic Policy" of Vladimir Lenin after the Bolshevik Revolution of 1917. Technology and engineering were both central to this style, yet such ideas as the need for "pure" art versus industrial production remain unresolved, and many architects refused to consider themselves Constructivists. The movement was formed by the brothers Naum Gabo and Antoine Pevsner, whose influential 1920 treatise *The Realist Manifesto* argued that Cubism and Futurism were not abstract and intuitive enough, and thus they sought to integrate the spiritual abstraction of artists such as the Russian painter Wassily Kandinsky into their movement. After the brothers emigrated from the Soviet Union in 1922, Constructivism began to move toward more functional and less theoretical concerns, and Constructivist architecture became more prominent within the movement.

One of the first Constructivist structures was designed in 1919 for the headquarters of the First Comintern in St. Petersburg by the Futurist artist Vladimir Tatlin. Also called "Tatlin's Tower," plans for this never-built monument reveal a dramatic spiraling **steel** high-rise enclosed with a **glass** curtain wall that recalls a more dynamic version of the Eiffel Tower in Paris. Lack of financing prevented the completion of many of these early works, and thus the origins of Constructivist architecture can be best understood through theoretical models such as the "Dynamic City," or the Prounen-Raum, designed by El Lissitzky in 1919. These theoretical plans, deeply inspired by painters such as the Suprematist artist Kasimir Malevich, sought to bring together the utopian and the everyday into workable solutions based on the new communal living arrangements encouraged by Lenin. In addition, both the automobile and industry were central to this modernist movement, and therefore new roads, more parking garages, and more efficient factories and government buildings formed the core of architectural commissions across Europe during the 1920s. Thus, Constructivist architecture shares many similarities in its spare style and universal design with the contemporary **International style**.

Ilya Golosov and **Konstantin Melnikov** were the primary architects of the new building type called the "workers' club," as well as the new communal urban apartment building. These structures provided a social outlet for workers that encouraged political and physical activity and sought to discourage them from either going to the pubs after work or returning home to their individual families. Golosov's Zuev Workers' Club, built in Moscow in 1926–1928, reveals this new style. The structure is formed as a white cube, but it has a three-story glazed cylinder that breaks away from the square corner of the building to create a dramatic and expressive affirmation of these new aesthetic and technological advances. The circle and square are both juxtaposed and balanced to create a visual harmony of static and dynamic forms. The interior consists of club rooms, a large foyer, and an auditorium, all connected by a stairwell set into the corner cylinder.

In addition to these workers' clubs, in the 1920s many Russian architects were dedicated to the construction of much-needed urban housing. The Narkomfin Building, constructed in Moscow by Moisei Ginzburg in 1928–1932, is one of the few remaining Constructivist apartment buildings, since most of them have been torn down to make way for the extensive construction projects of the 21st century. The Narkomfin Building is an excellent example of how apartments were designed for communal living. The exterior reveals a wide, five-story building made from **brick** covered in stucco to resemble **concrete**, with a strongly horizontal direction asserted by balconies at each level. No external decoration detracts from the purely functional aspects of the building, which does not rely on historical referencing for its importance. Built for the workers of the Commissariat of Finance, the apartments are narrow and vertical in plan, with communal living areas and kitchens on each floor. The narrow halls and stairwells as well as the narrow, stepped plan of each apartment maximized space while preventing the sectioning off of apartments into separate family dwellings. However, the building does not conform to basic safety codes; it will probably be torn down rather than restored.

Moisei Ginzburg was a theoretical architect and founder of the OSA Group (Organization of Contemporary Architects) in Moscow. His publication of *Style and Epoch* in 1924 reveals many similar ideas to **Le Corbusier**'s *Vers une architecture*, which was initially published in a series of articles from 1920 to 1923. Both architects argued for a dynamic and dramatic change in architecture to account for the growing urban population, new transportation possibilities, and the need for a cleaner city with a closer connection to nature. Thus, the communal aspects of the Narkomfin Building as well as the addition of a rooftop terrace were inspirational in the design of Le Corbusier's Unité d'Habitation apartment building constructed in Marseilles in 1947–1952. These buildings had a profound impact on modern urban public housing projects constructed through the 20th century.

COOP HIMMELB(L)AU. *See* DECONSTRUCTIVISM.

CORBEL. *See* ARCH.

CORBUSIER, LE (1887–1965). Charles-Edouard Jeanneret, known as Le Corbusier, initially trained as a painter but ultimately became the most famous modernist architect of the 20th century. Le Corbusier first studied with **Peter Behrens**, best known for his factory aesthetic in modernist architecture. During that time, he may well have met **Ludwig Mies van der Rohe** and **Walter Gropius**, both of whom were interested in developing a more spare style of construction based on a functional aesthetic formed by materials and structure rather than applied decoration. Early on, Le Corbusier also became interested in the philosophy of Purism, defined by a painter, his friend Amédée Ozenfant. Purism was a utopian ideal whereby art could be used to change the world. Art was therefore not just an aesthetic pursuit but could also elevate people to a higher level of social order.

Stonehenge, Salisbury Plain, England, c. 3100–1500 BC (Photo: Nancy Lee Palmer)

Pyramids at Giza, outside Cairo, Egypt, c. 2500 BC (Photo: Dawn St. Clare)

Parthenon, Acropolis, Athens, 400s BC (Photo: Dawn St. Clare)

Colosseum, Rome, AD 72–80 (Photo: Dawn St. Clare)

Pantheon, Rome, AD 128 (Photo: Dawn St. Clare)

Angkor Wat, Angkor, Cambodia, AD 800s–1200s (Photo: Nancy Lee Palmer)

*Anasazi "Great House" foundations, New Mexico, 900s–1400s
(Photo: Allison Lee Palmer)*

Uxmal Ceremonial Center, Mexico, 800s–1200s (Photo: Dawn St. Clare)

Machu Picchu, Peru, 1450s (Photo: Allison Lee Palmer)

Forbidden City, Beijing, 1368–1644 (Photo: Dawn St. Clare)

Castel del Monte, Puglia, 1240 (Photo: Allison Lee Palmer)

Notre Dame, Paris, 1200s (Photo: Dawn St. Clare)

Florence Cathedral, dome by Filippo Brunelleschi, 1420s (Photo: Dawn St. Clare)

Saint Peter's Church, Rome, begun 1505 (Photo: Dawn St. Clare)

Andrea Palladio, Villa Rotonda, Vicenza, Italy, 1560s (Photo: Dawn St. Clare)

Louis Le Vau, Versailles Palace, Versailles, 1660s (Photo: Nancy Lee Palmer)

Charles Garnier, Opéra, Paris, 1860s (Photo: Dawn St. Clare)

John Barry and Horace Jones, Tower Bridge, London, 1886–1894 (Photo: Allison Lee Palmer)

Gustav Eiffel, Eiffel Tower, Paris, 1889 (Photo: Dawn St. Clare)

Antoní Gaudi, Parc Güell, Barcelona, 1900s–1910s (Photo: Allison Lee Palmer)

Frank Lloyd Wright, Robie House, Chicago, 1909 (Photo: Allison Lee Palmer)

Gerrit Rietveld, Schroeder House, Utrecht, 1924 (Photo: Allison Lee Palmer)

Le Corbusier, Villa Savoye, Poissy-sur-Seine, 1929 (Photo: Dawn St. Clare)

Shreve, Lamb, and Harmon, Empire State Building, New York, 1930s (Photo: Dawn St. Clare)

Le Corbusier, Notre Dame du Haut, Ronchamp, 1955 (Photo: Dawn St. Clare)

With this thinking, Le Corbusier turned his attention to urban planning in the hopes of establishing a prototype for a healthy, clean, and well-organized modern city that would be an improvement over the noisy, crowded, and dirty cities that grew out of the Industrial Revolution. His city plans were laid out on a grid, with a uniform style, **skyscrapers**, broad avenues, and large parks. Unlike the Italian **Futurist** city plans, such as those of the same era by Antonio Sant'Elia, Le Corbusier's more practical city designs always sought to include nature. A theoretician as well as an architect, Le Corbusier wrote *Vers une architecture* in 1923 to express his ideas on the creation of an architecture befitting its time and place rather than echoing the buildings of the past. This treatise has mistakenly led scholars to consider Le Corbusier an anti-classical architect, but the timeless and universal aspects of classicism are instead the centerpiece of Le Corbusier's early work. In addition, he was the founder of the Congrès International d'Architecture Moderne (CIAM), which had a profound influence upon architecture across Europe in the first half of the 20th century.

In the 1920s, he began to design a series of private homes. During this decade, domestic architecture was an important topic of discussion in Paris, where a need for quickly constructed, inexpensive housing was in conflict with the continued desire for more traditional homes. Most of Le Corbusier's houses are therefore done in the **International style**, which developed in Europe after World War I as a simple, geometric mode that could transcend national boundaries. Le Corbusier's Villa Savoye, built in Poissy-sur-Seine outside of Paris in 1929, epitomizes this style and has become an icon of modern architecture. This home was built with the domino construction system, which consisted of reinforced **concrete** slabs elevated onto a central core of six very slender **steel** piers spaced apart like the dots on a domino. The square-spaced living quarters are then elevated onto a colonnade that continues around all four sides, thereby creating a floating effect much like a modern stilt house. Cars could park beneath the porch in a three-car garage, and one could then enter the home through the central core, which has a stair leading to the living quarters above. One long continuous window wraps around the square building, while a terrace is designed on the roof. Circular dividing walls add movement to the otherwise linear plan of the building.

Le Corbusier's homes were painted pure white, and with their elevation above ground, they were meant not to echo their surroundings, but to transcend them. The white concrete used in many other International style buildings can be interpreted as relating to the enduring white **marble** of antiquity, while the unifying use of squares and circles reveals clearly understood geometric shapes in a form of rationality, which is an inherently classical notion. However, one marked difference from classicism is in the proportions of the piers. In looking at the Villa Savoye, one might at first wonder if the thin-steel encased, free-standing *pilotis* are really able to support the thick upper living quarters of the villa, but this visual effect of weightlessness perhaps reveals a confidence in modern structural advances that allows for an inversion of the classical visual hierarchy of registers. These buildings recall a stripped-down version of classicism, which came to be seen as the essence of the International style. Buildings such as Le Corbusier's Villa Savoye were therefore increasingly described as "iconic" because of their ability to transcend time and place.

After designing a series of private homes, Le Corbusier was commissioned to construct an apartment building in Marseilles, France, called Unité d'Habitation (1946–1952). Here he used *béton brut*, or raw concrete, which allows for a more economical style later called **Brutalism**. His city layout of Chandigarh, India, in the 1950s, reveals Le Corbusier's expansion upon his modernist ideals on a large scale. There he created a loosely formed grid of government buildings for this new regional capital. Although most of these buildings follow the geometric principles of the International style, the Assembly Building in particular demonstrates the more expressive use of concrete that characterizes Le Corbusier's late works. His church Notre Dame du Haut, located on a hill in Ronchamp, France, was completed in 1955 in the style of **Expressionism**. Le Corbusier remains today a seminal figure in the establishment of a modernist philosophy of architecture, one that dominated architectural design through the 20th century.

CORTONA, PIETRO DA (1596–1669). *See* BAROQUE ARCHITECTURE.

COSTA, LUCIO (1902–1998). *See* NIEMEYER, OSCAR.

COTSWOLD COTTAGE. *See* TUDOR REVIVAL STYLE.

COTTE, ROBERT DE (1656–1735). *See* VERSAILLES PALACE, FRANCE.

CRITICAL REGIONALISM. Beginning with the **International style** that developed after World War I, modern architectural discourse has minimized regional influences by focusing instead on generalized formal and design elements devoid of any applied historical or decorative imagery. Because regional and historical architecture was considered inferior by adherents of this type of stripped-down modernism, geographical, climatic, and cultural differences were rarely expressed in architecture. Certainly, those architects who did work in such regional styles never received the international recognition that the architects of the more "avant-garde" style of modernism enjoyed. This modernist stylistic uniformity continued with **Post-Modern architecture**, which quickly became the dominant style for monumental, international commissions through the 1980s. Since then, however, architects, constrained by the limitations of this conformity, have sought to cultivate an increase in architectural diversity that responds more successfully to issues of weather, climate, local building materials, and regional cultural aesthetics.

Kenneth Frampton, in his 1983 article "Towards a Critical Regionalism: Six Points of an Architecture of Resistance," coined the term Critical Regionalism for this new architectural trend. Since then, regional architects have gone on to respond successfully to issues such as the need for low-cost housing, greater energy efficiency, and more aesthetically sensitive structures that reflect differing cultural and aesthetic backgrounds. In Egypt, Hassan Fathy sought to revitalize the use of mud-**brick** materials in private houses in a local style that has become increasingly popular with the work of his student Abdul El-Wakil, whose Halawa House, built in Agami, Egypt, in 1975, epitomizes this interest in regionalism. By creating a grand house with **Islamic** features and local materials, El-Wakil shows how the wealthy class need not look to European architectural models for their housing, but are ennobled by a return to their own native construction practices.

Critical Regionalism is not just regionalism, but it also challenges the architect and visitor to see how world culture and global concerns can be blended with regional issues to create a style that is more critically self-conscious and expansive. For example, **Tadao Ando**'s design for the Church of the Light in Ibaraki-shi, Osaka, built in 1989, is an extremely spare, concrete modernist structure, but it is also informed by Zen philosophy in its contrast between the solidity of the concrete and the immaterial nature of the light. Jørn Utzon's Sydney Opera House, completed in 1973 with the appearance of thin, billowing shapes on its roof, resembles the sails of boats on the Sydney harbor but with a very technically sophisticated use of concrete forms. Frampton also described **Alvar Aalto**'s buildings in these same terms, because they resisted the more universal modernist styles, materials, and technology that dominated mid-century architecture. His Baker House dormitory at the Massachusetts Institute of Technology (MIT) in Boston, completed in 1948, for example, is a brick structure that bends in its middle to create an undulating wall overlooking the Charles River. Thus, unlike the Post-Modernist application of historical references, Critical Regionalism seeks a fuller integration of global and regional concerns into the architectural setting of a structure. *See also* DECONSTRUCTIVISM; PEI, IEOH MING.

CUVILLIÉS, FRANÇOIS DE (1695–1768). *See* ROCOCO ARCHITECTURE.

– D –

DARBY, ABRAHAM III (1750–1791). *See* CAST IRON.

DE STIJL. *See* RATIONALISM.

DECONSTRUCTIVISM. Deconstructivism was first introduced to the public in a 1988 exhibition held at the Museum of Modern Art in New York City and organized by the American architect **Philip**

Johnson and theoretician Mark Wigley. This style is characterized by a desire among architects to "deconstruct" the traditional classical aesthetics of symmetry, balance, and harmony that had informed architectural design since antiquity. The previous generation of 20th-century architects had already made great strides in this direction. But although most **International style** architects had resisted any comparison to classicism in their architecture through the creation of a stripped-down style devoid of applied historical referencing, the universal regularity of the International style ultimately came to be considered classical. Deconstructivism, however, was primarily shaped by the philosophical ideas of the French philosopher Jacques Derrida (1930–2004), whose ideas on the subject were first expressed in the 1960s and published in his *On Grammatology*. Derrida was a linguist; he cultivated through the use of language the more general idea that nothing has one single, intrinsic meaning, but words, ideas, and images must always be understood in relation to their surrounding context.

Thus, the term "deconstruction" itself cannot be pinned to one specific definition, but must instead be seen as a constantly shifting process. Derrida also challenged basic assumptions of Western philosophy, whereby binary opposites have been constructed over time as a way of organizing information—but this processing of information involves setting up opposing viewpoints that always defer to the hierarchically "superior" view. In linguistics, then, one word is always "privileged" over its "opposite." For example, *presence* is privileged over *absence*, *life* over *death*, and *fullness* over *emptiness*. These three examples make us wonder if this particular hierarchy is the inescapable predicament of human existence, or if one can transcend this physicality, perhaps with the help of Eastern philosophy. Derrida's philosophy runs much deeper than this brief discussion, but this overview can at least serve as a platform for an analysis of Deconstructivist architecture.

Deconstructivist buildings appear to be distorted, off-center, twisted into more dynamic forms. This architectural dynamism has historical references to the early-20th-century Italian **Futurist** as well as Russian **Constructivist architecture** of the same period, both of which sought to create a politically and socially charged move toward newer forms of modernity. A good example of this new style is seen in **Zaha Hadid**'s Vitra Fire Station, built in Weil-am-Rhein, Germany, in 1989–1993, and in **Frank Gehry**'s Guggenheim Museum, constructed in Bilbao, Spain, in 1993–1997. Other Deconstructivist architects cited in the initial 1988 exhibition include Rem Koolhaus, a Dutch-born architect who currently teaches at the Graduate School of Design at Harvard University. A theoretician as well as an architect, Koolhaus has published widely on current issues such as globalization versus regionalism, prosperity and the consumer market, population growth and urbanism. His Casa di Musica, built in Porto, Portugal, in 2001–2005, opened to rave reviews complimenting not only its new engineering challenges, but also the balance between its intellectual foundation and its sensual beauty. This large structure appears to be a monumental rectangle that has been sliced away in its corners, cutting through its roofline, and shaving off part of its sides to create a geometric shape without name. Resting on one of the smaller sides of this shape, the building gives a "de-centered" appearance and a new appreciation for nonrectilinear shapes. Koolhaus's Seattle Central Library, opened in 2004, is an 11-story **steel** and **glass** structure that also appears fragmented, with shapes that seem to hover above the lower levels at sharp angles. This building was also meant to be a prototype for Koolhaus's ideas on cross-functional buildings, in that he hoped to include hospital units for homeless people within the context of the library.

Coop Himmelb(l)au, the cooperative group with a name that plays on the words for "heaven-blue" and cooperative construction, was established in Vienna in the late 1960s by Wolf Prix, Helmut Swiczinsky, and Michael Holzer, and now has offices worldwide. Their UFA-Palast, built as a movie theater in Dresden in 1993–1998, is part of a vast rebuilding of the city after the division between East and West Germany was dissolved. This contorted glass shape leans sharply to one side, providing what could initially be interpreted as an alarming vista. Bernard Tschumi, who was also represented in the 1988 exhibition of Deconstructivist architecture, used the principles of Deconstructivism in his design for the Alfred Lerner Hall at Columbia University in New York City, which was built in 1999 with one entirely glazed exterior curtain wall tilted at an angle to give the appearance of one giant window, slipping downward.

Daniel Libeskind's Deconstructivist buildings provoke a different reaction in that they appear to jut up and out from the comfort of their foundations. His Jewish Museum, completed in Berlin in 1999, gives this impression, as does, in a more powerful way, his addition to the Denver Art Museum, completed in 2006. This structure, called the Frederic C. Hamilton Building, is perhaps the most daring engineering feat to date. Made of titanium and glass, cantilevered pyramids thrust outward and upward, like a giant ship sailing forward. His 2002–2003 plans for the Memorial Foundations at the **World Trade Center** also include elements of Deconstructivism.

Finally, perhaps the most tied to the philosophical basis for Deconstructivism is Peter Eisenman, who worked with Jacques Derrida in the formation of his own theoretical discourse. Primarily a theoretical architect, his few commissions sometimes reveal a Deconstructivist style of architecture. His Wexner Center for the Arts, which opened on the campus of Ohio State University in Columbus in 1989, is a good example of his work. While one side of the building is made of **brick** to create a visual link to the old armory, the other sides of the building reveal Eisenman's more characteristic use of white **concrete**, punctured and uplifted to create a wider range of shape and form.

Ultimately, Deconstructivist architecture cannot be seen as simply a new stylistic emphasis; it also resulted in fundamental changes to how architecture is perceived worldwide. Greater architectural diversity tends to be more celebrated over the establishment of a dominant style, and regional influences are beginning to negate the imposition of a dominant culture onto architectural discourse. This regional sensitivity resulted in the formation of **Critical Regionalism** and shares a concurrent architectural development with Deconstructivism.

DJENNÉ, GREAT MOSQUE OF. *See* BRICK.

DOME. The dome, which is created from an **arch** turned on its axis 360 degrees, is traditionally considered one of the most important **Ancient Roman** architectural inventions. Although round temples were not new to Ancient Rome, the **Pantheon**, when it was built in AD 120, was unprecedented in its scale. Both the diameter and height of

the dome measure 143 feet, and it features a 30-foot-wide round oculus window in its center. Made of a volcanic rock called *tufa*, considered an early form of **concrete**, the dome also features coffering, a series of squares cut out of the concrete to reduce its weight and
provide a sense of rhythm and order to the dome's interior. The 20-
foot-thick walls are not solid, but built up of concrete layered with
arches to relieve the tremendous weight of the dome through the
walls. Despite the prevalence of domed structures in Ancient Rome,
most Roman buildings used a **stone** or **wood** vaulting system rather
than a dome. Domes constructed through the Middle Ages were
smaller and built of masonry with ribbing. Following the same design
principles as the pointed arch, they feature a pointed top capped by a
pinnacle.

The structural knowledge of the Ancient Roman semispherical
dome was lost over time, not to be rediscovered until the **Renaissance**. Until the early 1400s, the dome of the **Florence Cathedral**
and its octagonal drum remained open, given the overly ambitious
plan of earlier architects to construct the largest building in all of
Italy. In 1417, **Filippo Brunelleschi** was hired to complete the dome.
He had just returned from Rome, where his studies of Ancient Roman
architecture involved the careful measuring of specific buildings, including the Pantheon. Because of the preexisting octagonal drum,
Brunelleschi was not able to build a round dome like the Pantheon,
so instead he designed a modified solution that involved a double-
shelled dome with ribs set into the corners of the drum and a slightly
pointed top, capped by a lantern. This dome was the first since antiquity to employ ancient methods of construction and was therefore
hailed as the first "true" Renaissance building. Through the Renaissance, domes of all sizes were constructed, meant to recall the
grandeur of Ancient Rome. In the 1560s, **Andrea Palladio** introduced the dome in a domestic building, as seen in his Villa Rotonda,
built outside Vicenza. Thus, Palladio reintroduced in this rural home
for his upper-class patron both the ancient villa and the idea of the
imperial *domus* (of the word "domestic").

Domes became an almost mandatory feature of subsequent Re-
naissance and then **Baroque** churches, including **Saint Peter's
Church in Rome**, begun in 1505 and completed in the early 1600s.
But the domestic dome never became very popular outside of a num-

ber of **Neo-Classical** homes from the 18th century, such as **Richard Boyle**'s Chiswick House, built in West London in the 1720s, and **Thomas Jefferson**'s Monticello, built in Charlottesville, Virginia, beginning in the 1770s. By the 19th century, domes became increasingly important features of most government buildings constructed in the United States, in emulation of the original domed **United States Capitol, Washington, D.C.**, begun in 1803 by **Benjamin Henry Latrobe**. The most recent state capitol to receive a classical dome is in Oklahoma City, where the capitol dome was planned in 1914 but not completed until 1997.

While these domes all retain a historical referencing in their classical designs, new dome possibilities began to appear in the 20th century, as architects explored new ways of manipulating reinforced **concrete** in their domes. Pier Luigi Nervi's Palazzetto dello Sport, built in Rome for the 1960 Olympics, is a good example of his combination of engineering and aesthetics to create a thin concrete shell dome that spans a huge interior. These thin-shelled, organic-styled concrete roof coverings were more recently the source of inspiration for the Millennium Dome, a massive structure supported by masts that look like giant stakes driven through the top of the dome. Built in southeast London by Richard Rogers and the structural engineer Buro Happold for the year-long millennium celebrations held there in 2000, this building is currently an indoor sports arena.

Finally, the geodesic dome, another modern innovation, is a highly technical structure whereby a reinforced dome is created with intersecting lines. Although it is made from linear elements, it is ultimately a spherical structure created from a network of struts arranged around intersecting circles that lie on the surface of the sphere. Triangles are formed where the circles intersect and disperse the stress more evenly across the surface. This innovation is the sole man-made structure that can become stronger as it gets larger. Geodesic domes are mathematically complex, whereby a shape such as an icosahedron (a polyhedron with 20 faces, usually with equilateral triangles in each face) is used to measure out a pattern of triangles lying with minimal distortion on the surface of the sphere. The edges of the triangle are called *geodesics*. Although a variety of patterns can be used to create geodesic domes, the expense of creating a new pattern has standardized the dome into a few prevalent shapes.

The geodesic dome was built by Walther Bauersfeld in 1922 as a planetarium in Germany, but it was first introduced to the broader public at the American Pavilion of Expo '67 held in Montreal. Created by R. Buckminster Fuller, the American Pavilion dome was based on mathematical studies performed at Black Mountain College in Asheville, North Carolina, in the 1940s. Several **Bauhaus** architects, including **Walter Gropius**, taught at Black Mountain during this same decade, and from that point on, Fuller, an inventor, poet, and visionary, began to dedicate his work toward developing a utopian vision of improving human existence through more economical automobiles and homes. Fuller hoped that this strong, lightweight structure could be used for inexpensive housing, an idea that he developed further in his Dymaxion House, from 1945. This round home is made of metal covered in polished aluminum and resembles a flattened dome. The entire house is so lightweight that it can rotate around a central mast to improve air circulation. It also had other economical features, including rotating drawers and a fine-mist shower. Although this widely popular prototype of a home was never produced, a model can be found today in the Henry Ford Museum in Dearborn, Michigan. Domes, particularly the lightweight geodesic domes, continue to be modified for use in architectural construction today.

DOO WOP ARCHITECTURE. *See* VENTURI, ROBERT.

DURHAM CASTLE AND CATHEDRAL. Durham is located in northeast England, near Scotland. Therefore, it was an important frontier town after the Norman Conquest and grew to include a **Romanesque** fortified **castle**, a **monastery**, and a cathedral, all constructed from around 1075 through the 1100s. The sole entry into the enclosed castle complex was across a drawbridge flanked by guard towers. While many castles were surrounded by a moat, here the Wear River acted as a natural water boundary with **stone** walls built upon the natural rocky outcrop. The castle is a fine example of the *motte-and-bailey* type. Visitors then entered into the *bailey*, with the *keep* to the right, or east, and the Great Hall, once the largest in all of England, located straight ahead, while the cathedral was built to the south. The Great Hall was used for public meetings by the Prince-

Bishops of Durham, who lived in the adjoining castle, which is all part of Durham University today. The Durham complex was originally constructed in timber, and gradually replaced by stone through the years. A small chapel located next to the keep may have been the first stone building constructed, commissioned by William the Conqueror and built around 1075. The Cathedral of Durham was begun in 1087 to house the relics of Saint Cuthbert and is one of the best examples of Norman Romanesque architecture in Europe. The interior features an arcade of beautiful nave pillars carved in geometric chevrons and diamond-shaped patterns that alternate with compounded piers, all of which are topped by rounded **arches**, a short *triforium* gallery on the second story, and clerestory windows on the upper nave walls. Unlike **Gothic** churches, this design provides an A-B-A-B rhythm down the nave that is carried through in the ceiling as well. The cross-vaulted ceiling is one of the tallest in the Romanesque period, with intersecting ribs that span two bays instead of one, while in the transepts, the earliest example of four-part vaults arranged in rectangular bays appears. From Durham, this vaulting system then spread to continental Europe; it is found, for example, at Saint-Étienne at Caen in France.

– E –

EARLY CHRISTIAN ARCHITECTURE. Early Christian architecture grew out of ancient Jewish precedents, which consisted of religious structures built to solidify Hebrew authority in the ancient land around the eastern Mediterranean Sea, Canaan, which the Romans called Palestine. However, with the establishment of Christianity came a need for architectural spaces that could be used by believers to confirm, assert, and educate others about this new religion. Because Christianity held great favor among the common man, the earliest congregants rarely had enough political favor or wealth to build large-scale religious structures. In fact, prior to Constantine's Edict of Milan in AD 313, the Christian world was private. Christians gathered before altars in private homes, which came to be called the "house-church" or *ecclesia*, an ancient Greek word meaning "gathering of the called-out ones." The remains of a house-church in

Dura-Europos in modern-day Syria demonstrate this early development. The structure was visually prominent, which probably attests to
a lesser degree of persecution at this time than has traditionally been
thought. Many of these early *ecclesiae* reveal a mingling of early pagan, Jewish, and Christian symbolism.

As Christianity came to be increasingly tolerated, congregants began to build nonresidential places of worship. A particularly dramatic
growth of the Church occurred with the Emperor Constantine's ac-
ceptance of Christianity in Rome, which effectively ended the "Age
of Persecution" and contributed to the construction of many Christian churches and other buildings through the 300s, including a home
and baptistery for the pope-bishop of Rome. Hoping to distance
themselves from the visual symbolism of the pagan temple, early
Christians selected the Roman government building called the basilica
as a model for the earliest churches, while baptisteries and martyria
continued to be circular in format. A good example of the basilica-
plan church is the original **Saint Peter's Church in Rome**. Although
it does not exist today, it was begun around AD 320 by Constantine,
who wanted a large monument to mark the site where Saint Peter was
buried. The church of Santa Sabina, built in Rome around 422, remains one of the few early Christian churches to retain its original
form. This church's basilica plan, also called a longitudinal plan, has
a long, central nave flanked by side aisles. The nave is taller than the
side aisles, allowing a row of clerestory windows in the upper registers to illuminate the central interior. The entrance, at the western,
short end of the building, orients the visitor in a strongly axial direction down the nave, lined by a colonnade on either side, toward the
high altar, located in a rounded apse at the far end of the nave. The
high altar is elevated from the nave floor, demarking the choir area as
the most sacred space in the church. While the exterior of Santa
Sabina is a simple **brick** construction devoid of applied decoration,
the interior reveals marble flooring and a nave arcade of round arches
with fluted **marble** Corinthian columns. The nave also had now-lost
murals or mosaics in the register above the arcade and beneath the
clerestory windows.

Because the circular church, also called the centrally planned
church, was originally based on the ancient *tholos*, used as a funerary structure, the Christian context was often also funerary in func-

tion. The earliest surviving circular church is a mausoleum built around AD 340 for Constantina, the daughter of Constantine. Now called Santa Costanza, the church consists of a central domed area surrounded by a barrel-vaulted walkway called an ambulatory. The round arched colonnade that separates the ambulatory from the central area features a double layer of Composite columns. Marble and mosaics cover the interior walls and ambulatory ceiling. In Constantinople, the Emperor Constantine's funerary church (which does not survive today) was constructed as a centrally planned church with four equal arms, called a Greek-cross plan. With the fall of Rome, the Roman Empire moved first to Milan and then to Ravenna, an east-coast city important in Ancient Rome for its naval base and direct route to Constantinople. Therefore, Christian architecture in Ravenna exhibited a strong eastern influence that came to be called the **Byzantine** style. The Mausoleum of Galla Placidia in Ravenna dates to around 425 and was constructed as a Greek-cross-plan funerary monument for the half-sister of Emperor Honorius. Byzantine-style mosaics appear in the interior of the building, commemorating the martyrdom of Saint Lawrence. Once the city of Ravenna was captured by the Byzantine army of Emperor Justinian I in 540 from Arian Christian Ostrogoths who had lived in the city since 476, artistic influences reversed direction, stemming the transmittal of Roman culture into Constantinople, and instead bringing a fuller Byzantine style into Italy, a style that lasted there through the early years of the **Renaissance**.

EARLY JEWISH ARCHITECTURE. *See* TEMPLE OF SOLOMON.

EARLY MEDIEVAL ARCHITECTURE. The Middle Ages is broadly defined as the period between the fall of Rome, with its centralized imperial rule, and the revival of classicism in the **Renaissance**. Thus medieval architecture is often assumed, however wrongly, to turn away from classical influences and classical aesthetics. The Medieval period encompasses about 1,000 years of European history from the 5th to the 15th centuries and is traditionally broken down into the Early Middle Ages (400s–900s), which includes the Carolingian Empire (700s–800s) and the Ottonian Empire

(800s–900s), and the Later Middle Ages, which includes the **Romanesque** (1000s–1100s) and the **Gothic** (1200s–1400s). The expression "middle ages," or "medieval," refers to an early historical prejudice against this extensive historical time frame when the classical world was initially replaced by such regional groups as the Visigoths, the Ostrogoths, the Franks, the Saxons, and the Celts, who carved out local power and asserted their own beliefs, customs, and architectural practices. Since these cultures were ultimately unified under Christian authority in Rome, it was the Christian church that emerged during the Middle Ages as the most important patron of architecture. Medieval architecture consists of churches, **monasteries**, palace complexes, **castles**, and government buildings. Some of the earliest medieval churches built outside of Rome are found in Spain and were constructed by Visigoths who had converted to Arian Christianity in the fifth century, settled in Spain, and by the sixth century had established themselves as the elite class, ruling over the native peoples of the Iberian Peninsula.

The small Church of Santa Maria de Quintanilla de las Viñas located outside Burgos is one of the few surviving regional churches from the seventh century. It was originally a basilica-plan church with a nave and flanking side aisles that opened into the choir through two doorways. The choir was the same width as the church, and therefore gave the impression of either a transept or two flanking sacristies. Classical **Roman** architectural features blend here with regional pagan imagery, while Visigothic elements such as the notable horseshoe **arch** over the entrance to the apse attest to the rich confluence of cultures that typifies this period. Finally, the **Islamic** conquest of the Iberian Peninsula in 711 added another element to the rich cultural mix that informed both architectural style and sculptural decoration at this time.

The Carolingian Dynasty (768–877) is largely defined today by the rule of Charlemagne, or "Charles the Great," who was crowned Holy Roman Emperor in 800 by Pope Leo III in recognition of his work in establishing Christianity in the territories he conquered across modern-day France, western Germany, northern Italy, Belgium, and Holland. This alliance between secular and sacred Europe took place in a lavish ceremony held at Old **Saint Peter's Church in Rome**, where Charlemagne was compared to Constantine and urged to continue his expansion of Christian territories across Europe. Charlemagne began his career as a strong military leader among his native Frankish peoples, who had settled in an area around the Rhine River some three centuries earlier. He then rose in stature to become the leading secular authority in Europe. During his reign, he purposefully cultivated the use of Imperial symbols in his court in Aachen, Germany, to reinforce this alliance with Rome. Through his study of the Latin language and patronage of classically inspired art and architecture, Charlemagne revived the culture of classical Rome.

Charlemagne's palace complex in Aachen is largely destroyed today, but documents detail a lavish compound of houses, administrative buildings, and shops set near the hot springs outside central Aachen. Begun in 794, a partially surviving audience hall and his palace chapel are all that remain today. The chapel, constructed like an imperial mausoleum, recalls San Vitale (c. 520) in Ravenna, Italy, in its octagonal ground-plan, **dome**, and ambulatory, yet its original source is the Roman *tholos*, or round domed funerary building that was later adapted by **Early Christian** builders for use as a Christian *martyrium* or baptistery. The earliest example of this type of *martyrium* is Santa Costanza in Rome, the mausoleum built for Constantine's daughter around AD 340 and later modified for use as a church in the mid-13th century. Charlemagne would certainly have seen this and many other buildings during his visit to Rome, and these buildings would have helped him transfer this Imperial Roman style to northern Europe. Charlemagne's chapel is shaped into an octagon with a gallery topped by clerestory windows. Eight compound pilasters rise to a round arch above the clerestory level, and pairs of Corinthian **columns** repeat at both levels between the pilasters. These are the elements that make the most direct visual link to classical architecture. An ambulatory surrounds the central core at the ground level, while the eight corners follow through up into an eight-ribbed dome. The chapel also has a western façade with towers on either side that house spiral stairs leading to a second-story throne room and a third-story room that held the chapel relics.

Many other seminomadic peoples lived across Europe during this time, but what makes the Christian rulers important to the discussion of architecture is that they used permanent buildings as a potent symbol of unified authority. The Carolingian Empire was continued by the grandsons of Charlemagne but ended in the 9th century with almost no new architectural development. However, it was replaced in the 10th century by a powerful Saxon court from modern-day Germany and Austria, in what had been an eastern region of the Carolingian Empire. This new European power was called the Ottonian Empire, named after its three major rulers, Otto I (called "the Great"), Otto II, and Otto III, and it was this empire, due to its connections to the papacy and marriages in the Italic Peninsula, that led to the formal establishment of the Holy Roman Empire, which continued in some form down into the 20th century.

The Ottonians also sought to use architecture similar to the grand constructions in Rome as a means of defining their authority across various regions. Thus, their church of Saint Cyriakus, in Gernrode, Germany, begun in 961, reflects both Ancient Roman influences and local aspects of construction by German stonemasons. Its original façade was covered several centuries later with a protruding apse, but beneath the apse, one can still detect a tripartite division of the façade with three round-arched, bifurcated windows in the upper register of the central façade, which is flanked by round towers. The upper portions of the towers reveal a row of flat pilasters, carved in low relief to suggest the type of tower arcade that might have been found on an early Christian church in Rome. Aside from this fictive arcade and the window articulation, the exterior of Saint Cyriakus is very severe. Inside the church, the nave has three registers, while the nave arcade alternates round columns with square piers to create an A-B-A-B rhythm. Above the round arches of the arcade, a *triforium* gallery is formed with a different rhythm, in which six columns alternate with thick square piers down the arcade. The uppermost register features small arched clerestory windows. Transept chapels flank the choir at the east end of the basilica-plan church, while a side door allowed the nuns of the convent to enter the church through a separate portal.

Archbishop Gero of Cologne and Bishop Bernward of Hildesheim were important patrons of architecture during the Ottonian era, and the Benedictine Abbey Church of Saint Michael's, built in Hildesheim from 1001 to 1032, is one of the finer examples of Ottonian architecture. Destroyed in World War II, the church was rebuilt in the 1950s and is now considered a UNESCO World Heritage Site. The church features a choir at either end, in keeping with the layout of the Ancient Roman basilica, which lacks the strongly axial direction of most subsequent churches. Towers are located at each crossing, which provides a more complex exterior plan as well. On the interior, the nave arcade is articulated with alternating columns and piers in an A-A-B-A-A-B-A-A rhythm, while the walls rise up without a *triforium* into small clerestory windows located beneath the flat timber roof. This ceiling recalls Ancient Roman coffering more directly than at Saint Cyriakus, as here the ceiling is divided into more obviously square panels. The most famous feature of the Church of Saint Michael, however, is its set of bronze doors that rise up three times taller than human scale and are modeled with Biblical scenes in a narrative format that anticipates the intricate portal sculpture of the later Romanesque and Gothic eras. Both the Carolingian and Ottonian Empires were important in the formation of an architectural language that brought together the Ancient Roman world, early Christian symbolism, and important regional influences to accommodate the dramatic growth of the Church through the Middle Ages, a growth that continued through the next several centuries.

EASTLAKE STYLE. *See* VICTORIAN ARCHITECTURE.

EIFFEL, ALEXANDRE GUSTAV (1832–1923). *See* CAST IRON.

EIFFEL TOWER. *See* CAST IRON.

EISENMAN, PETER (1932–). *See* DECONSRUCTIVISM.

ERSKINE, RALPH (1914–2005). *See* HIGH-TECH ARCHITECTURE.

ESCORIAL, MADRID. During the **Renaissance**, the Spanish King Philip II not only governed much of the Iberian Peninsula but also parts of the Italic Peninsula, including Milan and Naples, as well as the Netherlands and colonies in the Americas. As the son of the Holy Roman Emperor, Philip II held vast power across Europe during the Protestant Reformation and therefore desired a palace complex that demonstrated a balance between the wealth of Spain and its piety. During his extensive reign (1556–1598), he was preoccupied with the expansion of Spanish interests in the Americas and the Netherlands, but in 1588, he lost his legendary Spanish Armada to his great rival, Queen Elizabeth of England. Nonetheless, the Spanish Crown had profited greatly from its colonial rule, and that wealth helped to establish Philip II's extensive art collection as well as to construct his palace about 28 miles outside of Madrid. Called the Escorial, it was not only a palace with administrative buildings, but also a **monastery** and a funerary complex to be used as a royal mausoleum for Spanish kings. It was built in a small town known for its iron foundry and was named *Escoria* after the iron slag deposits that were used in this region for a variety of products. Although forested, this region of Spain was less lush than other areas of the Iberian Peninsula, and thus the surrounding landscape as well as the local grey granite used to construct the Escorial lent an austere character to the complex.

The major Spanish Renaissance architect, Juan Bautista de Toledo, was working in Rome at the time; from 1546 to 1548 he had been **Michelangelo**'s main advisor in the construction of **Saint Peter's Church**. In 1559, Philip called him back to Madrid to complete the Escorial. While in Rome, Toledo was obviously steeped in the classicism of **Donato Bramante** and the **Vitruvian** principles so popular in Italian architecture at the time, for the Escorial reveals a classical balance and symmetry as well as architectural details. The Escorial's royal monastery of San Lorenzo includes a library, a school for the education of noble children, and a church with a crypt for royal burials, all built in white **stone**. Shortly after the death of Juan de Toledo, Juan de Herrera was hired to continue with the project. His plans included the enlargement of the entire complex by adding a second story to the wings and by creating a grander entrance with the addition of a large classical portico superimposed onto the front of the complex. Since Juan de Herrera had been de Toledo's apprentice and was also known as a humanist and mathematician, his work at the Escorial came to epitomize the introduction of Italian Renaissance classicism into Spain.

The complex is constructed in one vast square, with four-story outer walls that feature square towers in each of the four corners. The windows that line each of the four stories are lacking in any applied architectural decoration and therefore give the appearance of a somewhat fortified structure. Along the entrance wall, however, the front of the complex features a tall classical portico in the center, while two smaller porticoes appear equally spaced along the sides of the entrance wall, which then ends in each corner by the towers. The only part of the building that issues from the otherwise uniformly flat wall is the central portico, in which a two-story temple front is articulated with eight half-**columns** engaged to the wall and four on either side of the square doorway. Between the columns are three vertical rows of square windows, all of which are capped with an entablature of triglyphs and metopes, in keeping with the more austere Doric order used for the first column order. Then, a second register rises up through the center, with four Ionic columns, two on either side of sculptured niches above the central doorway. This entire aedicule is topped by a triangular pediment. Although the entire design recalls Bramante's more rigidly Vitruvian interpretation of classical architecture, it is not a strict copy of Bramante's principles. Instead, the façade portico, which rises in front of a mansard-styled roof, also has short, obelisk-shaped caps above the outer four columns at the lower register, which are then topped by balls.

The internal buildings of the complex are aligned on a grid pattern and dominated by the centrally located San Lorenzo, a Latin-cross-plan church that features two bell towers in the front to frame a view of the large **dome**, which in its size recalls the dome of Saint Peter's Church. Inside, the high altar is the most lavish part of the entire complex, with screens made of red granite and jasper, surrounded by gilded bronze sculptures, including kneeling figures of Charles I and Philip II. The library is equally beautiful, with wooden armoires lining the walls of long corridors that feature painted barrel-vaulted ceilings. The royal apartments, in contrast, are spare, with windows overlooking the basilica. The Pantheon, which is the mausoleum, features 26 **marble** funerary monuments to members of the royal family. Philip II's parents, Charles I and Isabella of Portugal, are buried there. The Escorial can be understood as Philip's demonstration of a more austere Catholic faith, cultivated in response to the growing Protestantism that was taking hold in the Netherlands and moving into Spain.

The entire project was completed in 1584, although subsequent rulers added more buildings to the surrounding area of the complex, including a summer palace and a theater. During the reign of Philip

II, a hunting lodge was also constructed about three miles away from the Escorial. Called *La Granjilla de la Fresneda*, this smaller complex, built from 1561 to 1569, consisted of a lodge, a small chapel, and monastic buildings, as well as the gardens of the king. Today, the Escorial and its surrounding community display some of the most important Renaissance monuments in all of Spain. *See also* ANCIENT ROMAN ARCHITECTURE.

ETRUSCAN ARCHITECTURE. Etruscan architecture is not fully understood today, given that Etruscan civilization predates Roman culture, and therefore Etruscan ruins very often lie beneath Roman ruins in modern-day Italy. Beginning in the Bronze Age, Villanovans lived in the northern part of the Italic Peninsula, while Greeks had settled the southern part. In the seventh century BC, Etruscan peoples, perhaps derived from the Villanovans, expanded their settlements through central Italy and spoke a pre-Latin language. They farmed and traded metals across much of Europe, including the whole Greek world and as far away as Phoenicia in modern-day Lebanon. For that reason, Etruscan architecture reveals a blending of **Ancient Greek** and **Ancient Near Eastern** styles and anticipates Roman design.

What is known of Etruscan architecture today consists of ongoing excavation work (mainly at funerary sites), ceramic funerary urns made in the shape of houses, and finally, written descriptions made by subsequent Romans, for example, the architect **Vitruvius**, who saw the remains of the vanquished Etruscan civilization firsthand. Etruscan cities were often located on hills to have a natural defense against rival city-states. The Porta Augusta in Perugia, from the 100s BC, is a rare example of surviving Etruscan construction. The monumental **arch** entranceway, made from local **stone**, provides a guarded entry into these walled towns. Above the arch is a lintel decoration of five circles carved in relief and separated by column designs that function the same way as Ancient Greek triglyphs. Two large towers flank the entrance. The structure of the arch developed gradually from the keystones used by previous cultures, but it was the Ancient Romans who developed the arch to its fullest potential.

From funerary urns it can be surmised that Etruscan homes had small open atria or courtyards, with shallow pools in the center that stored rainwater. From textual descriptions of an Etruscan temple, according to Vitruvius in the first century BC, these square temples, made of mud **brick**, were axially aligned and elevated on a platform called a podium. A front porch, supported by a row of four or six **columns**, was accessed by a single flight of stairs in the middle. These led up to a sanctuary that might be one room or else divided into three spaces accessed by three separate doors. The columns were typically made of **wood** or volcanic rock, and the capitals were modified from the Greek orders. The Tuscan order, used later in the Renaissance, was a modified Ancient Greek order devised by the Etruscans. The roofs of these temples, and perhaps the roofs of homes as well, were slanted and covered with terracotta tiles. Small terracotta figurines often decorated the edges of the roofline and the central ridgepole of the roof, perhaps in recognition of the many gods and goddesses borrowed by the Etruscans from the Greek pantheon.

Burial chambers designed to mimic domestic interiors also show Etruscan architectural aesthetics. The Tomb of the Reliefs in Cerveteri, outside Rome, dates to the third century BC and was carved out of rock, and then the walls were plastered and painted in white and red tones. Square posts, with ornate capitals like columns, were carved with low-relief images of jugs, household tools, and small human and animal figures. Around the edges of the room, raised ledges were carved and sectioned off to hold sarcophagi. Etruscan artisans also painted beautiful scenes of musicians, people dancing, and dolphins swimming, as seen on a wall painting in the Tomb of the Lionesses, dated around 480 BC, and located in the necropolis, or cemetery, at Tarquinia, outside Rome. Ultimately the Etruscans, unable to unify their city-states against sustained attacks by the Latin-speaking peoples in the area around Rome, succumbed to Roman domination. Despite the fact that little remains of Etruscan architecture, scholars have continued to improve their understanding of Etruscan culture in Italy through more sophisticated excavations done beneath modern-day cities.

EXPRESSIONISM. Expressionist architecture originally developed parallel to the aesthetic ideals of the Expressionist visual and performing arts in the European avant-garde from around 1910 through 1924. From its German, Dutch, and Danish origins, the term

Expressionism is now used to describe the style of any building that reveals an expressive, organic distortion of shape with reference to movement and emotions, symbolic or visionary works, or natural, biomorphic shapes. Not stylized in the same manner as **Art Nouveau**, Expressionism takes its inspiration from a more unusual massing of form. Less practical than the opposing **International style** of architecture, the earliest Expressionist buildings exist either on paper or were designed for temporary exhibitions or theatrical stage sets.

Expressionism in architecture was introduced by Bruno Taut, a German painter and visionary who sought to explore a highly utopian, socialist vision of modernist architecture. His Glass Pavilion, built for the Cologne Werkbund Exhibition of 1914, reveals a blending of **Gothic** and more exotic features in its pointed **dome** made of diamond-shaped panes of **glass** set atop a drum designed from piers that frame glass curtain walls. The entire structure rests on a base of **concrete**, formed like an earth mound elevated slightly off the ground. Although known today only in black-and-white photographs, Taut's structure was brightly colored, with stained glass to provide a symbolic, almost spiritual interior, much like that of a Gothic church. Taut's bold use of color is unique in early-20th-century modernist architecture. Original colors are rarely preserved on such extant buildings, but Taut's bright palette can be seen in his illustrations for *Alpine Architecture*, a utopian treatise published in 1917. Interest in a glass structure had existed in the previous century, and Joseph Paxton's Crystal Palace, built for the London Exhibition of 1851, initiated a debate on the merits of a glass house that did not reach its resolution until **Philip Johnson**'s famous Glass House was built in New Canaan, Connecticut, in 1949. Bruno Taut offered the idea that a glass house could create a transparency that would meld public and private and that would force honesty and shape more ideal human interactions. Taut's 1912 Falkenberg Housing Estate in Berlin and his housing complex built in Magdeburg in 1912–1915 both reveal his interest in bringing a humane functionalism, informed by the English garden city movement, to popular housing in Europe. As hostility toward Taut's political views mounted, he moved to Russia, then Japan, and finally to Istanbul, where he died after completing several municipal housing projects in Turkey.

The first major permanent Expressionist structure is considered to be Erich Mendelsohn's Einstein Tower, built in Potsdam, Germany, beginning in 1917 as an astrophysical observatory for the study of Albert Einstein's theory of relativity. Here Mendelsohn created a building with gentle curves and rhythms best described in musical terminology. Made to look like concrete, the shape of the building was actually created with plaster-covered **brick**, and Mendelsohn himself described the organic shape as an exploration on the mystery of Einstein's universe. In 1933, Expressionist art was outlawed by the Nazi Party as degenerate, but nonetheless expressive tendencies endured in later International style architecture. For example, the building that most closely follows Mendelsohn's curved shapes is **Le Corbusier**'s Notre Dame du Haut, built in Ronchamp, France, in the 1950s. Situated on a hill, the church features masonry walls of sprayed white concrete and a mushroom-shaped dark roof. The roof tilts on a slant, as if it is sliding down one side, while a bell tower grows out of the opposing side. Developing a more expressive late style, here Le Corbusier uses the symbolism of light and organic shape to reflect religious spirituality. The church is constructed with thick walls that are soft in appearance and have an assortment of variously sized square and rectangular windows spread across the exterior. These windows emit moving patterns of colored light in the interior of the church, creating a deeply moving ambience.

Other Expressionist architects include **Alvar Aalto**, whose Opera House in Essen, Germany, begun in 1959, features a white façade that appears to fold into curves like a piece of paper. Such later forms of Expressionism reveal a blending of modernist styles, which formed the foundation for the work of **Eero Saarinen, Bruce Goff, Frank Lloyd Wright**, and **Frank Gehry**. Thus, the legacy of Expressionism continues to inform **Deconstructivism, High-Tech architecture**, and the even more recent bulging, amoeba-styled buildings called "Blobitecture."

– F –

FEDERAL STYLE. The Federal style of architecture correlates with the Federal period of U.S. history, when, between 1783 and 1815, the Revolutionary War ended and the Constitution and Bill of Rights were written. Architecture of this period drew upon classical sources, just as classicism and Athenian democracy best reflected the political ideals of the founders of the American system of government. Simple, symmetrical buildings constructed in **brick**, with white trim and classical **columns**, Palladian windows, and the image of the American eagle in the gabled roofline—all are characteristics of the Federal style exterior. Interiors, however, are more opulent and recall the rich classical sources favored by the Scottish architect **Robert Adam**, a favorite of the 18th-century English aristocracy. Sometimes the Federal style reveals a slight French influence, with more rounded, **Rococo** elements on the exterior, in the manner of **Thomas Jefferson**'s private dwelling Monticello, located in Charlottesville, Virginia, begun in the 1770s. Thus, the Federal style is sometimes called the Adam or the Jeffersonian style, and is typified by **Charles Bulfinch**'s Old State House, built in Hartford, Connecticut, in 1796, and in his Massachusetts State House, located on Beacon Hill overlooking the Boston Commons, begun in 1798. Indeed, it is the Federal style so prevalent in the Northeast that best reflects the political as well as the aesthetic aspirations of the founders of the United States. *See also* GEORGIAN STYLE; NEO-CLASSICAL ARCHITECTURE.

FISCHER VON ERLACH, JOHANN (1656–1723). *See* ROCOCO ARCHITECTURE.

FLORENCE CATHEDRAL, ITALY. The Cathedral of Florence, begun in the late 13th century and completed almost 150 years later, epitomizes Florentine political and economic dominance in Italy during the **Renaissance**. Begun in 1296 by the architect Arnolfo di Cambio, the church was constructed on top of the foundations of an early Christian church dedicated to Santa Reparata, and was rededicated to Santa Maria del Fiore. Several architects, including the painter Giotto, continued construction. In the mid-1300s, Francesco Talenti took over and is credited with designing the **dome**, which, with its 138-foot diameter, was to be the largest dome constructed in Italy since antiquity. The church is a traditional basilica-plan construction, with side aisles flanking a wider central nave that leads the visitor to a massive crossing lined with side chapels and a high altar. The nave was finally completed in 1380, at which time the church lacked only its dome.

The dome project was problematic, however, as no architect was able to come up with a plan that would allow the builders to span the width of the drum with scaffolding, nor did the completed lower level allow for the use of external buttressing, aside from the *exedrae*, or side chapels, to help support the lower walls of the choir area. A competition was therefore held in 1418 requesting proposals for the dome, and several of these plans still exist in the Florentine archives today. Since the dome site was too high for scaffolding, stories tell of one ingenious plan that consisted of placing a massive pile of dirt in the nave crossing that would be tall enough to provide a platform for the construction of the dome. Upon completion of the dome, the dirt could be carried away by children, encouraged to help find gold florins buried in the soil.

The solution selected by the Arte della Lana, however, was that of **Filippo Brunelleschi**, an architect who had just returned from Rome, where he focused his studies on **Ancient Roman architecture**, including the **Pantheon**. Brunelleschi had already advised the construction of a tall drum, completed in 1410. On top of that, Brunelleschi's solution involved the construction of a double-shelled dome that had no lateral thrust, but instead directed its weight into the drum via a series of horizontal tension chains made of **wood** and **iron** set at the base of the dome. Without scaffolding, Brunelleschi designed hoisting machines that would bring materials up to the construction site, a great feat of engineering. Although concrete was used to build the dome of the Pantheon, its material components were unknown in the Renaissance, and therefore Brunelleschi used **brick** for the construction of his dome. Given the octagonal shape of the drum, Brunelleschi's solution was a mixture of the **Gothic** ribbed and pointed arch combined with a classical brickwork, oculus, and lantern. The brick played a pivotal role in the construction of the interior dome by creating, through the use of a herringbone pattern, brick layers that were interconnected. Vertical **marble** ribs and horizontal sandstone rings reinforced the overall shape of the dome, which was held together by oak beams tied together to form the outer ribs. **Arches** connected the two shells together, creating an internal walkway that allowed access into the lantern.

The church was consecrated in 1436, although the lantern was not fully completed until 1471, years after Brunelleschi's death. The arcade gallery that Brunelleschi designed to be located right above the drum was partly constructed in the early 1500s by Baccio d'Agnolo, but remains incomplete today. Brunelleschi's innovative solution to an overly ambitious project subsequently ushered in the Renaissance, with its classically inspired structures built on the scale of Ancient Roman monuments. Thus, "the Duomo," as the Cathedral of Florence came to be called, asserted with its wide diameter and great height the superiority of Florence during the early Renaissance, and on a scale that was not superseded until the next century, with the construction of **Saint Peter's Church in Rome**.

FLYING BUTTRESS. *See* GOTHIC ARCHITECTURE; NOTRE DAME, PARIS.

FONTAINEBLEAU, FRANCE. The **castle** of Fontainebleau, called a château, was built in France in the 12th century and renovated during the reign of François I, who ruled from 1515 to 1547. It became the largest château in all of France, as well as the first to demonstrate the **Renaissance** style as imported into France from Italy. The French monarchy had proven its military might over northern Italy, but did not, during the Renaissance, cultivate an artistic revival on the same scale as could be found in Italy. François I therefore sought to rejuvenate French artistic culture with not only the reconstruction of this rural palace, but also with the creation of a large court of artists made up mostly of Italian and Flemish expatriates and including, most famously, Leonardo da Vinci, as well as the Italian Mannerist painters Rosso Fiorentino and Francesco Primaticcio.

While these châteaux were very often traditional French late medieval rural **castles**, fortifications were often quite minimal by the time of the Renaissance. Instead, these royal country homes were transformed by the aristocracy into country seats, and they very often did not settle into one palace permanently but moved from one to another as they cemented political alliances, cultivated elite social discourse, and confirmed their authority outside the urban centers. François I was from the Valois Dynasty, yet unlike his predecessors, he sought to join the classically inspired humanistic discourse popular across Europe during this time; he is in fact credited with creating the largest royal library in France, originally at Blois, then at Fontainebleau, and finally in Paris, as the basis for the current National Library of France. François I's original home outside of Paris was the Château d'Amboise, which he also renovated, as well as the châteaux at Chambord and Blois. In Paris, he was instrumental in transforming the **Louvre Palace** from a late medieval structure to a Renaissance complex.

At Fontainebleau, a mixture of late **Gothic** through **Neo-Classical** styles is evident, as the building was used as a royal palace for almost five centuries. It began as a modest hunting lodge set next to the royal hunting forest in the small town of Fontainebleau, about 30 miles outside of Paris. From that, it became first, a classically inspired palace in keeping with the Renaissance interest in **Ancient Roman architecture** and its dissemination across Europe during the 1400s and 1500s, then a **Baroque**, and finally a Neo-Classical monument to French rule. In the 1520s, François I hired the French architect Gilles le Breton, together with the Italian architect **Sebastiano Serlio**, to enlarge the château and update its style to reflect his humanistic interests. He wanted to bring into France a more sophisticated courtly culture by moving away from feudal ideals and embracing the ideals of the Renaissance. Therefore, only one tower remains from the original 12th-century structure. The entire building grew to consist of a series of wings and towers linked by courtyards and galleries. The Gallery of François I is the most elaborate and historically important, as the first gallery in all of France. With frescoes and painted stucco molding designed by Rosso Fiorentino, it demonstrates the highly stylized, elongated, and elegant features of **Mannerism**. Primaticcio's main commission involved the renovation of the apartments of François' mistress, Anne, the Duchess of Étampes. Here Primaticcio combines classically inspired images with a light-hearted Mannerist style to create some of the first Mannerist works in all of France. François' son Henry II, who ruled from 1547 to his death in 1559, continued the renovations to Fontainebleau, hiring Primaticcio again and another Italian Mannerist artist, Benvenuto Cellini, to continue the work of transforming the interior into one vast program of painting, sculpture, and architecture.

Henri IV, who ruled until his death in 1610, continued the transformation of Fontainebleau, but by the later Baroque era, the royal artistic focus had shifted to **Versailles Palace**, which was also located outside of Paris and which was subsequently transformed by Louis XIV into a vast palace complex and administrative center. Later, when Napoleon I visited Fontainebleau and found all the rooms stripped of their furnishings, he replenished the interior and used the castle for his coronation in 1804. The pope was housed in a suite of newly restored apartments, and a Neo-Classical throne room was constructed for the occasion. Fontainebleau was the favored home of Napoleon, and since that time, the château has become a UNESCO World Heritage Site and a popular museum destination.

FORBIDDEN CITY, BEIJING. The Forbidden City, the name given the imperial palace complex in Beijing, China, was constructed during the Ming Dynasty (1368–1644) and remains important today as one of the few large-scale architectural monuments to survive the centuries of warfare that ensued at the end of the rule of this powerful dynasty. It is the world's largest surviving palace complex, covering 178 acres with about 980 buildings. The previous Yuan Dynasty, established in Beijing by the Mongol ruler Kublai Khan, lasted from 1280 to 1368. It set the tone for a period of great cultural divisions in that these foreign invaders set up their own court in northern China to rival the southern Chinese courts of the previous dynasties. It was the court of Kublai Khan that Marco Polo visited in 1271, and his very positive, well-publicized, and documented impressions of Mongol court life formed the basis of western understanding of Chinese culture for several centuries. The Mongol court was profoundly influential. Its emperors reached out to the west by encouraging travel across the vast, relatively safe Mongol territories that began at the borders of modern-day Hungary and extended across the Ukraine and through the vast Asian continent to China. These rulers were continuously thought of as outsiders in China, however, and so the establishment of the Ming Dynasty was predicated upon the removal of the Mongols from power in Beijing. But the subsequent reestablishment of "Chinese" rule there was initially no improvement because the Ming rulers were themselves despotic. Despite this, they continued the courtly focus by cultivating a highly artistic culture epitomized by the famous Ming porcelain that was exported worldwide. Architecture during the Ming Dynasty was complemented by a highly developed garden aesthetic, as well as an emphasis on a cosmological organization of city streets and buildings. Beijing continued to be the capital through the Qing Dynasty.

When the city of Beijing was constructed, the Mongols used traditional Chinese design principles in a grid-like layout. This geometrically organized city plan had first appeared in China in the seventh century during the Tang Dynasty (618–907). Its capital was Chang'an, a rectangular walled city with streets laid out evenly on a grid and with a walled imperial compound on its northern side. The streets were aligned to the cardinal points, suggesting a cosmological emphasis. Indeed, the principles of feng shui, which means wind and water, developed very early in Chinese history and are evident at Chang'an, where the imperial palace, located on the north, faced the preferred southern direction, while a broad avenue stretched to the southern entrance of the city and allowed the ruler to look over his territory. Each of the 108 blocks was its own walled neighborhood. Markets were located on the east and west sides of the town and were open during specific days and hours. The entire city is built on a piece of land topographically conducive to a balanced *qi*, or primal energy, with hills located to the rear of the city and waterways, in the form of man-made rivers or pools, traversed by bridges prior to entering the city gates. Such detailed regularity was intended to protect the city from evil spirits.

The Forbidden City was based upon the same principles when reconstructed under the rule of the third Ming emperor from 1402 to 1424, after the Mongol buildings had been razed by earlier Ming rulers. It is located in the center of the northern part of the walled city of Beijing and is surrounded by tall walls with towers in each of the four corners and with four doors, one at the center of each wall. The south side has the most impressive gated entrance with its long approach through the Meridian Gate, across the large open courtyard, and over a series of arched bridges that cross a curved waterway. After passing through another gated entrance, called the Gate of Supreme Harmony, the visitor enters another courtyard that has at its far end three buildings on raised platforms, one in front of the other, aligned on axis. The first building, called by the Qing name of the Hall of Supreme Harmony, is where the emperor would be seated in his throne room facing south, to watch ceremonies that took place in the courtyard. This building is the largest ancient **wood** structure in China, and the ceremonial center of the complex.

Beyond this building is the smaller Hall of Central Harmony, where the emperor could rest between ceremonies, and behind it, the Hall of Protecting Harmony, where royal ceremonies were rehearsed. Each of these buildings is constructed with a row of **columns** surrounding a continuous outer portico, and with a tiled, gabled roof. Following this axial direction, the next structures encountered after crossing a smaller courtyard are a set of three more buildings, one in front of the next, all smaller than the first architectural group but similar in design. Finally, the large Gate of Divine Might concludes the row of structures at the north end of the layered inner complex. These rooms form the core of the Inner Court, where Confucian lectures could be held and guests entertained. The central walkway, called the Imperial Way, was reserved for the emperor. Exceptions were the empress, who walked along the path at her marriage, and students after passing the imperial examinations. The Inner Court consisted of the main residential buildings for the royal family, with one structure for the emperor and the opposite building for the empress, while the central building, called the Hall of Union, is for both—that is, for the union of the *yin* and *yang*.

These buildings feature double gabled roofs with sculptures located in the corners of the upper gables, and in traditional **Chinese architecture**, the roof corners tilt up slightly to give the impression of weightlessness. The original pillars used for the exterior colonnades of the buildings were made from whole logs brought from the jungles of southwest China, but were replaced in the Qing Dynasty by pillars made with multiple pieces of wood. The Forbidden City today contains the largest collection of preserved ancient wood in the world. The large **stones** used for the sculptures were dragged to the complex on ice roads. Finally, the mostly original floors of the buildings are smooth **bricks** made by a unique and very slow firing process; walking on these floors causes a ringing sound.

The rigidly geometric layout of the entire complex symbolizes the role of the emperor as the Son of the Heavens, to maintain cosmic order that would then be translated into social harmony. The palace complex, surrounded by a moat, was enclosed by the Imperial City, then the Inner City, and then the Outer City. The highest officials lived closest to the royal compound and all commoners lived in the Outer City. While the early Ming emperors established their capital in the southern city of Nanjing and kept the Forbidden City as a secondary capital, Beijing gradually became the main capital of China in the 1400s. With the growth of Beijing, the complex is now located in the center of the city; since 1924, it has been open as a museum and houses the largest collection of Ming and Qing art in the country.

FOSTER, NORMAN (1935–). *See* CHINESE ARCHITECTURE; HIGH-TECH ARCHITECTURE; SKYSCRAPER; WORLD TRADE CENTER, NEW YORK.

FULLER, RICHARD BUCKMINSTER (1895–1983). *See* DOME; STEEL.

FUTURIST ARCHITECTURE. Futurism was an early-20th-century art movement founded by the poet Filippo Tommaso Marinetti and described in his *Manifesto of Futurism*, published in 1909. This organization of writers and artists included the Italian architect Antonio Sant'Elia, who held highly detailed theoretical views on modernist architecture that he documented in a series of powerfully rendered architectural sketches published in his *Città Nuova* in 1914. The treatise *Futurist Architecture* was published that same year, and attributed to Sant'Elia as well. As a socialist, Sant'Elia had many of the same concerns as Russian artists after the Bolshevik Revolution of 1917, and these concerns formed the aesthetic basis for an architectural style based on images of speed, energy, and the quick pace of "modern" life. Kinetic sculpture and abstract painting also influenced Futurist architecture. Sant'Elia was, furthermore, fascinated by industrial cities and modern systems of transportation, and he sought to integrate the two into his plans for a vast, highly mechanized modern city. Despite his untimely death in 1915 while fighting in World War I, many of the revolutionary designs he created had a profound influence on **Constructivist architecture** and on the modernist urban plans made by such **International style** architects as **Le Corbusier.**

– G –

GABRIEL, ANGE-JACQUES (1698–1782). *See* VERSAILLES PALACE, FRANCE.

GARNIER, CHARLES (1825–1898). Charles Garnier was the leader of the French academic tradition called the **Beaux-Arts** style, which was popular in France in the 19th century and in the United States in the early 20th century. Until the Impressionist painters resisted its influence in the last years of the 19th century, the Academy of Beaux Arts in Paris had exerted control over most of the artistic output in Paris during the 18th and 19th centuries, awarding scholarships, annual prizes, and even overseeing the selection of artists for major government commissions.

In the 1860s, Garnier received the important commission for a massive opera house in Paris, to be the focal point of a massive urban renewal plan designed by Georges-Eugène Haussmann and sponsored by Napoleon III. The Opéra, as it is called, is a rectangular building in the middle of a diamond-shaped piazza with a trident-shaped configuration of streets coming out of its corners and cutting wide diagonal avenues through the neighborhood. It displays an amalgamation of historical styles that can be characterized as ornate **Baroque**. The building was constructed with **cast-iron** supports covered by **stone**, and thus its more modern construction method is hidden behind a historical style that features a two-story façade with a ground-floor arcade and large rectangular windows on the first floor flanked by paired **columns** and topped by a richly carved entablature. The building's sides are articulated by projecting bays and gilded statues, and a shallow **dome** rises up from the middle. The ornately carved exterior prepares the visitor for the vast interior foyer, in which a massive staircase sweeps down from the upper foyer balcony, turns at the landing, and arrives, dramatically, at the entrance. The ornately decorated foyer provides a social context for spectators, who can move around the vast reception area and interact with this grand interior.

GAUDÍ I CORNET, ANTONI (1852–1926). Antoni Gaudí i Cornet is known for his beautifully organic "Catalonian Modernism," a regional variety of **Art Nouveau** that he developed in the northern Spanish region of Catalonia at the turn of the century. Barcelona had undergone a dramatic urban renewal beginning in the 1860s, and as a fiercely independent city whose residents still seek separation from Spain, artists there cultivated their own version of European *modernismo*. Thus, while the Spanish painter Pablo Picasso worked primarily in Paris, thereby bringing Spain into the early modern art discourse, Catalonian artists such as Joan Miró, Salvador Dalí, and Gaudí remained strongly connected to their Catalonian homeland. Gaudí's strangely unique style that demonstrates a creative mixture of organic elements, **Gothic** style, and modern inventions, was derided in its day but has fostered the most important architectural contributions to the city of Barcelona.

His most loyal patron was the wealthy industrialist Eusebí Güell, for whom Gaudí completed the Palau Güell in the late 1880s, a building now listed as a UNESCO World Heritage Site. A unique feature of this building, used to entertain important guests, was the reception room with peepholes for the owners to peer through before greeting their guests. In addition, the grand ballroom was built with small holes in the ceiling so that lanterns could be hung outside to illuminate the interior with star-like points of light. The Casa Mila, built in 1905, is an equally interesting apartment house. This building, nicknamed "The Quarry" due to its curved and angular rocky exterior, anticipated the biomorphic style of architecture seen in the work of such later architects as Erich Mendelsohn. The building is supported by a series of parabolic, or catenary arches, a type of **arch** invented in Catalonia. Gaudí also designed sculpted walls and benches for the Güell Park, located on the outskirts of Barcelona. Here, the playful curved benches are inset with colored **stone** mosaic, integrating the movement of the benches with the organic lines found in nature.

Finally, Gaudí's masterpiece, the building for which he is best known, is his Sagrada Familia, begun in 1884, and to this day not completed. This massive cathedral in downtown Barcelona was constructed with 18 towers in a fantastic pseudo-Gothic style that looks surreal, with looming pinnacles that appear to melt into each other, and pointed arches that seem to be formed from a giant grotto. While initially influenced by the writings of Gothic revivalists John Ruskin and Viollet-le-Duc in his use of pointed arches and pinnacles, Gaudí then seems to have dispensed with architectural regulations and traditions to create a highly expressive building of exuberant decoration that, in its unique and dramatic break with tradition, came to symbolize Catalonian nationalism. Perhaps the most unusual church ever constructed, this unfinished building is one of the most famous tourist destinations in Spain today. *See also* EXPRESSIONISM.

GEHRY, FRANK (1929–). Frank Gehry, the Los Angeles–based architect known for working in the **Deconstructivist** style, is best known for organic buildings that appear to question traditional aesthetic sensibilities and forms. His first architectural experiment consisted of the renovation of his private home in Santa Monica, California, purchased in 1977. Here he experimented by juxtaposing "unorthodox" building materials with the traditional materials of the original house. After receiving the Pritzker Architecture Prize in 1989, he designed the Walt Disney Concert Hall in Los Angeles, California, in 1991, and it opened in 2003. Built with a stainless **steel** exterior skin, this complex organic shape contradicts entirely any preconceived notions of building design and shape. Although derided for its unusual style, the concert hall itself is considered to have superior acoustics.

Gehry's design for the Guggenheim Museum in Bilbao, Spain, built in 1993–1997, is considered one of the most expressive buildings of the 20th century. It was designed to recall both a living creature and a giant ship. The building is a complex steel skeleton covered with a thin layer of titanium that shimmers either of golden or silver color, depending on the quality of the sunlight and the time of the day. Inside, a huge atrium recalls the sweeping forms of New York City's Guggenheim Museum, built in the 1950s by **Frank Lloyd Wright**. Standing as giant monuments to architecture, Frank Gehry's buildings have been criticized for neglecting pedestrians, for ignoring the surrounding urban context of the building, and for creating hazardous slopes and sliding roofs that do not work well in extreme weather. Nonetheless, Gehry's buildings set a new architectural standard, rising up and sweeping across in increasingly more complex feats of engineering upon which he overlays a highly expressive framework of architectural sculpture. *See also* EXPRESSIONISM.

GEODESIC DOME. *See* DOME.

GEORGIAN STYLE. The Georgian style of architecture, traditionally dated from 1690 to 1790, is the earliest distinctive style of European construction developed by North American settlers. After attaining a level of stability and prosperity that finally allowed them to turn their attention to a more stylized form of construction, they made use of more architectural details such as historical and geographical referencing, as well as more ornamentation. The Georgian style is named for the four British monarchs named George. It was King George III, the ruler from 1760 until his death in 1820, who lost the majority of the British territories in North America. Despite the great political divide that ensued between England and the emerging United States, cultural connections between the two countries remained strong, as evidenced by the great popularity of the Georgian architectural style, which in its later stages can also be called the **Federal style**. Georgian architecture, inspired by the Italian Renaissance architect **Palladio** as well as the English Baroque architect **Christopher Wren** and his successor **John Vanbrugh**, is characterized by a **brick** building of classical symmetry and proportion with a small portico at the center, rectangular windows trimmed in white and with nine or 12 panes of **glass**, and a hipped roof flanked by a chimney on either side. Earlier, more modest **wood** Colonial homes from the late 17th century, such as the Paul Revere house in Boston, were often renovated in the Georgian style with the addition of a taller, hipped roofline and the imposition of a more symmetrical appearance to the façade. *See also* COLONIAL ARCHITECTURE; NEO-CLASSICAL ARCHITECTURE.

GIBBS, JAMES (1682–1754). James Gibbs is best known for his monumental churches in London, as well as for his successful blending of **Renaissance** and **Baroque** architectural elements into an early-18th-century **Neo-Classicism**. Born a Catholic in Scotland, Gibbs revealed himself very early on as an excellent draftsman. He went on to study in Rome with the Late Baroque Italian architect Carlo Fontana. When Gibbs returned to London, he received a position as a surveyor to help with the planned construction of 50 new churches in London. His first commission for this project was the Church of Saint Mary-le-Strand in 1714. In 1722–1726, Gibbs constructed his most famous church, Saint Martin-in-the-Fields, in London. This building reveals the integration of a Palladian portico front with a basilica church plan, which has a spire rather than a **dome** rising from the roof of the building. This type of spire was widely copied across Europe in the 18th century and became popular in New England as well during the subsequent century. In 1728, Gibbs's *Book of Architecture* was first published, and in 1732, the publication of his *Rules for Drawing the Several Parts of Architecture* provided an English-language architectural manual used widely in England and the United States.

His most famous building, the Radcliffe Camera, was constructed in 1739–1749 in Oxford to house the university's science library. While the English architect Nicholas Hawksmoor can be credited with the idea for a round building, Gibbs created a beautiful fusion of Renaissance and Baroque features in this unique structure. The three-part design consists of a rusticated ground level topped by a two-story central section articulated with paired **columns** alternating with two registers of windows, which is then topped by a balustrade and then a dome capped by a spire. Highly sculptural, this building recalls the general classical column order in its overall layout, while its round design echoes the format of **Donato Bramante**'s small Tempietto, built in Rome in 1502. This building best embodies James Gibbs's desire to blend Renaissance classicism with Baroque grandeur into a more modern English context.

GILBERT, CASS (1859–1934). *See* SKYSCRAPER.

GINZBURG, MOISEI (1892–1946). *See* CONSTRUCTIVIST ARCHITECTURE.

GLASS. Glass results from the heating of a mixture of sand, lime, and sodium carbonate to a very high temperature. When different materials are added to the sand, glass can become transparent, translucent, or colored. While the origins of glass are shrouded in mystery, the **Ancient Egyptians** are traditionally credited with its invention, given their use of faience even before Egypt was unified into dynasties. Faience, a form of glass paste that is fired, was used by Egyptians to make small beads and to decorate clay pottery. The famous small blue hippopotamus, located in the Metropolitan Museum of Art in New York City, dates to about 1800 BC and illustrates this technique. Objects made entirely of glass date to the New Kingdom, beginning in 1550 BC, when glassmaking was limited to the royal workshops and created only for the royal families. These earliest glass objects are a core glass in which a clay model was formed, wrapped in cloth strips, placed on a skewer, and then dipped in molten glass. The clay was removed via the hole left by the skewer, and then small bits of colored glass were heated and molded into thin strips to be attached to the glass core in decorative patterns. Small animal-shaped vessels that held scented oils were often made of core glass during the Egyptian 18th Dynasty.

Architectural glass, however, was not introduced until the **Romanesque** period of the 11th century, when transparent and translucent glass was used for window coverings that allowed for the introduction of light, or even for interior liturgical partitions. The earliest method for creating glass windows was called the *crown glass* technique. In this case, a round piece of hot blown glass was cut away from the pipe and then spun around rapidly until it flattened out like a thin pancake. The piece would then be cut entirely off its pipe and shaped into smaller pieces that would fit into **iron** frames. This type of glass reveals a characteristic bull's-eye at the center point, where it remained attached to the pipe while being spun. Later, more sophisticated cutting of the crown glass resulted in a diamond-shaped piece, which reduced the distortion created by the varying thickness of the crown glass and allowed for a more intricate pattern of fenestration. Only in the 19th century was this process finally replaced by a less expensive process of creating sheet glass, which allowed for larger individual windowpanes. This type of glass still has subtle variations in thickness that are apparent in older buildings today, where one can see the effect of rippling on the glass. Float glass, used today for windowpanes, is a process invented in the 1950s and 1960s by the manufacturer Sir Alastair Pilkington of Pilkington Glass in England. Float glass provides the smoothest surface, is the least expensive flat glass to produce, and is used in architectural construction across the world.

Joseph Paxton's Crystal Palace, built for the 1851 London Exhibition, established a technological as well as a philosophical interest in creating a glass house. In 1938, **Walter Gropius** used thick glass blocks to create an entire exterior wall for his own house built in the **Bauhaus style** in Lincoln, Massachusetts, and in 1946 **Ludwig Mies van der Rohe** used a large single pane of glass to cover the façade of the Farnsworth House near Plano, Illinois. **Philip Johnson** took this idea to its conclusion with the construction of his own house made almost entirely of glass. His so-called "Glass House," built in New Canaan, Connecticut, in 1949, is often considered one of the most beautiful but least functional houses in the world. Free from constraints of a clientele, function, or money, Johnson created an exceptional home of glass walls set into a **concrete** frame and with concrete flooring. All the interior rooms flow together, and no interior walls touch the glass exterior. The bathroom is enclosed in a **brick** cylinder in the center of the small rectangular house, while the rest of the home enjoys privacy from its rural setting.

By the mid-20th century, large glass windows had become common in domestic architecture. The **Ranch style** house, for example, is characterized by both the use of larger glass windows and glass-paned sliding doors. These larger sheets of movable glass then necessitated the development of laminated and tempered glass to prevent their shearing into jagged strips if broken. Instead, this shattered glass holds together in a spider-web pattern. More varieties of chemically strengthened glass continue to be produced today to allow for further architectural possibilities, including not only the use of glass curtain walls on **skyscrapers**, but also load-bearing glass walls that are more energy efficient and soundproof.

GOFF, BRUCE (1904–1982). Born in Kansas, Bruce Goff received an architectural apprenticeship in Tulsa, Oklahoma, when he was merely 12 years old. Despite his lack of a formal education, Goff closely studied the domestic prairie style of **Frank Lloyd Wright** and went on to become a professor and then dean of the School of Architecture at the University of Oklahoma in the 1940s and 1950s. During that time, Goff was solicited by Harold C. Price to build the Price Tower in Bartlesville, Oklahoma, but he turned down the commission, and the building was subsequently constructed by Frank Lloyd Wright. Goff's eclectic style found favor in the college town of Norman, Oklahoma, where he built several homes, including the Ledbetter House in 1947 and the Bavinger House in 1950–1955.

The Bavinger House, built for Eugene Bavinger, a modernist artist in the School of Art at the University of Oklahoma, is an avant-garde home in its innovative mix of materials and an organic, expressive design. Built from **glass**, **steel**, and local rock, the house explores a huge range of textures and techniques that make Goff's buildings more unique than practical. Goff supplied the designs for the house, while the Bavingers constructed the home, which created a close friendship between architect and patron. The Bavinger House is built on a spiral, beginning with the entrance ramp that leads through the front door and into the round interior rooms. The center point of the house is capped with what looks like a flagpole, to which is attached wooden slats that curve around and up the pole in the shape of a seashell spiral. This spiral forms a stairway that leads up and around the home. The unorthodox shape of the house then requires suspension cables attached to the rooms to buttress the exterior. The rooms, including Bavinger's oval-shaped studio, appear to hang from this spiral framework, while the studio projects outward from an upper level of the home. The home cultivates a connection between home and nature that was unprecedented for its day, and Bruce Goff's exploratory style also allowed for a kind of free expression and organic appeal rarely seen in modern domestic architecture. *See also* EXPRESSIONISM.

GOLOSOV, ILYA (1883–1945). *See* CONSTRUCTIVIST ARCHITECTURE.

GOOGIE ARCHITECTURE. *See* VENTURI, ROBERT.

GOTHIC ARCHITECTURE. The Gothic style of architecture grew out of the **Romanesque** style to include even more sophisticated architectural structures that featured intricate ornamentation, vast interiors, and soaring roofs, with external flying buttresses, tall towers, and pinnacles. The Gothic style originated in the area around Paris called the Île-de-France during the middle of the 12th century, coinciding with the growth of the French monarchy and lasting until the 14th century. This northern European style came to be called "Gothic" due to the mistaken and prejudicial notion that it was introduced by the Germanic Visigoths, who were traditionally credited with the fall of the Roman Empire and therefore derided in subsequent centuries. This name has endured despite its initial mischaracterization and now represents an architectural style seen during its day as a more aristocratic and "modern" outgrowth of the older

Romanesque. Gothic buildings reveal pointed **arches** rather than rounded arches, more fenestration than Romanesque structures, taller ceilings with more slender internal supports, and an overall increase in architectural sculpture.

The Gothic style was found in private homes and civic buildings, such as town halls, but it is most famously seen in church design. Gothic churches appear across western Europe but are most common today in England, France, and Germany. The largest of these churches are the cathedrals, seats of the highest level of clergy, and therefore have a more extensive treasury and typically an urban setting. Notre Dame Cathedral of Chartres is an excellent example of this type, seen rising above the skyline of the town of Chartres in France. It was begun around 1134, and construction continued through the mid-13th century. These monumental structures were often begun in the Early Gothic style and completed later in the more ornate High or Late Gothic, after financial troubles or disastrous fires plagued their construction. Chartres Cathedral is a Latin-cross-plan church with a tall longitudinal nave, shorter side aisles, and projecting side arms called transepts, each with side entrances. As side entrances came to be increasingly used by the aristocracy to provide a path directly to the choir, the transept portals became more and more ornate. The choir extended from the crossing square, concluding with an apse encircled by an ambulatory with three chapels projecting from the interior wall. A narthex at the west façade entrance provides a transitional space from the physical world into the sanctuary, designated as the house of God on earth. The rich decoration of these churches is meant, then, not only to inspire the visitor, but to reflect God's authority through its beauty.

Because Gothic churches are taller and feature more fenestration than Romanesque churches, additional buttressing is needed on the exterior of the building. So-called flying buttresses were thus introduced. These consist of an external support pier attached to the wall at the top, and then angled outward toward the ground, where the weight of the masonry and gravity is dispersed. This system allows for an additional support that does not block the windows. In addition to the buttresses, Chartres Cathedral features a series of pointed pinnacles capping the buttresses and the transept corners, as well as pointed towers at the entrance façade. These pinnacles help to direct the weight downward, while at the same time directing the eyes of the visitor upward toward the heavens. It is this visual effect of soaring height that became the central characteristic of the Gothic style. The tripartite façade of Chartres has three portals in the central section, with three windows above, topped in the third register by a round window, called a rose window. This part of the façade is typically capped by an open arcade that forms the impression of a light latticework. Chartres Cathedral features towers that, because they were built during different times, do not match, but they nonetheless direct the eye upward.

The interior of Chartres Cathedral reveals a three-story nave with an arcade of compounded piers alternating with pointed arches at the ground floor. The engaged half- and quarter-columns of the piers rise through the nave wall, and each section follows through with the articulation of some aspect of the internal structure. For example, three column sections of each pier rise through the nave wall to meet the three ribs that branch across and intersect in the middle of the vault to create the four-part ribbed vaulting and the ribbed bay unit divisions of the nave ceiling. This very complex structural "skeleton," as it is sometimes called, gives visual clarity to an otherwise very complex building. A *triforium* gallery appears in the second register of the nave wall, and large, paired stained-**glass** clerestory windows fill the entire wall space of the top register of the nave. The façade windows allow light into the nave entrance of the church, while the most dramatic illumination is found in the choir area, where the entire wall is given over to tall stained-glass windows. The idea of light as a symbol of the divine, of enlightenment, is most fully articulated in the Gothic period.

The High Gothic cathedrals of Paris, Reims, and Amiens in France, of Cologne in Germany, and of Milan in Italy, all follow many aspects of the format seen at Chartres. The stonemasons in charge of construction, called the *capomaestri*, increased the height of these buildings and enlarged their fenestration with more daring engineering feats to the point at which they could build no more — signified by the collapse of the choir vault of Beauvais Cathedral in 1284. The Late Gothic style, consequently, is typified by smaller churches, such as Sainte-Chapelle in Paris, built in the 1240s by Louis IX to house his collection of Passion relics. The walls of this palace chapel are made up entirely of stained-glass windows separated from one another by slender columns and piers, with no other visible wall structure.

In addition, the Gothic era was ultimately a time of great learning, an enlightened age credited with the establishment of the earliest universities, which were built in the Gothic style. The continued use of the Gothic style across campuses today gives a visual link to this past and provides historical legitimacy to subsequent university buildings. The revival of the Gothic style, called the **Gothic Revival**, can be found in **castles**, private homes, and civic buildings through the next several centuries.

GOTHIC REVIVAL ARCHITECTURE. Gothic Revival architecture can be seen as part of the general trend of Romanticism that characterized mid-18th- through mid-19th-century European culture, and while it reached its high point from 1830 to 1870, a continued interest in the **Gothic** style appeared through the early 20th century. Revivalist movements were not new in architecture, but prior to this time, they had mainly centered on the revival of classicism, which by now had gone through at least four major renewals since antiquity. The Gothic Revival originated in England and was fueled by a more romanticized, nostalgic view of the Middle Ages. Romanticists favored the secular narratives of the feudal era with courtly romance and bravery in battle as the two central themes of interest, hence the widespread renewal of interest in the stories of Tristan and Iseult, Roland, and Arthur. The writings of Alfred Tennyson illustrate this type of Romanticism. However, in the Gothic novel of the 19th century, the sentiments that came out of these narratives are more sublime. That is, they escalate into more powerful emotions of passionate love, fear, and horror, very often set within the picturesque surroundings of the isolated, forgotten medieval **castle** or the haunted rural baronial estate. Neo-Gothic narratives include Mary Shelley's *Frankenstein* from 1818 and Edgar Allan Poe's *Fall of the House of Usher* from 1843.

Horace Walpole is credited with having written the first Gothic novel, titled the *Castle at Otranto*, published anonymously in London in 1764, and it is his country home, Strawberry Hill, that provides us with one of the earliest examples of the Gothic Revival style in ar-

chitecture. Having decided to renovate his rural home in Twickenham, England, in 1749, Walpole directed a 30-year transformation of
his house based on careful studies of medieval buildings in England
that had been renovated. His house features crenellations and projecting battlements, towers and round turrets, bifurcated windows
with pointed arches and decorative tracery. A fusion of the fortified
features of a feudal-era castle with the more open architectural elements found in a medieval church appears here. Inside the house,
rooms featured different medieval themes. Walpole studied illustrated books of tracery patterns and window designs to better understand medieval stylistic features, then adapted them for use in a more
fanciful way. For example, in his library, he borrowed features from
the then-destroyed old Saint Paul's Cathedral in London, which had
been documented in picture books, and his fireplace is modeled on a
medieval wall tomb. The ceiling blends real and imaginary family
coats-of-arms, which adds to the more fantastic character of the
Gothic Revival style. At Horace Walpole's death the house passed
through many owners with colorful lives, both friends and relatives,
yet none lived there very long, thus perpetuating the still-current idea
that the house is haunted. Finally, the property was sold to the public
in the mid-19th century, and although much of the original land was
gradually sold off, the house remains a museum today.

By the early 19th century, the Gothic Revival style came to be seen
as the national style of England, one that was historically native to
northern Europe and therefore more appropriate to English architecture than the equally popular **Neo-Classical** style, which derived
from Ancient Greece and Rome. As it gained popularity, the Gothic
Revival style developed its own philosophical underpinnings, which
gave it greater social relevance than it had held in 18th-century England. Thus, one of the best-known examples of the Gothic Revival
style is the Houses of Parliament, built in London in 1836–1880 by
Charles Barry and Augustus Welby Northmore Pugin after fire destroyed Parliament's earlier Westminster Palace in 1834. The predetermined Gothic style matched the Gothic style of Westminster
Abbey, located to the west of the new Parliament buildings, which
symbolizes the history of English monarchic power. Barry devised a
symmetrical plan to suggest a balance of that power with democratic
rule, while Pugin was responsible for the Gothic decorative detailing

on the Parliament buildings. Pugin had previously written about this architectural style, arguing that medieval architecture was morally superior to and more spiritually uplifting than the industrial, mechanized urban society in which he lived. This more philosophical interpretation of the Gothic style was further developed by John Ruskin in his books *The Seven Lamps of Architecture* (1849) and *The Stones of Venice* (1853), in which he romanticized the noble role of the medieval stonecutter.

George Gilbert Scott continued the Gothic Revival style in England with his construction of the monumentally sized Saint Pancras Railway Station in London in 1865 and with a proliferation of churches, chapels, and colleges constructed across England during the **Victorian** age. Perhaps the most famous example of the Gothic Revival style in England is Tower Bridge in London, built by John Wolfe-Barry and Horace Jones in 1886–1894. Prior to the construction of Tower Bridge, only London Bridge and newer bridges built to its west served downtown London. Tower Bridge responded to the need for an eastern bridge that could support the busy port along the Thames River. It was constructed as a movable bridge using hydraulics to raise and lower its *bascules*. The bridge therefore needed a massive framing to support this movable road; not only did the thick Gothic tower structures flanking the center function to enclose the mechanics and to support the road, but the style was also visually suited to the prevailing Gothic of old London.

The Gothic Revival found favor in the United States as well, where it is used most frequently in the construction of Roman Catholic and Episcopalian churches. Richard Upjohn's Trinity Church in New York City (1839–1846) is typical of this style. Born in England, Upjohn settled in the United States and is credited with introducing the Gothic Revival style there. College campus buildings are also frequently constructed in the Gothic Revival style, and are meant to provide a visual reminder not only of the Late Medieval origins of the university institution, but also of the high level of quality represented by the famous English colleges of Oxford and Cambridge as well as the Ivy League colleges found along the East Coast of the United States.

GRAHAM, BRUCE (1925–). *See* SKIDMORE, OWINGS & MERRILL.

GRAVES, MICHAEL (1934–). *See* POST-MODERN ARCHITEC-TURE.

GREEK REVIVAL STYLE. *See* ROMANTIC ARCHITECTURE.

GREEN ARCHITECTURE. Perhaps the most current of architectural movements today, Green architecture refers to ecologically sensitive construction that takes into account new environmental concerns and the psychological needs of people, who are seen as increasingly divorced from nature. This architecture is characterized by an energy-efficient organic design that blends into its natural surroundings. Like **Critical Regionalism**, Green architecture is typically made from local materials and takes into account its cultural context, but with an increased emphasis on energy-saving design and technical features that aid in the conservation and preservation of the earth's dwindling resources. Although nature-centered architecture is receiving a new emphasis now, it is not a new idea but can be found throughout history. In the early 20th century, **Frank Lloyd Wright**'s Fallingwater in Bear Run, Pennsylvania, from 1935 to 1939, was constructed atop a waterfall with local **stone**, **wood**, and **concrete** in the form of a series of horizontally oriented porches, patios, and open-plan interior spaces covered by continuous **glass** windows.

Although stylistically different from Wright's work, the rural churches of Wright's student E. Fay Jones in Arkansas are built upon these nature-centered principles. His Thorncrown Chapel (1980) in Eureka Springs, Arkansas, is made from thin pine timbers that cross each other to create a diamond-shaped support system for the glass walls. Rising from its wooded surroundings with a sharply gabled roof that directs the viewer's eyes upward, the chapel is spare in its modernism, yet with a subtle spiritual symbolism. The scale of the building is not overwhelming, as Jones instructed that no material be used that could not be carried into the wooded area by two men. Modeled on the late **Gothic** church of Sainte-Chappelle in Paris, the style of the Thorncrown Chapel is sometimes called "Ozark Gothic."

Renzo Piano, known for his **High-Tech architecture**, has also begun to focus on more "green" designs in his structures. In 1991 Piano was commissioned to design the Tjibaou Cultural Center in Nouméa, New Caledonia. With the advice of local Kanak peoples, Piano used native materials to create a series of 10 beehive-shaped structures joined together by a "spine" of low horizontal buildings that recall a native South Pacific village. These beehive structures are open at the top, giving an unfinished appearance that symbolizes the continued evolution of the Kanak peoples toward their final destiny, an idea central to Kanak belief systems. Using sophisticated technology within a traditional aesthetic, this structure alludes to both the past and the future and is sometimes called "eco-tech" architecture.

Jean Nouvel's Foundation Cartier, built in Paris in 1994, is also a highly technical structure, but in this case it is one that responds to the remnants of nature found in its urban context. Built on a busy, wide street, its esplanade boasts a line of cedar trees planted by François Chateaubriand, which are framed within a glass curtain wall constructed in front of the structure. The building itself is made from multiple layers of glass curtain walls that extend beyond and above the glass "box" of the actual building, thus blurring the distinction between interior and exterior space in a more sophisticated way than mid-century glass structures could achieve.

The next step in Green architecture is to increase efficiency in heating, cooling, water use, and lighting in these buildings to better preserve the earth's resources, while at the same time improving the quality of life with less expensive housing and increased levels of comfort in both the exterior and interior environmental ambience of these structures.

GREENE, CHARLES SUMNER (1868–1957) AND HENRY MATHER GREENE (1870–1954). *See* ARTS AND CRAFTS.

GRIFFIN, MARION MAHONY (1871–1961). *See* WRIGHT, FRANK LLOYD.

GROPIUS, WALTER (1883–1969). Walter Gropius, the leading designer of the **Bauhaus** School in Dessau, helped to bring graphic design to the forefront of artistic importance. He began his career by opening an architectural office with Adolf Meyer, and the following year he received his first important commission: to build the Fagus Shoe Company factory located in Alfeld an der Leine. Gropius's firm belief that workplace improvements in lighting and ventilation would increase workers' productivity is apparent in the large curtain windows that surround each of the three stories. The building has a **steel** frame to support the entire structure, thin **brick** piers to mask the vertical steel framing, and horizontal brick layers that separate each of the stories. The entire exterior wall can be considered a curtain wall in that it supports no weight but simply masks the interior. Thus, in this regard, Gropius's structural innovations reveal him to be a sophisticated engineer.

Only later did the Bauhaus School offer courses in architecture by professors committed to the establishment of modern architecture in Germany. The Bauhaus Building itself demonstrates these ideals. Built by Gropius in 1925–1926, the Bauhaus Building is a complex of three large cubes, which include classrooms, offices, and a dormitory in the back. It was meant to reveal an "honesty" of materials in its steel frame, which is covered by reinforced **concrete** punctuated by rows of windows to allow natural light into the studio areas. Raised parapets give the impression of a light structure that contrasts with the perceived "heaviness" of past styles. In 1932, an exhibition of **International style** architecture, as this European modernism came to be called, was shown at the Metropolitan Museum of Art in New York City. This exhibition was instrumental in detaching that style from its perceived German roots and allowing it to transcend national identities so that it would be accepted more widely, as happened in the United States.

Five years later, Gropius immigrated to the United States to accept a professorship at Harvard University's Graduate School of Design, and in this capacity he was able to hone his modern, utilitarian style of architecture in the United States. His first commission there was for his own house, the Gropius House, built in Lincoln, Massachusetts, in 1937. Inspired by **Le Corbusier**'s Villa Savoye, here Gropius blends industrial materials with native **stone** and New England–styled clapboards. Cantilevered concrete squares create cubes of space that intersect and are punctured with thin strips of fenestration. This economically produced home set the standard from which modernist domestic architecture was re-created for the next several decades throughout the United States.

GUIMARD, HECTOR (1867–1942). *See* ART NOUVEAU.

– H –

HADID, ZAHA (1950–). One of the few female architects to receive international acclaim, Zaha Hadid is the only woman to receive the prestigious Pritzker Architecture Prize (in 2004). Her architectural style is often consistent with the international movement called **Deconstructivism**, introduced in the 1980s with the intention of breaking down preconceived notions of architecture and provoking questions about what people hold to be aesthetically "true" in architectural design. Hadid, one of the leaders of this movement, was born in Baghdad and studied in London, where she opened her architectural practice in 1979. Her Vitra Fire Station, built in Weil-am-Rhein in Germany in 1989–1993, exemplifies this style, with its sharply angled walls that jut out of the framework of the building and provide an uneasy dynamism meant to suggest the function of the building as a fire station. The **concrete** exterior is a smooth, gray tone that blends into the sky. In 2006, the Guggenheim Museum of Art in New York City hosted a retrospective of Hadid's work, providing a venue for the rare entrance of a female architect into the "canon" of architecture.

HAGIA SOPHIA. *See* BYZANTINE ARCHITECTURE; ISLAMIC ARCHITECTURE.

HARDOUIN-MANSART, JULES (1646–1708). *See* VERSAILLES PALACE, FRANCE.

HASTINGS, THOMAS (1860–1929). *See* BEAUX-ARTS ARCHITECTURE.

HERRERA, JUAN DE (1530–1593). *See* ESCORIAL, MADRID.

HERZOG AND DE MEURON ARCHITEKTEN. This 21st-century Swiss architectural firm was established in 1978 by Jacques Herzog and Pierre de Meuron, both of whom were born in Basel in 1950 and educated in Zurich. Their parallel careers led to the development of a unique architectural style characterized by design elements that combine aspects of **Deconstructivism**, **High-Tech architecture**, and

Green architecture. In 2001, Herzog and de Meuron together won the Pritzker Architecture Prize. The commission that elevated Herzog and de Meuron into international prominence was their completion in 2000 of the renovation of the Bankside Power Station along the Thames River in London into the Tate Modern Art Museum. Retaining some of the open floor plan, industrial ductwork, and other materials of the original building, Herzog and de Meuron adapted the structure to include gallery space and a two-story **glass** roof extension to increase the space of the building and to make visible reference to its new function. On the exterior, the glass extension softens the stark, factory aesthetic of the original building. It is this creativity and innovative use of older materials that became the hallmark of Herzog and de Meuron's subsequent designs. In 2002, the team received a commission to build the Allianz Arena in Munich, which was completed in 2005. Made from **concrete** and a covering of inflatable air panels, the arena looks like a giant inflatable boat. The highly unusual materials used allow the building to light up at night into the colors of the various sports teams playing there. Otherwise, the dry air in the panels gives the impression of a white color from a distance, but at close range, the panels are transparent. This impressive building demonstrates the ability of these architects to work in a very creative way with highly technical materials.

In 2005, Herzog and de Meuron completed the Walker Art Center Expansion in Minneapolis in a Deconstructivist style. The solid wall of their additional wing rises up at an angle and crumples into a solid vertical tower articulated with two sets of large, irregularly shaped windows. The lack of symmetry or classical harmony, however, does not diminish the visual connection between the new addition and the preexisting structure. Instead, the new exterior provides a strongly sculptural presence that complements the museum collection's focus on modern sculpture. In the same year, Herzog and de Meuron also completed the new M. H. de Young Museum in San Francisco to replace the preexisting building, which had been damaged beyond repair in 1989 by an earthquake. Built near the San Andreas Fault, the museum presented a series of challenges that were both technical and symbolic. The new museum reveals a Deconstructivist style, the goals of which include a desire to offset classical proportions and balance, which ultimately can be seen as philosophically consistent with the building's location near the earthquake fault. It was constructed with ball-bearing sliding plates and fluid dampers to protect it from future seismic shifts, while the attached tower twists slightly to further affirm its precarious location. In addition, the building was also designed to blend into its parklike surroundings. The exterior is made from copper, which over time will turn green and match the neighboring trees, while the top of the building is cut out in sections and planted with trees to create an organic appearance. These innovative solutions to traditional issues of function, style, materials, and site will certainly continue to be central to the future designs of Herzog and de Meuron.

HIGH-TECH ARCHITECTURE. High-Tech architecture grew out of the **Post-Modernist** style of the 1970s and 1980s to reveal an increased focus on the artistic display of more highly technical aspects of construction. With the battle cry of "form follows function," early modern architects led the way in elevating the formal elements of buildings by stripping away all applied decoration. Yet in buildings such as **Walter Gropius**'s Fagus Shoe Company, built in Alfeld an der Leine, Germany, in 1911–1913, Gropius masked the **steel** frame of the building with thin **brick** piers. In the 1920s, the increasingly complex structural aspects of taller buildings pushed engineering innovations to their limits. Still, the structural components of these early **skyscraper**s remained hidden from view, despite their glorification in other types of constructions such as the famous steel Brooklyn Bridge, built in 1867–1883 by the Roeblings, or the Eiffel Tower, built by Gustav Eiffel in Paris in 1887–1889. In High-Tech architecture, the structural aspects of a building take on an aesthetic character themselves, while the utilitarian aspects are taken out of hiding and placed on the exterior of the building. The style was first described in *High Tech: The Industrial Style and Source Book for the Home*, published by Joan Kron and Suzanne Slesin in 1978. While the book demonstrates how industrial design and furnishings can be used within the home, its most famous examples are public buildings.

High-Tech architecture is best expressed in large urban civic structures or tall office buildings. The Centre National d'Art et de Culture Georges Pompidou, built in Paris in 1971–1977 by Renzo Piano and Richard Rogers, is one of the earliest examples of this style. This massive public building houses a museum of modern art, a public library, and centers for music and design, and because it is heavily used, the interior needed to remain as uncluttered as possible. Piano and Rogers therefore placed not only the steel frame on the outside of the building, but also the electrical wiring units, the air conditioning tubes and the water pipes, as well as the escalators, thus creating a vast exo-skeletal structure that contrasts vividly with the surrounding neighborhood. Each component was painted a different color, with the air conditioning ducts painted a bright blue, the elevators a rich red, the water pipes a green, and the electrical components a yellow.

High-Tech architecture is not a regional but an international style. Norman Foster's Hongkong and Shanghai Bank, built in Hong Kong in 1986, is another example of this style. This 47-story skyscraper features a white and gray steel frame on its exterior, with girders providing additional support. The building does not have the traditional service core, as earlier skyscrapers do, but instead it is located on the external east and west sides. Each floor is attached to this outer structure, and beneath the steel frame is a continuous line of curtain windows. A sophisticated computer tracks the sunlight and directs it into the building, reducing the need for artificial light. High-Tech architectural elements have gradually become more focused on these types of utilitarian innovations, with a desire to increase energy efficiency. For example, Ralph Erskine's "London Ark," a massive office building completed in London in 1992, looks like a giant ocean liner but is best known for its innovative use of a new, more efficient cooling system. High-Tech architecture will certainly remain focused on these issues as its style moves into the future.

HIROSHI, HARA (1936–2007). *See* JAPANESE ARCHITECTURE.

HOFFMANN, JOSEF (1870–1956). Josef Hoffman, a leader of the **Art Nouveau** architectural style, was born in Moravia and went to school in Brno with **Adolf Loos**. He then studied in Vienna under Otto Wagner and subsequently played a central role in founding the Viennese Secession, together with Joseph Maria Olbrich. Beginning in 1899, Hoffmann taught at the School for Arts and Crafts in Vienna, and later became the director of the school. A series of houses he constructed in Vienna, including the Carl Moll and Koloman Moser houses, reveal a more ornate style than that of Loos. After Hoffmann broke with the Secessionists, the wealthy industrialist Moser helped him found the *Viennese Werkstätte*, for which Hoffmann designed furniture and domestic objects in the **Arts and Crafts** style.

Hoffmann's Purkersdorf Sanatorium, built in 1904 on the edge of the woods outside Vienna, was commissioned by Viktor Zuckerkandl to be a modernist nursing home for the wealthy elderly. Zuckerkandl dictated much of the design, and in fact wanted a flat roof for the building. The building is a simple, white rectangle cut inward and outward to create cubic volumes that provide a three-dimensional façade together with a three-part vertical division of the exterior. The rhythmic arrangement of unarticulated rectangular windows, grouped in threes, reveals a restrained, well-proportioned structure. The bright, white interior, done in a very rational style, cultivates the appearance of a "sanitary" space. Hoffmann's subsequent Palais Stoclet, constructed in 1905–1911 in Brussels for the wealthy banker Adolphe Stoclet, was designed in a much richer style called the *Judenstil*, the Viennese version of the Art Nouveau style. Copper sculpture decorates the exterior of this subtly historicizing, organic building, while the interior is decorated with murals by Gustav Klimt. This is the style that provided impetus for Adolf Loos's attacks on architectural ornamentation and excess. With these buildings constructed in Europe in the first decades of the 20th century, historians have traced the beginning of the division between the sparer, geometric modernism and the more organic, expressive form of modernism that continued to define architecture through the rest of the century.

HOOD, RAYMOND (1881–1934). *See* ART DECO.

HORTA, VICTOR (1861–1947). *See* ART NOUVEAU.

HOWELLS, JOHN MEAD (1868–1959). *See* ART DECO.

HUNT, RICHARD MORRIS (1827–1895). Born in Vermont, Richard Morris Hunt was the first American-born architect to train at the famed École des Beaux-Arts in Paris. From there, he returned to the United States with a desire to elevate architectural standards by emulating the more lavish European styles. In the United States, the blending of **Romanesque**, **Renaissance**, **Baroque**, and **Rococo** came to be called the **Beaux-Arts** style, and this historicized style reflected the taste of the new wealthy class of the "Gilded Age." This period, from around 1885 to 1925, is characterized by a new prosperity, although the sinking of the *Titanic* in 1912 dampened in part the enthusiasm for such excess. Hunt opened the first American architectural school and helped to elevate the status of architects through his connections with wealthy American industrialists. As their favored architect, Hunt built more than six houses in Newport, Rhode Island, including the mansion for William Kissam Vanderbilt in 1888–1892. In the 1890s, for Cornelius Vanderbilt he constructed The Breakers, a 70-room Italianate mansion overlooking the ocean at Newport, and the famous Biltmore Estate in Asheville, North Carolina, the largest private mansion in the United States.

In 1893, Hunt was in charge of a group of architects hired to design the architectural setting for the 1893 World's Columbian Exposition in Chicago. This massive festival, very important in American popular culture at the time, celebrated Christopher Columbus's arrival in the Americas 400 years earlier and showcased every American invention and new trend of the time. Unlike the more structurally experimental buildings constructed at earlier world fairs, Hunt wanted to use a coherent Neo-Classicism to suggest permanence in these temporary buildings and to showcase the greatness of the United States and its democratic ideals, which hark back to classical Athenian values. The vast Court of Honor, created with a large pond in its center, was lined with **Neo-Classical** structures made of plaster and built on a scale that rivaled those of Ancient Rome. At the end of the broad vista of the Court of Honor, Hunt's Administrative Building, built to suggest a new "Renaissance" in the United States after the conclusion of the Civil War, dominated the skyline with its massive **dome**. This temporary city was clean, well organized, and beautiful, and demonstrated a new model for the increasingly crowded and industrialized American cities of the time. Frederick Law Olmsted, who had designed Central Park in New York City, oversaw the Exposition's landscape plans, which he used as a model of city park design.

Many of Richard Morris Hunt's buildings are open to the public today, and, as museums, they are monuments to the aspirations of this prosperous time in American history when the country began to develop into a world power. *See also* ROMANTIC ARCHITECTURE.

– I –

INCA ARCHITECTURE. *See* MACHU PICCHU, PERU.

INDIAN ARCHITECTURE. The structural, aesthetic, and symbolic characteristics of Indian architecture are traditionally seen within the shared cultural history of the peoples of the South Asian subcontinent, which includes modern-day India and the surrounding countries of Pakistan and part of Afghanistan to the northwest, Nepal and Bangladesh to the northeast, and Sri Lanka off the southern coast. India itself is divided by the Vindhya Mountains, which demarcate two distinct styles, one northern and one southern. The earliest known civilization in this region has been found in the Indus Valley of Pakistan and northwest India, along the banks of the Indus River, where an early culture flourished from about 3000 BC to 1750 BC. Mountain passes through the Hindu Kush linked India to the rest of Asia, and along these roads major trade routes were established and new waves of immigrants entered the subcontinent.

While Harappa was the first site discovered along this river, Mohenjo Daro is the best preserved. These cities were probably organized much like their contemporary city-states along the river banks of Mesopotamia and the Nile in Old Kingdom Egypt, yet they reflect perhaps more advanced architectural innovations and merit much further study. For example, their cities are built with a fired **brick** that is stronger than the sun-dried mud brick so widely used across a variety of cultures at that time. Mohenjo Daro, at its high point, maintained a population of around 30,000 people who lived in a very well-organized city built on a grid with wide streets and distinct neighborhoods. In the center of the seven-square-mile town is an elevated citadel complex surrounded by a wall. Inside the citadel are buildings that were probably used for governmental and religious purposes, and large pools used to store water. The rest of the city has covered drainage ditches. Tall houses, often designed with courtyards, lined the streets to create separate neighborhoods. Many of the artifacts found in the Indus Valley region suggest influences from Mesopotamia, yet here figures that might be priest-kings are sometimes shown in proto-yogic poses that reveal a more culturally specific belief system.

By the Vedic Period, which began around 1750 BC, an influx of nomadic shepherds from central Asia, called the Aryans, brought bronze tools, weapons, horses, and chariots that enabled them to assume control of the region and create a rich culture from which sprang Sanskrit, metaphysical philosophy, epic poetry, and most importantly, the sacred writings called the *Vedas*. The vast majority of architecture constructed through history has been built for religious purposes, and in this case the monumental and durable temples and shrines are all that remain from this broad time period; no secular architecture at all has survived. Sanskrit literature describes beautiful palace complexes, however, which surely vied for architectural authority with these religious structures, only to be destroyed by later rulers. During the Maurya Dynasty (c. 322–185 BC), Buddhism had become the official language of Hindu architecture, established by King Ashoka, who sought to impose a more peaceful quality to what he deemed to be a too-warlike culture. The **stone** monuments built under his reign probably replaced even earlier finely carved **wood** structures. Stylistically, it seems that Ashoka was inspired by the monumental stone buildings he would have seen on his military campaign to Persia, before his conversion to a pacifistic political philosophy.

The Great Stupa at Sanchi in central India is one of the earliest known religious structures in India. Originally built under Ashoka, it is the largest of a group of stupas that was begun in the second century BC and expanded upon through the centuries into an entire monastic complex. Stupas recall the original burial mounds made to hold the remains of the Buddha and therefore are built as solid, **dome**-shaped monuments to contain sacred relics in their solid core. Since some of the earliest stupas hold the actual remains of the Buddha, they are worshipped as his body, and it is believed that by walking around the stupa enough times, one can achieve *nirvana*, the liberation from rebirth. Surrounded by an elaborately carved railing, the stupa is built up on a base with four gateways (called *toranas*) aligned to the four cardinal points, with an entrance on the eastern side. The visitor can walk through a gateway and then around a platform that encircles the exterior base of the stupa. On the top of the dome, a square railing holds a mast or spire. While the outer railing separates the physical and sacred worlds, the dome railings define the world of the gods. In its center the mast, which links the physical and sacred world, holds three stone disks of diminishing sizes upwards, their diminishing diameters probably a reference to the Buddhist realm of existence—desire, form, and formlessness. At Sanchi, the stupas are made from dirt and rubble piled up to form a mound and covered in carved stone and finally, a white plaster made from lime and ground seashells to shine in the sunlight.

Rock-cut halls were also important in early Indian architecture. Caves were the traditional abode of ascetics across many religions, and beginning in the second century BC, Buddhist monks began to carve out more elaborate rock-cut halls in the rocky central region of India called the Deccan Plateau. The man-made Ajanta Caves line the rocky outcrop of the Deccan and are intricately carved and painted with religious images and scenes of courtly life. The cool, dark interiors provided an effective sacred space for meditation, and the rock-cut halls were either monastic living quarters (*vihara*) or prayer halls (*chaitya*) housing stupa shrines. The rock-cut hall at Karla, from the first century BC, is the largest early Buddhist *chaitya* known today. The entrance vestibule is flanked by columns and carved with fictive balconies and windows in emulation of a palace exterior. The internal façade has three entrances and one window to allow light into the cave; on the inside, the entire room is carved out to reveal a central hall lined with closely spaced octagonal columns set on rounded bases and topped with carved elephants, couples, and horses. The hall also includes side aisles, a barrel-vaulted ceiling, and a sacred stupa at the far end.

Only later, in the Gupta Period, are the earliest temples found. As distinct from the Buddhist stupa, the Indian temple was devoted to one or more of the deities of Hinduism. Northern Indian temples are slightly different from southern temples. The northern temples feature a platform upon which a tall cone-shaped *shikhara* rests and encloses the inner sanctum, called the *garbhagriha*, which contains a sculpture of the god to which the temple is dedicated. Like a stupa, the *shikhara* is topped with a spire that links the worldly and heavenly realms and is also understood to project downward through the exact center of the inner sanctum, the deity, and into the ground below. The Vishnu Temple at Deogarh in central India, dating to around 530, is the earliest surviving example of the early northern Hindu temple. Here the *shikhara* rests on a *mandala*-shaped platform, symbolizing the cosmos. The temple entrance is an elaborately carved doorway that demarcates the division between the physical and spiritual worlds. In more monumental northern temples, the platform has three additional conical towers called *mandapas*, which increase in height toward the *shikhara*. The Kandariya Mahadeva Temple, in Khajuraho in the Madhya Pradesh region, dates to around 1000 and exemplifies this format.

In the south, these elaborately carved temples are formed as a stone platform upon which rests a pyramidal tower, called a *vimana*, that houses the *garbhagriha* and rises in stepped cornices to a capstone that is carved to exactly the same size as the *garbhagriha*. The Rajarajeshvara Temple to Shiva, in Thanjavur of the Tamil Nadu region, dates to around 1000 and exemplifies the monumental version of the southern Hindu temple. All of these structures reveal a highly sculptural aesthetic, with an intricate system of architectural moldings, finials, cornices, and niches filled with sculpted images. Yet there is a mathematical precision that stabilizes the structure to its cardinal points, creates sophisticated shapes such as the parabolic arch, and provides a very precise system of measurements that symbolically link all aspects of the temple.

With the spread of Buddhist and Hindu beliefs to Myanmar (Burma), Malaysia, Singapore, Indonesia, Thailand, Taiwan, Laos, Cambodia, Vietnam, and other parts of Southeast Asia, early Indian architectural aesthetics as well as Chinese influences began to mingle with indigenous cultures. The Neolithic culture of this general region provided no architectural remains, nor did the subsequent Bronze Age culture that began around 800 BC, but both Indian and Chinese influences began to appear in the area by around 500 BC. The ceremonial complex of **Angkor, Cambodia**, is the best-known example of Khmer architecture.

The ceremonial complex in Bagan, Myanmar, is perhaps the most impressive site, however, with over 2,000 religious structures spread out on a vast, flat plain of 16 unobstructed square miles. Bagan was settled as early as the second century AD, but the Burmese capital was only established there by King Pyinbya in 874. Although the capital was subsequently moved, the complex reached its architectural high point after 1057, when King Anawrahta made Bagan a religious center. During the 200-year time span before Kublai Khan's army overran the site in 1287, each ruler commissioned the construction of Buddhist stupas or Hindu temples, often modeled on sacred mountains. The earliest major temple, the Ananda Pahto, was built during the reign of King Kyanzittha in 1084–1113. This is a symmetrical temple constructed in the early Mon style, with north Indian influences. The temple is set on a square base and rises like a beehive topped by a cone-shaped dome with a finial. With its recent controversial restoration, the dome and its surrounding pinnacles are now all gilded, while the rest of the temple is whitewashed. The interior of the temple, set in a cross-shape plan aligned to the cardinal points, is richly decorated and lined with carved sandstone reliefs of the life of the Buddha. The overall design concept of the temple is based on a cave in the Himalayas where several monks went for a period of contemplation; the temple commemorates both the cave and the endless wisdom of the Buddha. As the government begins to receive more outside visitors, scholars will undoubtedly be able to learn much more about these Southeast Asian stupas and temple complexes.

In the 1200s, northern India was invaded by Muslims, who brought a new culture to the Indian subcontinent. The result was the destruction of most of the important northern Indian temples and their replacement by Islamic buildings such as mosques and tombs as well as magnificent fortified government complexes and palaces constructed by the Turkish sultans, who ruled from the northern Indian city of Delhi. Of this Islamic influence, the Mughal Dynasty is best known for its architecture, epitomized by the famous **Taj Mahal, Agra**, in India. Western architecture was introduced into India only with British rule from 1858 to 1947, and India today, poised to become a world power, displays an international approach to architecture alongside its ancient structures. *See also* ISLAMIC ARCHITECTURE.

INTERNATIONAL STYLE. The International style can be understood as a highly codified application of basic principles of modern architecture that had been developing since the turn of the 20th century. However, modernity ultimately originated with the introduction of new materials and construction techniques in the middle of the 19th century, ones that allowed not only for such great feats of cast-**iron** engineering as the Eiffel Tower, constructed in Paris in 1887–1889, but also for taller buildings with **steel** frames and wider overhangs of cantilevered reinforced **concrete**. The recognition of these bold structural innovations helped to elevate the functional aspects of construction to a higher level of appreciation, whereby its scientific basis was upheld as the progressive model for the future. Architects then applied aesthetic principles to this new functionalism, arguing that applied decoration was a degeneration of "true" architecture. These ideas were in direct contrast to the prevailing **Art Nouveau** style, increasingly seen as ornamentally excessive, sensual, and aristocratic.

One of the first to voice a concern for this applied decoration was the Viennese architect **Adolf Loos**. Considered the founder of modernism, Loos wrote a manifesto titled "Ornament and Crime" in 1913, which explains these connections between excessive architectural ornamentation, decadence, and corruption. His buildings, such as the Steiner House in Vienna, from 1910, reflect these ideas. This structure protects its inhabitants with roofs and walls while providing light through plain windows that puncture the exterior where they are needed on the interior.

Loos's functionalism quickly spread across Europe. It is seen in the Fagus Shoe Factory, built in Germany in 1911 by **Walter Gropius**, and in the work of German architects Bruno Taut and Peter Behrens. Functional modernism quickly spread to the Netherlands, where it developed a more regional form of **Rationalism** called *de Stijl*, seen in the architecture of Gerrit Rietveld, and to France, as exemplified by the work of **Le Corbusier**. In Italy, Futurist architects sought a more dynamic approach to the fast-moving modern world, where future buildings would resemble great machines, while the next generation of Italian Rationalists, such as Giuseppe Terragni, created sparer geometric designs. The Russian Revolution of 1917 helped the spread of utilitarian modernism in Russia as well. Back in Germany, Gropius went on to establish the **Bauhaus** School of Design, which came to be seen as the final basis for the International style.

The term "International style" was coined by Henry Russell Hitchcock and Philip Johnson in an exhibition they organized at the Museum of Modern Art in New York in 1932. They called it "The International Style: Architecture since 1922" and subsequently published it in a manifesto in which they identified three fundamental principles of modern architecture. The first was a discussion of the expression of volume rather than mass in architecture. Now a building could be conceived of as a structural skeleton wrapped in curtain walls or windows that allowed for more unencumbered and flexible interior space. The second principle sought to define an aesthetic of regularity and balance rather than the more rigid symmetry favored by classical architects. The third principle included the rejection of any form of historical articulation or applied ornamentation, which they considered as merely arbitrary and unnecessary rather than degenerate. Instead, the materials themselves would be held up as intrinsically beautiful, and their carefully balanced arrangement would produce an aesthetic harmony of parts.

In the United States, the International style moved from its theoretical framework to a more practical application of its principles in the 1930s, when Gropius, **Ludwig Mies van der Rohe,** and **Marcel Breuer** joined **Richard Neutra** in the United States and established this form of modern architecture in private homes. **Louis Sullivan** experimented with its use in the urban **skyscraper,** and **Louis Kahn** and **Philip Johnson** introduced the International style to a variety of buildings constructed from the 1940s through the 1970s, including museums and office buildings. Because of the strict adherence to formal architectural principles and a disassociation with regional or national styles, the International style did not need to engage in the rather messy nationalistic concerns found in Europe during World War I, nor were International style architects compelled to respond to the political environment of the time. Instead, since this style of architecture was theoretically positioned "above" such concerns, its introduction into the United States was relatively smooth despite its avant-garde European origins. However, the International style was gradually supplanted by **Post-Modernism** and a reintroduction of historical referencing, regional concerns, and a fuller stylistic variety to architecture.

IRON. *See* CAST IRON.

ISLAMIC ARCHITECTURE. Islamic architecture is broadly defined as any construction based on the religious principles of Islam. Both religious and secular buildings reflect design principles of Islamic culture. These include mosques, funerary monuments, private dwellings, and fortifications built after the establishment of Islam in the 600s down to today. In the year AD 610, a wealthy merchant named "The Trusted One" was traveling outside Mecca, and later reported that one evening the angel Gabriel came to him and told him he would from then on be the messenger of God, given the task of reciting God's commandments. Thus, al-Amin (c. 570–632) became Muhammad, the "messenger of Allah," and established the religion of Islam, which means "submission to God's will." Islam officially began in 622, the year of Muhammad's flight from Mecca to Medina. Muhammad was politically important to the unification of Arabia under Islam by negotiating the more peaceful coexistence of warring communities and linking this diverse region together under the Arabic language. His four successors continued the work of establishing this religion across these diverse regions of the world, but with the rule of Ali, the fourth *caliph* after Muhammad, an internal divide resulted in the split between Sunnis and Shiites based on the legitimacy of his rule. Nonetheless, while Islam originated in ancient Arabia, it quickly spread across Africa, Asia, and parts of Europe. Therefore, although styles change over time and this broad geographical area of influence reflects varied and regional artistic traditions, Islamic buildings can be seen to reveal an enduring set of design principles intricately linked to the historical origins of Islam.

For example, during the earliest years, followers began to dedicate new buildings that would carve out a distinct culture and spread the word of Islam, yet Islam is based on a personal connection with God, and Muhammad himself taught from a simple mud-**brick** building next to his home in Medina and advised his followers against construction of elaborate architectural monuments. His own prayer building consisted of a simple square-walled courtyard surrounded by a covered portico on all four sides and a platform on the south side for Muhammad to speak from. The courtyard and the pulpit, called a *minbar*, are retained in later mosque designs. In addition, because the ancient square-shaped house that Abraham built for God, called the *Kaaba*, is thought to have been located in Mecca, this city became the most sacred site in all of Islam, to which Muslims even today direct their prayers. Therefore, the prayer wall of the mosque, called the *qibla* wall, always faces Mecca. Finally, the complete avoidance of divine, human, and certain animal likenesses can be seen in the architectural decoration. The Koran (Qur'an), the word of Allah, derives from the same religious tradition as that of the Jews and Christians. However, text and writing are so central to Islamic culture that mainly beautiful calligraphy, along with geometric patterns and images from nature, decorate its architecture.

The earliest Islamic architecture appears under the Umayyad Dynasty (661–750), when the political center of Islam moved from Mecca to Damascus and new mosques, palaces, and government buildings were constructed. Jerusalem was also considered a sacred city, and in 692, a shrine was constructed over a sacred rock in central Jerusalem that Muhammad was said to have climbed to meet God, the same rock where, it was said, God told Abraham to sacrifice his son Isaac and where the ancient **Temple of Solomon** was located. This octagonal, domed shrine, called the Dome of the Rock, was constructed by Syrian architects who had been trained in the construction of **Byzantine** domes and centralized spaces. The central **dome** is covered in gold leaf, while the eight surrounding walls that form an interior ambulatory are decorated with turquoise tiles and **marble**. An **arched** doorway flanked by a recessed portico supported by pillars articulates the entrance, while only a few windows are needed along the lower walls to allow light into the interior. The blue and white exterior tiles blend into the background sky, while the gold dome reflects light and therefore seems to hover above its tiled drum in a Byzantine style. Inside the building, pilgrims walk around the double ambulatory, reading the text written in golden calligraphy around the interior frieze. Above the calligraphic inscriptions are beautiful mosaics outlined in gold leaf that reveal intertwined, organic patterns that symbolize the gardens of Paradise. The center of the shrine, the most important part of the building, displays the sacred rock. The visitor will not at first see the rock, however, for it is bathed in light that streams down from windows in the drum of the dome, which ritualistically symbolizes the divine presence and the idea of enlightenment. The entire interior reveals a richness of material that blends **Ancient Roman** and Byzantine traditions into a new type of building.

This structure set a high standard of architectural construction and ornamentation, which was continued through the Umayyad Dynasty with the building of elaborate palaces and civic buildings. One of the few examples that remain today is the Palace Complex of Mshatta in modern-day Amman, Jordan, begun in the 740s but never completed. This hunting lodge features a fortified stone wall that enclosed a complex of courtyards, pools, a mosque, audience hall, and separate apartment wings. The front of the palace complex is decorated with a carved stone register that runs along the lower portion of the façade and features ornate designs often called "arabesques" in western literature. Here the designs are triangular shapes with rosettes carved into intricate organic interlaced patterns of animals set in nature. The use of the lion in these structures recalls, in particular, the similar decorations found on limestone reliefs located on the exterior walls of ancient Assyrian palace complexes. Although they would have been partially destroyed by then, they would certainly have been known to these Islamic caliphs.

It was during this first dynasty that the mosque format was codified to include a hypostyle hall arrived at through an open courtyard. Inside the hall, the far wall faced Mecca, and this *qibla* wall featured a niche in the center called the *mihrab*, where the Koran was located. The *mihrab* was often enclosed and contained a space for the ruler, called a *maqsura*, while a *minbar*, or pulpit, was located next to the *mihrab* and was used by the religious leader, or the *imam*, for prayers. Outside the mosque, tall towers, or minarets, connect to the courtyard wall and are used to call worshipers to prayer five times a day. The Umayyad Dynasty was overthrown in 750, but family members fled to Spain and continued to rule as local leaders from Cordoba for the next several hundred years. The Great Mosque of Cordoba, built in the 780s, survives from this time as a beautiful building created from local Roman ruins to feature a hypostyle hall of classical **columns** with double arches outlined in alternating stripes of white and red brick, which provide a greater height to the hall and allow for more air circulation. As Cordoba prospered under Islamic rule, the Great

Mosque was more ornately decorated to feature a golden *mihrab* created with an intricate network of intersecting ribs and gold patterned inscriptions.

The middle years of Islamic rule, under the Abbasid Dynasty of Baghdad, lasted until 1258 and can be characterized as a very prosperous time when literature and the sciences thrived. The monumental architecture during these years recalls the ancient Persian capital of Persepolis, and here mosques grew larger to include more congregational space. The Great Mosque at Samarra, begun in 847, was the largest ever built, and features a wide minaret that recalls the ancient Sumerian ziggurats native to this region of modern-day Iraq. A format developed in Persia (modern-day Iran) is called the four-*iwan* mosque, as it includes four large hypostyle halls with barrel vaults that each face toward an internal courtyard. Regional leaders also carved out their own architectural traditions, as seen in the **Alhambra** palace complex, built in Granada by the Nasrids, who were the last Muslim, or Moorish, dynasty to rule in Spain, from 1232 to 1492. This beautiful palace epitomizes the melding of Islamic aesthetics into both religious and political structures, as the two are really inseparable in Islam.

As Islamic culture became more and more diversified with a less centralized political structure, architecture became increasingly more varied. The Seljuk Turks, who ruled Anatolia, Mesopotamia, and Persia from 1037 to 1194, defined an eclectic style of architecture that combined elements from Syria in the northwest of their domain down to Persia in the southeast. They are best known for the creation of a small round, domed funerary monument called a *turbe*, which recalls both Armenian chapels and Bedouin tents. In addition, the Seljuks built *medresas*, or religious schools, which are more enclosed than a traditional mosque, and they also constructed many technically sophisticated bridges across Anatolia, with paved roads linking their extensive trade routes.

The Ottoman Empire, which overtook Seljuk control of Anatolia, provided a new prosperity and allowed the construction of many more fine examples of Islamic architecture. A type of mosque developed in Ottoman Turkey reveals a domed centralized plan that strongly resembles the Byzantine church of Hagia Sophia, built in Constantinople (modern-day Istanbul) in the 500s. In 1453, the Ottomans captured Constantinople, named it Istanbul, and ruled a powerful empire until 1918. During their empire, Hagia Sophia was converted into a mosque, with Koranic inscriptions added to the interior decorations and minarets built on the outside of the building. The architect **Mimar Koca Agha Sinan**, who built the Mosque of Sultan Selim in Edirne, Turkey, in the 1560s, was the best-known architect of the Ottoman Empire.

The oil wealth of 20th-century Islamic countries provided further impetus for the construction of monument architecture. The King Faisal Mosque, built in Islamabad, Pakistan, and sponsored by King Faisal of Saudi Arabia, was constructed in the 1980s by the Turkish architect Vedat Dalokay; it includes an enclosed congregational space for 300,000 worshippers and recalls in its wide, slopped roof a Bedouin tent, anchored in its four corner with minarets. The King Hassan II Mosque (1986–1993) in Casablanca, Morocco, is currently the second largest mosque in the world, slightly smaller than the Masjid al-Haram in Mecca. Designed by the French architect Michel Pinseau, the mosque is built out onto the Atlantic Ocean and features a glass floor so visitors can see the ocean beneath their feet. The mosque accommodates 25,000 people inside, while an additional 80,000 fit into the courtyard. The King Hassan II Mosque also features the tallest minaret in the world. By blending traditional Islamic architecture with modern technical innovations such as a heated floor and sliding doors and roof, this building certainly sets the stage for 21st-century Islamic architectural trends. *See also* BYZANTINE ARCHITECTURE.

ITALIANATE STYLE. *See* ROMANTIC ARCHITECTURE.

ITO, TOYO (1941–). *See* JAPANESE ARCHITECTURE.

– J –

JAPANESE ARCHITECTURE. The four islands that compose modern-day Japan are located off the coast of Russia, North and South Korea, and China. In **Prehistoric** times, this land mass was connected to the continent, and the Sea of Japan was a large lake upon which some of the earliest cultures flourished. With the end of the Ice Age, Japan was gradually transformed into a sophisticated island culture, protected by the sea from invaders and enjoying a fertile maritime society. Once agricultural communities were formed by Korean settlers who brought rice to the islands, Japanese material culture flourished, and here are found the earliest architectural remains from the Yayoi period (c. 300 BC–AD 300). Yayoi peoples lived in timber-framed and thatched **wood** homes with sunken floors and raised granaries. In subsequent eras, a more pronounced hierarchical society emerged, with royal tomb monuments and palace complexes, together with more ritualized religious structures. Early tombs were formed into a necropolis of earth mounds, topped by ceramic sculptures called *haniwa* that sometimes resembled domestic architectural structures. These unglazed ceramic forms probably symbolized aspects of the native Japanese Shinto belief system.

Shinto shrines have persisted throughout Japanese history and reflect the belief that the gods inhabit aspects of nature, such as waterfalls, mountains, trees, and even rocks. Often, a simple gateway called a *torii* signified a sacred natural site, devoid of any architectural construction. An early Shinto shrine built in the first century AD (during the Yayoi Period) is found at Ise, along the southwest coast of Japan. Rebuilt every 20 years, this shrine is a major tourist site today where pilgrims can venerate the sun goddess, the mother of the Japanese Imperial family. The unpainted cypress wood building rests on piles that raise the shrine off the ground. Only members of the royal family may enter the shrine's four-part interior through the doorway located under the porch at the ground floor. The thatched, hipped roof is held down by logs placed horizontally across the gable. The aesthetic principles seen here are consistent with the enduring characteristics of Japanese architecture in general, which include a preference for a natural setting with unfinished materials; a restrained design with a simple, harmonious layout; and careful attention paid to every aspect of construction, from the elaborate brackets joined without nails to the placement of the building on its site.

Shintoism was later supplanted by the advent of Buddhism from India. Temple monuments began to be constructed in Japan during the Asuka Period (AD 552–646). This monumental architecture was entirely new in Japan, given that earlier Shinto gods were often worshipped directly in natural surroundings rather than in architectural settings. (The Ise shrine is one exception and can be understood as an imperial monument that honors the ancestors of the royal family.) The Buddhist temple compound at Horyu-ji, in the central plains of Japan, built in the 600s, is one of the few surviving Buddhist temples from this early period and is the oldest original wooden building in the world. This small compound consists of two buildings: a solid five-story pagoda and a large worship hall called a *kondo*. These two balanced structures are located in a rectangular courtyard surrounded by covered walkways. Outside the sacred compound are monastic buildings, including classrooms, dormitories, a library, and a bell tower. During the end of the Heian Period (794–1185), a monastic complex reflects the ideals of Pure Land Buddhism, which was more spiritually direct than the esoteric principles of the earlier forms of Buddhism and therefore more widely popular. The Byodo-in, located in the Uji Mountains outside Kyoto, was originally built in the 11th century as a palace for the imperial counselor. Less austere than the Horyu-ji complex, this square temple faces an artificial pond and is flanked on three sides by connecting enclosed corridors elevated onto slender piles that end in elevated square rooms. The exterior walls, accented with a rich dark wood framework and reddish trim, are topped by a hipped roof with corners that tilt upward and reveal carved images of a phoenix in the corners of the gable. The tilted roof, which gives the impression of the phoenix taking flight, harks back to the earliest Chinese Buddhist temples, such as the Nanchen Temple on Mount Wutai in Central China, built in the 780s.

By the late 12th century a more meditative form of Buddhism, called Zen Buddhism, appeared in Japan. The highly cultivated Zen gardens, often made of **stone** or gravel carefully raked smooth, accentuate several carefully selected rocks and artistically pruned trees. Small Zen gardens provide the proper meditative surroundings for a variety of religious structures and anticipate the elegant simplicity of *shoin* architecture. *Shoin* buildings appeared in the Momoyama period (1568–1603) as upper-class homes that incorporated the elegant simplicity of the tearoom into their designs. The Japanese tea ceremony is perhaps this period's most famous and enduring tradition, in which a small group of people enter into a highly ritualistic interaction of contemplation and modest discourse. Tearooms were made of wood or bamboo, with mud walls, paper-covered windows, and a floor covered with tatami mats of woven straw. Diffused light enters through the thin paper window coverings, revealing a clear spatial arrangement to the interior, which is organized into asymmetrical square or rectangular shapes. A painted scroll or flower arrangement might be the subject of muted discussion. The *shoin* house is a simple rectangular structure defined by square or rectangular bay units with a timber framework and timber bay divisions that incorporate the tearoom aesthetic into a livable arrangement of verandas, alcoves that can be enclosed by decorated sliding doors called *fusuma*, and translucent rice paper screens called shoji that can further organize the interior space. Tatami mats cover the floors, and the wooden ceiling is divided into squares.

The **Katsura Palace**, built near the perimeter of Kyoto in the early 17th century, is perhaps the best example of this type of secular architecture. The palace is constructed as a series of buildings connected by covered walkways that harmonize with the surrounding woods. The rambling effect of the house provides ample opportunity to contemplate nature via the verandas constructed at the gable ends of the building blocks. The front of the palace contains guest rooms and the middle block is organized to entertain guests in tea ceremonies. The small block leading to the back of the house provides storage for books and musical instruments, and the back block features a series of small bedrooms and washrooms adjoining the servants' back wing. In addition to these aristocratic homes, large fortified **castles** were built during the Momoyama period in response to European influences in Japan. Himeji Castle, located near Osaka, dates to the first years of the 1600s and is one of the few surviving fortified imperial castles of the time. A labyrinth-like series of paths, steep stairs, guarded gates, and narrow ladders lead up the hill to the multiroofed and gabled white building complex called the White Heron. These are the complex structures of the warrior class, made famous in the history of Japanese martial arts.

From this period onward, Japan was increasingly exposed to western influences that are reflected in modern Japanese architecture, yet the traditionally nature-based, austere aesthetics of earlier Japanese buildings has continued, as exemplified in Toyo Ito's Silver Hut. Constructed in Tokyo in 1984, this structure maintains a strong contact with nature through its proliferation of windows. Its rooms, organized around a courtyard, reveal an open and flexible floor plan divided with partitions much like the early *shoin* homes. The light aluminum roof, supported on thin columns, consists of seven barrel vaults with glass lining the upper walls and parts of the vaulting, allowing for an almost transparent quality. A model of efficient contemporary urban design, this home reflects general trends still found in the more modest two- and three-story apartment house, called an *apato*. These apartments often have floors and *fusama* sliding doors as well as rice paper walls. Traditional Japanese style can be found in the more expensive modern hotels of Tokyo and Osaka as well as in many modern government buildings. However, the challenge for modern architects is how to integrate traditional Japanese principles of harmonious town planning and a proximity to nature into the construction of these increasingly crowded and industrialized cities.

Kenzo Tange's Yoyogi Gymnasium, built in Tokyo for the 1964 Olympics, reveals his desire to bring structural sophistication to Japanese architecture; it is a thoroughly modern concrete structure, yet with a sweeping, organic ceiling and a curved, asymmetrical floor plan that recalls traditional Japanese forms. **Tadao Ando** reveals a traditional Japanese restrained aesthetic in his Church on the Water, built in Tomamu in northern Japan in 1988 from **concrete**, **steel**, and **glass**, and with large windows that open directly out into its beautiful natural setting. Thus, the traditional emphasis on wood is largely replaced by concrete, but expressive qualities are retained. **Skyscrapers** were introduced in Japan later than in other regions of the world because of the danger of earthquakes, but with more sophisticated structural practices, major cities such as Tokyo are now filled with tall, earthquake-resistant buildings. One of the most unusual skyscrapers is the Umeda Sky Building in Osaka, completed in 1993 by the architect Hara Hiroshi with 40-story twin towers joined by a series of skywalks at various upper levels and capped by a rooftop observatory. Beneath the structures is an underground market, while gardens and a walking path surround the buildings at ground level. This business and apartment complex, in a **Post-Modern** style, responds to the pressing needs for housing and space in modern-day Japan, while at the same time it introduces a series of unique design features to late-20th-century skyscraper design. *See also* CHINESE ARCHITECTURE; INDIAN ARCHITECTURE.

JEFFERSON, THOMAS (1743–1826). Thomas Jefferson, the main author of the Declaration of Independence, was a self-taught architect very much interested in the ideals of the European Enlightenment. By the middle of the 18th century, the British version of **Neo-Classicism** had been introduced into North America, and this architectural style continued dominant in the colonies despite mounting hostilities with England. After the War of Independence, American Neo-Classicism, which dates from 1783 to 1830, came to be called the **Federal style**. In 1784, Jefferson traveled to France; after becoming the American minister to France a year later, he remained in Paris until 1789 and was exposed to **Renaissance**, **Baroque**, **Rococo**, and the prevailing Neo-Classical styles of architecture. Although in the 1770s he had already designed his private home called Monticello outside Charlottesville, Virginia, in the style of British Neo-Classicism, upon his return from Paris he completely redesigned it to feature a more elegant French design. Mingling the rather austere Palladian architecture popular in England with a more intimate French style that featured taller, narrower windows and French doors, Jefferson brought a new sophistication to Neo-Classicism.

When he was in France, he had seen examples of Rococo villas with a more intimate one-story design and less angular corners than the prevailing Neo-Classical style. Therefore, at Monticello, Jefferson minimized his second story and angled the wings of his home inward to soften its corners. The roofline, with a balustrade and a low **dome**, curves inward gently, much like the Rococo style. With the use of red **brick** instead of **stone**, and with contrasting white **wood columns** and white molding with black framing around the windows, the home is much more humble in its overall appearance. Thomas Jefferson can be credited with combining various elements of European architecture into a style that came to be uniquely North American.

JENNEY, WILLIAM LE BARON (1832–1907). *See* SKYSCRAPER.

JOHNSON, PHILIP (1906–2005). One of the most influential architects of the 20th century in the United States, Philip Johnson is known for developing his scholarly interests in aesthetics and architectural history into a monumental, modern architectural idiom. After traveling to Germany to study the work of modern European architects such as **Walter Gropius** and **Ludwig Mies van der Rohe**, Johnson returned to the United States in 1930 and went on to establish the Department of Architecture and Design at the Museum of Modern Art in New York City. In 1932, Johnson, together with the architectural historian Henry Russell Hitchcock, organized an exhibition of **International style** architecture at the Museum of Modern Art in New York, which helped to establish not only the term "International style" but also the criteria for this new modernism. By focusing on the formal aspects of these modern European buildings, which included a focus on functionality and a lack of applied decoration, Johnson and Hitchcock helped to make this spare modernism popular in the United States.

Johnson was deeply influenced by Mies's focus on rich materials, as seen in Mies's Barcelona Pavilion from 1929, and from that connection Johnson went on to experiment with the use of **glass** in his buildings, as seen in his famous private residence called the "Glass House," built with his associate Richard Foster in New Canaan, Connecticut, in 1949. Here Johnson was inspired by sketches of glass houses made by Mies van der Rohe, as well as Mies's Farnsworth House, built in Plano, Illinois, in 1946. Johnson sought to take these plans a step further by constructing an almost completely transparent home, built as a cube of glass with the most minimal support system and with internal partitions that loosely divide the living quarters and enclose only the bathroom. Set into a lush, country landscape, the home's privacy is ensured by its isolated setting rather than its walls. In 1959, Mies van der Rohe and Johnson built one of the earliest International style **skyscrapers**, the 39-story Seagram Building in New York City. This sleek bronze and tinted-glass office building on Park Avenue established a new corporate identity widely copied across the United States that was both discreet and elegant.

While Johnson's early work conformed to the International style, his later work is characterized by a reintroduction of historical references and symbolism, which became the hallmark of **Post-Modernism**. In 1968, Johnson formed a partnership with the American architect John Burgee, and the joining of Johnson's aesthetic sensibilities with Burgee's business skills resulted in a very prolific career for both that shifted the majority of Johnson's commissions from smaller works to more monumental corporate construction. Together they sought to infuse modern architecture with a greater symbolic, aesthetic, and visual variety by the inclusion of classical references, a new ornamentation, and a firmer integration with the surrounding environment. Their most famous building is the AT&T Corporate Headquarters, built in New York City in 1978–1983. This skyscraper is the first building to break away from the modern glass towers that dominated urban skylines across the United States; instead, Johnson's skyscraper is covered with an elegant granite veneer and features a tall central classical **arch** that rises through several stories, flanked by the **columns** of a colossal ground-floor portico. Thirty-six rows of tall windows mask the 80-story building, giving the illusion of a more human-scaled height. The most famous feature of the building, however, is the roofline, which is in the shape of a Chippendale highboy. Although many people did not initially appreciate Johnson's humorous connection between a "highboy" and a "highrise," the Seagram Building has since become an icon of Post-Modern aesthetics and has served to bring architecture down from its lofty, intellectual premise to a more popular vernacular language. In 1979, Philip Johnson was the first architect to win the newly established Pritzker Architecture Prize.

The so-called Lipstick Building, a skyscraper office building constructed by Johnson and Burgee in New York City in 1986, is an equally expressive commercial building. The structure received its unusual elliptical shape due to the developer's requirement to create a unique structure that would upstage its surroundings and overcome its undesirable Manhattan site. Johnson remarked that in this building, all offices could be considered "corner" offices, and in fact, this building housed the architectural firm of Johnson/Burgee until its gradual dissolution began in 1991. The Comerica Building, at One Detroit Center, was built in 1991–1993 by Burgee in consultation with Johnson, and reflects historical references consistent with Post-Modernism. This skyscraper stands out in the Detroit skyline because of its Flemish Renaissance–inspired stepped roofline and Neo-**Gothic** spires. Covered in granite, its sleek modernist façade typifies the new commercial architecture built in many American cities during the 1980s and 1990s, which was meant to create a unique silhouette rather than a uniform design. Highly influential in the development of 20th-century architecture, Philip Johnson helped to adapt the International style from its European origins into a widely popular American style, and then to point this modernist style into new, more diverse directions.

JONES, E. FAY (1921–2004). *See* GREEN ARCHITECTURE.

JONES, INIGO (1573–1652). Inigo Jones was the first architect in England to work consistently in the classical style adapted from **Ancient Roman** sources and seen in the **Renaissance** work of **Andrea Palladio**, whom Jones had studied while traveling in the Veneto. Jones is considered the leading proponent of Palladian architectural classicism during the **Baroque** age, for it was through a careful study of Palladio's Renaissance treatise *I quattro libri dell'architettura*, first published in 1570 and widely available in England by the 1600s, that Jones defined his own classical style. Jones's own copy of Palladio's treatise, filled with his own notes, is preserved today. Jones can also be credited with leading the shift away from Mannerism and toward a "purer" form of classicism that also drew upon the ideas of **Leon Battista Alberti, Donato Bramante, Sebastiano Serlio**, and Vincenzo Scamozzi in Italy.

England during this time was largely influenced by Italian culture, as can be seen in the writings of Shakespeare and the establishment in the next century of the English tourist industry that focused on Italy. Both James I of Scotland, who began his rule in Britain in 1603, and his son, Charles I, were avid patrons of art and literature. Despite this support, however, clashes between Protestant and Catholic powers led to instability during this century, and that is why most painters and sculptors were foreign-born artists invited to the Stuart court. The native Jones, however, sought to not only develop the ornate Jacobean architecture in England toward a simpler version of classicism, but he also injected this new classical Baroque style with a more theoretical framework, thereby helping to ennoble both historical construction and the profession of architecture in England. Jones was already an active member of the court, working on stage sets for the theater and temporary scenery for dramatic courtly entertainments called *masques*. His exposure to Palladio's work in Italy occurred when he was an artistic advisor for such wealthy collectors as

Lord Arundel. Upon his return from Italy in 1615 Jones was appointed Royal Surveyor of the Works, in charge of all royal architectural commissions for the Stuart court.

In 1619, Inigo Jones was commissioned by James I to rebuild an early **Tudor style** house that had burned to the ground. This new structure, the Banqueting House at Whitehall Palace in London, became the center of English courtly society. The **stone** façade of the Banqueting House is built in two stories of superimposed **columns** of the Ionic and then the Corinthian order, all of which rest on a basement story that acts to elevate the main floors of the building. Each bay of the seven-bay front reveals windows capped by alternating round and triangular pediments, while the second-story windows are rectangular. The corners of the façade are emphasized with paired pilasters rather than columns, to bring a visual conclusion to the building. Inside, the large hall is in the form of a double cube (110 feet by 55 feet by 55 feet), which is in accordance with Palladio's studies of proportion. This large, unencumbered interior was used mainly for banquets and masques, where spectators could gather in the balcony area above the large hall. Often, a temporary stage was built at one end of the room and musicians might be seated in the balcony above. In 1635, Peter Paul Rubens was commissioned to complete a large canvas painting of the apotheosis of James I, which was installed in the ceiling of the room. This building, with its painting, performance, and architecture, best summarizes the artistic interests of the Stuart court in Baroque England.

– K –

KAHN, LOUIS (1901–1974). Louis Kahn is best known for infusing a subtle poetic grace to modern architecture. Using mainly **concrete**, he provided a gentle rhythm to his designs, and that practice made him a famous architect of museums, where the gallery space itself came to be viewed as a work of art. Born in Estonia, Kahn settled in Philadelphia and taught at the University of Pennsylvania and Yale University, training some of the most important architects of the following generation, including Renzo Piano, Norman Foster, and **Tadao Ando**. His first public commission of importance was the Yale

University Art Gallery, built in New Haven, Connecticut, in the 1950s, and his most famous building is the Kimbell Art Museum, constructed in Fort Worth, Texas, from 1967 to 1972. This small museum features a parallel row of barrel vaults that enclose the main gallery space and provide a gentle, undulating rhythm to the exterior. Using post-tensioned reinforced concrete, Kahn makes the otherwise heavy material appear weightless. Inside the building, rectangular and square gallery spaces reveal an irregular floor plan that continues the idea of spatial rhythmic variety. This type of museum interior requires an active rather than passive participation by the visitor, who moves from small to large exhibition spaces that flow through the building. Known as an architectural philosopher, Louis Kahn infused his modern buildings with a subtle and enduring elegance. *See also* DECONSTRUCTIVISM; HIGH-TECH ARCHITECTURE; POST-MODERN ARCHITECTURE.

KATSURA PALACE, KYOTO. The tea ceremony is perhaps the most famous **Japanese** tradition and consists of a small group of people who come together not simply for a tea service but also for a highly ritualized modest discourse. Tearooms are typically made of **wood** or bamboo posts, with mud walls, paper-covered windows, and a floor covered with mats of woven straw called tatami. Diffused light enters through the thin paper window coverings, revealing a clear spatial arrangement of the interior, which flows in asymmetrically arranged square or rectangular rooms. A painted scroll or flower arrangement might be the subject of muted discussion. These structures are integrated with their natural surroundings, revealing a rustic simplicity and picturesque setting that characterizes the Katsura Palace. The Katsura Palace was constructed in the wooded perimeter of Kyoto in 1620 by the famous tea ceremony master and architect Kobori Enshu. At this time, the *shoin* house style was prevalent. Domestic *shoin* architecture first appeared in the late 14th century during the Muromachi Period (1333–1567), but was anticipated by the elegant simplicity of the highly cultivated Zen gardens developed to complement the more meditative form of Buddhism, called Zen Buddhism, that appeared in Japan in the late 12th century. These gardens, often made of gravel meticulously raked to accentuate several carefully selected large rocks or artistically pruned trees, provided the proper meditative surroundings for a variety of religious structures. The term *shoin*, at that time, referred specifically to a writing alcove or desk, and *shoin* architecture is characterized by an intimate display of rooms organized around the study or writing hall, which could also be used to entertain guests.

Shoin buildings are designed as simple rectangular structures defined by square or rectangular bay units with a timber framework and timber bay divisions that incorporate the tearoom aesthetic into a livable arrangement of verandas, alcoves, and open rooms. The rooms could be enclosed by decorated sliding doors called *fusuma*, while translucent rice paper made into screens called shoji could further organize the interior space. Tatami mats covered the floors, and the wooden ceiling was divided into squares. The measurement of traditional Japanese architecture is based on the standard shape of the tatami mat as a module, so a room would be called, for example, an eight-tatami room. What instigated this new architectural style was the increased desire among the military aristocracy, called the samurai, to emulate the elegant courtly culture of previous generations. They were the cultivated nobility who rejected the urban palaces and ornate architectural decoration for a more meditative, reductive approach to design.

Shoin buildings appeared in the subsequent Momoyama Period (1568–1603) in the form of upper-class homes that incorporated the elegant simplicity of the tearoom into their designs. The Katsura *rikyu*, or separate palace, is perhaps the best example of this type of secular architecture, and was constructed as a series of rooms connected by covered walkways that harmonize with the surrounding woods. The rambling design of the house and the verandas constructed at the gable ends of the building blocks provided ample opportunity to enjoy nature. Made of a light timber frame and a triangular truss in the tiled, hipped roof, the walls do not need pillars for support. The wood frame is plain, unpainted, or stained, and sometimes the bark is even left on parts of the timber.

The building is made up of three parts. The *Ko-shoin*, which is the more ornate *shoin*-style alcove, faces east at the front of the complex and is designed to accommodate two guest rooms, a warming room, and a small room for light snacks. The second section of the palace, located in the center of the block, is called the *Chu-shoin* and is designed in the more intimate *sukiya* style of farm cottages made elegant through the tea ceremony. This section contains the *tokonoma* alcove, where a single object of art or nature would be displayed for contemplation during the traditional tea ceremony. The *Chu-shoin* connects to the third alcove, called the *Shin-goten*, by a covered walkway that has storage space for musical instruments and a smaller tearoom for female guests. This too reveals the *sukiya* style, with its more rambling domestic layout. The *Shin-goten* is the rectangular rear alcove, which faces west and contains a series of small bedrooms and washrooms. To the north side of these private quarters is a series of servants' quarters. Verandas were built outside the building beneath the overhanging roof gables. Sliding doors and rice paper walls provide a smooth link between interior and exterior. A stone path leads to the entrance and toward the gardens that surround the structure. Although in some ways Chinese culture informed the architectural styles that developed in Japan, this complex certainly contrasts sharply with such rigidly symmetrical and axially directed architectural complexes as the **Forbidden City in Beijing**, where the buildings, elevated on a podium, were constructed with pillars, brackets, and highly ornate architectural sculpture.

KEYSER, HENDRICK DE (1565–1621). *See* CAMPEN, JACOB VAN.

KEYSTONE. *See* ARCH.

KHAN, FAZLUR RAHMAN (1929–1982). *See* SKIDMORE, OWINGS & MERRILL.

KOOLHAUS, REM (1944–). *See* DECONSTRUCTIVISM.

– L –

LABROUSTE, HENRI (1801–1875). *See* CAST IRON.

LATROBE, BENJAMIN HENRY (1764–1820). Benjamin Henry Latrobe, born to a prominent family in England, traveled widely and was highly educated, speaking over five languages. After being wounded while fighting in the Prussian army, he returned to London; beginning in 1790 he worked as the Surveyor of Public Offices. The premature death of his wife and the loss of his children's and wife's money to scheming relatives caused Latrobe to move to the United States in 1796. There he set up his architectural practice first in Virginia and then in Philadelphia, where his mother's family originated. In Philadelphia, Latrobe's most important early commission was for construction of the Bank of Pennsylvania, completed in 1801 and demolished in 1870. This building is credited with being the first Greek Revival style structure in the United States.

In 1803, Latrobe was hired as the Surveyor of Public Buildings of the United States and began to work in Washington, D.C., most notably on the **United States Capitol**, which he began that same year and modified throughout his life. Although this building assured Latrobe's enduring fame, he went on to complete several other important **Neo-Classical** buildings in the area, including the monumental Basilica of the National Shrine of the Blessed Virgin Mary, Baltimore, Maryland (1806–1821), which was the first Catholic cathedral in the United States; he also experimented with the **Gothic Revival** style.

LE VAU, LOUIS (1612–1670). *See* VERSAILLES PALACE, FRANCE.

LEDOUX, CLAUDE-NICOLAS (1736–1806). *See* NEO-CLASSICAL ARCHITECTURE.

LESCOT, PIERRE (c. 1515–1578). *See* LOUVRE, PARIS.

LIBESKIND, DANIEL (1946–). *See* DECONSTRUCTIVISM; WORLD TRADE CENTER, NEW YORK.

LISSITZKY, EL (1890–1941). *See* CONSTRUCTIVIST ARCHITECTURE.

LOOS, ADOLF (1870–1933). In 1913, Adolf Loos, one of the leading practitioners of modern, utilitarian architecture in Austria, wrote an

essay titled *Ornament and Crime* in reaction to the perceived aristocratic opulence of the popular **Art Nouveau**, or *Sezessionstil*, as it
was called in Vienna. In this text he argues that architectural ornament is a sign of degeneration and that "pure" form reveals an evolv-
ing, more sophisticated culture. Having studied in Dresden, the seat
of the **Rococo** style prior to its destruction in World War II, Loos was
no doubt strengthened in his anti-ornamental, utilitarian emphasis by
Dresden's highly ornate artistic culture.

One of Loos's earliest buildings is his Goldman and Salatsch
Building in Vienna (1909–1911). This commercial structure was constructed in a trapezoidal shape on a prominent curved intersection
across the street from the Imperial Palace in Vienna; its sparer façade,
despite the use of beautiful *cipollino* **marble** at the ground level, created a furor, as some critics considered Loos's building an insult to
what they considered "proper" architectural decorum. The four-story
structure, with a simple white exterior at the upper two levels and rectangular windows without additional articulation along the roofline,
was called "the building without eyebrows," yet its solid appearance
and subtle articulation became the trademark of Loos's style.

Loos's new architectural aesthetic can be seen best in his Steiner
House in Vienna, built in 1910. The reinforced **concrete** building is
covered with white stucco. Unadorned rectangular windows puncture
the exterior in an irregularly spaced pattern that suits the needs of the
interior space. No cornice caps the roofline, but instead a curved roof
with no overhang slants down for the run-off of rain and snow. This
gentle curve offers the one organic shape to an otherwise highly geometric building that in many ways anticipates the **International style**
of modernism first seen in Europe in the next decade. From dining
nooks to fireplace seating, Loos created inside the Steiner House
small, intimate spaces for different types of social interactions.

Then, in the Parisian house built for Tristan Tzara in 1926, Loos
designed an even more sophisticated space, to include a sequence of
rooms that adjoined to create a unique flow of space practically
suited to its small urban lot. On the exterior, Loos designed a rich
five-story façade with a two-story **stone** base topped by slightly textured stucco. At the ground level, two entrances angle inward to create a small portico with a balcony above. Offset windows in the upper three stories provide a geometric rhythm to the otherwise

unadorned exterior. The exterior of the Tzara house, with its window registers articulated at diverse heights, reflects the varied heights of the interior rooms. These height differentials reflect Loos's ideas on space, which he called the *raumplan*. *Raumplan* involves the conception of space in cubic shapes rather than in a two-dimensional plan. That is, instead of floor plans or sections, Loos conceived of his buildings as fully three-dimensional from the onset rather than creating a plan on paper that resulted, by default, in a three-dimensional conclusion.

Loos's Moller House, built in Vienna in 1927, provides a further elaboration on this idea. Inside the white, modernist exterior, the visitor is met by a series of rooms accessed at different levels with stairs that change directions and provide for elevated niches and connecting hallways. Beautiful **wood** paneling and built-in shelves and furnishings provide warmth to the otherwise spare interior. Loos's most ornate home, the Villa Müller, built in Prague in 1928–1930, features a cube-shaped exterior that recalls the International style, but with a material richness to the interior increasingly favored by his upperclass clientele. Travertine, colored tiles, rich green Italian marble, mahogany, and satinwood paneling appear on the interior. Loos wanted to reveal the true beauty of the materials he used, as well as their geometric shapes and cubic mass. In this regard, his style can be seen as classical in its enduring and timeless appeal.

LOUVRE, PARIS. The Louvre was initially a fortified **castle** built during the reign of Philip Augustus, king of France from 1180 until his death in 1223. He governed his territory from the Île de la Cité in the center of Paris and therefore located the fortification across from the island on the banks of the Seine River. Documents from 1198 first mention its name as the "Louvre," and in the 1300s, Charles V remodeled some of its wings into a more aristocratic setting. The exterior of the original Louvre Palace can be seen in the background of the October page of the beautifully illustrated manuscript titled *Les Très Riches Heures du Duc de Berry*, commissioned by the Duke of Berry and completed around 1410 by the Limbourg brothers. On this page appears a tall, square **stone** castle with towers and turrets in each of the corners, towers flanking a central doorway, and small windows in the upper registers. A model of this original structure can be found in the Louvre Museum today, and in the basement, visitors can see some of the original foundation walls of the castle.

During the **Renaissance**, King François I began an extensive renovation of the castle, demolishing the older structure completely. This work was begun in the 1530s and continued until the death of François in 1547 and the death of his son Henri II in 1559. François I was inspired by the emerging Renaissance style found in his court at **Fontainebleau** and at other châteaux along the Loire Valley and therefore hired Pierre Lescot to build a new wing to the Louvre in this new classical style. Lescot's west wing of the Cour Carrée, in the square court of the Palais du Louvre, was begun in 1546 and reveals the use of a classical symmetry and balance, with sculptural details in the **Mannerist** style designed by the French sculptor Jean Goujon. Because the turrets were replaced by round **arches** and because windows lined all three registers of the courtyard façade, the palace no longer had any of its original fortified appearance. Fluted classical pilasters flank each window. The ground-floor windows are crowned by an arch, and the second- and third-story windows are instead capped by rounded and triangular pediments. Although an urban palace, the gardens of the Louvre were very important to its initial design. The main living quarters on the *piano nobile*, or second floor, looked out over formal gardens in the area called the Tuileries garden.

Henri IV (ruled 1589–1610) continued the construction of the Louvre Palace along the Seine River with the Grande Galérie, a quarter-mile-long wing that was the longest freestanding structure in the world at the time. Louis XIII (ruled 1610–1643) continued the construction of the Denon wing and built the opposing Richelieu wing. The palace was then a U-shaped structure with a *cour d'honneur*, or Court of Honor, which formed the official entrance via a three-sided courtyard that led visitors to the central wing. In the latter 1600s, the palace was again the focus of a large-scale renovation, this time toward the more large-scale, theatrical **Baroque** style. Accordingly, in 1664, King Louis XIV invited the famous Italian architect **Gian Lorenzo Bernini** to spend a year in France to provide advice on the renovation of the palace. Due perhaps to nationalistic concerns, the French architect Claude Perrault was ultimately hired for these renovations, which he completed between 1665 and 1680. It was Perrault who introduced a classical balustrade along the roofline of parts of the palace, in keeping with the ideals of the Roman architect **Vitruvius**.

The palace served as the administrative seat of the monarchy until 1682, when Louis XIV moved his entire court to **Versailles Palace**, but the Louvre continued to be used and was opened as a museum in 1793. New additions continued to be added through the mid-19th century by Napoleon III, who created a Neo-Baroque wing. A pencil sketch made around 1899 by Louis-Ernest Lheureux, now located in the Musée d'Orsay, reveals an unrealized project for the addition of a Neo-Baroque pyramid at the entrance courtyard to commemorate the centennial of the French Revolution. In 1989, however, **I. M. Pei** was commissioned to build an entrance that could accommodate large crowds of visitors. He designed it as a metal and glass pyramid with entry into a broad subterranean foyer for the museum. The pyramid is 70 feet tall and contains about 673 panes of **glass** fitted into **steel** framing. (Rumors that 666 panes of glass were used for the pyramid caused a flurry of satanic legends and have been refuted.) The Louvre continues to function as one of the most important museums in the world, with additional renovations planned for the future.

– M –

MACHU PICCHU, PERU. The Inca ceremonial center of Machu Picchu, located in the Urubamba Valley 44 miles northwest of the Inca capital of Cuzco, Peru, is a stunning example of large-scale mountain-top **stone** construction. Machu Picchu, meaning "old peak" in the native Quechua language, was probably selected for its spiritual and cosmological significance and functioned both as a ceremonial center and a royal court. Constructed around 1450 but abandoned under unknown circumstances in 1530, it is likely that the ninth Inca emperor, Pachacuti, lived at Machu Picchu, from which he controlled the surrounding area. Although the Spanish *conquistadores* never found Machu Picchu, the collapse of the Inca Empire in Cuzco certainly contributed to the demise of Machu Picchu. Some scholars have wondered why this "hidden" mountain retreat was not used as an Inca stronghold against the Spanish, while other historians have argued that the sacred significance of Machu Picchu may have prevented it from being used as a citadel, where the Spanish could have destroyed the last remaining altar dedicated to the sun god Inti. Scholars have also long been puzzled by the seeming remoteness of Machu Picchu, located on a mountain ledge 2,430 meters above sea level with a drop-off of 600 meters down to the Urubamba River; perhaps the answer is that the complex was a secret stronghold for the Inca royal family.

On the other hand, future excavations might reveal that Machu Picchu was in fact located at the center of a busy network of Inca settlements in the valley and mountains along the Urubamba River. The nearby mountain peak of Huayna Picchu stands over Machu Picchu and can be visited via a narrow Inca path that runs along a ledge to its top. Furthermore, visible evidence of Pre-Columbian stone villages and terraced mountain ledges dot the countryside around Machu Picchu. Most of these have not yet been studied, but in 1981 a 325-square-kilometer area around Machu Picchu received a national protected status so that further archaeological work can be completed at some point. Perhaps in the future this most splendid example of Inca construction will be seen as the rural branch of Inca rule, the full administrative branch of which was located in the more urban setting of nearby Cuzco. A vast network of paths links these mountainous communities together with one long mountain road running from Cuzco directly to Machu Picchu.

Machu Picchu consists of 140 granite structures built in a concise five-square-mile urban plan that also includes open plazas and paved streets. The center is divided into three areas: a sacred area, an area of popular housing, and a section of more elaborate homes. The sacred area consists of an open square with a stone formation called the *intihuatana* which, with the *Temple of the Sun* and the *Room of the Three Windows*, functions as an astrological clock dedicated to the sun god Inti. *Intihuatana* can be translated as the "hitching post of the sun"; it is oriented to reveal the spring and fall equinox. The *intihuatana* at Machu Picchu is the last one remaining, as all others were destroyed by the Spanish in their attempt to introduce Christianity in South America. The popular housing zone consists of simple thatched dwellings and storage buildings, while the royal area, located over a slope, consists of houses decorated with reddish walls, trapezoid-shaped rooms, gables, and thatched roofs. Human remains also suggest the location of a nearby mausoleum. The stone buildings are all constructed with a superior dry stone wall technique called *ashlar*, in which massive stones are cut to fit perfectly together without mortar. Irregularly shaped rocks fit at perfect junctions, and the walls lean slightly inward, characteristic of Inca construction. Despite the sometimes severe earthquakes and the pillaging of Inca stones to build Spanish churches in Cuzco, Inca wall junctions remain perfectly tight, with no spaces or cracks or collapse. Without the wheel or the horse, the Inca used manpower and llamas to drag these large rocks up the mountains. Water fountains, water channels, and drains bring rainwater from a holy spring, and llamas roam freely around the area.

Stepped terraces surround the complex, often cut into the mountainsides with precipitous, vertigo-inducing drop-offs. On these terraces, the Inca cultivated different types of potatoes that could be preserved year-round. They also grew corn and ate llama meat that was dried and stored. Food storage areas were located across the Inca Empire, and some scholars argue that it was their success with food production and storage that allowed the Inca to carve out such a large empire, one that rivaled the Ancient Roman Empire in size. The *quipu*, a series of ropes tied in knots at different points, much like an abacus, was probably used as an accounting method to document food storage, tributes paid to the empire, and other practical governmental matters, but it is possible that the *quipu* (or *khipus*) functioned as more than an accounting method. Perhaps it was also used toward the end of the Inca Empire to transmit private communication at a time when the Spanish were asserting control over their world.

In the end, approximately 80 percent of the Inca died of European diseases, and Cuzco fell to the Spanish, along with the nearby Inca limestone-walled complex called Sacsayhuaman and the town of Ollantaytambo south of Cuzco, where the Inca retreated from the Spanish in Cuzco. The Inca community of Vitcos was the last Inca refuge, and the site of the final resistance against the Spanish. This was the settlement that Hiram Bingham had set out to find in 1911 when he came across Machu Picchu. Bingham did not discover Machu Picchu, for locals will confirm that it was never lost, but his best-selling book brought the ceremonial complex into popular knowledge. The location of the Machu Picchu artifacts at Yale University is currently under dispute in that the university has refused to honor the Peruvian government's request to have the objects returned to their homeland. *See also* MESOAMERICAN ARCHITECTURE.

MACKINTOSH, CHARLES RENNIE (1868–1928). One of the leaders of the **Arts and Crafts** Movement, Charles Rennie Mackintosh was instrumental in introducing modernism into Scotland. After attending the Glasgow School of Art in the 1880s, Mackintosh won a scholarship in 1890 to travel to Italy. His subsequent early work, such as the Glasgow Herald Building from 1893 to 1895, reveals a modernist approach to historical architecture. This **brick** building was designed by Mackintosh while working at the firm Honeyman and Keppie; its upper register, including the tower and decorative crenellations, recalls early Italian **Renaissance** palaces in Florence and Siena, while its lower register is sparer and conforms to the newer industrial designs of early modern architecture.

Mackintosh had remained friends with three other students from the time of his enrollment at the School of Art—Herbert McNair and the sisters Margaret and Frances Macdonald—and the four exhibited their graphic arts, furniture, and decorative arts in London, Turin, and Vienna. Through this collaborative work and his introduction to the Viennese Secession, Mackintosh developed his own version of the related Arts and Crafts style. Mackintosh's most important commission, the Glasgow School of Art, was begun in 1897 and reveals his mature style. This building was constructed in two phases. Initially, the center and east wing were built, and the west wing was added from 1907 to 1909. The rich **stone** façade reveals large studio windows and an offset entrance that is formally related to the east wing of the building. The entrance is arrived at via a gently curved stair topped by an iron bar that forms a slight **arch**, while the balcony and its paired windows found above the main entrance marks the location of the principal's office. The library was built in the west wing and features a two-story interior made of rich, dark **wood** illuminated by the second-story oriel windows. Creating a play between spare geometric designs and a lightly handed curved decoration, Mackintosh brilliantly combines the look of industrial uniformity with a handcrafted design to create one of the most beautiful library interiors in architectural history. His design for Hill House in Helensburgh, Scotland, in 1902, also combined his interests in architecture and interior design into an elegantly restrained domestic structure. That same year, Mackintosh designed the interiors for the International Exhibition of Modern Decorative Art in Turin, and through the next decade he remained busy in Glasgow with designing a series of tearooms. In 1915, Mackintosh left Glasgow to establish an architectural firm in London, but had little success there aside from various commissions for textile designs and furnishings. He moved to southern France in 1923 to focus the rest of his career on watercolor painting.

MADERNO, CARLO (1556–1629). *See* SAINT PETER'S CHURCH, ROME.

MAKI, FUMIHIKO (1928–). *See* WORLD TRADE CENTER, NEW YORK.

MANNERISM. Although the style of Mannerist architecture is relatively easy to recognize, scholars differ in their explanations of its origins and motivations. Mannerist architecture first appeared in Italy in the 1520s. It is sometimes thought to have developed out of the chaos that ensued in Rome after the city was pillaged in 1527 by members of the army of Charles V, the Holy Roman Emperor, who maintained an uneasy alliance with the papacy at the time. This latter-day sack of Rome, as it came to be called, created such a dramatic political, social, and economic disjuncture that, although the city recovered relatively quickly, its artistic culture was forever changed. In addition, because Raphael, the quintessential **Renaissance** artist, had died in 1520, his large workshop of painters and architects had dispersed across Italy, free to develop their own variations on the Renaissance style. Because Mannerism reveals a marked contrast to the rigid formality of the **Vitruvian** principles so carefully followed in Renaissance architecture, many scholars consider Mannerism to be a reaction against the Renaissance. More recently, however, Mannerism is simply seen as a natural expansion of Renaissance principles to encompass a broader definition of classicism. The term comes from the Italian *maniera*, which in turn comes from the word for "hand," or *mano*, in Italian. Thus, Mannerism has been interpreted as a highly "stylized" favoring of technical virtuosity. This definition is consistent with qualities found even before 1520 in court patronage in Florence and Rome, where paintings reveal an aristocratic elegance and grace in addition to the Renaissance ideal of *riposo*, or restraint.

In architecture, **Michelangelo Buonarroti** demonstrated an early example of Mannerist style in his Laurentian Library vestibule, built beginning in 1524 for the Medici family in the **Monastery** of San Lorenzo in Florence. The vestibule "breaks" several Vitruvian design principles concerning the use of **columns**, volutes, and niches. Here, Michelangelo crowds the wall with a classical articulation done in *pietra serena*, or dark **stone**. Paired columns sink into the wall, defying their use as a support system, and niches and corners remain empty while volutes are denied their supportive function. This same questioning of classical Vitruvian principles is carried over in Michelangelo's New Sacristy, built for the side of San Lorenzo to house the funerary monuments of Giuliano and Lorenzo de Medici. In this chapel, crowded walls ask more questions than resolve functional issues.

Another example of Mannerist architecture can be seen in the Palazzo del Tè in Mantua, begun in 1527 by Giulio Romano for Duke Federigo Gonzaga. Gonzaga hired Romano, who had just fled Rome that same year, to expand his hunting lodge into a suburban palace to entertain guests. Thus, the palace has horse stables, gardens, pools, and large rooms decorated with frescoes that feature playful, mythological narratives. Its Mannerist architecture is traditionally considered to be an equally playful yet very erudite commentary on Renaissance architectural rules, which Duke Gonzaga and his aristocratic guests would find enjoyment in critiquing. The one-story façade of the palace is designed with heavily rusticated stone and windows separated from each other by unequally spaced bays. It lacks symmetry and rationality—two main principles of Vitruvian aesthetics. The first courtyard also reveals a series of similar design elements. The bays are irregularly spaced and windows and niches are both blind. Engaged columns with Doric capitals do not line up with the triglyphs and metopes that appear in the frieze above. Instead, several of the metopes are punctured by attic windows, while some of the triglyphs appear to slip downward, and are therefore called slipping triglyphs.

Some of these same features appear in the Roman Palazzo Massimi alle Colonne, built in the 1530s by Baldassare Peruzzi on the site of the family palace, which had been destroyed during the sack of Rome. Peruzzi designed two adjoining palaces for the Massimi brothers on the irregularly shaped plot of land and joined the palaces with one curved façade that has a columned portico. Baldassare Peruzzi had previously worked in the shop of Raphael, where he was known for his perspective studies and fresco technique. He fled to his native Siena right after the sack of Rome but returned later that year to help with the reconstruction of the city. The Mannerist style was ultimately short-lived, but the shift in focus from Vitruvian classicism to more varied sources found further expression in the following **Baroque** age.

MANSART, FRANÇOIS (1598–1666). *See* VERSAILLES PALACE, FRANCE.

MARBLE. The **Ancient Roman** Emperor Augustus reportedly stated, "I found a city of **brick** and left it a city of marble." This sentiment echoes the love of marble found across the **Ancient Greek** and Roman empires during their high points. The term *marmaros*, or "shining stone," is Greek in origin, and certainly Ancient Greece is known for its white marble sculptures. A greater variety of marble colors and types became available after the Roman conquest of the Mediterranean, and the high cost of such marbles, logistically difficult to quarry and transport such great distances, bestowed an elevated level of prestige on the patron. Marble is a metamorphic rock made mostly of limestone, and its high polish is what makes it distinct from other **stones**. While white marble came from the famous quarry at Carrara in Italy, black, red, and green marbles came from the area around Greece, purple marbles were from Turkey and Egypt, and yellow marble was from Tunisia. Marble was increasingly used on architectural construction; thin slabs were hung onto brick walls while thicker slabs were used for floors. The use of marble as a symbol of wealth and high culture can be found in the subsequent **Renaissance**, **Baroque**, and **Neo-Classical** eras, and indeed, it has even continued into the 21st century.

The most famous marble structures from Ancient Greece are found on the **Acropolis** in Athens. The Acropolis, rebuilt with the large amounts of money the Athenians acquired after their defeat of the

Persians, was a powerful symbol of Athenian domination in the Greek Empire. At the Acropolis, built during the rule of Pericles in the mid-400s BC, architects and sculptors had access to unprecedented amounts of money, and the use of marble for the entire construction of these buildings stood as a powerful propagandistic tool for the Athenians. Prior to the construction of this complex, marble was used primarily for architectural sculpture, but in the grandest of monuments, such as the Parthenon, marble was used as the main structural component. The rectangular base of the Parthenon is a limestone platform made from large blocks of stone, which were carved out in rough blocks and then dressed. Greek marble came from either Mount Pentelus in Attica or a few islands such as Paros. The **columns**, triangular pediments, and architectural sculpture are all made of marble. Most of these sculptures, called the "Elgin Marbles," are now located in the British Museum in London, but negotiations to return them to their homeland continue.

The Romans were the first to cut marble into thinner slabs, called *opus sectile*, which could be used to cover **concrete** walls in a type of veneer. The use of a thinner marble reduced its cost and allowed the Romans to cover many more buildings in this stone than the Greeks could cover with solid blocks of marble. In Rome, the use of marble became widespread, and over 50 different types and colors were available in the Empire. The **Pantheon**, built in Rome in AD 118–125, is one of the best-preserved buildings from antiquity. Constructed from concrete to support a massive, unencumbered **dome**, the interior walls and floor were then covered in different types of marble to make patterns of contrasting colors and shapes.

This use of colored marble to make beautiful designs was further developed through the Middle Ages, when marble began to be used to cover **Romanesque** church floors, doors, and liturgical objects with a mixture of mosaics set within a colored marble framework. A historical marble craftsman named Cosmas, who supposedly came to Rome from Byzantium, is thought to be the source of this style of marble flooring, which is called *Cosmati* work. The first church pavement done in this particular technique is considered to be the Abbey at Montecassino, which was rebuilt at the end of the 11th century under the patronage of the Abbot Desiderius, who brought marble workers from Constantinople. In this style, mosaics, made from small pieces of stone and colored **glass** set into a paste, alternate with strips of marble laid in contrasting colors to provide a rich overall design. The original Cosmati work at Montecassino does not exist today.

Marble inlay was increasingly used in the Italian Renaissance as well; it expanded from its primary use on church flooring and furnishings to domestic furniture and other decorative pieces. In the 1600s, the use of marble was widespread. A beautiful example of colored marble inlay is found on the **Taj Mahal in Agra**, India, built by Shah Jahan in the early 1600s as a memorial to his favorite wife, Mumtaz Mahal, who died in childbirth. This beautiful funerary monument is made from white marble, but upon closer inspection, one can see that black marble inlay forms verses from the Koran while sapphire from Sri Lanka, lapis lazuli from Afghanistan, turquoise from Tibet, jasper from India, and jade and crystal from China were also used to create a beautiful inlay design of the garden of paradise, at the same time providing visual confirmation of the far-reaching power of the Mughal Empire.

The subsequent use of marble in later architectural styles has often resulted from a similar desire to recall the grandeur of historical monuments as well as to refer to the wealth and authority of the current patrons. **Richard Morris Hunt**, a **Beaux-Arts** architect who worked for wealthy families in the United States at the end of the 19th century, sought to introduce the great architecture of Renaissance and Baroque Europe in his monumental marble homes and civic and government buildings on the East Coast. For example, the "Marble House," built by Morris for William Kissam Vanderbilt in Newport, Rhode Island, in 1888–1892, was modeled on the Petit Trianon at **Versailles**, and this home was pivotal in the transformation of the seaside town of Newport from a small community of wooden cottages to a stone-lined resort for the wealthy.

MARI ARCHITECTURE. *See* ANCIENT NEAR EASTERN ARCHITECTURE.

MAYA ARCHITECTURE. *See* MESOAMERICAN ARCHITECTURE.

MCKIM, CHARLES FOLLEN (1847–1909). Charles McKim is one of the three architects of the famous firm McKim, Mead, and White, which did much to define monumental architecture at the turn of the century. Working mainly along the East Coast, the firm is credited with the construction of major government buildings, public libraries, and opulent homes in Providence and Newport, Rhode Island; Boston; and New York City. The firm was established by McKim in 1878 after he completed his studies at Harvard, at the École des Beaux-Arts in Paris, and then an apprenticeship in the shop of **Henry Hobson Richardson** in New York City. McKim was known as the idealist of the group. William Rutherford Mead, the oldest member of the firm, was considered the most pragmatic of the group; he met McKim while they were studying in Florence. During his training, Stanford White, the youngest of the group, also traveled widely, mainly around Paris. A social playboy, White's fame endured after he was murdered by his mistress's husband.

One of the first commissions completed by McKim, Mead, and White was the Boston Public Library, the first publicly supported municipal library in the country, built beginning in 1887. This white **stone** Renaissance Revival building dominates one entire side of Copley Square, right across from Trinity Church, which was erected in the 1870s by Henry Hobson Richardson. The Morgan Library, built in New York City in 1906 to house the collection of the wealthy industrialist J. P. Morgan, was also constructed in the Renaissance Revival style. The Rhode Island State Capitol, built in Providence from 1895 to 1903, is more overtly **Neo-Classical**, with its tall **dome** looming above the massive symmetrical building. Perhaps the most famous commission received by McKim, Mead, and White, however, was for Pennsylvania Station in New York City. Constructed in 1910, this massive building, truly a feat of engineering, was demolished in 1964. Built of **steel** vaults layered with stone **columns** and huge **glass** windows, this structure clearly demonstrated the ability of these architects to blend historicism with engineering to create an opulent American architectural style. *See also* BEAUX-ARTS ARCHITECTURE.

MEAD, WILLIAM RUTHERFORD (1846–1928). *See* MCKIM, CHARLES FOLLEN.

MEIER, RICHARD (1934–). *See* RATIONALISM.

MELNIKOV, KONSTANTIN STEPANOVICH (1890–1974). Konstantin Melnikov was the leading architect during the "New Economic Policy" of Vladimir Lenin after the Bolshevik Revolution in Russia. Melnikov was born into an impoverished family, but his father encouraged his artistic abilities and Melnikov was soon discovered by a wealthy engineer who paid for his entire education. Melnikov first studied painting after the 1917 Revolution, and in the 1920s he was encouraged to work in architecture, so he designed a series of modernist buildings that conformed to the new socialist ideals of the decade. Although Melnikov sought to distance himself from specific theoretical issues, his work is consistent with the Russian architectural avant-garde movement called **Constructivist architecture**, which focused on the creation of a new, modern machine for living. Melnikov's apartment buildings, parking garages, and workers' clubs were part of a larger building boom in Moscow that included modernist buildings constructed for all aspects of revolutionary education, public services, and recreation.

Melnikov's Soviet Pavilion at the World Exposition in Paris, from 1925, was his first work of international significance, and it most impressed people with its simple construction; it consisted of a **wood** building with a single-sloped roof easily assembled by a small number of workers in a short time. Throughout Melnikov's short-lived architectural career, the persistent rationing of building materials and heavy-handed bureaucratic oversight of architectural construction in Russia gave him the opportunity to create highly inventive solutions to traditional architecture, using alternate building materials and unorthodox structural components.

The workers' club was an entirely new building type, and Melnikov paved the way in defining this structure in a bold new dynamic style. His Rusakov Workers' Club, built in Moscow in 1927–1929, was located on a main road and designed with a fan-shaped triangular base upon which three cantilevered rectangles protrude out at slight angles at the upper story, separated by exterior glazing. On the interior, movable walls allow for a variety of different functions by creating larger or smaller auditorium configurations. The building, made from **concrete** and **glass**, is forcefully designed into strong cubical shapes that jut out at angles to symbolize the dynamic political situation in Moscow at the time. The back courtyard was made of **brick** to create a more intimate space in which to socialize. Melnikov's Kauchuk Factory Club, also built in Moscow from 1927 to 1929, is designed as a cylinder that boldly curves out into the surrounding space. The interior is formed into a large auditorium with a balcony level, while exterior stairs on the façade were created as a fire exit, in conformity with the new and highly innovative government-imposed architectural safety regulations. Although many Constructivist buildings are currently in danger of demolition, Melnikov's Svobada Factory Club is an exception in that it has recently been restored to its original red and white color. However, more preservation and restoration work is urgently needed in Moscow.

Melnikov explained that his architecture is like a tense muscle, based more on intuition rather than theory, and this is best seen in his own private house, constructed on Krivoarbatsky Lane in Moscow in 1927–1929. Melnikov designed his three-story home as two intersecting towers made of wood and brick, with a fanciful arrangement of rhomboid windows that give the effect of either a honeycomb or latticework. Melnikov is best known for his five workers' clubs in Moscow, built before his expulsion in 1937 from the architectural profession by the First Congress of Soviet Architects. Although he was initially embraced by this organization, Melnikov's desire to work as an individual ultimately led to his return to painting; he devoted the rest of his life to a successful career in portraiture.

MENDELSOHN, ERICH (1887–1953). *See* EXPRESSIONISM.

MESOAMERICAN ARCHITECTURE. Mesoamerican architecture refers to the structures of the various cultures that existed in modern-day Mexico and parts of Central America, including Honduras, Belize, Guatemala, and parts of Nicaragua. After the arrival of Hernán Cortés in November 1519, European influences began gradually and inextricably to alter the course of Mesoamerican history. Yet in Pre-Columbian Mesoamerica, many important cultures already existed: Olmec, Teotihuacan, Maya, and Aztec, together with their related civilizations and ancestors. Human existence in the Americas can be traced back more than 15,000 years, when Paleolithic peoples moved from North America through Mesoamerica, Central America, and into South America. Current scholars believe that these peoples entered the Americas via a land bridge along the Bering Strait. They cultivated squash, beans, potatoes, tomatoes, and corn, and they domesticated animals. Among these peoples is found the development not only of temporary shelters but also permanent architectural monuments that confirm the establishment of a hierarchical social structure and ritualized beliefs. Although Mesoamerican cultures developed in different ways, they were also closely linked by trade. For example, the Olmec peoples, who settled along the Gulf of Mexico, used jade and obsidian quarried in other parts of Mesoamerica. Through such contact, they developed similar religious beliefs, as seen in the ceremonial ball game and their creation of a mathematically sophisticated 365-day calendar. The architecture of these diverse communities also reflects a partially shared cultural background; what survives today reveals a series of monumental ceremonial centers with broad roads that led to intricately carved **stone** temples and massive stepped pyramids.

Based primarily on a study of the Maya, scholars have divided the history of this region into the Pre-Classic (1500 BC–AD 300), Classic (300–900), and Post-Classic (900–1500) periods. The Olmec peoples were the first culture to assert a surviving style of art and architecture during the Pre-Classic Period, when they established communities along the Gulf of Mexico by clearing the dense forestation for farmland and pastures, while constructing massive earth mounds used for political and religious purposes. Similar to the social structure first codified in Mesopotamia, these priest-kings probably had sole access to the sacred man-made mountains, while most people must have lived in **wood** and thatched dwellings clustered outside the ceremonial center.

The location, called San Lorenzo for its Spanish name, is the earliest known Olmec site, dating to about 1200–900 BC. La Venta rose to power around 900–400 BC, and both sites were abandoned around 400 BC for unknown reasons. While San Lorenzo displays the earliest evidence of a possible ball court, La Venta is known for its pyramidal earth mound that may have been stepped or tiered. The mound is oriented on a north-south axis and located at the south end of an open square. Stone-lined drainage ditches define the ceremonial center, suggesting that water may have been used in various religious rituals. Small carved jade figures, as well as larger basalt sculptures, have been excavated at La Venta. The jade carvings often feature a human head in the process of transformation into an animal, usually a jaguar, suggesting the shamanistic ritual of shape-shifting. The large basalt sculptures feature monumental heads, each different, which might represent the ruling elite. The strongly axial direction and design of Mesoamerican architecture refers to the three levels of the universe—the sky, the earth's surface, and the underground—linked together, much as in Buddhism, by a vertical line uniting the three. Further research on the Olmec culture suggests that the Olmec might have introduced writing to Mesoamerica, traditionally attributed to the Maya. They certainly played an important role in laying the foundation for the subsequent rise of the Teotihuacan and Maya civilizations.

Teotihuacan, located just outside modern-day Mexico City, became the first urban center in Mesoamerica, reaching a size of nine square miles at its high point (from AD 350 to 650) and a population of about 200,000 people, which made it the largest city in the world during its peak. This city was not only prosperous due to its thriving obsidian market, but farmers also cultivated the fertile land in the surrounding terraced hills. By the 750s, the ceremonial center burned, and Teotihuacan society declined, for reasons still unknown. However, because the later Aztecs maintained this center as the place where the gods created the sun and the moon, it was preserved until the 1500s as a sacred pilgrimage site and is therefore better preserved than many Mesoamerican monuments. Like the Olmec centers, Teotihuacan is designed in a strongly axial direction, with one broad north-south avenue flanked by a series of temples and pyramids, including the Pyramid of the Moon and the Pyramid of the Sun. Mesoamerican pyramids form an interesting comparison to the **Ancient Near Eastern** stepped *ziggurats*, such as the Nanna Ziggurat in Ur from the 2100s BC, and the **Ancient Egyptian** stepped pyramids, such as that of King Djoser from the 2600s BC. Similar in width to many of the largest Egyptian pyramids, those at Teotihuacan are shorter; they do not rise up into a point but lead up a flight of stairs that pauses at several platforms and finally arrives at a flat top with a temple. Due to its elevated height, the temple certainly would have been used to provide a closer connection between god and man.

Rather than assuming a specific typological influence from one region of the world to another, however, it is entirely possible that this type of monument appeared simultaneously across a variety of cultures simply in imitation of elevated natural shapes. The Pyramid of the Sun at Teotihuacan was built over a cave with a spring and is covered in a veneer of painted stucco over stone. Both this and the smaller Pyramid of the Moon are each surrounded by a flat, open square with a series of platforms that emulate on a smaller scale the form of the pyramids. At the far end of the center, the Temple of the Feathered Serpent features a slope-and-panel construction, in which the sloping base supports a panel that is intricately carved with geometrically squared and abstracted images of the feathered serpent. Increasing in size several times, the newer temple would each time completely encase the older version, probably to accommodate a larger population and to update the style and imagery found on the temple. This urban center also features a residential area, which is highly unusual in that housing in most cultures is built outside the ceremonial center. Here, the palaces of the elite reveal a stratified culture; the largest homes, some with as many as 45 rooms, are located closest to the center of the complex, while more modest homes are found farther away from the religious complex. All are one-story buildings, however, with rooms arranged around a series of courtyards and protected by tall walls. Another unusual aspect of these homes is that they feature the true fresco technique of wall painting, traditionally attributed to **Ancient Roman** or **Renaissance** societies. In this technique, paint is applied to stucco before it fully dries, so that the paint sinks into the plaster and creates a permanent bond, creating an extremely durable surface.

While these frescoes give us a better idea of Teotihuacan culture, it is the Maya civilization, located directly across Mesoamerica in the area of the Yucatan in modern-day Mexico, Guatemala, Belize, and Honduras, that has been the most thoroughly studied Mesoamerican culture to date. That is because this civilization existed during the arrival of the Spanish colonizers in the early 1500s. Because the Maya, like the Inca of South America, built their cities in very fertile tropical areas, they could produce a high yield of food on relatively small plots of land. Therefore they were able to maintain heavily populated urban centers. The Maya are best known for their hieroglyphic writing and sophisticated mathematical principles such as the concept of zero, used before it was understood in Europe. This mathematics allowed for the creation of a remarkably accurate annual calendar unmatched in Mesoamerican culture. Maya architecture is best seen at Tikal and Palenque, as well as the later Chichen Itza and Uxmal. While many other Maya sites are currently under excavation, these cities all reveal the use of architecture for display, that is, to support a rigidly hierarchical society by suggesting its superiority and authority through monumental construction.

The city of Tikal, which could accommodate 70,000 inhabitants at its height, featured a ceremonial center entirely elevated on a platform that connected the buildings via elevated paved roads running out toward the residential areas. One of the main pyramids, called Temple of the Giant Jaguar, encloses the tomb of Ah Hasaw, who ruled Tikal in the first decades of the 700s. The stepped pyramid has nine tiers, which probably symbolize the nine layers of the underworld and thus its funerary context. Steep, narrow stairs run across the tiers and rise directly up to a shrine at the top. This shrine consists of two narrow rooms with a steeply corbelled vault on the roof. A carved crest, called a roof comb, is located on top of the roof; it was originally painted in bright colors, much like the reds, yellows, white, and earth tones of Maya ceramics. The main pyramid at Chichen Itza reflects an even closer connection between astronomy and architecture: during the evenings of the fall and spring equinox, the setting sun casts an undulating shadow that seems to run up and down the central stairway. These pyramids of Post-Classic Maya architecture continue to feature a stepped pyramid of nine tiers, topped by a square platform and temple, but at Chichen Itza, the pyramids are shorter and wider. With the use of more columns and broader lintels, these structures feature broader galleries and larger interior spaces. The monuments are always surrounded by open spaces cut out of the dense forestation, suggesting human control over nature. In addition, the pyramids rise above the tree canopy, which would have allowed for a rarely held unobstructed view of the land, accessible only to the priest-king. Because the Maya ball courts, which consist of an open, rectangular space enclosed by tall walls, are found in close proximity to these religious monuments, ritualistic connotations have always been associated with the ball game. The actual rules of the game—and the fate of the losing team—remain shrouded in mystery, although Maya ceramics and carved stele reveal dramatic scenes of human bloodletting and sacrifice.

These fascinating rituals are also seen in the later Aztec culture, in which the Aztecs added to earlier Mexica and Maya beliefs their own set of gods and goddesses. It was the Aztec capital of Tenochtitlan that greatly impressed the army of Cortés. Upon their arrival in 1519, they enthusiastically described the straight causeway and the city, which seemed to appear magically out of the water like a shimmering image of monumental stone buildings. This description comes from the fact that Tenochtitlan was originally located on an island in Lake Texcoco, which was connected to other islands via elevated roads traversing the surrounding marshland. The Aztecs rose in power from their origins as a nomadic people living in central and northwest regions. They settled around modern-day Mexico City and established a powerful empire beginning in the 1200s. Once the Spanish soldiers conquered the Aztec Empire, they settled in the area of Tenochtitlan and began to build what would become the center of Mexico City, with the Cathedral of Mexico City occupying the site of Tenochtitlan's ceremonial center. Only in the 20th century have reconstructions allowed visitors to better understand the monumental architectural sophistication of the ancient Aztec Empire. *See also* MACHU PICCHU, PERU.

MICHELANGELO BUONARROTI (1475–1564). Michelangelo Buonarroti was born into a prominent Florentine family during the final decades of the early **Renaissance**. Trained first in painting, which was considered the most elevated of the arts, Michelangelo then turned his attention to sculpture and made a point throughout his career to champion the cause of sculptors by propagating the idea that sculptors, like painters, could be divinely inspired in their work. Michelangelo was hired initially by the Medici family in Florence and exposed to classical ideals via the Neo-Platonic Academy set up by the Medici to highlight the ideas of Plato. Due to his spiritual discourse, Plato was considered most suitable of all the pagan philosophers to the Christian world. By linking the artistic act of creation to both religious beliefs and these Platonic ideals, Michelangelo was able to elevate the status of artists, and mainly sculptors, to the degree that many of them became internationally famous and very wealthy. After having completed his famous Pietà in 1500, his David in 1504, and finally, his Sistine ceiling project in 1512, Michelangelo turned to architecture.

The Medici family, who had been expelled from Florence for a brief time, returned in 1515 with a renewed desire to establish authority in the city, and that authority was made powerfully visual through the commissioning of various architectural projects. That year, Michelangelo was called back to Florence from Rome and made chief architect to the Medici family. In the 1440s, **Filippo Brunelleschi** had built the Medici church of San Lorenzo, located right behind the family palace, but San Lorenzo never received a **marble** façade, and to this day it is covered in a rough-cut **brick** edged in layers with ridges meant to support large blocks of **stone** facing. At San Lorenzo, Michelangelo was commissioned to finish the façade, build another sacristy across from Brunelleschi's "Old Sacristy," reface the Medici library held at the **monastery** of San Lorenzo, and complete a stairway leading up to the reading room of the library. Beginning just after 1515, he designed a classicizing façade for San Lorenzo, which exists today only in its original wooden model that would have been used by builders to complete construction. The three-part marble façade would have risen up in a square shape, matching the taller height of the nave and masking the lower heights of the side aisles. Probably due to Michelangelo's multiple commissions for the Medici, this façade was never completed. Instead Michelangelo built the "New Sacristy" to house funerary monuments for Lorenzo and Giuliano de Medici. This sacristy was so big that the height of its **dome** towered over the church and echoed the large dome of the **Florence Cathedral**. Architectural parallels such as this made visually concrete the political connections between the Medici family and Florentine government.

Inside the chapel, Michelangelo began to experiment with a new flexibility in his use of classical references. Instead of carefully mimicking the principles of the Roman engineer **Vitruvius**, as **Bramante** had done, Michelangelo created a more crowded wall, articulated with a darker stone called *pietra serena*, which stands out against the white wall background. Fluted pilasters are pressed into the four corners of the room, niches stand empty over the doorways, volutes do not support entablatures, and additional decorative elements not described by Vitruvius appear on the wall. This new style, which is not so much a breaking away from classical ideals but an expansion of classicism, is called **Mannerism**.

The library stairwell, which dates to the 1520s, also reveals this new Mannerist style. Never before has a stairway received so much attention, which in the Renaissance helped to emphasize the idea that even the most functional elements of a building could be created in a beautiful, artistic way. The Laurentian Library, located off the ground floor in one of the upper-story wings of the courtyard of the Monastery of San Lorenzo, had a narrow vestibule or foyer, which could have hampered Michelangelo in his stairway design. Nonetheless, Michelangelo was still able to design a monumental stair based on the idea, or conceit, of flowing water. Thus, the steps come down from the top in wider increments, and curve at their edges to suggest the idea of water pooling at different levels as it flows downward. The main stairs are broken about two-thirds of the way up at a landing that opens onto the sides to allow side stairs to "flow" downward as well, thereby creating a tripartite stair at the bottom, separated into its three parts by a classical banister. The walls of the room are articulated in a manner similar to those of the New Sacristy. That is, pairs of columns sink into the wall, suggesting that their function is merely decorative rather than part of the support system. Blind niches, or niches devoid of sculpture, also function as blind windows that do not open to the outside, while pairs of **columns** sink into the corner, negating the idea of the corner as structurally reinforced from two walls that come together at a 90-degree angle. Typical of the Mannerist style, here Michelangelo uses classical motifs but in a manner different from that proposed by Vitruvius.

In the 1530s, when the Medici once again began to lose political favor in Florence, Michelangelo returned to Rome and worked for Pope Paul III on major commissions at **Saint Peter's Church** and the Capitoline Hill. At Saint Peter's, Michelangelo picked up where Bramante had left construction, at the crossing beneath the proposed dome. Because Bramante's piers were cracking, Michelangelo had to reinforce them, modifying the ground plan slightly and building the walls around the south end of the transept. After his death, the dome was finally completed in the 1580s by his student Giacomo della Porta.

For the Capitoline Hill project, Pope Paul III envisioned a new government center that would match the grandeur of Saint Peter's. Earlier government structures on the Capitoline Hill include a Senate building and an office building with a long loggia, or open porch, both of which were constructed in the 1300s. The entire site was located in downtown Rome on a hill that was accessible by a dirt path leading to an irregularly shaped unpaved piazza, or urban square. Michelangelo's plan involved renovating the buildings and adding a new classical façade to each, paving the piazza, and making the area symmetrical. Directly across from the old office building, he added one that angled slightly away from the Senate building to the same degree as the opposite structure, thereby bringing symmetry to the piazza in the form of a slight trapezoid. The new façade was built to match the opposing renovated façade, both with an open loggia and colossal columns that ascended through both stories of each building and were topped by a Roman-style balustrade with roof sculpture. The center of the piazza was designed with an intricately patterned oval shape of intersecting marble lines that frame a bronze equestrian figure of the Roman emperor Marcus Aurelius. This sculpture, placed on a tall pedestal, served to anchor the entire program by recalling imperial Rome and thus providing historical validity to the current Renaissance political system. Furthermore, during the Renaissance this equestrian figure was thought to be a statue of Constantine, who would have provided an additional historical link to the establishment of Christianity in Rome.

The entire complex provides powerful expression of Michelangelo's skill in adapting classical architectural style and symbolism to current Renaissance issues. It also highlights his ability not just as a painter and sculptor, but as an architect as well. Indeed, these works show that Michelangelo epitomizes the ideals of the true Renaissance man.

MICHELOZZO DI BARTOLOMMEO (1391–c. 1472). *See* RENAISSANCE ARCHITECTURE.

MIES VAN DER ROHE, LUDWIG (1886–1969). Ludwig Mies van der Rohe's dictum "less is more" came to be understood as the underlying rationale for German modernism. Director of the **Bauhaus**

School of Dessau from 1930 until the Nazis closed it in 1933, Mies van der Rohe worked in the **International style** made famous by **Walter Gropius** and **Le Corbusier**, but he tempered his constructions with beautifully rich materials of contrasting texture and color. This style is evident in his model house built for the German Pavilion of the International Exposition held in Barcelona in 1929. The interior, designed in an open, geometric plan of balanced rectangular spaces, reveals a strongly structured building that serves as a backdrop for the display of stainless **steel** accents, tinted **glass** windows, and rich **marble**, a huge slab of which is used for the entrance partition. The stainless steel Barcelona chair, still used today, was first seen in this house. The house thus shows how Mies van der Rohe balanced the spare International style with beautiful details to give elegance and warmth to his interiors.

Unable to develop his career in Germany, Mies van der Rohe emigrated to the United States in 1937 and settled in Chicago, where he taught at the Illinois Institute of Technology. In 1951, Mies completed the small Farnsworth House in Plano, Illinois, as a weekend retreat for Dr. Edith Farnsworth. This modest home created a new paradigm in modernist domestic architecture and is therefore perhaps his most famous work. The one-story rectangular home, elevated on steel piers, features a flat roof and exterior walls made entirely of glass. This geometric home is the first "glass house" constructed in the United States. Built with precast **concrete** floors and concrete roof slabs held in place by a steel frame and with glass curtain walls, the isolated setting of the home allowed for privacy despite its transparent exterior walls. Concrete steps lead to an open porch, while the interior rooms are divided by beautiful **wood** partitions that recall Mies's German Pavilion in Barcelona.

Mies is also known for his glass **skyscrapers**, inspired in their design by the previous generation of architects working in Chicago, such as **Louis Sullivan** of the "Chicago School." In 1951, Mies constructed his famous glass skyscraper apartments on Lake Shore Drive in Chicago, numbered 860 through 880. His skyscrapers are further stripped down to form a giant square tower of glass, as seen in his Seagram Building, designed with **Philip Johnson** in New York City in 1954. This tall building came to epitomize post–World War II skyscraper design, but in addition to the traditional steel beams encased in concrete, Mies added custom-made bronze beams along the outer wall to echo the internal structure of the building and to reveal his love of elegant materials. The glass curtain wall was darkly tinted to increase privacy, reduce glare, and add a more dignified external appearance to the office building. It was ultimately this building type, symbolic of a clean efficiency, that dominated corporate architecture through the end of the 20th century.

MINOAN ARCHITECTURE. *See* ANCIENT AEGEAN ARCHITECTURE.

MISSION STYLE. *See* ARTS AND CRAFTS; COLONIAL ARCHITECTURE.

MODERN ARCHITECTURE. *See* BAUHAUS ARCHITECTURE; INTERNATIONAL STYLE; RATIONALISM.

MONASTERY. Western European monastic communities began to develop into more formalized **brick** and **stone** architectural compounds during the reign of Charlemagne in the 800s. Monasteries, which function as a place of prayer and are inhabited by people separated from the secular world, are found in many religions, including Buddhism, Hinduism, and Christianity. When the more hermetic form of individual Christian monasticism began to develop in the third century into a larger, more codified community of members, the monastery became an architectural entity as well as a way of life. Accordingly, monasteries began to develop into a complex of buildings suited to the needs of the community, to include churches or abbeys, dormitories, refectories, hospitals, and other such buildings that allowed for greater self-sufficiency. Although some monasteries became the center of urban communities, most were originally located in rural settings on large tracts of land cultivated by the community members. Many monasteries were surrounded by walls to more effectively partition the spiritual space of the monastery from the distractions of secular life.

From the Order of Saint Benedict, established at the Monastery of Montecassino in Italy in 529, came the regulations followed by most subsequent monasteries across Europe. Both the Abbey of Saint

Riquier at the Monastery of Centula, built in 799 and later destroyed but known today through early drawings and archaeological evidence, and the plan for the Benedictine monastery of Saint Gall, drawn around 817, reveal a logical and clear approach to monastic construction that recalls **Ancient Roman** urban planning. At Saint Gall, the monastic plan was drawn in a grid-like pattern with the abbey church located in the center of the rectangular site, while the remaining buildings are organized in a hierarchical yet highly functional group around the four quadrants of the plan. These buildings include the refectory, a brew house, a bake house, a hospital for the poor, a school, and a workroom for artisans, among other buildings. The plan is efficiently divided to allow public entrance to the guest house, hospital, and school, while the more private areas, such as the convent for novices, are located behind the church.

Finally, the monastic community of the Cluny Abbey, established in 909, grew to become the best-endowed monastery in all of Europe by the 12th century. Although much of the monastery was later destroyed, its existing town house in Paris, built from 1485 to 1510, is one of the finest examples of late medieval urban civic architecture in France. *See also* EARLY MEDIEVAL ARCHITECTURE.

MOORE, CHARLES WILLARD (1925–1993). *See* POST-MODERN ARCHITECTURE.

MOORISH ARCHITECTURE. *See* ISLAMIC ARCHITECTURE.

MOSQUE. *See* ISLAMIC ARCHITECTURE.

MUGHAL ARCHITECTURE. *See* TAJ MAHAL, AGRA.

MYCENAEAN ARCHITECTURE. *See* ANCIENT AEGEAN ARCHITECTURE.

– N –

NASH, JOHN (1752–1835). *See* ROMANTIC ARCHITECTURE.

NATIVE AMERICAN ARCHITECTURE. Although most Native Americans today have abandoned their traditional homes in favor of housing based on European models, textual and visual sources can tell us much about the earliest truly "American" dwellings. Native Americans inhabited North America for many centuries prior to European intervention, and since they lived in diverse communities across the entire continent, their architecture is extremely varied. In general, Native American architecture consists of monumental and permanent ceremonial centers and domestic dwellings, which were typically built as temporary or seasonal shelters. While nothing remains of the earliest Native American dwellings, giant earthworks that date to before 1000 BC have been excavated and reconstructed. Much like the **Prehistoric** burial mounds found at Newgrange, Ireland, or the later **Etruscan** burial mounds, early Native American ceremonial centers reveal funerary mounds where the deceased were buried with a variety of precious objects. Objects found in surviving mounds located across Louisiana, Mississippi, and Ohio reveal a rich culture of trade. Copper, stone, shells, and other goods from diverse regions of the continent were used to make jewelry, religious objects, and tools. By the time of the Mississippian culture (c. AD 900–1500), mounds had developed into complex ceremonial centers. The Great Serpent Mound in Adams County, Ohio, dates to around 1070 and reveals the shape of a giant snake formed out of the earth. Twenty feet wide and 1,250 feet long in its writhing shape, it appears to slither up a ridge to a mound of rocks shaped like a giant egg.

Cahokia, in East St. Louis, Illinois, is perhaps the largest known early Native American urban center in North America. Dating to around AD 1150 and built where the Illinois, Missouri, and Mississippi Rivers come together, the reconstructed site features six square miles of construction, including an enormous earth mound in the center of the complex, an open plaza in front, and smaller mounds at the periphery of this central area enclosed by a wooden fence. Housing encircled the ceremonial center and accommodated up to 20,000 people. The central earth mound, covering 15 acres, was built up in four elevations, with a flat summit that featured a rectangular temple and a platform that might have been used for sacrifices. A circle of wooden posts oriented to the cardinal points allowed the inhabitants to anticipate the changing of the seasons, much as at **Stonehenge**. A victim of urban encroachment, Cahokia is in urgent need of restoration. The Pre-Columbian site of Spiro, located in eastern Oklahoma, is an equally important mound site located at the center of the vast Mississippian trade route. Inhabited from c. 850 to 1450, this 150-acre area consists of 12 platform mounds; burial sites have been looted through the 20th century and are in need of protection.

While mud **brick** and **wood** were primarily used for architectural construction in the middle of the North American continent, in the Southwest, **stone** remains reveal complex communities. The Mogollan people lived in the mountains of New Mexico, and the Hohokam of Arizona were known for their sophisticated system of irrigation, but it was the Anasazi peoples who constructed what are called the great houses of the Southwest. The Anasazi culture, in the corners of New Mexico, Colorado, Utah, and Arizona, dates to around 900–1400. Known for their sophisticated masonry, wide paved roads that linked together over 70 communities, large stone dwellings, and kivas, the Anasazi are the best known of all ancient Native American cultures for their architectural achievements. Their great houses were essentially multilevel apartments that sometimes reached five stories and were made of stone with timber roofs covered in thatch. Kivas, or ceremonial gathering centers, were built underground and feature circular rooms with seating platforms that run along the walls. This subterranean room is entered via an opening in the roof, where a ladder can be pulled down or up to monitor access. Near the entrance, a square hole was dug into the ground to symbolize the navel of the earth. At Chaco Canyon, one such great house complex has 30 kivas, interspersed with living areas and rooms used for food storage. Today, the Hopi and Zuni peoples maintain multistory mud-brick pueblos that hark back to the Anasazi dwellings and are used as either permanent dwellings or for family gatherings.

When the Europeans settled in North America, the displaced Native Americans began to move westward and adopt a more nomadic lifestyle that included the tepee. The tepee, a temporary dwelling that is light and can be assembled quickly and repeatedly, is constructed with three or four long poles placed on a vertical tilt and lashed together to form a point. The posts are then filled out with additional poles and covered with animal hides to form a protective barrier against adverse weather. A smoke hole opens up at the top of the te-pee, which has a hearth in the center of the interior dirt floor. Tepee linings were often painted, beaded, or embroidered with personal and symbolic images and stand as testament to the aesthetic value of these dwellings.

NEO-CLASSICAL ARCHITECTURE. The revival of classicism is a recurring theme in the history of architecture. From the earliest establishment of an architectural canon in **Ancient Greece** and its further codification in **Ancient Rome**, architects throughout time have been inspired by classicism. In the 800s Holy Roman Emperor Charlemagne modeled his palace in Aachen upon the ancient architecture of Rome, which he saw firsthand during his coronation there. Beginning in the 1300s, the earliest stylistic intimations of the **Renaissance** appeared, developing into a complete classical revival all through the 1500s. It was during this time that an increased interest in the study of Ancient Rome, called antiquarianism, resulted in the first regulations against the destruction of Roman ruins, in the form of a papal bull that disallowed the pillaging of the Roman forum by local stonemasons in search of reusable **marble**.

The architectural treatise titled *De architectura*, written by the Roman architect **Vitruvius** in the first century BC, was rediscovered in the early years of the 1400s and translated from the original Latin into vernacular Italian; it was widely consulted during the Renaissance for its discussion of the appropriate use of **columns**, capitals, and other elements of classical architecture. By the **Baroque** era, architects added to their repertoire of Vitruvian classicism new sources of ancient architecture that resulted in a more varied, often more sculptural and dynamically eclectic, style of construction. Classicism then went through another transformation into the **Rococo**, in which Vitruvian classicism was entirely replaced by a highly ornate, organic, and decorative style that retained a limited assortment of classical elements. By the middle of the 18th century, however, a confluence of social, philosophical, and political events resulted in the reintroduction of a more overt style of classicism and the introduction of Neo-Classical architecture. Neo-Classicism was named in the 19th century. In the 18th century it was simply called the "new" style.

The study of Roman antiquity was considered during this century to be an important aspect of the education of aristocrats, who would often complete their university education with a tour of Europe, called the "Grand Tour." While the Grand Tour included Paris, southern France, and other important cities in Europe, most travelers spent the majority of their time in Italy. This cultural phenomenon resulted in a lively art market, where tourists would commission their portraits and buy landscapes of Rome, such as the architectural prints by Giovanni Battista Piranesi, or Venetian landscapes by artists such as Canaletto. These were increasingly popular among English tourists after the publication of John Ruskin's book *The Stones of Venice* in 1853. New archaeological discoveries aided in the definition of this style, as Herculaneum was discovered in 1737 and Pompeii in 1748. Part of this thriving art market included the collecting of newly discovered Ancient Roman sculpture and pottery, and the hiring of scholars to classify and categorize these objects.

Cardinal Alessandro Albani built one of the largest collections of ancient art in Rome and hired the German librarian Johann Joachim Winckelmann to study his collection. In 1755, Winckelmann published a small book titled *Thoughts on the Imitation of Greek Works in Painting and Sculpture*, and in 1764 he published *The History of Ancient Art*. These tremendously important books are taken to signify the birth of the discipline of art history and the enduring importance of classicism in the aesthetic canon of both art and architecture. Winckelmann ultimately gave Albani's collection academic legitimacy, which is a modern concept, as is this self-conscious selection of a particular style based on theoretical reasoning. In his text, Winckelmann provided the first formal analysis of ancient art and did not consider any political, environmental, or religious influences. This is an important distinction, because its purely formal approach gave classicism great flexibility in its use. For example, although it can generally be seen as a reaction to the "frivolous" French **Rococo** aristocracy, it was also very much an international movement. Also, paradoxically, Neo-Classicism became the style favored by the wealthy, as the classical qualities of simplicity, elegance, order, and virtue were taken over by the upper class to reflect their social status. However, classicism was also used by the middle class as a quest for truth and liberty against governmental corruption.

This classical revival swept across Europe, where wealthy art patrons who championed the superiority of classicism over the Rococo commissioned the construction of Neo-Classical homes to accommodate their art collections. Neo-Classicism was increasingly seen as morally and intellectually superior to the decadent Rococo and was embraced by those patrons who styled themselves as more enlightened than the older generation of aristocracy. Thus, the Chiswick House, designed by the owner **Richard Boyle**, Lord Burlington, in West London in the 1720s, is modeled on **Andrea Palladio**'s famous Renaissance Villa Belvedere (Rotunda) located outside Vicenza. The Scottish architect **Robert Adam** established a more opulent interior design to these English Neo-Classical homes, epitomized by his richly decorated, yet classical Syon House located in Middlesex, England, from the 1760s.

Neo-Classical architecture involved more than the style of individual homes, however, for it was also employed to regularize streets and neighborhoods. John Wood the Elder was instrumental in introducing this emphasis of classicism to England. His native town of Bath had been a provincial Roman settlement, and his dream was to rebuild the town, then a spa resort, along a better organized and regular classical construction. Although much of his urban plan was never completed, the Circus, a wealthy housing project located in the center of the town, was begun in the 1750s and completed by his son John Wood the Younger. The Circus was named for its circular arrangement of town houses, which opened up at three points in the circle into broad, straight avenues. Each town house, modeled on the Roman **Colosseum**, had the same three-story façade, which provided a visual unity to the project.

In France, Neo-Classicism during this period was considered the "true" style of architecture, as seen in the Panthéon (Church of Sainte-Geneviève), begun in Paris in the 1750s by **Jacques-Germain Soufflot**. This large domed church with a colossal portico topped by a triangular pediment reflects Soufflot's architectural studies in Rome and the Palladian influences that were so prevalent in the 18th century. The chaotic climate that the French Revolution created in Paris resulted in a strange provenance history for the Panthéon, however, and the French ultimately failed to fully establish Neo-Classicism in Paris, although the style enjoyed wide favor in the paintings of

Jacques-Louis David and the sculpture of Jean-Antoine Houdon. More than a style, however, classicism was a powerful philosophy intricately linked to the French Revolution. Classicism came to be seen as a utopian ideal, in which cities could be efficient and well organized by following the classical ideals of symmetry and order.

The French Neo-Classical architect Claude-Nicolas Ledoux designed a city center for Chaux, in southern France. Though never built, it demonstrates these egalitarian notions with a circular plan that has wide streets radiating out from the core and a uniformly designed grouping of private houses and government and commercial buildings. Étienne-Louis Boullée was also an architectural idealist, creating both austere Neo-Classical homes as well as very imaginative plans that were more theoretically based. His illustration of a theoretical funerary monument for Isaac Newton, which dates to the 1780s, reveals a massive sphere set into a platform meant to symbolize an orbiting planet. Walking into the enclosed cenotaph, the visitor would see only a small monument in the corner, lit by small holes in the roof to give the impression of a starry sky. Deeply imaginative, both Ledoux and Boullée designed Neo-Classical monuments not for their contemporary France, but for a better future.

Neo-Classicism is evident in Germany as well, as seen in the Berlin Altes Museum, built by **Karl Friedrich Schinkel** in the 1820s, and in the United States, where it was the style selected to symbolize the new democratic government established after the War of Independence. **Thomas Jefferson**'s home at Monticello, in Charlottesville, Virginia, was modified in the Neo-Classical style after Jefferson's trip to Paris in 1784. In the first years of the next century, **Benjamin Henry Latrobe** built the **United States Capitol** in Washington, D.C., in the Neo-Classical style later modified by **Charles Bulfinch**. From that time, Neo-Classical style endured to inspire architects throughout the 19th, 20th, and 21st centuries. *See also* COLONIAL ARCHITECTURE; FEDERAL STYLE; GEORGIAN STYLE.

NEO-GOTHIC ARCHITECTURE. *See* GOTHIC REVIVAL ARCHITECTURE.

NEO-RATIONALISM. *See* RATIONALISM.

NEOLITHIC ARCHITECTURE. *See* PREHISTORIC ARCHITEC-
TURE.

NERVI, PIER LUIGI (1891–1979). *See* CONCRETE; DOME.

NEUMANN, JOHANN BALTHASAR (1687–1753). Balthasar Neumann is known today as the leading **Rococo** architect of the early
18th century in Europe. Born in Bohemia, he moved to Würzburg,
Germany, in 1711, and in 1717 he began to work for the prominent
Schönborn family, who held the prince-bishopric of Würzburg. The
Rococo style originated at the beginning of the century in the courtly
culture centered in Paris, and from there it rapidly spread to the major courts of Europe, becoming specifically popular in Germany and
Austria. Although the Rococo grew out of the preceding **Baroque**
style of architecture, it replaced Baroque monumentality and classical organizational features with a more intimate style. Even large
Rococo exteriors appear smaller and more personal, with their
rounded corners and ornate decoration, while the interiors, which received a greater architectural focus during this time, have curved
walls and rounded ceilings. This intimacy did not suggest social fa-
miliarity between classes, however, for the very ornate, richly gilded
Rococo interiors are purely aristocratic. The royal Residenz in
Würzburg, built from 1719 to 1744, typifies this style. The invited
guest would be entertained in the Kaisersaal, or Imperial Hall, an
oval-shaped room lavishly decorated with **marble** floors, gilded
wood, stucco walls, and an intricately curved, vaulted ceiling featuring pastel frescoes painted by the Italian artist Giovanni Battista
Tiepolo. Windows on the walls and round clerestory windows allow
dappling light to reflect off the crystal chandeliers. Modeled on the
Baroque Hall of Mirrors at **Versailles**, the Kaisersaal is more ornate
and playful in its decoration.

This style is also effectively used by Neumann in church design,
seen in his famous Vierzehnheiligen, built near Staffelstein, Germany, from 1743 to 1772 as a pilgrimage church dedicated to 14
saints known as the "14 Holy Helpers." This massive church, whose
tall towers are rounded at the corners and flank an undulating central
bay, is both monumental and intimately elegant. Inside, Neumann
uses an ingenious system of six overlapping ovals in the floor plan.

The Roman Baroque architect **Francesco Borromini** was the first to base his ground plans on the oval shape, making them a feature of Baroque architecture, but Neumann's interlocking ovals of different sizes is even more sophisticated. Despite this complexity, Neumann's interior is so well organized that a colonnade, despite its curvatures, directs the visitor toward the richly decorated high altar at the eastern end of the church. A large shrine anchors the center of the nave and is dedicated to the 14 patron saints of the church. One of the most beautiful Rococo churches in existence, the Vierzehnheiligen remains an important pilgrimage church today.

NEUTRA, RICHARD (1892–1970). In addition to **Marcel Breuer** and **Walter Gropius**, Richard Neutra is credited with introducing the **International style** of modern architecture in the United States. Born in Austria, Neutra first trained with **Adolf Loos** and worked with Erich Mendelsohn before coming to the United States in 1923. Unlike many European architects who fled Europe during World War I and settled along the East Coast, Neutra worked in California, where he built modern homes for movie industry clients. The Kaufman House, built in Palm Springs in 1946, is perhaps his most famous home. Since it was built as a vacation home in the desert climate of southern California, Neutra constructed a white building with a strong horizontal design of overhanging cornices that protect inhabitants from the bright sun and heat. Large sliding glass doors provide a link to the surrounding nature, while movable outdoor patio partitions allow flexibility in outdoor use. Much like the prairie-style homes of **Frank Lloyd Wright**, Neutra's free-flowing interior spaces open up the floor plan to maximize the living and dining room areas, thereby allowing for the entertainment of a large number of guests. While Wright's homes respond to the surrounding Midwestern environment, however, Neutra's houses are more consistent with the California **Ranch**, which is a more elegant version of this popular house style introduced in the 1930s. Neutra also helped to make the domestic swimming pool popular; they first appeared in the homes of the wealthy but gradually became more commonly found in middle-class homes. The Kaufman House, together with Wright's homes from the 1930s, the Gropius House built by Walter Gropius in 1937, and the Breuer House I, built by Marcel Breuer in 1938, are considered some of the most important examples of early modernist domestic architecture in the United States.

NIEMEYER, OSCAR (1907–). Oscar Niemeyer is perhaps the best-known Latin American artist of the 20th century. Born in Rio de Janeiro, Niemeyer graduated from the Escola de Belas Artes in 1934 with an engineering degree and became an architect in Brazil, specializing in the use of reinforced **concrete** to design buildings in the **International style**. Niemeyer first worked with Lucio Costa, credited with the introduction of modernism to Brazil. From there, Niemeyer adapted the International style aesthetic to suit his own culture, and accordingly, he developed a more "free-form" modernism based on the theme of the Brazilian *jeito*, a sensual style best known in Brazilian music and dance.

Early on, Niemeyer joined the Brazilian Communist Party and received numerous government commissions, the most famous of which was his construction of a new capital for Brazil, called Brasilia, located in the center of the country. This monumental project to relocate the entire government outside of Rio represents a bold plan of self-determination, testament to the incredible architectural idealism of the day inspired by the utopian city plans of **Le Corbusier** and others. Now designated a UNESCO World Heritage Site, the urban layout for Brasilia was designed by Niemeyer's friend and mentor Lucio Costa, and Niemeyer devoted much of his life to constructing the buildings needed for the city. All of the buildings are unified with a modern style and white concrete materials set into a sprawling yet organized space that symbolizes modern efficiency. The National Congress Building is the centerpiece of Brasilia. It has a uniquely designed platform of windows supporting a flat roof with what appears to be a large white bowl resting on one side of the broad roof, balanced by a pair of tall columnar structures of office space on the other side. Here Niemeyer enriches the International style vocabulary with unexpected shapes to create a more plastic design that is poetic and expressive. The most innovative building in Brasilia, however, is Niemeyer's cathedral, constructed in the shape of a hyperboloid, or double curves that intersect, to create a **dome**. The structure's white concrete ribs pinch inward to form the dome and then curve outward to create a modern, open lantern. The hyperboloid dome was first pioneered by Russian engineers and consists of stacked sections of hyperboloids. The city of Brasilia was inaugurated in the 1960s, and although many people were convinced of its failure, it gained in popularity over the years and is currently home to more than 2.3 million inhabitants.

In 1947, Oscar Niemeyer was invited to teach at Yale University but was unable to obtain an entrance visa due to his political leanings. Vindicated a year later, Niemeyer then came to the United States as one of the internationally elected board members, together with Le Corbusier, in charge of overseeing construction of the United Nations Headquarters in New York City, a complex completed in 1952. In 1961, the Brazilian president was deposed, and eventually Niemeyer moved to Paris, where he built the French Communist Party Headquarters in the 1960s. Niemeyer then returned to Brazil in the 1980s, won the Pritzker Architecture Prize in 1988, and when he was 89 years old, constructed perhaps his most unique building, the Contemporary Art Museum in Niterói, outside Rio de Janeiro. This highly sculptural white concrete building resembles a saucer elevated on a massive pier, with entry ramps that lead up into the gallery level of the building. Meant to appear like a flower, the entire building is surrounded by a reflecting pool. Ultimately, Oscar Niemeyer was important to the establishment of the International style in Latin America, where his works merit further study; yet his later, more sculptural works are aligned with **Expressionism**.

NORMAN ARCHITECTURE. *See* DURHAM CASTLE AND CATHEDRAL; ROMANESQUE ARCHITECTURE.

NOTRE DAME, PARIS. Notre Dame is perhaps the best-known **Gothic** cathedral in the world, probably due to its location on a small island in the Seine River in central Paris called the Île de la Cité. It has been central to many prominent historical events, including Napoleon's coronation as emperor in 1804 and the French celebration of their liberation from the Nazis in 1944. The impetus for construction of the cathedral came about when a new bishop, Maurice de Sully, decided around 1160 that the older cathedral was not grand enough for its role as the parish church of the "kings of Europe." Therefore, the decision was made to demolish the older church and build a larger one in the new Gothic style. Construction began in 1163, when the cornerstone was laid by either the bishop or Pope Alexander III, and the nave was completed by 1200. The interior and west façade were not finished until 1250. During the reign of King Louis VII, the construction of Notre Dame became the major task of the Bishop de Sully, who spent his life overseeing its financing. During its construction, the Gothic style developed from its early phases into the High Gothic, which is why stylistic changes are evident in different parts of the building.

The earliest Gothic style is epitomized by the Abbey Church of Saint-Denis, located several miles north of central Paris. This Benedictine **monastery** houses several tombs of the French royal family as well as the relics of Saint Denis, the patron saint of France. After a fire destroyed part of the older church, Abbot Suger in the 1130s oversaw the financing for the construction of the new church. Having traveled widely, Suger sought to introduce a new style of architecture at Saint-Denis, and his tireless work resulted in the first true Gothic church, which became the source for many other Gothic churches constructed across France in the next several centuries. Unlike most buildings, the west façade of Saint-Denis was completed first, by around 1140. A tripartite façade appears here with twin towers, only one of which can be seen today because the other did not survive damage it sustained in the 19th century. Although the general layout of the façade recalls the **Romanesque** church of Saint-Étienne in Caen built in the 1060s, it is much more elaborately carved with architectural sculpture. On the interior, sophisticated vaulting and supports allowed for larger stained-**glass** windows that let more light into the building. The vaulted ceilings were more open and spacious than in Romanesque structures, with thinner **columns** that provided a more "weightless" appearance. The pointed **arches** also allowed for a taller ceiling and more wall space for fenestration than the Romanesque round arch provided.

These are the Gothic features adapted for use at Notre Dame. With more fenestration came the need for more sophisticated buttressing; the first use of true flying buttresses is found at Notre Dame, where the buttresses are attached to the upper register of the outer clerestory wall and then "fly" out from the wall, attaching again into the outer walls of the lower-level side aisles and area. Pinnacles top the areas where the buttresses angle into the side walls, and these bring more vertical weight down into the wall supports. Flying buttresses are a crucial feature of Gothic architecture. The additional support is certainly needed, given the large windows in relation to the masonry walls. The more traditional attached buttresses, such as are seen at Saint-Étienne at Caen, would have obscured the windows. In addition, Gothic churches are typically built on a Latin-cross plan, with a long vaulted nave flanked by lower side aisles, a transept with side doors at the crossing of the church, and a well-lit choir area, sometimes with an ambulatory circling around the choir and chapels radiating from the ambulatory.

At Notre Dame, the transepts are suppressed, and the ambulatory allows for visitors to walk around the choir without disturbing the mass. Notre Dame does not have projecting choir chapels as do later Gothic cathedrals, such as at Amiens. The elevation of the church is typically designed with a two- or three-story interior, to include a *triforium*, or balcony above the nave arcade, and then clerestory windows above the triforium. Gothic arches, as seen in the nave arcade, are always pointed, a feature that allows for an increase in height within the radius of the arch and thus more room for tall windows as well as the visual effect of a soaring interior height. At Notre Dame, the three-story interior is articulated with thick piers that line the nave, separating the central area from the side aisles. The side walls are defined by the arcade, a *triforium*, and then a register of clerestory windows. From the massive piers spring ribs, some of which curve around into the pointed arches that define the arcade, while others travel vertically upward to demarcate the bay unit divisions and to merge into the ceiling. There they become the ribs used for the cross-vaulted roof support. At Notre Dame, the nave vaulting is a six-part system, where three ribs intersect each other. The ribs help to direct the weight of the masonry and of gravity through the support system of piers and walls, and they also help the visitor to visualize how the building is measured out based upon geometric principles. Therefore, a seemingly complex structural system is laid bare by ribbing that functions as an exoskeleton, much like the way the flying buttresses function on the exterior of Notre Dame. The Gothic cathedral also appears weightless in that the pointed arches direct the visitor's eye upward toward the clerestory windows, where light streams in on a sunny day, creating patterns of colored light on the walls of the church. Certainly at this time the interior space would have been overwhelming to the visitor, unaccustomed to seeing such large-scale architectural constructions.

In addition, Gothic churches are even more elaborately decorated with architectural sculpture, placed at pivotal points, mainly on the exterior of the building. The magnificent decoration served both iconic and didactic purposes. It was meant to glorify the sacred space as the house of God on earth, but it also constituted didactic narratives of such events as the Last Judgment, the Coronation of the Virgin, and various episodes in the life of the Virgin, for example, her Visitation and the Annunciation. Such is the case with Notre Dame, where the façade faces west and reveals a tripartite division, with three arched entrance portals, each with a set of double doors surrounded by portal sculpture. The portal sculpture is arranged around the doors to include standing figures, called jamb figures, which flank the entrance, while a central figure stands in the *trumeau*, a carved post located between the double doors. Above the doorway is the lintel, and the *tympanum* is the space that extends from the lintel to the point of the arched doorway frame. Both are intricately carved with scenes related to the Virgin Mary and then framed by a series of stone blocks called *voussoirs*, which attach together around the arch into registers called *archivolts*, which are also carved.

The main façade of Notre Dame also has three horizontal registers, with the entrance portals at the ground floor, topped by a round, centered rose window, which allows light into the nave entrance. The rose window is flanked by bifurcated (two-part) arched windows on either side. The registers are then divided by a frieze of carved figures standing in niches. Above the second register is a carved latticework entablature that one can see through in the center of the church. This feature gives the appearance of weightlessness to the upper portions of the structure. Finally, twin towers appear on either side of the façade. Notre Dame in Paris is rare in that its façade towers match. Very often, due to the extensive time frame needed for the completion of the Gothic cathedral, the towers were completed in different Gothic styles. Differing Gothic styles can be seen inside Notre Dame, however; the clerestory windows in the nave were reconstructed in the latest building campaign after 1225 into larger double-lancet windows topped by smaller rose windows. Although in the coming centuries, architectural styles would shift toward a more classical design, appreciation for these Gothic churches continued in northern Europe, and the Gothic style was revived periodically into one **Gothic Revival** or another. In any event, Gothic churches continue to inspire people to think about the high motivations, the huge cost, and the incredible logistically complex construction that fueled an entire economy centered on architectural endeavors in the Middle Ages.

NOUVEL, JEAN (1945–). *See* GREEN ARCHITECTURE.

– O –

OLBRICH, JOSEPH MARIA (1867–1908). *See* ART NOUVEAU.

OLMEC ARCHITECTURE. *See* MESOAMERICAN ARCHITECTURE.

OTTOMAN ARCHITECTURE. *See* SINAN, MIMAR KOCA AGHA.

OTTONIAN ARCHITECTURE. *See* EARLY MEDIEVAL ARCHITECTURE.

OUD, JACOBUS JOHANNES PIETER (1890–1963). *See* RATIONALISM.

– P –

PALEOLITHIC ARCHITECTURE. *See* PREHISTORIC ARCHITECTURE.

PALLADIO, ANDREA (1508–1580). Andrea Palladio is best known for establishing an enduring tradition of classicism, not only in the Veneto during the High **Renaissance** but also through subsequent generations of classical architects who looked to the Palladian style for their architectural references. Probably born in Padua to a modest family, Andrea di Pietro della Gondola was initially trained as a stonecutter but moved to Vicenza, where he met the humanist scholar Giangiorgio Trissino. Trissino accepted Andrea di Pietro into his informal academy and renamed him "Palladio," after the name Pallas from the ancient pantheon. Through Trissino, Palladio was introduced to the writings of **Vitruvius** and traveled to Rome to study Roman architecture firsthand. Throughout his life, Palladio wrote guidebooks to Roman buildings, illustrations to supplement Vitruvius's ancient treatise on architecture, and finally, his own book on architecture, titled *I quattro libri dell'architettura,* published in 1570. His book was devoted to both technical questions and the classical orders as well as to a discussion of classical buildings, including ancient domestic, civic, and religious architecture. He illustrates the book extensively with his own drawings of classical buildings as well as his own architecture. It was this text, printed in many editions through the next several centuries, that helped disperse the Palladian style across Europe and America, as exemplified by the classicizing buildings of **Inigo Jones** and **Christopher Wren** in 17th-century England and **Thomas Jefferson**'s and other **Neo-Classical** structures in Washington, D.C., from the 18th century.

Palladio constructed numerous palaces in Vicenza, over 40 villas in the surrounding countryside, and two major churches in nearby Venice. Because the Veneto was very lush and fertile but swampy, various land reclamation projects were sponsored throughout the Renaissance to create more farmland for the increased population on the Italic Peninsula. This farmland was so expensive that agricultural pursuits came to be viewed as more appropriate for the wealthy class, and thus the idea of the "gentleman farmer" was born. This rural landowner then needed a home befitting his high social status, so the Renaissance villa was introduced. The villa had been fully developed in Roman antiquity and specifically adapted for upper-class life in the countryside, but during the Middle Ages villas were replaced by fortified **castles** needed for the more politically unstable feudal age. The Renaissance villa was therefore modeled on those known from antiquity. Palladio's Villa Rotonda, also known as both the Villa Capra and the Villa Belvedere, is his most famous work. Constructed in the 1560s, the Villa Rotonda is a square building with an elevated porch on each of its four sides. The matching porches are supported by a row of six Ionic **columns** capped by a triangular pediment featuring sculpted figures in the center and on the corners of the pediment. This overall design recalls the **Pantheon** in Rome. The villa also has a **dome**, an architectural element reserved in the Early Renaissance for churches; however, Palladio probably saw the dome on **Ancient Roman** imperial homes and connected its domestic use to the Latin word *domus*.

This careful study of classical antiquity can also be seen in his church of San Giorgio Maggiore in Venice, built beginning in 1565. Here Palladio created a traditional basilica-plan church, also called a Latin-cross plan, but with a taller nave flanked by shorter side aisles, much like **Leon Battista Alberti**'s church of Sant'Andrea in Mantua, built in 1470. While the upper register of Alberti's façade was never completed, Palladio successfully resolved the design problem of this height variance by creating the look of two façades, one superimposed upon the other and linked together to unify the front. The center of the façade features a tall portico with four engaged colossal half-columns that support a triangular pediment. A dome looms behind the pediment, marking the crossing of the church, where the nave meets the side aisles in the interior. The interior of the church continues with similar half-columns attached in clusters to the side walls of the nave, creating a very sculptural colonnade of the massive compounded columns needed to support the dome. The nave ceiling has a barrel vault modified with slight groins to better direct the weight through the compounded columns rather than over the **arches** of the nave colonnade.

One of Palladio's final commissions was for the Teatro Olimpico in Vicenza, commissioned in 1580 by the Accademia Olimpica as a permanent site for their productions. Palladio was one of the founders of the Academy, and had studied Ancient Roman theater design in both the writings of Vitruvius and in the nearby ruins of the Ancient Roman Teatro Berga in Vicenza. Palladio died after creating the initial designs for the theater, and the stage was then completed by his student Vincenzo Scamozzi, in keeping with classical precedent. Completed in 1585 and used for the first time in a performance of Sophocles's *Oedipus the King*, the building is important today as the oldest surviving Renaissance stage. Thus, all three of these buildings represent Palladio's interests in classical antiquity; more importantly, they reveal his ability to adapt classical principles to Renaissance needs in a harmonious and beautiful way.

PANTHEON, ROME. The Pantheon, built as a temple to the Roman gods, stands today as one of the most famous engineering feats of **Ancient Rome**. Begun in AD 118 by the Emperor Hadrian, this building features a huge portico lined with eight **columns** that support a triangular pediment inscribed with the name of Marcus Agrippa, the Roman statesman who commissioned an earlier pantheon on this site. Rising above the pediment is a **dome**, which although unremarkable from the exterior, given its simple drum and shallow dome shell, was the largest built in antiquity. The dome, 143 feet in diameter, is made of a volcanic rock called *tufa*, used to create an early form of **concrete**. This concrete was carved out into concave squares to reduce the weight of the material and to direct gravity down into the 20-foot wide walls of the building. The center of the dome has a round open window called an oculus, which, together with the entryway, provides the only sunlight into the large, unencumbered interior. The walls of this round temple, which act as the drum to support the dome, are covered in colored **marble**. Seven niches in the wall originally held statues of various ancient gods.

The dome, actually an **arch** rotated on its axis, is a Roman invention. Although the Romans are also traditionally credited with the invention of the arch, the arch was in fact developed over time and within a variety of cultures that employed the use of the keystone. The arch is a much more sophisticated structural system than the earlier **post-and-lintel** structure because its shape, in addition to the keystone, directs more weight to the posts than would a straight lintel. Because the space beneath the lintel or arch is a void, almost all weight must be shifted to the posts or side walls, which become increasingly thicker as the arch or lintel becomes wider. Since lintels are inherently weaker than arches, columns might be used to support large interior rooms that have flat roofs, but an arched room need not be encumbered on the interior with wall divisions or internal columns. Instead, thick external walls can be used to buttress the interior space. The round arch can therefore be used in a variety of ways to manipulate interior space. An arch that is repeated creates a barrel vault, while two barrel vaults that intersect at a 90-degree angle form a cross vault, or groin vault. Finally, the arch that rotates in a circle becomes the dome. Because of their invention of the arch and the dome, Ancient Romans earned a great reputation for architecture that was overwhelming in scale and vast in its open interior spaces.

In the early 600s, Pope Boniface designated the Pantheon a Christian church, which preserved it from destruction. The design of the massive dome later became a great source of inspiration for classicizing architects from the **Renaissance** onward, and today the Pantheon is one of the most visited sites in all of Italy.

PARIS OPÉRA. *See* GARNIER, CHARLES.

PARTHENON. *See* ACROPOLIS, ATHENS; ANCIENT GREEK ARCHITECTURE.

PAXTON, JOSEPH (1801–1865). *See* CAST IRON; GLASS.

PEI, IEOH MING (1917–). I. M. Pei is one of the most prolific modernist architects of the 20th century. Pei was born in China and grew up in the prosperous city of Suzhou, known for its beautiful gardens and historic homes. At the age of 17, Pei began his studies in the United States, which culminated in a graduate degree from Harvard University, where he studied with **Walter Gropius**. Very much influenced by Gropius and other **International style** architects such as **Le Corbusier** and **Marcel Breuer**, Pei established his own firm in 1955 and began to work in a style of modernism that incorporated aspects of the **Bauhaus** style, **Brutalism**, and **High-Tech architecture**. I. M. Pei first experimented with the linking of **concrete** square and rectangular spaces to create a crisp, geometric appearance, as seen in his National Center for Atmospheric Research, built in Boulder, Colorado, in the 1960s. This style, often called Brutalism, was further refined in Pei's more intricately shaped, interlocking triangles that form the East Wing of the National Gallery of Art, built in Washington, D.C., in the 1970s. After winning the Pritzker Architecture Prize in 1983, Pei was commissioned to create a new entrance for the **Louvre, Paris**. Here he revisited the triangle shape proposed by a much earlier architect and refined it in his famous **glass** pyramid entrance constructed in 1989.

The Christian Science Center, built in Boston in 1968–1974, combines Pei's interest in concrete and **steel** construction with his desire to include natural elements to form a quiet oasis in an urban setting. This 14-acre campus is the corporate headquarters of the Christian Science religion. In the center of this arena-shaped area is a broad reflecting pool surrounded by buildings and linden trees to separate the campus from its urban context and to create an oasis in the middle of Boston. The complex includes a 28-story administrative **skyscraper** on one side, while a band of administrative buildings with an open loggia lines the opposing side, stopping short of the preexisting mother church and angling out from the square to frame the church. The spare, geometric aesthetic of these modern buildings is softened by the rounded edges of the roof cornice above the loggia. The church had been built in a Romanesque Revival style in 1894, and the dome was added in 1906. A tall portico with colossal columns was built in 1975 to form a visual connection with the newer buildings. Pei's administrative skyscraper provides a visual balance to the opposing church, while his modernist buildings are all constructed with a concrete that matches the color of the granite used for the older church. Finally, the reflecting pool is edged with granite cut in a round shape to create a slow, shallow waterfall around the entire area of water. The subtle sound of falling water is soothing, and the reflections of the surrounding buildings move across the surface of the water in a manner that recalls the numerous pools of water found in the gardens of Suzhou, where Pei grew up.

The idea of a reflective surface is carried into I. M. Pei's next Boston commission, the Hancock Tower, completed in 1977. There was a concern for the preservation of the historical aesthetic of Copley Square, which is framed by the Old South Church built in the **Gothic Revival** style in 1873, Trinity Church, built by **Henry Hobson Richardson** in 1877, and the Boston Public Library, constructed in 1895 by **Charles Follen McKim** in the Renaissance Revival style. Pei's ingenious solution involved the construction of a 60-story obelisk-shaped commercial office tower made with a blue tinted glass curtain wall that reflects its surrounding buildings. Seen from a distance, the blue glass renders the building almost invisible. Like most skyscrapers, the glass curtain wall is hung on a steel frame. A combination of the large size of the glass panes and its tinting and reflective coating began to stress the tape bond that holds the double panes together, and glass has subsequently fallen off the sides of the building. Studies of this dangerous situation have resulted in superior glass bonding methods found in later **Post-Modernist** and High-Tech architecture and seen in I. M. Pei's 72-story Bank of China office building, constructed in Hong Kong in the 1980s.

Pei's most recent building, the Suzhou Museum (2006), reflects a distinctly Chinese rendition of modernism that blends traditional eastern aesthetics with a more spare western modern style. This interest in incorporating regional elements into the prevailing international architectural style is often called **Critical Regionalism**. With this work, Pei has come full circle, thereby establishing himself as one of the most enduring modernist architects of the 20th century, fully capable of working within the full range of architectural styles that exist today.

PELLI, CESAR (1926–). Born in the mountainous northern Argentine city of San Miguel de Tucumán, Cesar Pelli first studied architecture at the university in Tucumán and then at the University of Illinois in Urbana-Champaign. His first architectural position was in the firm of **Eero Saarinen** in New Haven, Connecticut; he assisted in the construction of Saarinen's Trans World Airport Terminal, built at JFK Airport in New York (1956–1962). This building reveals Saarinen's expressive architectural style, which Pelli later modified in his own urban **skyscrapers**.

Pelli received some of his first important commissions while dean of the School of Architecture at Yale University in 1977–1984. During this time, he built the World Financial Center that surrounded the **World Trade Center in New York City**. Through the 1980s, Pelli experimented with the creation of a more expressive design for his skyscrapers, first modeling them on **Art Deco** skyscrapers such as the Empire State Building, as seen in his Wells Fargo Center, built in Minneapolis, Minnesota, in 1986–1988. Both buildings feature a stepped format along the shaft, resulting in a summit narrower than the base of the building. He used this recessed crown also in his 60-story Bank of America Corporate Headquarters, built in Charlotte, North Carolina, in 1990, but here the sides of the building bulge out slightly, creating a less linear and more expressive overall design.

Pelli's characteristic curved façades, **glass** and metal designs, and great attention to the external lighting of the building created a dramatically luminous silhouette, which is best seen in his most famous structure, the Petronas Twin Towers built in Kuala Lumpur, Malaysia, in 1998. Briefly considered the world's tallest buildings, the Petronas Towers remain the world's tallest twin towers. Although the twin towers of the World Trade Center consisted of 110 stories while the Petronas Towers have 88 stories of office space, the Petronas Towers include a mall and various other areas of entertainment on the ground floor, creating a vast space at street level. Made from reinforced **concrete**, **steel**, and glass, these towers bulge, curve, become narrower, and almost end in a pinnacle, thus recalling the minaret in **Islamic architecture**. Because steel is expensive in Malaysia, Pelli used more concrete in his design than is found in most skyscrapers built outside of Asia. For this reason, the towers are extremely heavy and are therefore set very deeply into a foundation of bedrock. Linking the two towers is a two-story skywalk at the 41st floor, which provides an additional safety exit as well as a unique design to the towers. Interestingly, a different construction company was hired for each tower and a competition was set up between them that today can be used as a comparative case study of cost and construction issues. Cesar Pelli, best known for his skyscrapers, remains important today in his transformation of the urban landscape to include such expressive and structurally superior monuments of **Post-Modernism** and **High-Tech architecture.**

PERRET, AUGUSTE (1874–1954). Auguste Perret, the first architect to use reinforced **concrete** in domestic architecture, was born in Belgium and worked mostly around Paris. *Béton armé*, or ferro-cement, a concrete threaded with **steel**, was introduced by François Hennebique for use in industrial buildings in the 1890s, and Auguste Perret and his brother Gustave became the leading contractors of ferrocement in Paris. Reinforced concrete not only increased the strength of the material, but it also solved the problem of the *monolithic joint* by integrating the bonding material with the building material rather than bonding the separate pieces together with a weaker adhesive.

Perret's first project was an eight-story concrete apartment building located in Paris at 25 bis Rue Franklin, built in 1903–1904. This structure has a unique open-plan arrangement, with large interior rooms that anticipate the modernist domestic architecture of the 1920s and even the **Ranch style** homes of the 1950s. Roof terraces, also very innovative, were added to allow occupants an outdoor space to garden and to enjoy free air off the street. Instead of designing an inner courtyard, as was traditional at the time, Perret created a recessed façade, set back from the street with angles to allow more windows—and therefore more light into the building. The concrete frame is visible on the exterior of the building and mimics **wood** construction. Because Perret was interested in texture and decorative detailing, the façade was also covered with floral patterns made from the concrete building material rather than attached to the façade. Because of Perret's organic use of concrete, his style has often been described as poetic.

Perret's Church of Notre Dame du Raincy, built in 1922–1924, was created with a shallow vaulted concrete shell that rests on thin **columns**. **Glass** curtain walls are set into thin concrete frames. This building is also one of the earliest examples of the use of exposed ferro-cement, but its style retains historical elements. On the interior, Perret exploits the appearance of a traditional **Gothic** skeletal structure with concrete instead of masonry. Reinforced concrete ultimately became the primary building material of the 20th century, and architects elected to focus on either its technical or aesthetic applications in the creation of new forms of modernist architecture. *See also* BRUTALISM.

PERSIAN ARCHITECTURE. *See* ANCIENT NEAR EASTERN ARCHITECTURE.

PERUZZI, BALDASSARE (1481–1537). *See* MANNERISM.

PIACENTINI, MARCELLO (1881–1960). *See* RATIONALISM.

PIANO, RENZO (1937–). *See* GREEN ARCHITECTURE; HIGH-TECH ARCHITECTURE.

PISA CATHEDRAL COMPLEX, ITALY. Pisa Cathedral and its surrounding buildings form a **Romanesque** complex unequalled in all of Italy in its large scale, high quality, and unique style. Constructed from 1063 to 1350, this complex consists of a large cathedral, a separate baptistery that rivals the cathedral dome in height, and a separate bell tower, called the *campanile*, which is the famous "Leaning Tower of Pisa." Next to the cathedral is an enclosed courtyard with the *camposanto*, or cemetery. At the time these buildings were constructed, Pisa was a powerful port city, one of the most prosperous on the Italic peninsula. Pisans negotiated control of the Mediterranean trade routes from the equally powerful merchant leagues of Venice, Amalfi, and Genoa, and Pisan merchants went on to dominate the western Mediterranean Sea over their greatest rivals, the Muslims. Muslim control of the neighboring Iberian peninsula, which they called Al-Andalus, reached back 700 years, and by 1000 it included not just all of Spain, but parts of Portugal and France as well. In 1063, when the Pisans won a decisive military victory over Islamic forces, this victory was seen as a monumental event not just for Pisa but for the entire Christian world, and it precipitated the construction of the Pisa Cathedral.

More important than Florence or Siena during this time, Pisa enjoyed a highly sophisticated Romanesque culture. Romanesque architecture is generally characterized by its use of rounded **arches** and other features that recall **Ancient Roman architecture**, but Pisa's cosmopolitan interests are imprinted on the varied stylistic influences seen at the Pisa Cathedral complex. There, Byzantine and Muslim aesthetics blend with Roman classicism. The motivation for the use of classical elements in the Romanesque period is different from that of the more philosophically extensive **Renaissance** brand of antiquarianism, however. Romanesque classicism was meant specifically to recall not only the architectural grandeur of Ancient Rome, but also to confirm its historical importance as the first official seat of western Christianity, established there in the 300s under the reign of Constantine. From that beginning was created a powerful Roman papal court with political and religious control over large portions of Europe. Thus, the decision to construct a cathedral at Pisa and to dedicate it to the newly popular Virgin Mary was a clear reference to the Christian victory over the Muslims in Spain.

The cathedral is built of white **marble**, with a unique west façade that includes three entrance portals and then four shorter registers of blind arcades, two that rise up to the height of the side aisles and two more that reach into the taller nave roof. The exterior walls are decorated with colored **stone** inlay, much like the Romanesque and

Gothic buildings found in Venice. This colored stone provides a somewhat Eastern aesthetic, and is followed through with Corinthian **columns** topped by carved human and animal heads. Inside the cathedral, the nave is flanked by pairs of side aisles and topped by a flat timber roof, intricately carved into squares called coffering, in emulation of Ancient Roman basilicas. The interior walls are articulated with greenish marble to create a striped effect, a feature found in other central-Italian churches, such as at the Cathedral of Siena, built in the next century. At Pisa, the walls are divided into three registers, with a round-arched arcade running the length of the nave toward the high altar, then a *triforium*, or gallery level, and finally, a row of small clerestory windows. In general, Romanesque churches are thicker and more austere than is found in subsequent **Gothic architecture**, and the windows are markedly smaller and lack stained glass. In Italy, Romanesque windows tend to be even smaller than those found in northern European structures, given the greater amount of direct sunlight found in southern Europe. Moving toward the high altar of the Pisa Cathedral, wide transepts, also called the arms of the church, extend from the dome crossing. The high altar features a monumental **Byzantine** mosaic of Christ as Judge.

Outside the cathedral the baptistery, located in front of the west façade, is a round structure divided into three registers and topped by a large tiled dome. At the ground level, a blind arcade features rounded arches, but the upper registers begin to demonstrate, through their pointed arches and an increase in architectural sculpture, the subsequent Gothic style that was in existence by the time the Pisa Cathedral complex was completed. The camposanto is architecturally simpler in design than the cathedral and baptistery, but the blind arcade is carried through on the exterior to create a visual link to the complex. Finally, the campanile, like the baptistery, is a free-standing structure designed with seven registers of arcades that lead up to a lantern. The tower was begun in 1173, and its current lean, which resulted from an improperly laid foundation, was evident during construction. Attempts to shift the weight of the tower at the upper levels of construction resulted in a slightly bowed shape. The tower currently leans at 5.5 degrees, and while over the years attempts have been made to stabilize the structure, most architects have agreed that the lean should not be corrected but that the subsoil must instead be stabilized. Benito Mussolini was the first leader of the 20th century to tackle this project, but the **concrete** base poured into the surrounding soil during this project only made the tower lean even further. More recently, the tower underwent a sophisticated restoration, concluded in 2001, to provide a subterranean support system that one hopes will prove successful in arresting any further tilting. It is this combination of unique stylistic features and interesting construction history that has made the Pisa Cathedral complex so famous today.

PORTA, GIACOMO DELLA (c. 1533–1602). *See* SAINT PETER'S CHURCH, ROME.

POST-AND-LINTEL. The earliest, simplest method for spanning a space is the post-and-lintel system of upright posts to support a horizontal beam, called a lintel. The width of the lintel is limited not only by its tensile strength, but also by the length of the materials possible for use as a lintel. Often, a series of posts must be used to increase the overall width of an enclosed space, creating a room encumbered by **columns** or wall divisions. Although most structures employ a post-and-lintel system, one of the more famous examples of the use of a post-and-lintel is **Stonehenge**, constructed in the Salisbury Plain of Wiltshire, England, around 2750 BC. Here, five pairs of vertical megaliths called *trilithons* are formed in the shape of a horseshoe, and each pair was capped by a lintel. This group was surrounded by an outer circle of megaliths capped by a continuous lintel of massive horizontal **stones**. Other **Prehistoric** structures include individual freestanding post-and-lintel stone formations found across Europe, called *dolmens*.

Stone post-and-lintel structures are found throughout the **Ancient Near East** and **Ancient Egypt**, while **wood** was also used throughout Europe in post-and-lintel construction. By the 18th century, the replacement of stone and wood lintels by **cast-iron** and then **steel** frames has allowed for a gradual increase in unobstructed room widths that rival the size of **domed** interiors, yet with flat roofs and broad interiors supported by metal framing.

POST-MODERN ARCHITECTURE. Post-Modern architecture was established in the 1970s to bring historicism and playful ornamentation to the more austere modern **International style.** International style was increasingly considered too intellectualized, serious, and repetitive, and thus a style that ultimately did not respond to the needs of the broader public. The leaders of this new movement were **Robert Venturi** and Denise Scott Brown, who expressed these concerns in the book *Complexity and Contradiction in Architecture*, first published in 1966. In the later *Learning from Las Vegas* (1972), they developed further a desire to elevate the comfortable, more popular vernacular style of architecture into the realm of serious architectural discourse. Post-Modern architects such as **Philip Johnson** and **Aldo Rossi** then developed a neo-eclectic formula for construction, which reintroduced a broad variety of historical and philosophical issues.

Michael Graves is perhaps the best-known Post-Modern architect. Graves was initially categorized in 1972 as one of the "New York Five," and went on from his architectural firm in Princeton, New Jersey, to construct what is considered the icon of Post-Modernism, the Portland Public Service Building (Portland, Oregon, 1982). This 15-story-tall office building with a copper figure of "Portlandia" in front of it makes a series of playful references to the **Beaux-Arts** amalgam of historical styles used at the turn of the 19th century for large government and civic structures. It features a massive applied exterior design of two colossal fluted **columns** with a large trapezoidal top to cover the two "columns" like a giant classical capital. The clear exaggeration of these classical features gives a playful quality to the **skyscraper**, reducing the seemingly self-important severity that modern skyscrapers traditionally engender. Michael Graves also constructed buildings for Walt Disney World, including Orlando's 1990 Dolphin Resort, which reveals a playful mix of "high" and "low" architectural elements. Robert Stern's version of Post-Modernism is very conducive to fantasy vacationlands, and he also constructed a series of buildings for Walt Disney World.

Charles Willard Moore also used exaggeration in his Post-Modern designs. His Piazza d'Italia, a small square built in New Orleans in 1978, exemplifies this idea. With a mix of loud, sometimes clashing colors, Moore's work provides the visitor with a fusion of such historical elements as columns, **arches**, and colonnades with frieze inscriptions. Sometimes Moore's constructions border on kitsch, through such nontraditional materials as large graphics and neon lights. However, at the Piazza d'Italia, the classical references to Italy very clearly depict a classical urban square located somewhere in Italy. The piazza's enclosed areas and stepped seats that flow into open areas encourage the visitor to spend time there.

Other Post-Modern architects include the Italian Carlo Scarpa, the Spanish architect Ricardo Bofill, and the Argentine architect **Cesar Pelli**. Because of the more eclectic and vernacular interests of Post-Modern architects, the style continues to be viable today, in conjunction with the more recent styles of **High-Tech architecture** and **Critical Regionalism.**

PRAIRIE STYLE. *See* WRIGHT, FRANK LLOYD.

PRANDTAUER, JAKOB (1660–1726). *See* ROCOCO ARCHITECTURE.

PREHISTORIC ARCHITECTURE. The earliest known architecture in human history is found in the prehistoric period called the Upper Paleolithic Age, which dates from around 40,000 BC to around 7000 BC. While earlier humans lived in Africa and Asia, the receding Ice Age and the extensive climate changes that occurred in Europe during these years set the stage for dramatic changes in the life of Neanderthal and Cro-Magnon humans, which allowed for a more settled lifestyle and more extensive forms of shelter. Archaeological evidence of early architecture is difficult to reconstruct because most structures were created with fibrous materials that decay over time. Instead, architectural anthropologists have argued that Paleolithic humans did not "invent" architecture, but gradually began to define and structure their surrounding environment to create spaces that allowed them to better understand their place in the world. Thus, surviving **stone** tools that were clearly used to cut plant materials must suggest the creation of camping sites during a period that predates traditional notions of architectural origins. However, if architecture is defined in its most general sense as a human-made enclosure created with an aesthetic intent, it is easy to understand how a choice of camping sites, selection of building materials, and use of new techniques such as binding, bundling, and staking were not only functional aspects of architecture but could also reveal simple aesthetic principles such as categorical polarity and proportional harmony.

Cro-Magnon peoples made tools of bone and antler carved with images of animals and other organic forms, while also painting images of hunting scenes on the internal walls of caves. Such images not only reveal a socially organized society, but one that demonstrates the earliest form of an aesthetic context in such creations. That aesthetic quality can also be found in the earliest known shelters. These structures are typically oval huts made of branches, animal hides, or even bone, with a hearth in the center. Larger huts might have more than one fire pit, with the interior space sectioned into different task areas. Although most **wood** dwellings do not survive over time, a Paleolithic village excavated at Mezhirich (in the Ukraine) dates to around 15,000 BC and reveals a cluster of huts made of woolly mammoth bones. The bones provided an intricate framework for structures that were probably covered by animal hide. The huts range in diameter from 13 to 33 feet, and 15 hearths have been excavated, revealing ashes and charred bones. In some cases, the dirt floors were colored with powdered ocher.

From the Mesolithic to the Neolithic era, architecture became more fully developed. People began to domesticate animals and wild grasses, which meant that life was less transient, necessitating more permanent dwellings. As humans started to hunt and farm, communal tasks were divided up in a more sophisticated way, and dwellings and villages reflect this increase in human collaboration with a more structurally complex architectural system. Most buildings during this time were made of timber with a **post-and-lintel** structural system, in which timber formed a flat roof that spanned the width of the room and was supported by posts. The posts could then be filled in with woven branches covered with mud, which would dry to create a sturdy wall structure. This technique is known as wattle and daub. Larger structures might have a ridgepole, a long horizontal beam running down the middle of the roof and supporting a slightly slanted roofline, which was then supported internally by additional vertical posts running down the middle of the open room. In the northern areas of Europe, dwellings were made of masonry, and many of these stone structures have survived today. One such example, which dates to around 3100 BC, is the village of Skara Brae, located on the Orkney Islands off the coast of Scotland. This village consists of a cluster of rectangular dwellings linked by covered passageways. The buildings are made of layers of flat stones, stacked up without mortar but layered to slope inward slightly and form a corbelled structural system. In this system of corbelling, the walls rise up and come together gradually; the smaller open roof would likely have been covered with wood and turf. Inside the dwellings, stone seats, stone bed enclosures, a hearth, and storage niches create a clearly defined interior.

Stone ceremonial structures also began to appear in the Neolithic Age. Large stone alignments can be found across Europe, such as the *menhir* alignment at Menec in Carnac, France, from around 3700 BC. Here rows and rows of large vertically placed rocks called megaliths appear, which when placed upright individually are called *menhirs*. Circular stone arrangements are also found across Europe, and they are called "cromlechs." These sites certainly had a ceremonial function much like the permanent megalithic tomb structures that also appear in the Neolithic period. The tomb site at Newgrange in Ireland is the most elaborate system of passage graves known today. This complex dates to around 3000 BC and consists of a series of burial chambers made of large rocks placed vertically into the ground and then covered with smaller rocks and dirt to create a mound. The construction rocks were engraved with abstract geometric designs of circles and spirals. Narrow entrance passages, which give the name "passage grave," lead into the central burial chamber, which is aligned so that on the summer solstice a ray of sunlight shines directly into the center of the burial area.

Clearly, the cyclical nature of life, with the passing of the seasons, and the agrarian cultures were central to the religious beliefs of Neolithic peoples. This emphasis is seen even more clearly at the most famous Neolithic site of **Stonehenge** on the Salisbury Plain in England, which dates from between 2700 and 1500 BC. This "henge," or circle, is made of megaliths formed into a post-and-lintel system to create a circle surrounded by a ditch. Inside the circle, a second group of stones forms a horseshoe shape. Much has been written about the logistics of bringing these large stones to this region of England, as well as the mathematical precision needed to calculate the exact day of the summer solstice, the morning in which the sun rises directly over the heel stone, as can be seen from the center of the horseshoe.

Current research continues to reveal more Paleolithic and Neolithic sites from France, Spain, northern Italy, Greece, Central Europe,

Siberia, Iran, and into Africa; with this research, more architectural examples from this era will probably be revealed and can give us a better understanding of prehistoric culture.

PUEBLO STYLE. *See* NATIVE AMERICAN ARCHITECTURE.

PUGIN, AUGUSTUS WELBY NORTHMORE (1812–1852). *See* GOTHIC REVIVAL ARCHITECTURE.

PYRAMIDS OF GIZA, EGYPT. An entire funerary complex, called a necropolis, or "city of the dead," can be found in Giza outside of modern-day Cairo. In this complex are located the so-called Great Pyramids of Giza. Traveling from Cairo, one can begin to see these three huge pyramids rising from an entire complex of buildings constructed for three pharaohs from Dynasty 4 of the Old Kingdom. The largest, made for the pharaoh Khufu (ruler from 2589 to 2566 BC), covers 13 acres of solid rubble that rises up along four slanted faces to a height of about 480 feet at the central point. Granite and smooth limestone originally covered each pyramid and some of it remains on the top of the pyramid of Khafra (d. 2532 BC). The smallest pyramid, dedicated to King Menkaura (2532–2503 BC), still has some of the original red granite along its base. These pyramids were made of solid **stone**, except for the internal burial chamber beneath the pyramid and the various sham chambers, false passageways, corridors, and escape routes that descended diagonally into the pyramid either toward or away from the burial chamber. The original entry, sealed after burial, might well be several stories up on one face of the pyramid, making subsequent entry almost impossible except for the most dedicated tomb robbers.

Since Ancient Egyptians worshipped a sun god, these pyramids might have symbolized the rays of the sun. The elevated processional path that leads past the monumental Sphinx toward the pyramids follows an east-west direction toward the setting sun. Around the complex is a series of temples, built in the **post-and-lintel** system and made of granite and alabaster. More recent excavations at the site reveal an entire town built for the manual laborers, who spent a lifetime constructing these monuments. Given that each stone, quarried nearby, might weigh about 2.5 tons, the process of rolling the stones on logs or dragging them on smooth wet sand from the quarry to the pyramid, and then pulling the stones up wooden ramps that sloped to the top, was not only a feat of engineering, but of extremely intense physical labor. It is no wonder the Ancient Greeks considered the Pyramids at Giza one of the Seven Wonders of the World. *See also* ANCIENT EGYPTIAN ARCHITECTURE.

– Q –

QUEEN ANNE STYLE. *See* VICTORIAN ARCHITECTURE.

– R –

RAINALDI, CARLO (1611–1691). *See* BAROQUE ARCHITEC-TURE.

RANCH STYLE. The Ranch style of domestic architecture was origi-nally based on the sprawling, single-story Spanish Colonial ranches of the Southwest but was modified as a suburban middle-class home in the 1930s to better accommodate the dramatically increased need for single-family housing in the United States, a need that peaked in the 1950s. The Ranch house first appeared in the quickly growing state of California, where the automobile allowed for easy access from the city to the suburbs and their less expensive, larger lots. Ranch homes featured large lots with big yards and a rambling, one-story style that dominated the space. Ranch homes feature a **brick** exterior with a front porch at ground level, covered by a long, low roofline and a hipped roof, shuttered windows, and simple trim. In-side, the houses feature a simple, open floor plan, often in an L shape, where sleeping areas are divided from living areas.

Like the Usonian houses first adapted by **Frank Lloyd Wright** for more popular use, Ranch homes have a centrally located kitchen styled as the core of family life. Sliding glass doors open up into the backyard, echoing Wright's interest in the integration of the exterior and the interior of his homes. The Ranch house goes a step further, however, with the inclusion of a more informal recreational room in addition to the living room, and the addition of an attached garage. The increased length of a house with an attached garage provides an imposing façade and symbolizes the central importance of the automobile to this house design. **Le Corbusier** had incorporated automobile parking at the ground level of his Villa Savoye of 1929, but there the main living areas were elevated, in keeping with the more traditional domestic format of the *piano nobile* set above ground-floor storage areas.

The most important aspects of the Ranch house, which have given this house style such an enduring appeal, are its "livability" for middle-class families, its flexibility in floor plan, and its simple, clean lines that allowed such homes to adapt easily to a variety of climates and blend into different types of neighborhoods. By the 1950s, the California Ranch, the Midwestern Ranch, and the Colonial Ranch were varieties of the Ranch house, the decade's most popular house type in the United States.

RAPHAEL SANZIO (1483–1520). *See* RENAISSANCE ARCHITECTURE.

RASTRELLI, FRANCESCO BARTOLOMEO (1700–1771). This Russian architect, whose family originated in Italy, is best known for his highly ornate Late **Baroque** and **Rococo architecture** found in and around St. Petersburg. Rastrelli arrived in Russia in 1715 with his father, a sculptor, and both went to work for the Russian aristocracy to cultivate a sumptuous, native Rococo style for the royal family. By 1730, Rastrelli had become the Senior Court Architect.

Rastrelli's Winter Palace, built in St. Petersburg in 1754–1762 for Catherine the Great, appears as a richer, more elaborate version of **Versailles Palace, France**. This visual parallel to French aristocratic architecture helped to confirm the cultural authority of the Russian monarchy at the time. (The first Winter Palace, built by Rastrelli in the 1730s, had been demolished to allow room for this grander structure.) While light pastel colors were commonly used in Rococo paintings and interior spaces, here a light green color is introduced on the massive exterior, accentuated by white **columns**, more forcefully disengaged from their walls than at Versailles, and topped by highly ornate gold capitals. With a wonderful view across the Neva River, this building is now used to house part of the Hermitage Museum.

The Catherine Palace, built in Tsarskoye Selo, or the "Tsar's Village," in 1752–1756, allowed the royal family to escape urban life for the carefully cultivated countryside. Built in the Rococo style with later **Neo-Classical** additions, the building is painted a light blue with white columns topped by gold capitals, while gold onion **domes** provide an exotic, almost playful, appearance to the exterior. With the addition of formal French-styled gardens and a courtly culture in emulation of the French ideal, Catherine I was able to confirm her cultural superiority at a time when monarchic rule was just beginning to be questioned in French intellectual circles.

In Kiev, Rastrelli built the Church of Saint Andrew in 1749–1754 for Empress Elizabeth. Kiev was the center of Eastern Orthodox faith at the time, and this particular site, located on a steep hill, was thought to be the location where the Apostle Saint Andrew erected a cross during his visit to the region. Due to the awkward terrain, the church was built with **cast-iron** steps that lead the visitor up to an entrance platform. The structure, built on a square plan with a vivid green onion dome and four corner towers that look like minarets topped by smaller onion domes, has light blue walls covered by a profusion of white columns.

These elaborate Rococo buildings helped to provide a beautiful visual symbol of powerful political rule in Russia in the mid-18th century, and despite their adherence to French Baroque and Rococo architectural principles, Rastrelli nonetheless created a uniquely eastern version of the Rococo style that remains an important historical symbol of high Russian culture.

RATIONALISM. European modernist architecture of the 1920s and 1930s was defined as a functional style of construction stripped of applied decoration, whereby the intrinsic characteristics of a building's materials were brought to the forefront of its design, allowing for a better understanding of the true beauty of the structure. Modern architects maintained that two forms of beauty existed: one that was sensual and emotional and therefore prone to degradation, and one that was more objective and therefore reflected a "higher" form of beauty, timeless and universal. The idea that architects should aspire to a more objective, rational approach to architectural design is philosophically classical in origin, but the stylistic qualities of Rationalist architecture did not include overt classical Greek or Roman references that might trap the building in a specific time or place. This thinking runs parallel to the ideas of the **Bauhaus** artists in Germany, led by **Walter Gropius** and **Ludwig Mies van der Rohe**, to French Purism, epitomized by the disciplined buildings of **Le Corbusier**, and to the Utilitarian forms of architecture developed after the Russian Revolution of 1917 by architects such as Vladimir Tatlin. The Rationalist style was most fully developed in the Netherlands, where its regional variant is called *de Stijl*, and in Italy, where it is called *razionalismo*. Distinctly different in style, these two forms of Rationalist architecture confirm the idea that the **International style**, as this general European phenomenon of modernism later was called, did not, in fact, transcend national or cultural differences. These national differences can be seen, for example, in the works of Giuseppe Terragni in Italy and Gerrit Rietveld in the Netherlands.

While German avant-garde modernism was brutally suppressed during Adolf Hitler's reign, Rationalism thrived in Italy under the rule of Benito Mussolini, who saw an underlying classical ideal that fit with his interest in Roman antiquity. For Mussolini, Rationalism was a natural modern outgrowth of the Ancient Roman Empire, the greatness of which he sought to restore during his own rule through both conquest and construction. Giuseppe Terragni was the leader of the Rationalist movement in Italy. He was born in Lombardy in 1904 and studied at the Milan Polytechnic before establishing his ideas in the *Gruppo Sette* manifesto, published in 1926 by seven like-minded Italian architects. These architects built upon the work of the previous Italian Futurists, such as Antonio Sant'Elia, who wanted to bring Italy further into the modern world by rebuilding the country in the form of a giant, dynamic machine. The dynamism that formed the central characteristic of Futurism was based in part on the thriving Italian automobile industry, which consisted at this time of Fiat, established in Turin in 1899, and Alfa Romeo, begun in Lombardy in 1910. Certainly, the advent of the automobile played a major role in the design of modern architecture in general, causing homes such as the Villa Savoye, built outside Paris by Le Corbusier in 1929, to feature a carport and ground-level garage. Rationalism differed from Futurism, however, in its greater focus on efficiency and its rejection of the more chaotic elements of Futurism. Rather than dynamism, Rationalism was more focused on a universal timelessness.

Terragni's most famous building is his Casa del Fascio, built in Como in 1932–1936 as a regional administrative center for the Fascist government. The white reinforced-**concrete** building is a perfect prism, set off-center with four rows of five large openings on the left two-thirds of the building's façade and a thick, uninterrupted wall surface that takes up the right third. The rectangular openings have windows throughout to flood the interior with light and provide a transparency meant to symbolize the supposed openness of the Fascist regime. This building conforms to the three principles of the International style: the primacy of volume rather than space, the design of regularity rather than symmetry, and the lack of applied decoration. In particular, the façade of the Casa del Fascio demonstrates the principle of regularity, and it is this distinction that separates Terragni from the more stripped-down **Neo-Classicism** of other early 20th-century Italian architects such as Marcello Piacentini. Piacentini is best known for his design of EUR, the Esposizione Universale di Rome, in 1938–1942, and the Via della Conciliazione in front of **Saint Peter's Church in Rome**.

In the Netherlands, both J. J. P. Oud and Gerrit Rietveld worked in an equally geometric style, but instead of the classically inspired white surfaces of Terragni's buildings, Rietveld in particular experimented with primary colors. As a member of *de Stijl* ("the style") which was a movement formed by the painter Piet Mondrian, Rietveld sought to design both buildings and furniture to create a uniform ambience in his interiors. His Schroeder House, built in Utrecht in 1924, is further influenced by the geometric structure of Analytic Cubism, because he did not seek classical symmetry but a more dynamic equilibrium of colors and shapes. The exterior of the building is made of gray and white squares of reinforced concrete, pieced together in vertical and horizontal sections with cantilevered squares and balconies jutting out in an asymmetrical design that negates the traditionally flat exterior wall surface. Small sections of colors accent the exterior surface and prepare the visitor for the inside of the house, which is entirely given over to bold primary colors. Wall partitions can be moved back and forth throughout the house to create different room arrangements and maximize interior flexibility. Although the owner of the house was quite wealthy, she requested a house that was modest in addition to elegant.

Although Rationalism was short-lived, perhaps due in part to its utopian ideals, Neo-Rationalist tendencies can be found in the **Post-Modern architecture** of the Italian architects **Mario Botta** and **Aldo Rossi**, and in the current work of Richard Meier in the United States. Richard Meier was born in Newark, New Jersey, and established his profession in New York City. In 1972 he was identified as one of the "New York Five," which consisted of a group of architects under the mentorship of **Philip Johnson**. Meier worked primarily in an updated version of the International style and was influenced mainly by Le Corbusier in his use of highly geometric forms stripped of any external decoration. His extensive career includes the recent construction of the Barcelona Museum of Contemporary Art in 1995 and the Getty Center in Los Angeles, which opened in 1997. The exterior of the Barcelona Museum employs a series of white squares and rectangles pieced together in a three-dimensional form, much like Rietveld's Shroeder House, yet with the restrained, classical white concrete of Terragni's buildings. Thus, in the works of Rossi and Meier, it is clear how Neo-Rationalist architects continue to find meaning in the early 20th-century European modernist style of Rationalist architecture.

REINFORCED CONCRETE. *See* CONCRETE.

RENAISSANCE ARCHITECTURE. The time after the Middle Ages, from around 1400 to 1600, can be characterized as an age when the classical world of Ancient Greece and Rome enjoyed a renewed and broad-based popularity. Thus, in the mid-19th century, the term "Renaissance" was given to this period because its culture reflected a "rebirth" of antiquarianism. Building upon late medieval advances in higher education and the arts, as well as the end of the feudal society and the growth of city life, the Renaissance enjoyed an increasing economic prosperity and a relatively stable political structure. The newly emerging merchant class provided more venues for architectural patronage that complemented and expanded upon the continued patronage of the nobility and the Catholic Church. Thus, architecture flourished.

In addition, "humanism" emerged as a philosophy based on the Ancient Greek ideal of a human-centered world, blended in the Renaissance with Christianity to provide a balance between the secular and sacred worlds. Architects, like artists working in other media, enjoyed an increase in social importance and came to be viewed by the end of the Renaissance as creative geniuses rather than just skilled craftsmen. This more prominent position came about with the merging of the medieval role of the *capomaestro*, or "headmaster," who oversaw construction of a building, and the more intellectual approaches of the Renaissance scholar or artist, who sought to better understand the philosophical and aesthetic aspects of classical architecture. The design of a Renaissance building therefore required more than just geometry and pattern books. It required the aesthetic background of a painter, the three-dimensional studies of a sculptor, together with a mathematical examination and philosophical study of historical structures—all combined to produce a more intellectually based role for the architect.

The Renaissance architect was not trained in the profession of architecture, which did not yet exist as a separate career; rather, artists became architects via a variety of professions. **Filippo Brunelleschi**, widely considered the first Renaissance architect, is a good example. Trained as a goldsmith in Florence, he traveled to Rome around 1402 after losing a commission to create a set of bronze doors for the Baptistry of Florence. In Rome, Brunelleschi embarked on a sustained study of **Ancient Roman architecture**, including the **Pantheon**. He returned to Florence to build the largest **dome** since antiquity for the Florence Cathedral, later called the "Duomo." After that, Renaissance architecture spread across Italy and then throughout Europe, defining itself with such elements as the classical **column**, the portico, the triangular pediment, the round **arch**, and the dome. Aesthetically, Renaissance architecture is based on symmetry and a logical and clear system of proportion that harks back to the Ancient Greek ratio studies of the human body. In order to better understand classical architecture, Renaissance artists relied heavily not only on existing buildings in Rome, but also on the sole surviving ancient treatise on architecture, written by **Vitruvius** in the first century BC and titled *De architectura*. This manuscript was rediscovered in 1414, and copies of it became immediately popular among Italian Renaissance artists and scholars, spawning a whole series of Renaissance treatises written by architects such as **Leon Battista Alberti**, **Sebastiano Serlio**, and **Andrea Palladio**, all modeled in part on this ancient manuscript.

Because of its connection to classicism, Renaissance style is widely considered to have been born in Italy—more specifically, in the prosperous central region of the peninsula. It was in Florence in the early 1400s that the Renaissance first appeared, largely a result of the great interest in architecture demonstrated by patrons such as the Medici family, who used buildings to glorify their political power in much the same way as the Ancient Romans. For example, the Medici Palace, built by Michelozzo di Bartolommeo in the 1440s, set the design standard for the Tuscan palaces of many subsequent patrons, including the Rucellai and the Pazzi families. In order to become a rationally designed urban home, the Medici Palace softens the features of the fortified medieval **castle**, such as rough-cut **stone**, towers, crenellations, and irregularly arranged doors and windows. This late-medieval-style palace is also epitomized by the Palazzo della Signoria (the Palazzo Vecchio), built in the 1290s and used as the main government building in Florence. This is a tall building made of rusticated stone, with a small entrance door that was guarded at all times. External windows are located at irregular intervals across the façade to suggest a four-story building. Some windows are in the **Gothic** bifurcated style, with two vertical sections and pointed arches at the top, while the others are unadorned square shapes. The top of the building has an attic that juts out from the wall surface and provides a room of open windows used by the guards. It is capped with crenellations along the roofline, a feature that is sometimes called a battlement. Finally, a tall bell tower, also with a battlement, rises to the right side of the building. Inside the building, a large courtyard based upon classical models welcomes the visitor and brings light to the internal rooms.

In contrast, the three-story Medici Palace is built with rusticated stone at the lower level but with smoother masonry at the upper levels, where round-arched windows divided in the middle by slender classical columns are placed equidistant from each other. In addition, the stories are clearly separated by an entablature, and the second and third stories are visually linked by the placement of windows one exactly atop the other. The ground floor originally had a series of arched doorways that entered into shops, but they were closed in the early 1500s by **Michelangelo**. Entering the building, the visitor would first come upon the large classical courtyard in the form of a rectangular arcade of thin columns with composite Corinthian capitals and round arches. From there, the visitor would ascend the stairs to the house's large front hall, which was used to entertain guests. This second story, called the *piano nobile*, was the central living floor of the house. On the way, one would pass the beautifully decorated chapel, located in a small alcove off the stairwell. The bedrooms were then located toward the back of the house, with the children's and servants' rooms in the third story.

These grand Renaissance *palazzi* reveal what is called the "theory of magnificence"; even though private, their beauty and grandiosity were intended to be a source of pride for all Florentines. This palace style quickly spread across all of Italy, and excellent examples can be seen in Rome, Siena, and Urbino in the 1400s. In the next century, the Palazzo Farnese, begun in Rome by Antonio da Sangallo the Younger and completed by Michelangelo in the 1540s, is an even larger palace with an even clearer articulation on the exterior. This three-story building features smooth masonry throughout, with entablature bands that run beneath each row of windows to demarcate each story. In the *piano nobile*, the windows feature the new rectangular format, with alternating semicircular and triangular pediments on top of each, whereas simpler triangles cap the third-story windows. A heavy cornice tops the building, and stonework runs down the corners of the building. Stone is also used in the center of the building to provide a focus to the central door. More architectural elements are used to articulate and clarify different aspects of a building, in keeping with the Renaissance desire for a rational and logical design.

As the feudal era waned, fortified architecture also gave way to more open and classically inspired rural homes as well. Although Andrea Palladio was best known for his Renaissance villas, many similar country homes can be found across Italy. The Medici Villa, located at Poggio a Caiano in the hills outside Florence, was built by Giuliano da Sangallo in the 1480s and epitomizes this new Renaissance architectural type. This country home is not surrounded by busy streets and flanked by other urban homes and thus can have open porticoes on the front and back of the building. The front façade features a tripartite plan, with three stories divided into three parts vertically as well. The whitewashed masonry provides a smooth exterior surface. The ground floor, which housed the equipment needed for the farm, features an arched loggia with three sets of three arches that jut out from the wall to provide an open porch on the *piano nobile*. The *piano nobile* is reached via two sets of stairs that curve up toward each other from the ground floor. The center of the façade features a classical portico entrance, with six columns that support a triangular pediment. Above that are rows of windows at the third story, and the building is capped by a simple roof with a clock tower rising from the middle. It is this overall design that formed the basis for Palladio's subsequent villas, built in the Veneto in the 1500s.

The Renaissance classical aesthetic can also be seen in church architecture at this time. The small church of Santa Maria delle Carceri, located in Prato, outside Florence, was built by Giuliano da Sangallo in the 1480s. This Greek-cross-plan church, with transepts located on all four sides, conforms to the Renaissance desire for perfect symmetry. It is considered the earliest church of this type in Renaissance Italy to be modeled on Brunelleschi's earlier versions in Florence and on Alberti's discussion of the perfect form of this church in his treatise on architecture. It is a small square building with a dome over the central core, elevated on a drum surrounded by round, or oculus, windows. The arms, or transepts, which extend outward from this central square, measure one-half the width of the square and are covered by barrel vaults. The articulation of the interior, done in *pietra serena*, or dark stone, follows the number symbolism as first established by Brunelleschi. As such, the dome features 12 ribs and rests upon the square crossing that rises up to meet the round dome via transitional triangular sections called pendentives. Thus, 3, which refers to the Trinity, multiplied by 4, which often refers to the Evangelists, results in the 12 ribs, or 12 apostles. Ultimately, although given a Christian interpretation, symbolic values for these numbers can be traced back to ancient scholars such as Pythagoras. Of the three basic geometrical shapes employed by Sangallo here, the circle, in keeping with Christian tradition, was considered the most perfect. With no predetermined beginning or end, the circle referred to the idea of infinity, and thus, to God himself. In the next century of the Renaissance, **Donato Bramante** took this plan a step further in Rome in 1504 with his small church of San Pietro in Montorio, called the Tempietto.

The Church of **Saint Peter's in Rome**, begun by Bramante, served as inspiration for the next generation of architects as they provided visual symbolism to the continued strength of Roman Catholicism despite the advent of the Protestant Reformation. In France, François I (who ruled from 1515 to 1547) sought to introduce this new Renaissance style to his country with a major artistic campaign centered in Paris and at his country home, the **Fontainebleau Château**. In Paris, the medieval-styled **Louvre Palace** was updated with classical elements added by Pierre Lescot. In Spain, the Renaissance style was introduced in the court of Philip II (ruled 1556–1598), who hired Juan Bautista de Toledo and Juan de Herrera to build the **Escorial** outside Madrid, both as his palace complex and as a **monastery**. In the Protestant break with the papal church and the establishment of the Church of England, Tudor and Elizabethan architecture reveal a blend of late medieval **Gothic** elements with regional influences. The Tudor style, later called the **Tudor Revival**, continued to be popular in England and then in the United States through the 19th century.

Renaissance style maintained a lasting significance for architecture, with classical revivals appearing repeatedly until the modern era. With the birth of humanism and its intellectual underpinnings, architects came to be seen not simply as manual laborers who specialized in stonemasonry, but as intellectuals who, with a better understanding of classical ideals, created a theoretical base for architecture that established a new aesthetic imbued with symbolic meaning. These ideas continued into the next century, when they were reformulated to fit the needs of the ensuing Counter-Reformatory Church in Rome and the increasingly powerful aristocratic culture across Europe. This new era is called the **Baroque**. *See also* ANCIENT GREEK ARCHITECTURE.

RIBERA, PEDRA DE (c. 1681–1742). *See* COLONIAL ARCHITECTURE; ROCOCO ARCHITECTURE.

RICHARDSON, HENRY HOBSON (1838–1886). Henry Hobson Richardson was the second American-born architect to study at the École des Beaux-Arts in Paris, after **Richard Morris Hunt**. Richardson was born in Louisiana and studied first at Harvard and then in Paris. He worked in many styles during his career but is best known for his adaptation of the **Romanesque**, which came to be called the "Richardsonian Romanesque." Although many private homes feature this Romanesque style with its red **brick** exterior walls and heavily rusticated red **stone** around doorways and windows, Richardson's most famous buildings in this style are his public structures in Boston and Chicago. Richardson's Trinity Church in Copley Square, Boston, was built after the Great Fire destroyed part of the city in 1872. The monumental church features a Greek-cross plan with a central square tower at the crossing. The façade was originally flat with front towers, but Richardson later added a highly sculptural porch modeled on the Romanesque Church of Saint-Trophime in Arles, France. Trinity Church epitomizes the Richardsonian Romanesque with its heavily rusticated stone walls, round **arches**, square towers, and the use of pink granite, red sandstone, and a red clay roof.

In Chicago, Richardson was hired to build the Marshall Field Warehouse in 1885–1887 (demolished in the 1930s). This commercial building revealed a balance between subtle historicism, as seen in the rusticated stone and arched windows that recalled a Florentine **Renaissance** palace, and a cleaner, more modern design devoid of **columns** and porticoes. The building suggested solidity in its use of granite and sandstone together with its wide corner piers and the beautiful rhythm seen in the rows of small rectangular and larger arched windows. Since the city of Chicago was still recovering from its Fire of 1871, many new buildings were being constructed, yet it was Richardson's warehouse that set the standard for the next generation of architects in Chicago, called the "Chicago School." *See also* SKYSCRAPERS.

RICHARDSONIAN ROMANESQUE. *See* RICHARDSON, HENRY HOBSON.

RIETVELD, GERRIT THOMAS (1888–1964). *See* RATIONALISM.

ROCOCO ARCHITECTURE. The Rococo style of architecture first appeared in the French court in the early years of the 18th century and can be seen in some ways as an outgrowth of the late-17th-century **Baroque** age. But while Baroque architecture was monumental and propagandistic, Rococo architecture was more intimately aristocratic, more sculptural, organic, and ornate. From France, it quickly spread to Germany, Austria, and then across the rest of Europe. It was a style that mirrored the highly refined culture increasingly cultivated by the aristocratic class to distinguish itself from the growing middle class. It is sometimes thought of as a more playful and less serious reaction to the overly formal classicism that continued during the Baroque age. When the Rococo first appeared, the reign of Louis XIV was drawing to a close.

This king was credited with the construction of the Baroque **Versailles Palace** in the 1660s. But at his death in 1715, the Duke of Orléans, who served as regent to the underaged Louis XV, moved the royal court back to Paris. There the Rococo style thrived with the construction of elegant urban palaces. Because these urban homes lacked the sprawling space of the rooms at Versailles, their Rococo interiors were more intimate, with elaborate decoration and furnishings, and often with mirrors that reflected light and gave the illusion of a larger space. Much like Versailles, these homes were used for such aristocratic social gatherings as masked balls and theatrical and musical performances, but also for the newly popular intellectual gatherings called salons, where current literature or philosophical ideas were discussed. The Rococo is sometimes described as a feminine style, given that women of the court often hosted these gatherings and became very important in the patronage of art.

The Hôtel de Soubise, built in Paris in the 1730s, features a room called the Salon de la Princesse. Designed by Germain Boffrand, it is an excellent example of the Rococo style. In this oval-shaped room, the visitor is greeted by an elaborate display of gilded stucco decoration on the walls and ceiling, with light from the chandeliers reflected off the mirrors that line the walls. No straight lines are evident in the room; instead, organic shapes called *arabesques* encircle the entire wall space, leaving nothing blank. Rococo paintings by Charles-Joseph Natoire, shaped like curved trapezoids, fit into the spaces between the mirrors and the curved molding of the ceiling. This integration of painting, sculpture, and architecture appeared in the Baroque age but became more popular in domestic rooms during the Rococo era.

The Rococo style soon spread to Germany, where the French architect François de Cuvilliés refined its exterior design in the small hunting lodge called the Amalienburg. Built in the 1730s in the park of the Nymphenburg Palace in Munich, it was named after the Electress Maria Amalia of Austria. This single-story building is pink with white trim and curves out from the side wings toward the central entrance. Here the undulating lines used by Baroque architects such as **Francesco Borromini** are continued in this aristocratic, domestic Rococo format. **Johann Balthasar Neumann** then expanded its use for the lavish Residenz, built for the Prince-Bishop of Würzburg. The general design of the Imperial Hall is based upon the Hall of Mirrors at Versailles, but its curved oval shape and highly sculptural ceiling give the room a more lively sense of movement than its counterpart at Versailles. Neumann employed this same style for his church of Vierzehnheiligen, near Staffelstein, Germany, begun in the 1740s.

In Austria, the Benedictine **Monastery** Church at Melk, built above the Danube River by Jakob Prandtauer (beginning in 1702) also reveals a gently curved façade with rounded twin towers. Inside the church nave, the piers undulate inward and outward, creating a rhythmic vista toward the elaborately decorated high altar. The monastic library at Melk similarly displays this ornately curved style. Perhaps the most impressive Rococo complex is Schönbrunn Palace, located in Vienna. This UNESCO World Heritage Site features a palace complex on the scale of that at Versailles, with beautiful gardens in the formal French style. It was begun in 1696 by the architect Johann Bernhard Fischer von Erlach for Emperor Leopold I; its massive scale is Baroque, but over the years it was updated in the Rococo style at the request of Empress Maria Theresa of Austria. Fischer von Erlach, born in Graz, is perhaps the best-known Austrian architect of the Rococo era.

These royal palace complexes served to confirm authority and to provide cultural centers for the European elite, who traveled from one palace to another not only for entertainment but also to cement political alliances. Many of these palaces were connected in part by the only existing paved rural roads of the time, for they were built with roads that radiated outward toward surrounding courts. Probably because Rococo culture originated in France, the French language became the official language of the court, learned by young aristocrats across Europe to Russia, where the Romanov Dynasty used the French language, European aristocratic cultural traditions, and Rococo architecture to cultivate a political link with the rest of aristocratic Europe. These palaces were therefore designed for an entire courtly culture, and rulers would host artists and performers to showcase their high taste. For example, Mozart's stay at the Rococo Palace of Schwetzingen outside Heidelberg has had a lasting influence even today, since the complex hosts an annual festival in his honor.

Finally, Rococo architecture spread to more modest regions of Italy, Spain, and Portugal, where it began to appear in civic buildings, local churches, and smaller palaces. The town of Lecce in southern Italy epitomizes the exuberance of the Rococo in the farthest reaches of its European influence, and in Spain its regional variant, sometimes called the *Churrigueresque*, or the Late Baroque, style, is seen in Pedro de Ribera's Portal of the Hospicio de San Fernando, built in Madrid in the 1720s. It is this Spanish version of the Baroque and Rococo styles that spread to North and South America, where it developed into the Spanish Colonial style. *See also* COLONIAL ARCHITECTURE.

ROEBLING, JOHN AUGUSTUS (1806–1869) AND WASHINGTON AUGUSTUS ROEBLING (1837–1926). *See* STEEL.

ROGERS, RICHARD (1933–). *See* CONCRETE; DOME; HIGH-TECH ARCHITECTURE; WORLD TRADE CENTER, NEW YORK.

ROMANESQUE ARCHITECTURE. The Romanesque style, named for the classical Roman features that characterize it, dates to the 11th and 12th centuries and features a thriving artistic culture. Medieval monastic communities enjoyed a continued growth, and towns often grew up around these religious centers because they provided goods and services as well as a degree of political stability. Cities also became more important than in the early years of the Middle Ages, although most people still lived primarily in agricultural communities spread across the continent. This agrarian culture was the central feature of the feudal era, when landowners living in fortified **castle** compounds offered some stability and protection to the local people in exchange for a certain percentage of the goods produced on their land. In addition to the landowners, who increased their authority either through marriage alliances or by battle, the clergy maintained authority mainly in the urban communities. The Holy Roman Empire then contributed an additional layer of aristocratic authority to this mix, and while sometimes these leaders forged a unified power structure, more often than not they vied for an increase in their own power.

Because of this increasingly complex political environment that was not yet fully codified, fortified castles came to symbolize Romanesque culture. Medieval castles line the countryside of Europe today, and while some are small, abandoned, and crumbling structures, others have been rebuilt or remain well preserved. Nonetheless, all types of castles have stirred the imagination of many people who romanticize this era, known for its chivalric codes and ideas on courtly love. The Romanesque castle, as the seat of both aristocratic life and military life, was often the scene of great battles. Castles grew out of Frankish military structures adapted for use by the Normans, who first built castles from **wood**, and only later began to construct larger compounds from **stone**. Initially, castles were of the quickly built mound-and-bailey type, which featured a round ditch dug out to create a moat. The loose earth was then piled into the center of the ditch and used to create a wall for a tower, which was then surrounded by a wood wall called a palisade. This structure was adjacent to the outer courtyard, called the bailey, in which the garrison and livestock were located. Masonry castles became popular during the Crusades, as Christian soldiers were able to see firsthand some of the massive stone **Byzantine** castles of eastern Europe.

The Krak des Chevaliers, a UNESCO World Heritage Site, is located in Syria along the border with Lebanon and is perhaps the best preserved Crusader castle in the world. A smaller, fortified stone structure had initially been built on this site by the Emir of Aleppo in 1031, which was captured during the First Crusade of 1099. It was then used over the years by the Crusaders and given to the Knights Hospitaller, who oversaw a dramatic expansion of the fortifications. During the Ninth Crusade of 1272, King Edward I of England stayed there and, greatly impressed by its architecture, was inspired to construct similar castles in England and Wales. The Krak des Chevaliers features a massive exterior of thick masonry built up on a hill. The wall has a walkway on top of it and towers located at various intervals around its circumference. This wall is then separated from a taller inner wall built up on an earth and rock mound, called a rampart, which forms the castle. A moat and drawbridge allow access to the castle. In the later **Gothic** era, the Hospitallers added internal courtyards and halls. The interior decoration of the Krak des Chevaliers makes it one of the best-preserved castle interiors in the world.

It was this castle type that became the most popular across western Europe, as seen in England's Tower of London and Italy's Castel del Monte. The former is a massive square crenellated castle built by William the Conqueror beginning in 1078 to house the aristocracy, the treasury, the garrison, and the prison of London. The concentric Castel del Monte in the southern Italian region of Puglia was built by Frederick II in 1240 to defend his provincial territories. **Durham Castle** in England is an important example of Norman Romanesque architecture. While the medieval castle was supplanted in the **Renaissance** by the urban palace and then the rural villa, these massive structures continued to be inhabited and remain very architecturally important today.

The highly fortified appearance of the castle, symbolizing the need for greater political stability, was mitigated by an increasingly prosperous, flourishing culture that witnessed the construction of many other types of buildings. The launching of the Crusades at the end of the 11th century and the increase in travel for military purposes, to establish new trade routes, and for pilgrimages, provided ample motivation for the construction of many other forms of monumental architecture, including beautiful cathedrals and great civic buildings. This growth in architectural construction aided in the establishment of a vibrant market for building materials and a large work force of manual laborers who more and more often were not tied to the land for their survival. Increasingly, stone replaced timber across Europe as a more durable and stronger material that allowed for larger structures, resisted fire, and recalled the buildings of **Ancient Rome**. Thus, a head master, or *capomaestro*, was typically trained as a stonemason. He created the layout and design for a building based upon the needs of the patron, and he directed a team of stonemasons who constructed the building. Construction required careful on-site supervision and was probably based on wooden building models, as paper was still too rare and expensive in Europe at this time to be used for extensive sketches of designs and for measurements. Stone blocks were individually carved and fitted together to create sophisticated structures with **arches**, vaults, and complex programs of architectural sculpture.

Churches were the most sophisticated of Romanesque structures, and typically consisted of basilica-plan buildings with beautifully decorated façades, tall flanking bell towers, wide projecting transepts, and elevated sanctuaries, often with ambulatories and with larger and larger windows that allowed more light into the interiors. The space where the nave and the transepts, or side arms, meet is called the crossing, which increasingly was used as the basic unit of measure for the entire church, with geometry organizing the interior. The taller nave ceilings necessitated a more sophisticated support system than was traditionally found in early medieval structures, and so **brick** and stone barrel vaults and cross vaults with semicircular ribs became more common as time went on.

The Cathedral of Santiago de Compostela in Spain, built from 1078 to 1122, is an important early Romanesque structure that exhibits these features. Built to accommodate the larger crowds that visited such pilgrimage churches, Santiago also has additional chapels running around its eastern side to house an increase in liturgical objects, works of art, and relics. After entering through the elaborately carved portal at Santiago, the viewer faces a tall two-story nave with compounded piers running down the nave arcade. The compounded pier, a Romanesque invention, consists of a cluster of half-**columns** joined together to create a stronger structure than an individual column. This greater strength allowed Romanesque builders to construct taller ceilings. At Santiago, the ceiling consists of a barrel vault separated into bay units by rounded masonry ribs. One set of engaged columns within the compounded pier then rises through the nave wall to meet the ribs, thereby dividing the wall very visibly into its bay units. Each of these bay units has a two-part arched window in the upper gallery from which light is filtered into the nave. More light enters via windows at the high altar and in the octagonal lantern that rises up over the crossing. The more sculptural effect achieved by the piers also provides a greater structural clarity to the church interior, a hallmark of Romanesque architecture. The lower side aisles are covered with groin vaults, which also help to disperse the weight of the nave roof into the outer walls.

Another Romanesque church of interest is Saint-Étienne in Caen, France, begun in 1060. Established by William, the Duke of Normandy, at the time of his conquest of England, this church features a tall façade flanked by some of the tallest towers of the era of Romanesque art. Because of this great height, external wall piers called buttresses are attached to the façade, creating a three-part division to the front that helps support the structure. The façade also rises up into three stories, and the center of the façade is articulated with a row of three windows in the two registers above the entrance, providing an overall unity to the exterior of the building. On the inside, the nave arcade features compounded piers that divide the nave into bay units, and a gallery above the arcade from which a sexpartite vault system springs. This vaulting, dating to the later 12th century, is characterized by bay units of three ribs each that intersect in the middle to form six parts, thus forming the most sophisticated structural system to date.

During this era, architectural sculpture became more complex. It was centered at the portals of the church where all visitors would pass from the physical world into the "house of God." The Romanesque church portal typically consists of a pair of wooden doors surrounded by an elaborately carved rounded arch that rises above the basic **post-and-lintel** framing of the doorway. A pier is located between the two doors, which is sometimes intricately carved and called a *trumeau*. Flanking the doors is a series of engaged columns called jamb columns, and above the lintel is a round arch called a *tympanum*. Surrounding the *tympanum* are several rows of square carved stones called *voussoirs*, which form several semicircular layers called archivolts. A good example of this architectural sculpture can be found on the west portal of the Cathedral of Saint-Lazare in Autun, France, from around 1130. It features a scene of the Last Judgment in the *tympanum*.

Although the Romanesque style originated mainly in Germany, France, and England, it spread across Europe, and examples in Italy include the Church of Sant'Ambrogio in Milan, begun in 1080, and the unique **Pisa Cathedral Complex**, begun in 1063.

ROMANO, GIULIO (c. 1499–1546). *See* MANNERISM.

ROMANTIC ARCHITECTURE. Romantic architecture takes its cue from the movement called Romanticism, which first developed in England during the late 18th century and the Industrial Revolution of the 19th century. It was motivated by a reaction against the rational, classical ideals of the 18th century and introduced a more nuanced understanding of aesthetics, emotions, the deeper sensibilities that motivate people, and of course, the sublime, which draws upon the image of a vast, untamed, and powerful nature for its inspiration. Romanticism spread from Europe to the United States, and is best known in literature, seen in the writings of François-René Chateaubriand and Jean-Jacques Rousseau in France, William Blake and William Wordsworth in England, Johann Wolfgang von Goethe and J. C. Friedrich von Schiller in Germany, and Ralph Waldo Emerson and Edgar Allan Poe in the United States.

In architecture, Romanticism often evokes past styles, such as the **Gothic** style, seen in the mid-19th-century **Gothic Revival**. Other types of Romantic architecture are illustrated in a variety of styles considered "exotic" due to their displacement into a "foreign" setting in a more fanciful, less accurate format. Examples of exotic architectural styles include Egyptian-influenced homes, Asian-styled homes, and even Swiss chalets. These homes contain such "exotic" elements as Egyptian columns and small sphinx sculptures, or Japanese-inspired rooflines, or a Swiss chalet A-frame as a decorative overlay to the traditional European building type. Inspired by Napoleon's military campaign to Egypt, which initiated the first modern, sustained research on **Ancient Egyptian** culture, Egyptian-influenced architecture was very popular in France and England from the 1790s through the first decades of the 19th century.

The Oriental Revival of the early 1800s can be attributed to increased trade with India and China in the later years of the 18th century. The most famous example of this fanciful, Indian-inspired style is seen in the Royal Pavilion in Brighton, England, built by John Nash in 1815–1822 as a seaside home for King George IV when he was the prince regent. The building features a series of onion domes along the roof, with minarets flanking the central dome while the roofline features exotic-styled pointed crenellations capped by balls. The front porch is partially covered with a latticework screen with Moorish horseshoe arches and pseudo-Gothic bifurcated windows.

The interior of the pavilion is done in a Chinese style, with richly decorated rooms suited to a vacation home.

Neo-Classicism also enjoyed a continued popularity in the form of the mid-19th-century Greek Revival style, which can be considered a Romantic style. Romanticism is also seen in the introduction of the Italian country villa style during this period, called the Italianate style. However, what makes the Italianate style different from the nearly continuous classical revival that characterizes architecture from antiquity onward is the motivation for its use. In this case, it specifically refers to the more Romantic notion of a nostalgic longing for this Italian **Renaissance** building type rather than to the more noble philosophical and sometimes political issues that are traditionally pinned to the various classical revivals.

In America, these ideas can be seen in the most ornate Italianate style house in the United States, which is the famous "Breakers House" built overlooking the ocean in Newport, Rhode Island. Designed by **Richard Morris Hunt** in the 1890s for Cornelius Vanderbilt, this 70-room mansion features a three-part **stone** façade where porticoes open at both the ground level and the upper story to allow views of the surrounding countryside. The central porticoes are flanked by wings on either side. While many more modest Italianate homes are made of **wood** and feature modified Victorian woodwork, this stone house represents the more monumental form of the Italianate style. Clearly a vacation home for the wealthy, The Breakers takes its cue from the Italian Renaissance villa type to create a visual reference between the Vanderbilt family and the established aristocratic families of Europe, who were widely viewed at this time as more culturally refined than their American counterparts.

The Swiss chalet–style home, also considered a vacation home, became popular in both Europe and the United States after it was introduced in a pattern book published in 1850 by Andrew Jackson Downing. This type of home, originating in the Alps, was more economically amenable to the middle-class than the more "exotic" Indian style, and therefore it found favor during the first several decades of the 20th century, primarily in the mountain regions of the United States.

Finally, the Octagon House, with its eight-sided shape, was introduced during this era as well, and several hundred of them, built on the East Coast and in the Midwest during the 1850s and 1860s, survive today. Introduced in a pattern book published by Orson S. Fowler in 1849, the octagonal house was considered to be very economical, efficient in floor plan, and better lighted than a traditional square building. Fowler's ideas on indoor plumbing and central heating were very forward-looking for his day, and although the Octagon House did not ultimately become widely successful, its economical design and practical features paved the way for subsequent designs created to accommodate the influx of middle-class homeowners in the 20th century. *See also* TUDOR REVIVAL STYLE.

ROSSI, ALDO (1931–). Although most **Post-Modern architecture** is generally seen as overtly historical, sometimes **Mannerist**, and even playful or humorous, Aldo Rossi cultivated a more formal Post-Modern style that is reductive, rational, and formal. By reducing his buildings to their basic geometric components, Rossi is often said to have a Neo-Rationalist style and is compared to the Italian Rationalist architect Giuseppe Terragni. But Rossi's combination of shapes and materials is unexpected. Exemplifying this style is Rossi's New Town Hall, built in Borgoricco, outside Venice, Italy, in the 1980s. This is a rigidly symmetrical building, in which Rossi takes industrial materials and elements such as the exhaust chimney that rises up in front of the building, the metal roof, and the large, frameless windows, and then unifies them with the more enduring evocations of such classical structures as the **Ancient Roman** temple and basilica. It is the way that Rossi combines these elements, however, that is unique, and his buildings provoke a sense of mystery much like the paintings of Giorgio de Chirico. *See also* RATIONALISM.

RUSSIAN CONSTRUCTIVISM. *See* CONSTRUCTIVIST ARCHITECTURE.

– S –

SAARINEN, EERO (1910–1961). Eero Saarinen, the Finnish-born American architect who first studied architecture with his father, Eliel Saarinen, is known for his curvilinear, organic constructions.

One of the first 20th-century architects to question the stark aesthetic that characterized early modernism, he sought instead to imbue his structures with a more expressive quality. Raised around the Cranbrook Academy of Art in Michigan, where his father taught, Eero displayed an early interest in architecture, studied at Yale University, and then traveled around the world before returning to Michigan to teach at Cranbrook. He later established an architectural firm in New Haven, Connecticut.

Eero Saarinen's early career was linked to that of his father. In 1942, Eliel Saarinen completed the first contemporary church designed in the United States, the First Christian Church in Columbus, Indiana. The modernist building set in motion a series of architectural commissions in this small town that established it as one of the premier locations for modernist architecture and public sculpture in the United States. Eero Saarinen's Irwin Union Bank was the second modernist structure in Columbus, completed in 1954. Here the architect sought to diminish the imposing, formal design of the traditional bank and instead to build a structure that was more open and welcoming. Accordingly, this bank, which is surrounded by trees, features large glass windows on the exterior and an open, well-lit interior. The town of Columbus today features over 70 important buildings constructed by numerous internationally known architects, including Gunnar Birkerts, **Cesar Pelli**, **Robert Venturi**, and **I. M. Pei**.

The Trans World Airport Terminal, built at JFK Airport in New York (1956–1962), is Eero Saarinen's most famous work and demonstrates his desire to integrate the function of the building into its design. Here, the walls swoop upward like a bird in flight, and the huge roof, made of reinforced **concrete**, is shaped like two broad wings. The inside of the terminal features broad spaces that flow from one to another, providing an open interior where people can move quickly from ticket counters to gates. As flying was becoming a more accessible mode of travel, record numbers of people were beginning to fly. Thus the TWA Terminal, with its innovative design, records this period of excitement in air travel, the booming travel industry, and American idealism.

Eero Saarinen's Gateway Arch in St. Louis, known as the "Gateway to the West," is a famous tourist destination that has come to symbolize the city as well as to express American idealism in terms of modern American technical innovations. Designed just before his death, the **arch** was completed from 1963 to 1965 by Saarinen's partners Kevin Roche and John Dinkeloo. At a cost of 15 million dollars, the arch is a feat of engineering. It stands 630 feet tall, is made of stainless **steel** wrapped over reinforced concrete, and is shaped like a parabolic arch of equilateral triangles. With its internal elevators for visitors to travel to the top, it has become one of the most famous tourist destinations in the Midwest. *See also* EXPRESSIONISM.

SAARINEN, GOTTLIEB ELIEL (1873–1950). *See* SAARINEN, EERO.

SAFDIE, MOSHE (1938–). After World War II, the need for inexpensive urban housing created innovative apartment designs based on the utopian urban ideals of **Le Corbusier**. Most of these urban apartment buildings were constructed using raw **concrete** formed in bold rectangular shapes in a style called **Brutalism**. Within this historical framework, the Israeli-born architect Moshe Safdie introduced a more spatially complicated apartment complex called Habitat '67 as part of the permanent housing exhibition created for the 1967 World Exposition in Montreal. The overall design consists of prefabricated modules placed together in a stacked, zigzag pattern to create rooms, courtyards, and roads elevated at different levels. This multilevel format recalls ancient Mesopotamian dwellings that were traditionally clustered together with shared walls and a stepped pattern of differing building heights. These regional considerations anticipated the architectural style called **Critical Regionalism**, which has been popular in domestic architecture of the 21st century. The Habitat is also very practical in its modular system, which featured an internal structure to allow for easy expansion of its components. Safdie's innovative apartment designs provided a welcome alternative to the traditional high-rise apartment blocks of the modern era.

SAINT PETER'S CHURCH, ROME. Because Saint Peter's, located in the Vatican in Rome, is the "mother" church of Roman Catholicism, it has historically been one of the most important pilgrimage sites in the world. Even during the **Renaissance**, a new structure was needed to accommodate the large crowd of visitors, and in 1505 a reconstruction campaign was initiated by Pope Julius II. Old Saint Peter's, as the original church came to be called, was so revered that during its reconstruction detailed sketches were made to document its earliest appearance. Old Saint Peter's followed the traditional basilica-style plan, which was based upon such **Ancient Roman** government buildings as the Basilica of Maxentius, located southeast of the Imperial Forums in Rome and begun around AD 306. Emperor Maxentius requested that this rectangular basilica, his administrative seat, not be constructed with a **columned** interior such as seen in the earlier Basilica Ulpia (AD 113). Instead, the building featured groined vaults down its tall center and two shorter side aisles, with barrel vaults to buttress the center and provide room for clerestory windows above. The vaults were made of **brick** and **concrete** and allowed for a large, unencumbered interior space. Most Roman basilicas were entered from the longer sides of the building, but Maxentius's entrance was at one of the short ends, allowing for a strongly axial direction toward the apse at the far end. Although Constantine later added a side door, this original axial direction, as well as the tripartite interior division, was adapted for use in the earliest Christian churches. These churches either employed a columned interior and flat timber roof or piers to support a vaulted roof. The basilica format, instead of a traditional temple plan, served to distance this new religion from that in which the pagan gods were still worshipped, although the classical rotunda was often still used for baptisteries and funerary monuments. Despite the government-supported pagan religious beliefs, Emperor Constantine is credited with ending the persecution of Christians in Rome and allowing them to worship in public.

Old Saint Peter's Church dates to Constantine's reign and was constructed beginning in AD 326 on the site where the apostle Saint Peter was buried. This burial site came to include a full crypt that lies beneath the church. Old Saint Peter's was a large basilica church with a long nave separated from the double side aisles with rows of columns that supported a timber roof. Clerestory windows allowed light into the nave, and the entrance was placed on an axis with the high altar, located at the far end of the church. Toward the apse was an early, less fully formed, proto-transept called the *bema*, and a high altar that featured a large triumphal **arch**. Saint Peter's bones were placed beneath the altar, and a large *ciborium* was constructed over the altar to commemorate this location. To enter the church, the visitor walked up a series of stairs that served to elevate the sacred space, passed through an arched entrance that led into an open courtyard lined with a covered colonnade, called either an *atrium* or a forecourt, and then walked through the *narthex*, or church foyer, and into the nave. The narthex, which provides a transitional area from the secular world to the sacred, was retained on many early Christian churches, but is rarely used today.

Because Old Saint Peter's had been restored on several occasions, by the time of the Renaissance, it was in such poor shape that Julius II decided to rebuild it as the largest Christian church in the world. At the time, Christianity had been fully established across Europe, but the city of Rome, which never fully recovered its ancient grandeur through the Middle Ages, did not reflect its importance as the seat of the papacy. Therefore, the renovation of Saint Peter's Church eventually included the completion of the Vatican apartments with frescoes by Raphael, the completion of the Sistine Chapel with **Michelangelo**'s frescoes, and the construction of numerous other administrative buildings, gardens, paved paths and roads, and a large square, or *piazza*, in front of the church.

This monumental project was initiated by **Donato Bramante** in 1506, but only a few years later, his death and the death of Pope Julius II briefly interrupted construction. Bramante had designed a massive domed, centrally planned church, which, by the time of the Renaissance, was considered the superior church plan due to its perfect symmetry. In this case, the domed church also functioned as a *martyrium* (a sacred edifice, usually a tomb, built to commemorate a Christian martyr or saint). Disagreements began almost immediately, however, resulting mostly from the concern that a centrally planned church cannot accommodate the same number of congregants as a church with a long nave. The resulting dispute concerning the idealistic views versus the realistic church plan led to a series of proposals for a basilica-plan church, and Michelangelo's design from the 1540s was selected. Michelangelo retained Bramante's original centrally planned design but reduced the number of smaller internal rooms and reinforced the central piers, which already showed signs of cracking. He began construction in the crossing and around the back of the church, and he created a **dome** design, but it had to be constructed after his death by his student Giacomo della Porta, who in the 1580s lengthened the height of the drum but otherwise retained the essential features of Michelangelo's plan.

By the late 1500s, the Counter-Reformation led to the larger, more theatrical and sculptural **Baroque** style that was showing its first signs of development. The reforms of the Council of Trent included encouragement for the use of basilica-plan churches, which could accommodate the large crowds of people anticipated in the fight against the Protestant Reformation. Therefore, in 1606, Pope Paul V commissioned Carlo Maderno to complete Saint Peter's in a modified basilica plan that would include a wide three-bay nave attached to Michelangelo's design, a narthex, and a wide façade. The façade is truly monumental, with a colossal portico entrance of disengaged columns superimposed onto the center of a tripartite design, with pilasters on the sides and two tall stories, a thick entablature, and then a high attic level capping the façade. The dome rises above the façade, but twin bell towers that were initially planned for the sides of the façade were never completed due to problems with cracking. The cathedral complex was finally completed in the 1650s by **Gian Lorenzo Bernini**, who constructed a huge oval piazza that stretches out like the arms of the church to encircle its congregants. This oval piazza comes out from the smaller trapezoidal entrance square, or forecourt, right in front of the narthex.

Because Saint Peter's was originally designed as a centrally planned church (also called Greek-cross-plan) but received a longitudinal nave, it ultimately illustrated the basilica, or Latin-cross-plan, church. This solution was a compromise and resulted in two high altars. In the 1620s, Bernini completed a massive bronze *baldacchino* over the crossing altar of Saint Peter's, and in the 1660s he finished the bronze "Cathedra Petri," or Chair of Saint Peter, over the apse altar. Although the majority of the church was finally completed in the Baroque era, the importance of Saint Peter's as the "mother" church of Roman Catholicism today means that its interior decoration remains an ongoing process. *See also* EARLY CHRISTIAN ARCHITECTURE.

SANGALLO, ANTONIO DA (THE YOUNGER) (1484–1546). *See* RENAISSANCE ARCHITECTURE.

SANGALLO, GIULIANO DA (c. 1443–1516). *See* RENAISSANCE ARCHITECTURE.

SANSOVINO, JACOPO (1486–1570). Jacopo Sansovino is credited with introducing to Venice the classical architecture that was developed further in the next generation by the famous Venetian **Renaissance** architect **Andrea Palladio**. Jacopo Sansovino was born in Florence but spent most of his early years working in Rome. During this time, the papal court in Rome sponsored many architectural commissions to restore the city to its ancient grandeur, and so the High Renaissance style flourished there during the first two decades of the century. However, in 1527, Rome was pillaged by members of the army of Holy Roman Emperor Charles V. The Holy Roman Empire and the Papacy had been maintaining an uneasy alliance, and indeed the Emperor was in northern Italy at the time to help drive the French out of the region. His victory so drained the imperial treasury that the majority of his soldiers abandoned their duties after finding out that they would not receive their salaries. Around 35,000 of these soldiers, together with their commanding officers, marched on Rome to loot the city, and Rome was nearly destroyed. Most of the leading artists and architects, including Jacopo Sansovino, fled the city along with many other people.

In 1529, Sansovino settled in Venice and became the chief architect to the Procurator of San Marco. It is in the central piazza of San Marco that Sansovino's most famous buildings are located, including the Mint, called the "Zecca"; the small portico called the "Loggetta" that adjoins the belltower, or campanile; and the library, located across from the Doges' Palace. The library, built by Sansovino in the 1530s, is innovative in design and format. It effectively provides the final link to the traditional branches of city life. These include the economic center, located in the thriving market area behind the library; the religious authority, symbolized by the adjacent Cathedral of San Marco; the secular political power, represented by the Doges' Palace; and finally, the new Renaissance interest in the intellectual aspirations of its citizens, represented by the library itself.

Libraries had been built prior to Sansovino's structure, but this is the first library to attain such a prominent location and to be so fully integrated into a city's identity. The library mimics the general appearance of the opposing Doges' Palace by following the same long, rectangular shape and the two-story open portico. The Doges' Palace, however, is larger and has an additional third story, marking its central importance in the city. The architectural importance of the library is that it replaced the **Gothic** style, which had continued to be very popular in this northern Italian city, with a Renaissance classicism imported from Rome. Accordingly, Sansovino's columns are not the fanciful versions separated by Gothic arches and exotic decoration that characterize the Doges' Palace. Instead, he used the **Vitruvian** Doric and then Ionic capital orders to support each story, together with rounded arches that form the open porch areas and are flanked by smaller columns. Finally, a classical Roman balustrade runs along the roof. The levels are separated by classical molding that serves to create a rational design, in keeping with classical principles. Thus, here Sansovino successfully brought to the city of Venice both the style of classical antiquity and its Renaissance symbolism.

SANT'ELIA, ANTONIO (1888–1916). *See* FUTURIST ARCHITEC-TURE.

SCAMOZZI, VINCENZO (1548–1616). *See* PALLADIO, ANDREA.

SCARPA, CARLO (1906–1978). *See* POST-MODERN ARCHITEC-TURE.

SCHINKEL, KARL FRIEDRICH (1781–1841). Architecture in Germany often followed a different path from the major stylistic innovations that came out of Italy, France, and England during the **Renaissance** and **Baroque** ages. This different approach was due in part to the fact that the late medieval **Gothic** style of architecture was claimed as a German innovation and therefore continued to be popular into the Renaissance and Baroque ages. It was supplanted only in the early years of the 18th century by the aristocratic, courtly style of the **Rococo**, which originated in France. By the middle of the 18th century, however, **Neo-Classicism** had been introduced into Germany, largely a result of the pioneering work of the first art historian, the German scholar Johann Joachim Winckelmann. Winckelmann spent most of his life in Rome, working to establish stylistic categories for ancient art and to better understand the distinctions between

Ancient Greek and Roman artistic innovations. By making historical links between Ancient Greek and ancient German cultures, Winckelmann was able to lift classicism out of the clutches of Italian culture and give it equal claim to being German in origin.

It is with these nationalistic underpinnings that subsequent German architects such as Karl Friedrich Schinkel, working in the Neo-Classical style, became so popular in Germany. Schinkel was born in Prussia, studied architecture in Berlin, and then traveled to France and Italy before returning home to a French-controlled country. After the French were expelled from Prussia, Schinkel was hired as the Surveyor of the Prussian Building Commission to help revitalize his country. He built numerous Neo-Gothic buildings but is best known for such Greek-inspired Neo-Classical works as his Neue Wache, built in 1816–1818, and the Schauspielhaus, built in 1819–1821. Schinkel's most important commission, however, was for the Altes Museum, built in the 1820s. Located on a small island on the Spree River in downtown Berlin directly across from the royal palace, the museum was built to house the royal art collection. Eighteen Ionic **columns** line the raised portico of the massive Neo-Classical entrance, which is elevated by a tall set of wide stairs. Tall windows line the exterior walls, and interior courtyards also help solve the need for diffused lighting inside the museum. Schinkel's version of Neo-Classicism endured through the next century and came to be seen as a national German architectural style.

SCOTT, GEORGE GILBERT (1811–1878). *See* GOTHIC REVIVAL ARCHITECTURE.

SCOTT BROWN, DENISE (1931–). *See* VENTURI, ROBERT.

SECOND EMPIRE STYLE. *See* VICTORIAN ARCHITECTURE.

SELJUK ARCHITECTURE. *See* ISLAMIC ARCHITECTURE.

SERLIO, SEBASTIANO (1475–1554). Born in Bologna, Sebastiano Serlio worked in Rome for the architect **Baldassare Peruzzi** until the city was sacked in 1527 by the army of Holy Roman Emperor Charles V. He then relocated in Venice, where he began writing a series of influential treatises on architecture. The first published volume, called *Regole generali d'architettura*, was printed in 1537 and was meant to be the fourth volume of a series of seven books on architecture. A total of five books were ultimately published, with a sixth book just recently identified and published along with the original series. In the first two books, Serlio provided information on geometry and perspective, while Book 3 comprises an overview of **Ancient Roman architecture**. Book 4 is focused on the adaptation of classical rules to more modern architectural elements not found in Ancient Rome, such as fireplaces. Book 5 provides a discussion of the classical **column** orders, and here Serlio added the Tuscan order, a fusion of the Doric and Ionic, to the canon first established by **Vitruvius** and elaborated upon by **Leon Battista Alberti**. Serlio then illustrates 12 temple designs using these orders. What is innovative about Serlio's architectural treatise is the way in which he was able to combine tradition and invention, or *invenzione*, which allowed for greater flexibility in the use of the classical architectural vocabulary. This more varied use of classicism is consistent with Serlio's training in **Mannerism**.

These books attracted the attention of King François I, and in 1540 Serlio, together with several other Italian **Renaissance** and Mannerist artists, was invited to the royal court at **Fontainebleau**. There they introduced Italian Mannerism to France and helped to reinvigorate French Renaissance artistic culture. At Fontainebleau, Serlio oversaw the construction and decoration of the château; while in France he received several other commissions for country palace designs. His greatest contribution, however, was the dissemination of his treatise to architects such as **Andrea Palladio**, who illustrated his *I quattro libri dell'architettura*, published in 1570, with the same lavish detail as Serlio, and across Europe, where architects did not necessarily have access to Roman models and therefore could not always study classicism firsthand. The high-quality images therefore served as important models for instruction across northern Europe and inspired subsequent architects such as **Christopher Wren** in the establishment of classicism in English **Baroque architecture**.

SHINGLE STYLE. *See* VICTORIAN ARCHITECTURE.

SHREVE, LAMB, AND HARMON. *See* SKYSCRAPER.

SINAN, MIMAR KOCA AGHA (1489–1588). The best-known architect of the Ottoman Empire, Sinan was the chief architect to the sultans Selim I, Süleyman I, Selim II, and Murad III. For 50 years, Sinan oversaw every major building constructed around the empire. With such powerful royal patronage, Sinan was provided with a large workshop that aided in the construction of over 300 buildings. Sinan began his career in the Ottoman military, which he joined in 1512, and where he was able to study carpentry and math. As a member of the Janissary Corps, the sultan's household troops and bodyguards, Sinan traveled widely, and after the capture of Cairo, he was promoted to chief architect in charge of rebuilding bridges, roads, and houses, and converting churches into mosques. Through his military experiences, Sinan learned what structural deficiencies might lead to the easy destruction of a building, and he therefore sought in his own work a more sophisticated engineering, which resulted in some of the largest, most monumental structures of his day. In 1539, he became the Architect of Istanbul and then the Architect of the Empire, receiving the title of "Koca," or "Elder."

Sinan's best-known buildings are his Süleyman Mosque in Istanbul and his Selimiye Mosque in Edirne. The imperial mosque built for Süleyman "the Magnificent" in Istanbul was the center of a group of buildings in the *kulliye*, or palace complex, which included schools; a hospital; a *hamam*, or bath; a soup kitchen; and a *caravanserai*, or traveler's inn. Begun in 1551, the complex was completed rapidly, before the end of the decade. The mosque is based on the church of Hagia Sophia, built in Istanbul in the 500s and subsequently converted into a mosque. Like Hagia Sophia, the Selimiye Mosque has an interior space formed on a 1:2 ratio that emphasizes the massive central **dome.** The windows that encircle the drum make the dome appear to hover, weightless, above the centrally planned interior. With the Selimiye Mosque in Edirne (1569–1575), Sinan further modified his ideas by creating a dome set upon an octagonal drum with eight external piers to buttress the dome. This provides support for the window-lined drum as well as for the windows located in the walls beneath the dome. Structurally daring, this proliferation of windows around a dome allows for an extremely well-lit, unencumbered interior. Since this mosque is two feet taller than the dome of Hagia Sophia, Sinan achieved his dream of constructing the tallest dome in the world, while the mosque also features the tallest minarets in the world. Sinan's architectural innovations were formed from a more practical, empirical knowledge rather than the classically inspired theoretical basis from which construction was derived in western Europe during the **Renaissance**. In this regard, Sinan was able to stretch the prior structural limitations of domed, unencumbered space to create some of the most daring religious structures in history. *See also* ISLAMIC ARCHITECTURE.

SKIDMORE, OWINGS & MERRILL. One of the largest architectural firms in the world, Skidmore, Owings & Merrill (SOM) was formed in Chicago in 1936 by Louis Skidmore and Nathaniel Owings, and in 1939 John Merrill joined the group. In 1937, the New York City branch opened, and offices are currently found around the world. Skidmore, Owings & Merrill is best known for high-quality commercial real estate, while the "**glass**-box" **skyscraper** has become its trademark. The first building that gave SOM international attention was the Lever House, built in New York City in 1952 as the corporate offices for the British soap company. Designed by Gordon Bunshaft and located in the high-rent district of Park Avenue, this **International style** skyscraper was built with the first glass curtain wall in New York City. The sleek, 24-story rectangular box is made of a stainless **steel** frame that supports the blue-green tinted glass windows, sealed to keep dust and dirt out of the building. The skyscraper rests on a two-story platform at ground level, which includes a terrace and cafeteria at the open third story. The steel framing is designed with tracks to allow window washing scaffolding, stored on the top level, to move up and down the exterior with ease. A 25-million-dollar renovation of the Lever House has just been completed, allowing the contemporary visitor to enjoy the original glass color and the beautiful sheen of the steel framing.

In 1969, Fazlur Khan, the primary structural engineer for SOM, designed the 100-story John Hancock Center in Chicago, which was for a time the tallest building outside of New York City, and it remains one of the tallest residential buildings in the world. The exterior of this skyscraper is braced with X-shaped stainless steel bars that provide additional support to the outer walls, thus the ability to support an open interior space without a massive structural system needed in its core. The structural innovations found in this building anticipated the **High-Tech architecture** of the next decade and paved the way for ever-taller skyscrapers. The Sears Tower, built in Chicago in 1970–1973, was designed by Fazlur Khan and Bruce Graham of Skidmore, Owings & Merrill. This 108-story building is stepped inward in three phases from its base to its top, providing a visual organization to the building by breaking up the "shaft" of the skyscraper into smaller parts, much like the three-part division seen in the earliest skyscrapers. With these tall buildings began the race for ever higher structures, and the Sears Tower was quickly superseded in height by the "supertall" Petronas Twin Towers built in Malaysia in 1996 by **Cesar Pelli**, then by Taipei 101, built by C. Y. Lee and Partners in Taiwan in 2004, and finally, by the Burj Dubai, a 164-story skyscraper currently under construction in the United Arab Emirates by Adrian Smith of Skidmore, Owings & Merrill, due to open in 2009.

In addition, David Childs of Skidmore, Owings & Merrill rebuilt the **World Trade Center** 7, which was consumed by fire and collapsed after the bombing of the World Trade Center Twin Towers in New York City on September 11, 2001. This 52-story structure is smaller than the original building, as it was designed to accommodate a park around the structure and additional safety and environmental features within the building. The architects of Skidmore, Owings & Merrill continue to excel at large-scale projects, which number over 10,000 worldwide and include such large-scale design commissions as the Boston Transportation Planning Review, completed in the 1970s, and a series of subsequent "supertall" structures found around the world.

SKYSCRAPER. The skyscraper first developed in the United States as urban property became more expensive and cities were increasingly crowded. A skyscraper does not have a specific style or height requirement but is generally considered taller than what is often called a "high-rise." The skyscraper was initially an economic solution, but it went on to become a symbol of American architectural ingenuity, in spite of the fact that the idea was generated with the older **cast-**

iron framed buildings constructed in England during the Industrial Revolution, such as the flax mill built in Shrewsbury in 1797.

Henry Hobson Richardson anticipated the development of the skyscraper in the United States with his Marshall Field Warehouse, built in Chicago in the 1880s and demolished in the 1930s. On the exterior, the building featured seven registers of fenestration grouped to demarcate several tall warehouse floors on the interior. Although this building, with its rusticated **stone** and **arched** windows, resembled at first glance a **Renaissance** palace, its clean lines and lack of exterior sculptural detail also show a break from the **Beaux-Arts** tradition in which Richardson had been trained. The building set the stage for the subsequent construction of many more austere skyscrapers in Chicago, in a style sometimes called the "Chicago School." The skyscraper originated in Chicago because of the large amount of construction that took place there after the Fire of 1871; by the turn of the century, the building type had quickly spread to all major urban areas of the United States. Skyscrapers were made possible with the introduction of **steel**, which by the mid-19th century was beginning to be mass-produced through a more efficient and economical method. Steel was superior in its tensile strength to iron and allowed for greater structural possibilities, which were immediately explored by architects. In addition to the industrial production of steel, the invention of the electric passenger elevator in 1889 made the skyscraper logistically feasible.

Chicago's first steel-framed buildings were constructed by William Le Baron Jenney. Jenney's two earliest steel-framed buildings have been demolished, but in 1891 he constructed the Leiter II Building on State Street, which still exists as the city's oldest department store. Built with a tall, fenestrated gallery level at the street, the structure rises with six registers of double windows capped by a thick cornice. Piers anchor each of the four corners, providing the building with several stripped-down historical references that give a visual organization to the structure. Jenney's Manhattan Building, also constructed that year in Chicago, is a 16-story building—unprecedented for its day—with a façade of bay windows that allow considerable light into the building. Granite sheathes the first three stories, while a lighter, less expensive **brick** is used on the upper registers. **Louis Sullivan**'s Wainwright Building, constructed in St. Louis in 1891, is even more austere, yet it maintains a basic organization seen in its clearly articulated tripartite division that mimics the **column**. Here the street-level story forms a base delineated by a cornice, while the middle of the building rises up like the shaft of a column and is capped with a heavy cornice at the roofline, much like a capital.

Sullivan's firm was in Chicago, but by the early 1900s New York City began to dominate skyscraper construction. The Woolworth Building, constructed in 1911–1913 by Cass Gilbert, is a good example of the restrained historicism that continued to pervade skyscraper designs. At 55 stories tall, it was built with a clearly articulated base at the street level, and then a wide shaft rises punctuated by cornices that provide visual pauses to minimize the building's vertical consistency. From the shaft, a spire rises, tiered three times and topped with a pinnacle. These features provide the building with a more austere form of the **Gothic Revival** that continued to be popular through the early 20th century. By 1930, **Art Deco** was the skyscraper style of choice, seen in the Chrysler Building and Empire State Building in New York City. William van Alen, who built the Chrysler Building in 1928–1930, and the architectural firm of Shreve, Lamb, and Harmon, who completed the Empire State Building in 1931, vied for "tallest-building" status, and indeed the Empire State Building held the honor for 40 years.

The first **International style** skyscraper built in the United States is the Philadelphia Savings Fund Society Building (PSFS), constructed by George Howe and William Lescaze in Philadelphia in 1931. This 32-story rental office tower is an elegant polished black granite and glazed brick building with copper, brass, and stainless steel detailing. A big sign with "PSFS" written in block letters angled across the top of the tower fully integrates the design of the building with its corporate identity. By the middle of the century, **Ludwig Mies van der Rohe** and **Philip Johnson** also began to use the International style in their skyscrapers, resulting in such **glass** structures as their Seagram Building in New York City. Constructed in the 1950s, this skyscraper has a clearly articulated street level and then a shaft that rises up in a dark glass curtain wall, uninterrupted by cornices or any other applied decoration, and capped by a smooth top. These International style buildings continued to grow taller, and when the seven-building **World Trade Center** was completed in

1973 by Minoru Yamasaki, its "twin" towers stood 110 stories tall and were briefly the tallest structures in the world, soon surpassed by the Chicago Sears Tower.

More sophisticated structural advances characterize Norman Foster's Hongkong and Shanghai Bank, built in 1986, which is a good example of **High-Tech architecture.** This 47-story-tall building has exterior girders that allow for a more open interior space and a reduced need for a strong structural core. By the 1990s, "supertall" skyscrapers began to challenge existing structural advances. **Cesar Pelli**'s Petronas Twin Towers, built in Malaysia in 1996, is an 88-story twin tower with a two-story skywalk at the 41st story. Currently, the tallest building in the world is the 164-story Burj Dubai, under construction in the United Arab Emirates by Adrian Smith of **Skidmore, Owings & Merrill**. These "supertall" buildings not only fulfill the need for dense urban housing but also challenge existing architectural innovations in their technical sophistication.

SMITH, ADRIAN (1944–). *See* SKIDMORE, OWINGS & MERRILL.

SMITHSON, ALISON (1928–1993) AND PETER SMITHSON (1923–2003). *See* BRUTALISM.

SOUFFLOT, JACQUES-GERMAIN (1713–1780). The leading French architect of the 18th-century **Neo-Classical** style, Jacques-Germain Soufflot worked during a turbulent time of French history, which ultimately erupted in the French Revolution. By the middle of the 18th century, the Neo-Classical style was increasingly viewed as the favored style of the Age of Enlightenment, while the "decadence" of the prevailing **Rococo**, seen as the aristocratic style, became discredited in France. The Church of Sainte-Geneviève, also called the Panthéon, built in Paris by Soufflot from 1755 to 1792, epitomizes this reemerging classicism. Here, Soufflot combined the ancient and **Renaissance** classicism he saw while traveling in Italy with the monumentality of the **Baroque** style to create a massive church with a colossal columned portico that supports a triangular pediment. Like that of **Christopher Wren**'s Baroque Cathedral of Saint Paul in London, Soufflot's **dome** rises up on a tall drum that features a colonnade of freestanding **columns**. Despite its importance, the chaotic time leading up to the Revolution impeded construction of the church and led to its unusual history. During its construction, the French government, needing to replenish its treasury after losing its colonial territories to England during the Seven Years' War, took over the property with the intention of selling it. Then, in 1791, the church was transformed into a secular Temple of Fame that honored those who died in the French Revolution. Under Napoleon, the building reverted to a Catholic church, then a nondenominational religious temple, and then a physics laboratory. Today the Panthéon remains one of the most important architectural monuments in Paris, while Soufflot is credited with the establishment of a monumental form of the classical idiom in 18th-century Paris that created a definitive break with the Rococo.

SOUTHEAST ASIAN ARCHITECTURE. *See* ANGKOR, CAMBODIA; INDIAN ARCHITECTURE.

SPANISH COLONIAL ARCHITECTURE. *See* COLONIAL ARCHITECTURE.

STEEL. Steel, an alloy of iron and trace amounts of carbon, is a stronger material than **cast iron**. Known since antiquity, steel began to be produced with some degree of efficiency only in the mid-19th century, with a new industrial procedure called the Bessemer process. The first structural use of steel in architecture is found in William Le Baron Jenney's early **skyscrapers** built in Chicago, and one of the most famous early steel skeletal structures is the Fuller Building in New York City, better known as the Flatiron Building. Constructed in 1902 by Daniel Burnham, this **Beaux-Arts style**, 285-foot-tall skyscraper was constructed in a triangular shape to accommodate the area where Fifth Avenue and Broadway intersect at an angle. Steel was stronger, lighter, and less expensive than cast iron; its introduction as the skeleton frame of large-scale buildings altered the course of architectural history.

Steel constructions often featured technically challenging designs as well. Steel was also used for suspension bridges, as exemplified in the Brooklyn Bridge, constructed by John Augustus Roebling and his son Washington Augustus Roebling in the 1860s–1880s. John Roebling had invented twisted wire cabling to replace the chains previously used in bridge suspensions, and when completed, the Brooklyn Bridge in New York City was the longest in the world. Heavy steel cables hang from two massive stone towers that feature paired pointed **arches** flanked by pilasters. R. Buckminster Fuller, an early technical architect, also used steel for his geodesic **dome** constructed for the United States Pavilion at Expo '67 in Montreal. In many ways, Fuller's dome anticipated the focus placed on the highly technical architectural style introduced in the 1980s and called **High-Tech architecture**. These buildings were increasingly constructed from a stainless steel exoskeleton that more effectively resists corrosion, and architects were increasingly exploring the use of titanium, such as **Frank Gehry** in his **Post-Modern** buildings. His Guggenheim Museum in Bilbao, Spain, from the 1990s, is completely covered with Grade 1 titanium that features a slight rippling effect to create a softer texture to the exterior. Despite the introduction of these new materials, steel continues to be structurally superior and therefore central to technically sophisticated design and construction.

STERN, ROBERT (1939–). *See* POST-MODERN ARCHITECTURE.

STICK STYLE. *See* VICTORIAN ARCHITECTURE.

STONE. The Neolithic era of **Prehistoric architecture** has traditionally been called the "Stone Age" because of the appearance of stone tools and other implements, as well as large-scale stone constructions. The earliest masonry structures are Neolithic settlements from around 3100 BC, such as the one at Skara Brae, located on the Orkney Islands off the coast of Scotland. This island had little forestation, and its rocky coastline provided ample masonry for this seaside village. Houses were built in square shapes with rounded corners, made with layers of flat stone stacked without the use of mortar and slanted slightly inward to create a partial corbel. The smaller roof opening was then thatched. Inside the rooms, stone was used to create partitions for bedding and niches for storage. A hearth area with a low stone bench was located in the middle of the room. The houses were linked with covered passageways. Tomb mounds were also created from large rocks, called megaliths, and were placed into a **post-and-lintel** structural system to create passageways into the tomb interiors. Such monumental rocks were often transported large distances, and furthermore, the fact that different types of stones came to symbolize different aspects of society demonstrates the beginnings of a socially stratified culture with codified rituals. **Stonehenge**, located in the Salisbury Plain of Wiltshire, England, dates to around 2750 BC and is the most famous example of a large-scale stone monument.

The Inca of Peru devised a unique and structurally superior method of stone construction as seen at the mountainous town of **Machu Picchu, Peru**, built around AD 1450. Here the stone buildings are all of a superior dry stone construction technique called *ashlar*, in which massive stones are cut to fit perfectly together without mortar. Irregularly shaped rocks fit at perfect junctions while the walls lean slightly inward, which is characteristic of Inca construction. Despite the severe earthquakes and the pillaging of Inca stonework to build Spanish churches in Peru, surviving Inca wall junctions remain perfectly tight with no spaces or cracks or threat of collapse. Making these architectural feats more impressive is the fact that the Inca did not have the wheel or the horse, and therefore used manpower and llamas to drag large rocks up these mountains.

Despite the prevalence of stone monuments across almost all cultures, stone structures came to be primarily associated with **Ancient Greek** and **Ancient Roman architecture** because of the beautiful white **marble** found mainly in the area around Greece. The term *megalith* comes, in fact, from the Ancient Greek encounter with these large (*mega*) stones (*lithos*). Subsequent stone constructions built throughout the Middle Ages and in the Renaissance then came to recall this enduring classical history and to express an alliance with the papacy or the Holy Roman Empire. The use of stone to signify architectural authority continued in the early-20th-century **Beaux-Arts style**, when architects such as **Richard Morris Hunt** and **Charles Follen McKim**, inspired by the idealized but temporary "White City" constructed for the World's Columbia Exposition held in Chicago in 1893, went on to build stone structures across the major East Coast cities of the United States, including the Metropolitan

Museum of Art in New York City and the Public Library in Boston. Although more recent buildings are formed from **steel** skeletons and feature curtain walls of **glass** and other materials, stone is still often used to provide a more historically based, "grand" curtain wall for buildings. *See also* BRICK.

STONEHENGE, ENGLAND. Stonehenge is perhaps the best-known example of Neolithic ceremonial architecture in Europe. Constructed as a *henge*, or circle, of massive, megalithic **stones** in the center of the Salisbury Plain in Wiltshire, England, and dated to around 3100 to 1500 BC, this monument provides fragments of information about these earliest structured cultures. The Neolithic period is characterized by a gradual thawing of the Ice Age, which brought about newly temperate lands, more diverse animals, and greater possibilities of more sophisticated standards of living. The bow and arrow replaced the less accurate spear, dugout boats created more opportunities for fishing, and the stone tools from the previous Paleolithic era of **Prehistoric** times became more varied and functional, paving the way for the establishment of agriculture and then the domestication of animals. This more settled lifestyle allowed for an increasingly complex social structure that hinged upon communal rituals, and one major factor in the recognition of a Neolithic society is the evidence of more permanent settlements. By the end of the Neolithic era, communities enjoyed a more stable lifestyle. They stored foods, traveled and traded, and began to construct monumental ceremonial architecture in addition to their more simple **wood** and thatched dwellings. Since this ceremonial architecture was for the most part constructed of stone, many examples still exist today.

Prehistoric ceremonial architecture was probably constructed for two main reasons, for funerary needs and for agricultural calculations. While the appearance of tomb architecture suggests structured religious beliefs, these monuments are also often fused in function with their more cosmological use in determining the changing of the seasons. The tomb mounds at Newgrange, in Ireland, date to around 3000 BC and epitomize both functions, with passage graves aligned to the summer solstice. Stonehenge does not overtly function as a funerary monument, but tomb monuments have been found nearby, thereby fueling speculation about its function or functions. Clearly, the site had long been important to Prehistoric peoples. Human habitation can be found in the area as early as 8000 BC, when Mesolithic postholes, with pine posts sunk upright into the ground, were excavated near the modern-day parking lot of Stonehenge. It is thought that at least three of the posts are aligned in an east-west arrangement. This use of timber postholes is not previously known in England, but examples from this time can be found in Scandinavia. The region of Wiltshire was heavily forested during this time, and evidence shows that Neolithic peoples began to clear land near the stone monuments to create farmland and pastures; the location of Stonehenge would certainly not have been remote to these Neolithic peoples, as one might assume from its current spare geography.

Stonehenge is a circle of stones set up vertically to function as posts. Some are covered with a continuous row of lintels, and the entire arrangement is surrounded by a round banked ditch. The **post-and-lintel** structural system is the oldest in the world, and appears here very clearly despite the fact that some of the lintels have fallen and some posts have collapsed. The circle was probably laid out with a type of cord to measure the circumference of the circle from its center point. Cords woven from plant fibers were also probably used to haul and hoist the stones into place. What makes Stonehenge unique is not that it is the largest *henge* in Europe, but rather that evidence of its continued rebuilding over a thousand years suggests that it was extremely important, perhaps centrally located in a major regional center. In the earliest phase of construction, a massive ditch was built, dug down into the chalky subsoil to create a white outer circle for the monument. Bones of deer and oxen, as well as stone tools, have been found in the ditch. A broad path led from this outer circle to a single sarsen, or gray sandstone, which is set vertically into the ground. This huge stone, weighing 35 tons, was brought from a quarry located about 23 miles away. The logistics of the use of such huge stones, brought from far distances, remains a wonder to modern scholars. Clearly, the sarsen stone itself held symbolic meaning that did not allow for its replacement by a more conveniently located stone. This stone is traditionally called the heel stone and is an important point of reference for the seasonal changes demarcated at Stonehenge.

During later phases of construction, the distinctive inner core of the stone complex began to take shape. Today it consists of a central horseshoe-shaped grouping of five pairs of sandstones, each topped with a lintel. These post-and-lintel pairs are called *trilithons*. The central *trilithon* is taller than the other four, standing about 24 feet tall. At the center of the *trilithon* grouping is one single stone, called the altar stone. Surrounding this group is a circle of megalithic sarsen stones, some weighing as much as 50 tons. All the stones are set vertically into the ground, each one standing approximately 20 feet tall. This circle was topped by a continuous lintel, some of which is intact today. All the stones are tapered slightly at their tops to give the appearance of stability. The lintels are held together by rocky projections cut into one rock, secured into a hole carved out of adjoining rock. Between these two megalithic rings was a smaller ring of bluestones. This type of blue dolerite must have held some specific symbolic value, for they were brought from a quarry in modern-day Wales, located around 150 miles away. Many of the stones original to this circle were reused in later construction campaigns, when some of them were placed inside the horseshoe arrangement around the altar stone. Now, if one were to stand at the altar stone on the morning of the summer solstice, what appears is the sun rising directly over the heel stone, located out near the ditch. Therefore, it is clear that Stonehenge functioned, at least in part, as an ancient "sundial," which marked the changing of the seasons by measuring the movement of the sun within this circular arrangement. This knowledge would certainly be important to this primarily agricultural society, and ceremonial centers such as Stonehenge may have been used to celebrate planting and harvesting rituals.

SULLIVAN, LOUIS (1856–1924). One of the prominent members of the Chicago School, Louis Sullivan was instrumental in establishing what is considered the most innovative building type in the United States: the **skyscraper**. Sullivan was born in Boston and trained at the Massachusetts Institute of Technology, which housed the first university-based architectural program; he settled in Chicago in 1875. In Chicago, he became acquainted with the technical innovations in architecture, including the use of **steel**. Steel constructions were first introduced in Chicago by the architect William Le Baron Jenney, and subsequent architects favored this stronger, lighter material because it allowed them to build taller structures in cities that were increasingly crowded and therefore limited in space. With this technical know-how, the first elevator was introduced in 1889, making a tall skyscraper logistically feasible.

Sullivan's Wainwright Building, constructed in St. Louis in 1890, is one of the first buildings of this new type. This building reveals a design introduced for these increasingly vertical structures: a three-part division in emulation of the classical **column** with its base, shaft, and ornate capital. The base is the shops, located at street level and designed with tall windows for the display of merchandise. A mezzanine level, also with tall windows, serves as an "attic" to the storefront level. From there a thick entablature divides the building's base from its shaft, which is articulated with seven horizontal registers of windows. The building is capped with a tall frieze and wide cornice, both of which are carved out with a decorative pattern that can be easily seen from street level. This frieze also serves as an attic level to conceal the mechanics of the elevators. Thus, the original skyscrapers were made in a traditional classical proportion system. A U-shaped interior plan allowed light to the internal rooms. Sullivan went on to apply the design principles he established for the early skyscraper to his Carson Pirie Scott Department Store, built in Chicago in 1899. In keeping with his famous motto "form follows function," these buildings reveal Sullivan's careful balance between technical aspects of construction and his more subtle use of historical references.

SUMERIAN ARCHITECTURE. *See* ANCIENT NEAR EASTERN ARCHITECTURE.

– T –

TAJ MAHAL, AGRA. The Taj Mahal, an impressive mausoleum located on the bank of the Yamuna River at Agra in northern India, was built in 1632–1648 by Emperor Shah Jahan as a funerary monument for his favorite wife, Mumtaz Mahal, who died in childbirth in 1631. Now a UNESCO World Heritage Site, the complex consists of a series of buildings and intricate gardens constructed by many architects and gardeners, but the principal architect is considered to have been

Ustad Ahmad Lahauri. Legends include various stories about how architects were required to sign contracts testifying that they would not reveal construction secrets from the mausoleum or design subsequent similar buildings. This emphasis on architectural secrecy is not unique but was apparently common in antiquity, although firm documentation has yet to be found concerning how, specifically, secrets were maintained about such locations as royal treasuries, burial tombs, and royal palace layouts.

The Taj Mahal is perhaps the most famous example of Mughal architecture in India and reveals a dramatic departure from the prior Hindu and Buddhist architectural monuments constructed throughout India. Instead, it demonstrates a melding of **Islamic**, Persian, **Indian**, Turkish, and **Byzantine** architectural styles. Islam was introduced into India in the AD 700s, yet this initial Islamic settlement around the Indus River did not become markedly strong until three centuries later, when newly converted Turkish Muslims traveling across Central Asia began to settle in larger numbers in northern India. Gradually, Turks began to carve out regional centers of Islamic authority based in Delhi, and from the 1200s onward, these rulers, called *sultans,* began to construct monumental palaces, fortifications, mosques, and funerary monuments. This culture laid the foundation for Mughal advancement into India in the early 1500s. The Mughals were both Turkish and Mongol, and they unified power in northern India to become emperors. The first Mughal emperor was Muhammad Zahir-ud-Din, who ruled briefly from 1526 to 1530 after conquering Delhi and establishing his empire across Central Asia. His successors unified northern India under Mughal rule. This long-standing dynasty lasted until 1858, when the last Mughal emperor was exiled to Burma (Myanmar) by British forces seeking greater control over India.

Mughal architecture consisted primarily of Islamic structures, which had already been established in India, but these newer buildings also reveal such newly introduced stylistic features as the horseshoe **arch** and onion **dome**. These can be found at the Taj Mahal. The delicately carved white **stone** building is set into a carefully cultivated garden that features long rectangular pools and is divided into four parts, separated by broad paths lined with straight rows of fruit trees and flowers. The tomb monument rises up at the end of this formal Persian-styled garden, an unusual feature given that mausoleums were traditionally located in the center of gardens. New research, however, reveals the remains of another garden, called the Moonlight Garden, located behind the mausoleum and across the Yamuna River. That being the case, the river itself, symbolizing the River of Paradise, became a part of the complex, with the mausoleum located in the center of this two-part garden complex. Further excavations are expected to provide a more definitive understanding of this interesting discovery.

The mausoleum itself is flanked by a smaller mosque on one side and a matching resting hall on the other. These structures are linked to the central tomb by a broad platform that visibly unites all three parts of the complex into one whole. Yet the side buildings are made from a red stone that allows the white **marble** tomb monument to stand out dramatically from its surroundings and to shine in the sunlight and be reflected in the water of the shallow pools. The tomb monument itself has a minaret at each of the four corners of its marble platform. The minarets are divided into three vertical parts, echoing the three vertical divisions of the tomb monument. While the minaret is an Islamic architectural feature used to call the faithful to prayer, here each minaret is topped by an open porch, or *chattri*, that traditionally appeared in earlier Indian palaces. The tomb itself is a perfectly square building, but the corners are cut at angles to suggest a subtle octagonal shape.

The façade is further divided into three parts and has a tall curved and pointed arch niche above the central door. Each side of this door displays two pairs of these arched niches, one atop the other, for a total of four smaller arches on each side, with the outer niches set into the angled corners. This feature differs from the arch shape found in western Europe and is called an *iwan*. Cutting into the façade in such a way causes light and shadows to play off the front of the building, creating a richer appearance than if the façade were flat. On the top of the monument, octagonal *chattris*, located one in each corner of the building, surround the central onion dome that rises up above them on a delicately carved drum. The surface of the marble monument has blind arcades carved into it, while the entrance doors are framed by black marble inlay of verses from the Koran; very subtle colored stone inlay is found above the *iwan* arches. The stone inlay stands as testament to the far-reaching mercantile prosperity of the Mughal Empire and consists of sapphire from Sri Lanka, lapis lazuli from Afghanistan, turquoise from Tibet, jasper from India, and jade and crystal from China. The stones are set in a delicate floral pattern that echoes the surrounding garden and symbolizes paradise, thus contrasting the beauty of the physical world with the funerary context, as concluded inside the monument, with cenotaphs of the emperor and his wife.

TANGE, KENZO (1913–2005). Kenzo Tange, one of the premier 20th-century architects from Japan, witnessed the development of his home country out of the devastation of war and into a prosperous, modern world power with international economic interests. Tange's modernist architecture therefore reflects the worldwide cultural developments that occurred during the second half of the century. Born in Osaka in 1913, Tange went to the University of Tokyo, where he was introduced to the architecture of **Le Corbusier**. In 1946 he opened the Tange Laboratory to engage Japanese architects in the broader international architectural arena.

In 1949, Tange's architecture became known worldwide with his designs for the Hiroshima Peace Memorial Park and Museum. The central building, raised on pilotis in the style of Le Corbusier, is reached via a bridge designed by Isamu Noguchi. The **concrete** structure of the museum follows the **International style**, but with screened windows found in traditional **Japanese architecture**, while the central monument is designed in the shape of a parabolic **arch**. This commission, with its blend of technical innovations, traditional architectural elements, and an organic aesthetic focus, set the stage for Tange's future work. In the 1960s, Tange became interested in the integration of his technical designs with more spiritual considerations and a focus on urban plans. His National Gymnasium Complex in Yoyogi Park, Tokyo, built for the 1964 Olympics, reflects this vision. The arena, made for swimming and diving competitions, is designed as two semicircles connected slightly off-center from each other, with either end elongated to form two beautiful curves. The roof is suspended on two massive **steel** cables connected to concrete piers, giving the overall impression of a shell. The 1972 Munich Olympic Arena built by Otto Frei was clearly inspired by Tange's arena design.

In the 1970s, Tange was involved in several urban projects, including new town projects in Bologna and Catania, Italy. His expansion of the Minneapolis Art Museum (1975) doubled its space and gave Tange a foothold in the United States, where he taught for several years at various different universities.

When Tange won the Pritzker Architecture Prize in 1987, he was working in Tokyo on several structures to revitalize the downtown area. These buildings include Saint Mary's Cathedral, the Akasaka Prince Hotel, and the City Hall Complex. The hotel is designed as a **skyscraper** that steps outward from its central rectangle into a series of wings that break forward to create a jagged U-shaped building. This monumental structure moves away from the traditional box-like format of skyscrapers to carve out an entrance area in keeping with Tange's interest in the creation of human-scaled urban space. His Fuji Television Building, built in Tokyo in 1996, achieves the same innovative result with its large-scale rectangular design cut out in the middle with an open, grid-like structure that links the two wings and supports internal walkways, an elevator shaft, and a circular auditorium in the upper left quadrant of the building. The unique design of this structure gives the appearance of a lightweight but strong steel skeleton with large windows that light the interior rooms and an efficiency of movement between the internal spaces via a series of walkways on each level. The discreet, serious appearance of earlier corporate structures is replaced here by a more whimsical yet still highly visually organized design. Tange's Fuji Television Building, with its blend of technical and aesthetic considerations, thus provided a new vision for corporate architecture of the next century.

TATLIN, VLADIMIR (1885–1953). *See* CONSTRUCTIVIST ARCHITECTURE.

TAUT, BRUNO (1880–1938). *See* EXPRESSIONISM.

TEMPLE. *See* ANCIENT EGYPTIAN ARCHITECTURE; ANCIENT GREEK ARCHITECTURE; ANCIENT ROMAN ARCHITECTURE; CHINESE ARCHITECTURE; INDIAN ARCHITECTURE; JAPANESE ARCHITECTURE; MESOAMERICAN ARCHITECTURE; TEMPLE OF SOLOMON.

TEMPLE OF SOLOMON. Although earlier Israelite architecture existed in Egypt, perhaps the best-known Jewish structure from antiquity is the legendary Temple of Solomon, built in Jerusalem by King Solomon to house the Ark of the Covenant. After David conquered Jerusalem in 1004 BC, he resolved to build a great temple; he turned this task over to his son, Solomon, who initiated construction shortly after his rule began. Biblical accounts of construction describe the **stone** that was quarried from beneath Jerusalem, the timber that was sent from Lebanon, and the vast underground cisterns that brought water to the temple. The Book of Kings attributes the overall plan for the temple to a trade agreement between Hiram of Tyre and Solomon. The building was thought to have a portico at its entrance, elevated by a series of steps and supported by two large **columns**. Wings on either side gave the temple a tripartite division, with a tall, angled roof and a ridgepole that ran down the middle of the building and allowed for clerestory windows to light the interior. Clearly, the Temple of Solomon blended architectural traditions found across Mesopotamia and down into Egypt. Its stone courtyard recalls ancient Canaanite architecture, while the two large fire pillars that topped the front portico are Phoenician, and the hypostyle hall and clerestory windows reveal **Ancient Egyptian** influences. Pillaged many times through its history, the "First Temple," as it came to be called, was completely destroyed by Nebuchadnezzar in 586 BC. The Second Temple was begun in 516 BC, later to be destroyed by the Roman Emperor Titus. *See also* ANCIENT NEAR EASTERN ARCHITECTURE.

TEOTIHUACAN ARCHITECTURE. *See* MESOAMERICAN ARCHITECTURE.

TERRAGNI, GIUSEPPE (1904–1943). *See* RATIONALISM.

TOLEDO, JUAN BAUTISTA DE (d. 1567). *See* ESCORIAL, MADRID.

TSCHUMI, BERNARD (1944–). *See* DECONSTRUCTIVISM.

TUDOR REVIVAL STYLE. Tudor Revival, an outgrowth of the Tudorbethan style (c. 1835–1885), was introduced in England in reaction to the perceived overly ornate **Victorian architecture**. It appears most often in domestic buildings from around the 1910s through the 1940s. Accordingly, it is culturally related to the advent of the **Arts and Crafts** movement in mid-19th-century England and the ensuing Mission style and Bungalow style homes found in the United States. Modeled on the more picturesque aspects of medieval cottages and English country houses, Tudor homes feature steeply gabled roofs with exposed dormers and exposed beams on the exterior walls, often filled in with stucco or a **brick** herringbone pattern. A few Tudor homes have thatched roofs, but the majority of them feature thick shingles that suggest a thatched appearance. In England, this more rustic cottage is also called the Cotswold Cottage, a domestic form popular from the 1890s to 1940s. These revivalist styles are all related to **Romantic architecture** in their general philosophical principles of nostalgia. This style of house was then introduced in the United States, where it continued to be popular through the 1970s. *See also* TUDOR STYLE.

TUDOR STYLE. English architecture from the Tudor Period (1485–1603) combined elements from the late **Gothic** Perpendicular and the **Renaissance** styles to create a uniquely regional style favored in England from the Renaissance and in the United States up until the early 20th century. Campus buildings at Oxford and Cambridge reveal a Gothic Revival style with Tudor elements, such as the four-centered **arch** and the oriel windows that project out from the wall. Hampton Court Palace, built in southwest London in 1515–1521, is a good example of the Tudor style in its references to late Gothic elements. The most characteristic examples of the Tudor style, however, are found in domestic buildings that employ **wood**, **brick**, and thatching. Tudor houses are characterized by a wattle-and-daub construction with the addition of decorative half timbering or brick on the walls, placed in horizontal, vertical, and diagonal patterns. William Shakespeare's mother, Mary Arden, was born in a Tudor-style farmhouse built in the early 1500s outside of Stratford-Upon-Avon, which is preserved today as a museum of the Tudor period. The half-timber exterior wall decorations signaled a high level of prosperity among the rural families who constructed such homes in the Renaissance. *See also* TUDOR REVIVAL STYLE.

– U –

UNITED STATES CAPITOL, WASHINGTON, D.C. In 1803, **Benjamin Latrobe** was hired as the Surveyor of Public Buildings of the United States and began to work in Washington, D.C., most notably on the United States Capitol, which he began that year and modified throughout his life. The Capitol was originally designed in 1792 by William Thornton in the **Neo-Classical style**; it featured wide wings meant to house the Senate and House of Representatives. After a series of architects struggled with the logistics of construction, Secretary of State **Thomas Jefferson** hired the more experienced Latrobe to oversee the work. Latrobe added a monumental stairway leading up to the entrance of the building and created a large colonnaded portico to emphasize the front of the building. After the building was damaged in the War of 1812, Latrobe repaired the side wings and introduced on the interior a more opulent **marble** style, while modifying the interior Corinthian capitals to include corn and tobacco leaves instead of the traditional acanthus leaves. Final renovations were completed later in the century by **Charles Bulfinch**, who is credited with creating a taller **dome**.

The Capitol, in its Neo-Classical style, symbolizes the democratic principles upon which the United States was founded. The building rises above Capitol Hill at the east end of the National Mall in downtown Washington, D.C., and has over 16 acres of floor space. Its three-story white exterior is divided into three parts, with a central portico topped by the dome, flanked by two broad side wings set back from the entrance portico. The ground floor is made of a more rusticated **stone**, while the upper registers are smooth. Windows on each of the three stories alternate with colossal pilasters across the wide façade. The central portico is also divided into three parts, with its own wings receding and articulated with four **columns** each, while the main part of the portico reaches out with a colonnade of eight columns topped by a triangular pediment. The entire roofline is capped by a classical balustrade. Above that, the dome stretches up onto a two-tiered drum; the lower portion of the drum features a freestanding colonnade, while the upper part of the drum is lined with windows. The dome itself alternates ribs with oval oculus windows and is capped by a lantern topped by a colossal bronze statue of the

Allegory of Freedom. As one of the most important buildings in United States history, this Neo-Classical structure provided a strong visual link between the new United States government and the philosophical and political ideals of Ancient Greece. *See also* ANCIENT GREEK ARCHITECTURE.

UPJOHN, RICHARD (1802–1878). *See* GOTHIC REVIVAL ARCHITECTURE.

USONIAN HOUSE. *See* WRIGHT, FRANK LLOYD.

UTZON, JØRN (1918–). *See* CONCRETE; POST-MODERN ARCHITECTURE.

– V –

VANBRUGH, JOHN (1664–1726). John Vanbrugh, a successor to **Inigo Jones** and then **Christopher Wren** in England, is known for his heavy, theatrical, **Baroque** style of architecture, which was well suited for the monumental buildings constructed in England during this time. Coming from a wealthy family of merchants, Vanbrugh was very politically active throughout his career and at one point landed in the Bastille. As a Restoration playwright, he attained both fame and notoriety for his bawdy and satirical works, the most famous of which are *The Relapse* (1696) and *The Provoked Wife* (1697). Vanbrugh was very forward-looking in terms of his desire for greater social equality.

His most famous building, Blenheim Palace, located north of London in Woodstock, was built beginning in 1705 for the national hero the first Duke of Marlborough. It recalls **Versailles** not only in its vast scale and rural setting, but also in its Baroque, theatrical organization. The palace is entered through a gate into a vast court that is almost as large as the piazza of **Saint Peter's in Rome**. Then, after dismounting from horses and carriages, the visitor entered the central building through a forecourt. From that core, massive wings spreading out from either side are organized around a series of internal courtyards. The symmetrical complex is built up as if the buildings were stuck together to create the whole. This way, the complex is broken down into smaller units that make it more visually accessible and provide a rhythm to the overall appearance. Towers that recall a medieval **castle** cap each corner. A huge lawn opens up behind the garden façade of the palace, bordered on either side by a small wooded area. As at Versailles, this space was used for outdoor entertainment and performances of music, theater, and dance. The garden was originally planned as just a small garden for vegetables and herbs, but the surrounding landscape was enlarged dramatically by Lancelot "Capability" Brown in the 1760s. Instead of designing one of the very popular French gardens with a geometrical and formal setting of boxwood hedges and rose bushes, Brown created what is now called a "picturesque" setting, with a vast lawn of grass surrounded by undulating lines of trees in a more relaxed, yet still artfully arranged, natural setting. Thus, Blenheim, which is the largest domestic palace not built for the royal family, was an important villa prototype for the monumental rural home increasingly popular in the 18th-century English countryside.

VELDE, HENRY VAN DE (1863–1947). *See* ART NOUVEAU.

VENTURI, ROBERT (1925–). Although Robert Venturi has sought to reject architectural labels throughout his career, he, together with his wife, Denise Scott Brown, is nonetheless considered the founder of the **Post-Modern** architectural style. This style is the result of their architectural philosophy, which is based upon a desire to free architects from rigid, inflexible modernist "rules" and instead allow for a less "bombastic" and more varied approach to design that takes into account each individual commission. By rejecting what they considered the repetitious, impersonal, and self-important qualities of **International style** architecture, Venturi and Scott Brown instead championed the vernacular. Turning **Ludwig Mies van der Rohe**'s famous motto "less is more" into the motto "less is a bore," Venturi sought to enliven architecture with regional distinctions, historical references, and popular culture. This new style is best described in Venturi's *Complexity and Contradiction in Architecture*, first published in 1966, in which he spells out the need for architecture that is not homogeneous but more realistically reflective of our varied culture. In his later book *Learning from Las Vegas*, published in 1977, Venturi argues for the importance of both "high" and "low" architecture by validating a variety of regional, vernacular architectural styles, such as Googie and Doo Wop, that were prevalent in the 1950s and 1960s and featured exaggerated futuristic designs with bright colors and boldly cantilevered overhangs. These styles were typically found in diners, bowling alleys, and other roadside structures.

Venturi's architecture firm (established first with John Rauch and then with Venturi's wife, Denise Scott Brown) is called Venturi, Scott Brown and Associates. The Vanni Venturi House, built for Venturi's mother in 1961–1964 in Chestnut Hill, Pennsylvania, is a good illustration of these ideals. The broad triangular façade that echoes the slanted roof defines the quintessential "house" shape in America, but it is then cut down through the middle to create a broken triangle. Like **Mannerism**, Venturi's historical references question the rigid conformity of "classical" architecture. An irregular floor plan with oddly situated stairs adds further complexity to the interior of the house. Although Venturi and Scott Brown's Guild House, a retirement home built in Philadelphia in 1963, has been derided for its purposefully mundane and ugly design, their theoretical approach to such buildings has opened a lively public discourse on the merits of aesthetically pleasing architecture. While aesthetics have traditionally been central to architectural considerations, Venturi and Scott Brown have demonstrated that aesthetics are of little concern for the vast majority of people, who instead prefer the architecture of the "ordinary."

The Seattle Art Museum, built in 1991, is a more recent expression of Venturi's architectural ideals. Built with a curved façade made of incised concrete and topped with a row of windows, the museum features a broad stairway called the "Art Ladder," which leads the visitor into the exhibition space. Befitting its surrounding urban area, the museum does not impose a "heroic" façade or any historical preconceptions about museum space. Instead, the visitor is led into the exhibition space through an undulating, human-scaled structure that provides a gradual transition from the street level to the museum. In 1991, Venturi won the Pritzker Architecture Prize. Influenced by Venturi and Scott Brown's ideas on architecture, many subsequent architects such as **Philip Johnson** began to infuse their buildings with a more varied architectural vocabulary that freely borrowed from both "high" and "low" genres of historical architecture.

VERSAILLES PALACE, FRANCE. Versailles Palace, located outside Paris, epitomizes the classicizing **Baroque** style of architecture popular in France in the 17th century. Louis XIII originally commissioned Philibert Le Roy to build it in 1624 as a small hunting lodge, but it was dramatically expanded by his son, Louis XIV, beginning in the 1660s, to become the largest château at the time in all of France. In 1682, Louis XIV moved his entire administrative court from the **Louvre Palace** in Paris to Versailles. The court consisted of 20,000 nobles, 5,000 of whom lived in the palace while the rest lived in the town of Versailles. This number was in addition to the 14,000 staff and military who lived at the palace as well. French monarchs continued to use Versailles as their administrative seat until they were forced to return to Paris in 1789 as a result of the French Revolution.

Prior to the reign of Louis XIV, the French monarchy had experienced a period of instability beginning with the assassination of Henri IV in 1610, which left Henri's nine-year-old son, Louis XIII, and his wife, Marie de' Medici, together with the powerful Cardinal Richelieu, in control of the Crown. During this time, the nobles gradually attained more power, carving out their own alliances and regions of authority. The same situation occurred in the next royal generation, when Louis XIII died in 1643 at a relatively young age, leaving his five-year-old son, Louis XIV, and his wife, Anne of Austria, who ruled as coregent with Cardinal Mazarin. When Cardinal Mazarin died in 1661, Louis XIV began to assert his authority. One of his main goals was to bring absolutist rule back to the monarchy, with more control over the nobility. It was primarily for this reason that Louis XIV moved his entire court to Versailles, where he could detach them from Paris and create a more centralized government. Louis XIV went on to assert himself as a powerful and firm ruler; he governed for a longer time than any other monarch in French history.

During his rule, Louis XIV continued to revitalize the arts and culture in the French court. The French Royal Academy had been founded in 1635 and the Royal Academy of Painting and Sculpture in 1648. The establishment of the Royal Academy of Architecture during Louis XIV's rule in 1671 reemphasized the ideals of the **Ancient**

Roman architect **Vitruvius** as well as the **Renaissance** architect **Andrea Palladio**. In order to construct Versailles, Louis hired artists away from his finance minister, Nicolas Fouquet, after accusing him of using money from the Crown for his lavish construction at Vaux-le-Vicomte. These artists included François Mansart and Louis Le Vau, whose architectural taste can be characterized as a restrained, classicizing Baroque, but the final additions to the palace, completed between 1738 and 1760 during the reign of Louis XV, were made according to the newer **Rococo** and **Neo-Classical** styles.

The construction of Versailles Palace under Louis XIV is divided into four major building campaigns. The first, dating from 1664 to 1668, consisted of alterations to the original palace and garden to accommodate 600 guests invited for the first large-scale public event held there during the reign of Louis XIV. The three-story form of the hunting lodge remained, but was enlarged. Louis Le Vau oversaw the initial design for the palace; as the campaign progressed, Charles Le Brun was hired to oversee the interior decoration, while André Le Nôtre designed the vast formal gardens. During the second campaign, from 1669 to 1672, the new palace, called the *château neuf*, was constructed around the older **stone** and **brick** hunting lodge, enveloping the older building on the north, south, and west sides.

Since Louis XIII had already obtained a deed to the city of Versailles in 1632, a large portion of the native population was already in service to the Crown at the time Louis XIV moved there, simplifying the logistics of construction and maintenance. The north side was constructed with a suite of rooms on the *piano nobile*, or second floor, for the king, while the south *piano nobile* wing had a suite of rooms of equal size for the queen, the scale of which was unprecedented at the time. The western side of the palace had a terrace that connected the royal apartments and overlooked the gardens. The ground floor consisted of the service quarters and grand stairwells. The third floor of the original structure, or *château vieux*, was the center of the palace, with private rooms for the king and rooms for the children and servants. Private rooms included a guardroom, an antechamber, a private room for eating, a council room, and rooms for clothing and the king's wigs, which numbered more than 500. The north and south wings were conceived of by Louis Le Vau as a suite of seven rooms each, with a hallway that ran continuously through each room and thus facilitated public access throughout each suite. The rooms were given celestial symbolism, with each room named after a planet and its corresponding god or goddess: Diana as the Moon, Mars, Mercury, Jupiter, Saturn, Venus, and Apollo as the Sun God. Many connections between Louis XIV and the Sun God Apollo were made throughout the decorative program of the palace, as well as in propagandistic dialogue.

The third building campaign, begun after the death of Le Vau, was overseen by Jules Hardouin-Mansart from 1678 to 1684. During these renovations, the famous Hall of Mirrors was built from the originally open garden terrace on the *piano nobile* and lengthened to include three of the royal apartment rooms—those of Jupiter, Saturn, and Venus. In the Hall of Mirrors, Hardouin-Mansart added the huge mirrors along the wall opposite the windows, which were quite expensive at the time, and light reflected from the arched windows overlooking the gardens into the mirrors, creating an ephemeral, richly spacious interior. The barrel-vaulted ceiling was filled with allegorical, propagandistic narratives glorifying the reign of Louis XIV. Hardouin-Mansart reconfigured the rooms of the remaining king's suite to be used for billiards, balls, playing cards, music, and the serving of food to guests, and he added a small apartment suite for the king's collection of "rarities." This collection was modeled on those amassed by Italian Renaissance princes and kept in their *studioli*, or private studies. Hardouin-Mansart also regularized the garden façade to match the wings.

It was during the time following the Treaty of Nijmegen in 1678 that Louis gradually began to move his court to Versailles, making the move official in 1682. His famously intricate court etiquette evolved during this time, centered on his morning *lever* (in which Louis got up and dressed), which was described as parallel to the morning sunrise and the symbolism of Apollo. This courtly ritual, which provided daily structure for the vast nobility by keeping them entertained and out of political power, was quickly emulated across Europe, including Russia. In addition, Louis added the Orangerie, and it was during this third campaign that the majority of the interior decoration and gardens were completed. During the final campaign, which dates to 1701–1710, the Royal Chapel was built by Hardouin-Mansart and Robert de Cotte.

The palace, as it was finally constructed, consisted of a three-story central core, flanked by massive wings that created a huge, U-shaped *cour d'honneur* where horses and carriages arrived and departed. From there, guests entered the **marble**-floored, open forecourt and then proceeded through the main entrance at the ground floor to be escorted up to the *piano nobile*. Still today, the entrance consists of three doors separated by tall paired **column**s, topped by a gilded balustrade, and then three **arched** windows in the *piano nobile*. The brick walls are articulated with classical pilasters and other Vitruvian details that help to organize the flat exterior walls and provide them with a visual rhythm. The central structure has a *mansard* roof in front of which is a continuous classical balustrade. The garden façade reveals rusticated stonework on the ground floor, punctuated by arched windows, while the taller *piano nobile* is more ornate, with tall arched windows and three porticoes of paired columns demarcating the central garden entrance foyer and relieving the visual conformity of the broad façade. The third floor acts as an attic level, with a shorter register of smooth stone and square windows, all capped by a classical balustrade with sculpture located at various points across the roofline. The Royal Chapel, built in the first years of the 18th century in a Rococo style, has elegant white fluted Corinthian columns supporting an oval-shaped interior space made of marble. The barrel-vaulted nave ceiling is painted with frescoes and framed in the more organic, curved lines of the Rococo.

The gardens are an important element of the architectural design in that they expand outward the various areas used for the entertainment of the nobles. André Le Nôtre organized the vast cultivated area in an axial direction, along a broad avenue from which a trident of streets angled away. Broad vistas contrasted with private, enclosed gardens. The most formal gardens were located near the palace and the less formal areas melded into the forest beyond. Classical fountains and sculpture designate particular areas of the garden, which were used as gathering spots or for entertainments. Several garden buildings were constructed over the years, the first of which was the Baroque Grand Trianon, built in 1669 by Hardouin-Mansart for Louis XIV as an escape from the rigors of palace life at Versailles. The Rococo-styled Petit Trianon was constructed in the 1760s by Ange-Jacques Gabriel for Louis XV as a gift to his mistress, Madame de Pompadour. The

Petit Trianon was given to the young Queen Marie Antoinette by King Louis XVI at the beginning of his reign in 1774; she had the elegantly rustic Hamlet constructed nearby in the more informal style favored by late-18th-century French nobility just prior to the French Revolution. The events of the French Revolution ended courtly life at Versailles by forcing the royal couple to return to Paris, where they were later held for treason and executed by guillotine.

VICTORIAN ARCHITECTURE. Victorian architecture consists of a variety of styles that correspond with the long reign of Queen Victoria, who ruled Great Britain from 1837 to 1901. In the United States, Victorian architecture appeared from the 1860s until the turn of the century and can be categorized into the Second Empire style, Stick, Queen Anne, Shingle, and Folk Victorian styles, which are typically found in domestic constructions. The Richardsonian Romanesque style (1870s–1900s) also dates to this period and was sometimes integrated into Victorian homes. At this time, dramatic changes in construction materials and processes, spurred by the Industrial Revolution, allowed architects to realize more challenging designs than the traditional rectangular building. For example, the balloon frame, made of lighter **wood** held together with nails, replaced the heavier timber framing of prior buildings and allowed for a more varied manipulation of wood decoration. As the custom-made decorative detailing of wealthy homes became less expensive, Victorian homes began to feature more elaborate woodwork, decorative overhangs, wrap porches, turrets, and other elegant features.

The overall appearance of these homes was typically that of an asymmetrical design and multicolored wood, although **brick** was often used in the Richardsonian Romanesque house style. In the interior, these two- or three-story Victorian houses were formal and elegant, the last domestic house-type that maintained the formality of the upper-class lifestyle. Beautifully carved wooden stairs at the entrance foyer set the stage for elegant interior detailing. The parlor was located off the front foyer, followed by the family living room and formal dining room, which were often divided by large sliding wooden doors, while the kitchen, located at the back of the house, was separated entirely from view by a traditional door that was kept closed. The more elaborate Victorian homes featured a separate back entrance to the kitchen, a butler's pantry, and a separate set of stairs leading from the kitchen to the servants' rooms located at the back of the second floor.

The Second Empire–style house, popular from 1855 to 1885, featured low-hanging Mansart roofs, dormers, elaborate cornice designs, and cornice brackets. These houses were traditionally built as town houses, with a flat front façade placed at the line of the street. Contemporaneous with the Italianate and **Gothic Revival** homes, the Second Empire–style house lacked the busier details of these more picturesque homes and was therefore considered modern, with clean lines more appropriate to the urban setting. The Stick-style home, popular from 1860 to 1890, was a wooden home with a gabled roof that featured diagonal wooden trusses in the gables. The horizontal wood boards on the exterior walls were often overlaid with vertical or even diagonal boards, called "stickwork," to lend variety to the surface, while porches were braced with diagonal pieces of wood attached to columns that echoed the wall designs. Often cross-gabled and with towers and dormers, Stick houses featured fine design details and are seen as a transitional style from the Second Empire to the more ornate Queen Anne style.

The Queen Anne style, built mainly from the 1880s through the 1910s, was even more varied in its exterior design and became the dominant style of the last two decades of the 19th century. Featuring an irregularly shaped roofline with a façade-facing gable, the Queen Anne house was typically a wood home with shingles in the gable, bay windows, and a wrap-around porch. The decorative detailing of the Queen Anne style is the best known aspect of the Victorian home. With slender, turned porch **columns** that resemble furniture legs, delicate spindle work in the porch frieze, gables, and wall overhangs, this highly sculptural style is sometimes called "gingerbread" or "Eastlake," from the contemporary English furniture designs of Charles Eastlake.

The Shingle-style home (1870s–1900) featured a simpler exterior detailing but is noted for its continuous wall cladding of wood shingles. Given its style name by Vincent Scully in the 1950s, these homes are often found in rural settings or at seaside resorts from coastal Maine through the middle of the East Coast, where the more rustic, less formal design was conducive to use for vacation homes.

Finally, the Folk Victorian, popular from around 1870 to 1910, was a smaller version of the ornate Queen Anne style. With a single gabled roof, these one-story homes were offered as a less expensive version of this ever-popular style of house.

VIENNESE SECESSION. *See* ART NOUVEAU.

VILLA. *See* ANCIENT ROMAN ARCHITECTURE; PALLADIO, ANDREA; RENAISSANCE ARCHITECTURE; VANBRUGH, JOHN.

VITRUVIUS POLLIO, MARCUS (c. 80 BC – c. 25 BC). Vitruvius was an **Ancient Roman** architect and engineer famous for his treatise on construction called *De architectura*, known today as *The Ten Books on Architecture.* Little is known of the life or architectural constructions of Vitruvius. Born in Rome around 80 BC, he was probably an army engineer under Julius Caesar and then an architectural advisor under Augustus, to whom he dedicated his architectural treatise. This book remains important today as the sole existing practical treatise written in Ancient Rome.

Unlike the theoretical discussions of Greek artists, Vitruvius described actual Roman building materials and practical plans for a variety of different building types, and he also laid out an aesthetic code for architects to follow. The three fundamental architectural considerations he discussed are *firmitas, utilitas,* and *venustas*, which meant that buildings were to be strong, useful, and beautiful. Vitruvius agreed with **Ancient Greek** architects that buildings were to be constructed according to systems of human proportions and that buildings imitated things found in nature, such as **columns** that were modeled on tree trunks. Thus, in addition to the Greek Doric, Ionic, and Corinthian orders of columns, he discussed the Composite order as a late variant of the Corinthian. This order first appeared on the Arch of Titus in Rome, from AD 82. Vitruvius also defined more specifically the idea of the "Vitruvian Man," drawn in the Renaissance by Leonardo da Vinci as a nude male body with arms outstretched within both a circle and a square system of measurement.

Beginning with a preface dedicated to the Emperor Augustus, the treatise is divided into 10 books. The first focuses on the education of the architect and describes the fundamental design principles of construction. These include order, eurythmy, symmetry, propriety, and economy, and then the ideals of commodity, firmness, and delight. Vitruvius then focused on practical concerns of site, climate, and materials. He discussed different building types such as temples, homes, recreational buildings, fortifications, and machines. His fullest discussion dealt with the capital orders and the idea of symmetry. Chapters on color, harmonics, and astrology complete the text. The book encompasses not only discussions of architectural style, but also landscape architecture and garden designs, as well as such engineering concerns as plumbing, aqueducts, and machines used for the military and for entertainment. Architects in antiquity were considered technicians, or technical advisors, and had a wider range of commissions than contemporary architects.

In 1414, Vitruvius's text was rediscovered in a northern European library by the Florentine scholar Poggio Bracciolini, who promoted it widely. Such **Renaissance** architects as **Leon Battista Alberti** in the 1400s and **Andrea Palladio** in the 1500s modeled their own architectural treatises on Vitruvius. The treatise was first translated from its original Latin into the Italian vernacular, and copies were then printed in many different languages and found across all of Europe, which helped to make popular the enduring, so-called Vitruvian style of classical architecture from the Renaissance through the **Neo-Classical** era.

– W –

WAGNER, OTTO (1841–1918). *See* HOFFMANN, JOSEF.

WALPOLE, HORACE (1717–1797). *See* GOTHIC REVIVAL ARCHITECTURE.

WARREN, WHITNEY (1864–1943). *See* BEAUX-ARTS ARCHITECTURE.

WETMORE, CHARLES (1866–1941). *See* BEAUX-ARTS ARCHITECTURE.

WHITE, STANFORD (1853–1906). *See* MCKIM, CHARLES FOLLEN.

WOOD. Wood has always been used most commonly in the construction of domestic structures that do not require the same level of durability as temples and funerary monuments, which are more typically constructed from **brick** or **stone**. Timber became more prevalent in northern Europe after the end of the last Ice Age, so wood post–framed huts with thatched roofs dating to **Prehistoric** times were constructed across Europe. Neolithic timber shelters were built with vertical corner and side posts placed in a large rectangular shape and topped with a timber-framed roof that could support thatching. The roof was constructed with a long timber ridgepole, a horizontal beam that formed the gable of the roof, while smaller, slanted poles called rafters ran perpendicular to the ridgepole. These were lashed together for support while rows of posts lining the center of the space supported the ridgepole from below. The walls were filled in with wattle and daub in a process whereby twigs were woven together like a basket and then covered with mud or clay. While timber structures were probably far more prevalent than masonry, it is the more durable bone and stone materials that are prevalent enough to be studied today. Nonetheless, timber architecture endured despite its more flammable nature, and even **Ancient Romans**, known for their masonry, often constructed timber ceilings in their northern European settlements, given the scarcity of stone in many regions of Europe.

The architectural tradition of timber continued through the **Early Medieval architecture** of the Vikings. Settling in northern France in the early 10th century, the "northerners," called the Norsemen, built in masonry and also wood. Their wooden structures were of two types: horizontally stacked logs lashed together at the corners (the so-called "log cabin") or the vertical constructions introduced in the Neolithic era. Each method was then completed with wattle and daub and enclosed with thatch. Although most roofs were gabled with a ridgepole, sometimes a naturally forked piece of timber was cut into two equal pieces and used for the corners of a gable. This is called *cruck* construction. Most buildings, however, featured a more elaborate **post-and-lintel** construction consisting of a series of lintels supporting a triangle of rafters to divide the internal space into three parts supported on the interior with two rows of posts, much like the format of a church, with lower side "aisles" and a taller "nave." On the inside, a hearth was located in the middle, and the doorway was off to the side to minimize the circulation of air across the hearth.

Although most of these constructions have not survived, a few beautiful examples of timber stave churches still exist in Norway. The Borgund stave church located in Sogn, Norway, dates to around 1125 to 1150. Four large timbers, or staves, form the core for the building, which features a series of smaller rooms encircling the rectangular core and a round apse attached to the high altar, with its own three-tiered conical shingle roof. The shorter side rooms help to buttress the taller central core. The walls are formed by vertical timbers slotted together, and the entire structure is capped by a steep wooden shingled roof formed into varying heights to protect the walls by allowing for snow and rain to run easily off the building. The central core has an additional three-tiered pinnacle that rises above the structure, and the corner gables feature carved crosses and dragons consistent with their symbolism and inviting comparison with the gargoyles found on later **Gothic** churches. These stave churches are then decorated with intricate interlaced patterns much like the decorations found in Viking carvings and Celtic manuscripts; although most of these buildings have not survived, some of their tracery can be found in museums today.

In some cultures we see a more extensive use of wood than other available building materials. This is particularly true in Japan and China, where natural building materials conform to religious and aesthetic ideals, and are used in Shinto temples and Buddhist shrines. In fact, the oldest original wood building in the world is thought to be the Japanese temple compound at Horyu-ji located in the central plains of Japan, which dates to around 711. This small compound consists of two buildings: a solid five-story *pagoda* and a large worship hall, called a *kondo*. These structures are located in a rectangular courtyard that is surrounded by covered walkways. The largest collection of ancient wood buildings in the world is the **Forbidden City in Beijing**, dating to the early 1400s. Many of its buildings feature massive timber construction using native trees such as the Chinese evergreen called Pheobe zhennan. The Golden Carriage Palace, built in the center of the Forbidden City in 1406, is supported by a total of 72 single-post pillars that are each over 59 feet tall. Exceptional in their own right, these buildings are also important due to the survival of their original wood materials.

In more recent times, wood has retained its appeal either because of tradition or due to its abundance as a building material. In the United States, the American frontier was initially covered with log cabins, and wood continues to be favored in American domestic construction. The early-20th-century **Arts and Crafts** bungalow homes feature exposed wood beams, built-in wood cabinets, and other such features that are similar in their general aesthetic to **Japanese architecture**. In addition to the use of wood as a building material, Shingle- and Stick-style **Victorian** homes also highlighted hand-crafted wood decorative detailing on their exteriors. In Europe, wood has remained popular in Scandinavian house construction and in Swiss chalets and other rural and vacation homes. Despite the gradual introduction of stronger and more durable building materials, wood, now regularly treated to protect it from water and insect damage, will certainly remain popular as a natural and aesthetically pleasing building material.

WOOD, JOHN (THE ELDER) (c. 1704–1754). *See* NEO-CLASSICAL ARCHITECTURE.

WORLD TRADE CENTER, NEW YORK. The World Trade Center was planned in 1960 as a seven-building complex to form the economic center of New York City, but the buildings went on to symbolize a broader image of American prosperity. The idea for the center was initiated by David and Nelson Rockefeller, and Minoru Yamasaki was hired to design the towers. The lower Manhattan site was ideal, given that this part of the island has deep bedrock deemed adequate to support the 110-story "twin towers" that formed the centerpiece of the complex. Construction began in 1966, and Tower 1 (to the north) was completed in 1970, while Tower 2 (to the south) was finished in 1972. For one year, the twin towers were the tallest structures in the world, standing at 1,368 and 1,362 feet tall respectively, but they were surpassed in height in 1973 by the Chicago Sears Tower, built by the firm of **Skidmore, Owings & Merrill**. Structurally innovative, the twin towers were some of the earliest "supertall" **skyscraper**s in the world.

When construction began, a **concrete** wall was built underground as a slurry wall to keep water from the Hudson River out of the foundations of the buildings. Then a six-level basement was completed in each of the "twin towers." The soil displaced from these foundations was added to the landfill used to create Battery Park. The towers were designed as **steel**-framed cubes, with each floor a self-supporting unit. Steel piers lining the perimeter of the buildings, as well as a strong central core of piers, supported the outer lateral loads and the force of gravity. The central core was used for the elevator shafts, stairwells, restrooms, and utility rooms, while unencumbered office space filled the rest of each floor. The buildings were conceived of as hollow tubes surrounding a strong central core. The intended result was a wind sway minimal enough to be absorbed by the lightweight outer walls, a significant improvement over previous curtain wall structures. The floors were constructed of four-inch-thick concrete slabs laid on steel decks with floor trusses between the piers. The windows on each floor were relatively narrow, at 18 inches wide, intended by Yamasaki to help enclose the space to limit any fear of heights or sense of vertigo that might plague the inhabitants of the higher-level offices. Nevertheless, the narrow windows, along with the great height of the buildings, were considered too impersonal. Lewis Mumford argued that the large scale had no real function aside from what he termed "technological exhibitionism." Indeed, the towers were initially difficult to fill with renters, and only in the 1980s were they considered fully occupied.

After one relatively small accidental fire and one prior bombing attempt, on September 11, 2001, Al Qaeda suicide hijackers flew planes into the twin towers, resulting in their total collapse. The other buildings in the complex were also affected. WTC 7 collapsed, WTC 3 was crushed by the weight of these structures, and WTC 4, 5, and 6 were subsequently demolished. The official death total currently numbers 2,750, which was a challenging figure to reconstruct given the dearth of human remains found at the obliterated site. After eight and a half months of clearing debris 24 hours a day, the Lower Manhattan Development Corporation was given the task of selecting the future construction on this valuable piece of real estate. Hoping to balance the use of the site as a historical memorial and a future economic center, the advisory committee selected the overall site design created by the Polish-born American architect Daniel Libeskind, whose Jewish Museum in Berlin, constructed in 1999 in the style of **Deconstructivism**, provided him international recognition. Libeskind planned five buildings and a memorial clustered around a sunken field that maintains the foundations of the destroyed twin towers and the original slurry wall. This central area is to feature a museum and a memorial titled Reflecting Absence, selected in 2004 from a competition design submitted by Michael Arad and Peter Walker. The office towers, three of which are to be designed by Norman Foster, Richard Rogers, and Fumihiko Maki, all known for their **High-Tech architecture**, are clustered around Libeskind's Freedom Tower, which rises 1,776 feet, in reference to the date of American Independence. Seventy stories would be used for offices space, restaurants, and shops, while the top 30-story spire is to have gardens. The three currently planned glass office towers will range in height from 946 to 1,254 feet tall, and will be completed in 2011–2012, while a fifth building is now being designed. WTC 7, not part of Libeskind's project, has already been rebuilt by the firm of Skidmore, Owings & Merrill.

WREN, CHRISTOPHER (1632–1723). Christopher Wren is considered the most important English **Baroque** architect after **Inigo Jones**. He was born into an intellectual family and initially taught astronomy and math, with architecture as a secondary interest. However, Wren went to Paris in 1665, and there he met **Gian Lorenzo Bernini**, the famous Roman Baroque artist who was visiting as a guest of King Louis XIV. He also became interested in the renovations for the **Louvre Palace** that were under way. These experiences shifted his focus to architecture, and after he returned to London, he was hired in 1669 as the King's Royal Surveyor-General. The core of London had been destroyed in a fire in 1666; architectural commissions were so plentiful that Wren is credited with constructing around 53 buildings in London during his lifetime, including the Royal Observatory and the Library at Trinity College in Cambridge.

His most famous building, however, is the massive Cathedral of Saint Paul, begun in the 1660s as a renovation of the original medieval structure; the commission became a full construction project after the Great Fire of 1666 destroyed the medieval church completely.

Wren's massive church went through several modifications before he arrived at what appears today—a monumental two-story structure with an open portico of Corinthian **columns** at both levels of the façade. The resulting deep narthex is capped on either end by large clock towers, much like those originally planned for **Saint Peter's Church in Rome.** The nave is longer than the compromise solution found at Saint Peter's, and the **dome** is equally massive. Wren's interior dome is very classical in that it is made of masonry with an oculus, while on the exterior the dome is covered by a layer of lead over **wood.** The tall lantern is additionally supported by an internal cone of **brick** in the upper dome. The drum of the dome is encircled with freestanding columns that visually match the double, open colonnade on the façade. Christopher Wren was buried in the crypt of this cathedral, and on his tomb marker is written, "If you want to see his memorial, look around you."

WRIGHT, FRANK LLOYD (1867–1959). Frank Lloyd Wright, the best-known American architect of the 20th century, designed both public buildings and private houses to develop a uniquely modern American style of architecture. Born in Wisconsin, Wright first studied engineering at the University of Wisconsin but left his studies to apprentice with **Louis Sullivan.** By 1893, he had opened his own architectural studio, specializing in domestic structures. Wright's goal was to create a house design that took into account the surrounding geography in order to better integrate homes into nature. This type of home, characterized by strong horizontal lines and large windows, is called the Prairie style house. First introduced in the Midwest, this house was typically a one-story dwelling with a heavy overhanging roofline that provides a horizontal echo of the flat landscape.

Wright's most famous Prairie style home is the Frederick C. Robie House, built in Chicago in 1906–1909. The warm **brick** exterior spreads out to include terraces edged in white **concrete** and a dramatically cantilevered roof over the terrace sections. A wide chimney cluster rises from the center of the building, providing a sole vertical element that monumentalizes the symbolism of the family hearth. The floor plan of the house is open, with rooms that flow from one into another, much like **Japanese architecture.** In the Robie House, the living room flows into the dining room; the rich **wood** molding, ceiling beams, bookshelves, and niches found throughout the house unify the open space of the interior.

One of the founders of the **Arts and Crafts** Movement in Chicago, Wright often designed his own furniture to match his houses. In addition, he and his assistant Marion Mahony Griffin designed modern lighting and heating systems for his homes, bringing a higher level of comfort to the domestic space. New research has shown, in fact, that much of his furnishings, lighting, mosaics, and murals were actually completed entirely by Griffin. Griffin was the second woman to graduate from MIT, in 1894, and was one of the first to receive an architectural license in the United States. She was Wright's first employee at his studio in Oak Park. In her 14-year tenure with Wright, Griffin created the beautiful watercolor sketches that Wright has become known for, and like Wright, Griffin was influenced in her style by Japanese prints.

By the 1930s, Wright was building his "Usonian Home," a less expensive adaptation of his Prairie House that was more visually suited to a varied geography. Ultimately, Wright designed over 362 homes across the United States, 300 of which survive today. His most daring home is the Edgar Kaufmann House, also called Fallingwater, built in 1937 in Mill Run, Pennsylvania, outside of Pittsburgh. This house is literally built into the landscape, right on top of a small cliff with a waterfall and a pool of water that runs off into a creek. A large boulder was integrated right into the hearth. With water running beneath the house, Wright then added widely cantilevered concrete slabs to create terraces across the exterior of the home to echo the stepped horizontal slabs of rock located around the waterfall. Worried about the structure of these slabs, the builder secretly placed steel inserts in the concrete despite Wright's objections.

The Price Tower, located in Bartlesville, Oklahoma (1952–1956), is the only cantilevered concrete **skyscraper** built by Wright, who was hired upon the advice of **Bruce Goff**, Dean of Architecture at the University of Oklahoma. While Wright learned the structural aspects of skyscrapers during his apprenticeship with Louis Sullivan, the design of this 19-story building is novel. Here Wright created a central core of elevator shafts with the floors cantilevered outward like branches attached to a tree trunk. Described as "the tree that escaped the crowded forest," this building is now the Price Tower Arts Center, and plans for an addition to the museum, commissioned to **Zaha Ha-did**, are under way.

Although Wright is best known for his housing designs, his most famous building is the very prominent Solomon R. Guggenheim Museum, located on Fifth Avenue in New York City. Built between 1943 and 1959, the museum is in the shape of a giant seashell, with tan concrete terraces that spiral down and inward onto a rectangular ground-floor base. The organic design of this building creates a dramatic break from the very geometric surrounding buildings that maintain the straight lines of the street. The museum houses a collection of modern art meant to be viewed on a descending spiral ramp beginning at the top of the broad foyer of the museum and sweeping slowly downward to arrive again at the entrance foyer. The museum visit begins with an elevator ride, and visitors can focus on the works of art that line the descending walls as they walk slowly downward, without having to navigate a labyrinth of galleries. This building, much like Wright's houses, was ultimately meant to be highly accessible to people. It is this accessibility blended with a high level of aesthetic beauty that ensured Frank Lloyd Wright's widespread and enduring appeal, an appeal that continues to be a source of inspiration for architects today. *See also* EXPRESSIONISM; GREEN ARCHITECTURE.

– Y –

YAMASAKI, MINORU (1912–1986). *See* SKYSCRAPER; WORLD TRADE CENTER, NEW YORK.

– Z –

ZAPOTEC ARCHITECTURE. *See* MESOAMERICAN ARCHITECTURE.

Bibliography

CONTENTS

This bibliography is not exhaustive, but is meant to provide an introduction to resources for further reading on the general areas covered in the dictionary. The bibliography contains a mixture of current studies together with earlier seminal texts on architecture organized into chronological periods and covering the cultures, styles, and architects discussed in this volume. Included are volumes of architectural terminology, historical overviews, monographs, exhibition catalogues, and collections of essays, with a small selection of pertinent articles and Internet sites. Special emphasis is given to heavily illustrated, recently published volumes in English that provide color images of many more buildings than can be illustrated in this dictionary.

The study of architecture in its historical context began in Renaissance Italy. This era was characterized by an intense interest in classical antiquity, called antiquarianism, which quickly spread across Europe through the next several centuries. It was this interest in the history of classical architecture that laid the foundation for the first architectural publications, which were printed shortly after the advent of the printing press in the mid-1400s. These first publications ranged from the theoretical treatise by the Ancient Roman engineer Vitruvius, whose first-century BC manuscript *De architectura* had just been discovered in the early 1400s, to the prolific number of Renaissance treatises on architecture such as Leon Battista Alberti's *On the Art of Building in Ten Books* from the 1400s to Andrea Palladio's *Four Books of Architecture* from the 1500s. All of these books are easily accessible today as inexpensive Dover publications and help the reader better understand the foundation of architectural history.

The first comprehensive overview of architectural history was written by Sir Banister Fletcher in 1896 and titled *A History of Architecture*. Now in its 20th edition, this survey remains the definitive text on historical western architecture. Spiro Kostof's more recent *History of Architecture: Settings and Rituals* (1995) provides a more thematic overview of architecture and includes more non-western buildings in the canon of architecture. A good general dictionary of architectural terminology is John Fleming, Hugh Honour, and Nikolaus Pevsner's *Penguin Dictionary of Architecture and Landscape Architecture* (2000), while Cyril M. Harris's *Illustrated Dictionary of Historic Architecture* (1983) provides an extensive collection of line drawings of some of the most significant buildings in history. Finally, the *Illustrated Encyclopedia of Architects and Architecture*, edited by Dennis Sharp (1991), provides the most thorough biographic catalogue of architects to date.

Ancient architecture of Europe, the Near East, and North Africa is typically studied within the framework of anthropology and archaeology, and therefore ancient buildings are rarely discussed outside a fuller cultural framework. The books on Prehistoric architecture found in this dictionary reflect this interdisciplinary focus, and include the overview of Stonehenge by Aubrey Burl titled *A Brief History of Stonehenge, One of the Most Famous Ancient Monuments in Britain* (2007). In 1980, the architectural anthropologist Lawrence H. Keeley, in his seminal study *Experimental Determination of Stone Tool Uses*, offered a fuller examination of stone tools that has extended our understanding of the origins of the built world further back into the Paleolithic Age. Interest in the study of Ancient Near Eastern architecture initially came from biblical descriptions of ancient monuments and descriptions of the Seven Wonders of the World. The recent book by Enrico Ascalone, *Mesopotamia: Assyrians, Sumerians, Babylonians* (2007), makes use of more current archaeological studies of this region, often called the "cradle of civilization," to provide an overview of Mesopotamian architecture. The standard text on Ancient Egyptian architecture remains Alexander Badawy's *History of Egyptian Architecture* (1966), while Dieter Arnold's *Encyclopedia of Ancient Egyptian Architecture* (2003) provides an excellent, thorough, and scholarly alphabetical reference. In addition, recent archaeological discoveries have transformed our understanding of monumental construction in Ancient Egypt, and include Rosalie David's *Pyramid Builders of Ancient Egypt: A Modern Investigation of Pharaoh's Workforce* (1997).

Ancient Aegean architecture was first understood via textual descriptions of Knossos, Tiryns, and Troy found in the epic writings of Homer, and early-20th-century German and English archaeologists were able to discover various ancient Mycenaean and Minoan settlements using Homer as their guide. Donald Preziosi's *Aegean Art and Architecture* (1999) provides the most detailed overview of these important pre-Hellenic cultures. Ancient Greece is perhaps the most thoroughly examined area of architectural history, and texts abound on the subject of Greek architecture and aesthetics. A. W. Lawrence's *Greek Architecture*, now in its fifth edition (1996), is the traditional overview of the subject, while the Parthenon, perhaps the best-known building from classical antiquity, is discussed in Vincent Bruno's *Parthenon* (1996). A comprehensive overview of Ancient Roman architecture is found in Axel Boethius's *Etruscan and Early Roman Architecture* (1992), while a more focused study of the best-known Ancient Roman building is found in William MacDonald's *Pantheon: Design, Meaning, and Progeny* (2002). Early Semitic architecture remains less well studied in the history of architecture, but the standard overview of Early Christian and Byzantine architecture is Richard Krautheimer's *Early Christian and Byzantine Architecture* (1984).

The architecture of Asia includes Indian, Chinese, Japanese, and Southeast Asian structures. Although the scholarly focus has been on ancient monuments in these areas, major monographs on contemporary Japanese and Chinese architecture can be found in the bibliography as well. Christopher Tadgell's *History of Architecture in India: From the Dawn of Civilization to the End of the Raj* (1990) provides a nice overview of the earliest Asian culture, while interesting new research on the symbolism of the famous Taj Mahal in Agra is published in Elizabeth Moynihan, ed., *The Moonlight Garden: New Discoveries at the Taj Mahal* (2001). Qinghua Guo's *Visual Dictionary of Chinese Architecture* (2006) is an excellent reference book on this region of Asia, while Antony White's recent *Forbidden City* (2006) provides a focused overview of the most famous architectural complex in Beijing. Michiko Young's *Introduction to Japanese Architecture* (2003) is a nicely illustrated, well-written overview of the general characteristics of Japanese architecture from pre-Buddhist culture to modern Japan. Finally, the architecture of Southeast Asia is less well studied, but Michael Coe's *Angkor and the Khmer Civilization* (2005) provides a good overview of this most famous architectural site in Cambodia.

While non-western architecture in general can be studied further in Dora Crouch and June Johnson's *Traditions in Architecture: Africa, America, Asia, and Oceania* (2000), Mesoamerican architectural studies typically focus on the Maya, with Mary Ellen Miller's text *Maya Art and Architecture* (1999) remaining the main source for this area of study. Similarly, South American architectural research is focused on the Inca, as detailed in Nigel Davies' *Ancient Kingdoms of Peru* (1998). Finally, Peter Nabokov and Robert Easton's *Native American Architecture* (1990) provides the best historical overview of native architecture in North America.

European architecture from the Middle Ages onward has been more thoroughly studied than that of these ancient cultures, exclusive of Ancient Greek and Roman architecture. Research on medieval architecture, for example, tends to be broken down into different stylistic and geographical categories, with Byzantine and Islamic architecture in the east and Carolingian, Ottonian, Romanesque, and Gothic architecture in the west. Byzantine architecture developed in the Ancient Roman settlement of Constantinople, and can be further examined in Cyril Mango's *Byzantine Architecture* (1976), while the most famous Byzantine building, Hagia Sophia, receives a thorough examination in Rowland Mainstone's *Hagia Sophia: Architecture, Structure, and Liturgy of Justinian's Great Church* (1997). A well-illustrated overview of Islamic architecture is Henri Stierlin's *Islamic Art and Architecture* (2002), while the mosque in particular is more fully examined in Martin Frishman and Hasan-Uddin Khan, eds., *The Mosque: History, Architectural Development and Regional Diversity* (2002). Studies on early medieval architecture in western Europe also focus on monasteries, castles, and cathedrals. Roger Stalley's *Early Medieval Architecture* (1999) is a good overview of the early centuries of this era, while Nicola Coldstream's *Medieval Architecture* (2002) provides a thematic overview primarily of later Romanesque and Gothic architecture. Christopher Gravett's *History of Castles: Fortifications around the World* (2001) and Wolfgang Braunfels's *Monasteries of Western Europe* (1973) provide a more focused examination of two of the most favored building types of the Middle Ages.

Pre-modern architecture begins at the time of the Renaissance and continues through the 18th century. By this time, the position of the architect and the place of architecture in society are more clearly defined, and the dictionary reflects this broader methodological approach to architecture. Still used in the classroom is Peter Murray's *Architecture of the Italian Renaissance* (reprinted in 1997), with Henry Russell Hitchcock's *German Renaissance Architecture* (1982) covering northern European work. The monographic studies on major Renaissance architects tend to favor the Italians and include James Ackerman's *Architecture of Michelangelo* (1986) and his *Palladio* (1974), while beautifully illustrated books on various Renaissance building types include Thorsten Droste and Axel M. Mosier's *Châteaux of the Loire* (1997). Stylistic examinations of 16th-century European architecture tend to focus on Mannerism and include John Shearman's textbook *Mannerism* (1991), while Baroque architecture of the 17th century is traditionally covered in a broader variety of regional studies, including Anthony Blunt's *Art and Architecture in France, 1500–1700* (1999) and John Varriano's *Italian Baroque and Rococo Architecture* (1986). Important monographs include Howard Hibbard's *Bernini* (1965) and the most recent publication on Inigo Jones by Giles Worsley, *Inigo Jones and the European Classicist Tradition* (2007). Volumes on individual buildings include those written on the Saint Peter's Church in Rome and Versailles Palace in France. Finally, the architecture of the 18th century is almost exclusively focused on the Rococo style and the Neo-Classical revival, discussed in the textbook overview by John Summerson, *The Architecture of the Eighteenth Century* (1986).

By the 19th century, more overt methodological issues developed within the study of architectural history that began to add richness to traditional viewpoints about architecture. Robin Middleton and David Watkin's *Architecture of the Nineteenth Century* (2003) provides an overview of the century, while the many new styles are addressed in such books as Megan Aldrich, *Gothic Revival* (1997); Peter Davey, *Arts and Crafts Architecture* (1997); Arthur Drexler, *The Architecture of the École des Beaux-Arts* (1978); and Klaus-Jurgen Sembach, *Art Nouveau* (2007), published in the beautifully illustrated Taschen series.

By the early 20th century, stylistic categories exploded in number; they are documented in a series of manifestos written by European architects who proclaimed the advent of more modern architectural styles every decade. Ulrich Conrads, ed., in his *Programs and Manifestoes on Twentieth-Century Architecture* (1975), includes a collection of such treatises. Both World War I and World War II inspired a deep questioning of architecture, its theoretical underpinnings, its implied hierarchy, and its methodological construction. Kenneth Frampton's *Modern Architecture: A Critical History* (reprinted 1992) and Reyner Banham's *Theory and Design in the First Machine Age* (1980) led the way in addressing these issues. New styles and techniques brought architecture into the "modern" world. The most pivotal study of early-20th-century architecture is Henry Russell Hitchcock and Philip Johnson's historical text *The International Style: Architecture since 1922* (reprinted 1997), while monographs such as Philip Johnson's *Mies van der Rohe* (1978) and Gilbert Lupfer, Paul Sigel, and Peter Gollse, *Walter Gropius, 1883–1969: Promoter of a New Form* (2004) abound. Finally, the advent of the automobile transformed domestic architecture, as discussed in Tim Benton's well-illustrated volume titled *The Villas of Le Corbusier and Pierre Jeanneret, 1920–1930* (2007).

Leland Roth's *Concise History of American Architecture* (1980) provides the best overview of architecture in the United States prior to the advent of Post-Modernism. Eighteenth-century architecture in the United States shared many of the same developments as European architecture of the same era, as seen in the plethora of Neo-Classical structures found across the country. The most important Neo-Classical buildings are discussed in the books by William Beiswanger et al., *Thomas Jefferson's Monticello* (2001), and by Henry Hope Reed and Anne Day, *The United States Capitol: Its Architecture and Decoration* (2005). By the 19th century, the Gothic Revival was introduced in the United States, as is discussed in Elizabeth Feld, Stewart Feld, and David Warren's *In Pointed Style: The Gothic Revival in America, 1800–1860* (2006). This led the way for the introduction of increasingly varied architectural styles in America. Art Deco is one such style, discussed in Carla Breeze, *American Art Deco: Modernistic Architecture and Regionalism* (2003).

Bibliography on domestic architecture in the United States is extensive, and includes field guides as well as scholarly studies of style and architects. Virginia McAlester and Lee McAlester's *Field Guide to American Houses* (2000) will help the reader identify local house styles, while Thomas Heinz's *Frank Lloyd Wright Field Guide* (2005) provides a thorough catalogue of all the works of this most famous American architect. Manufactured housing in the United States has a fascinating history, and Dover reprints of many original catalogues are easily found today, including the *Aladdin "Built in a Day" House Catalog, 1917* (reprinted 1995). Janet Foster's *Queen Anne House: America's Victorian Vernacular* (2006) also illustrates one popular house style, while more scholarly studies have been published by Vincent Joseph Scully, a leading teacher of American architecture, including *The Shingle Style and the Stick Style: Architectural Theory and Design from Downing to the Origins of Wright* (1971) and *Frank Lloyd Wright* (1960).

By the early 20th century, new technological advances such as steel framing, reinforced concrete, glazed curtain walls, and skyscraper construction challenged traditional assumptions about architecture, and here the literature focuses on 20th-century architecture primarily in the United States. These technological advances are first discussed in Peter Collins's historic *Concrete: The Vision of New Architecture* (1959), while Matthew Wells's more recent *Skyscrapers: Structure and Design* (2005) is a nicely illustrated overview of this most important building type of the later 20th century.

Finally, these increasingly sophisticated constructions are the focus of Post-Modernist architecture, which takes into account more historical, regional, technological, and environmental factors in architectural design. Diane Ghirardo's *Architecture after Modernism* (1996) provides a good international overview of the significant buildings of the latter half of the 20th century, while the most recent architectural style, Green architecture, is best illustrated in James Wines, *Green Architecture* (2000). Architects continue their involvement in the publication of manifestos; the best-known of these include Robert Venturi and Denise Scott Brown, *Complexity and Contradiction in Architecture* (reprinted 2002) and Rem Koolhaas, *Delirious New York: A Retrospective Manifesto for Manhattan* (1997). Finally, *The Phaidon Atlas of Contemporary World Architecture* (2004) is a massive, beautifully illustrated volume of current architecture that anticipates styles to come.

I. GENERAL SOURCES

Ching, Francis D. K., Mark M. Jarzombek, and Vikramaditya Prakash. *A Global History of Architecture.* Hoboken, N.J.: Wiley, 2006.

Fleming, John, Hugh Honour, and Nikolaus Pevsner. *The Penguin Dictionary of Architecture and Landscape Architecture.* 5th ed. Baltimore: Penguin, 2000.

Fletcher, Sir Banister. *A History of Architecture.* 20th ed. Edited by Dan Cruickshank. 1896; Oxford: Architectural Press, 1996.

Harris, Cyril M. *Illustrated Dictionary of Historic Architecture*. New York: Dover, 1983.

Kostof, Spiro. *A History of Architecture: Settings and Rituals*. Oxford: Oxford University Press, 1995.

Norwich, John Julius, ed. *Great Architecture of the World*. Cambridge, Mass.: Da Capo Press, 2001.

Pevsner, Nikolaus. *A History of Building Types*. Princeton, N.J.: Princeton University Press, 1976.

Placzek, Adolf K., ed. *Macmillan Encyclopedia of Architects*. 4 vols. New York: Free Press, 1982.

Rudofsky, Bernard. *Architecture without Architects: A Short Introduction to Non-Pedigreed Architecture*. Albuquerque: University of New Mexico Press, 1987.

Salvadori, Mario. *Why Buildings Stand Up: The Strength of Architecture*. New York: Norton, 2002.

Sharp, Dennis, ed. *Illustrated Encyclopedia of Architects and Architecture*. New York: Watson-Guptill, 1991.

Sutton, Ian. *Western Architecture from Ancient Greece to the Present*. New York: Thames and Hudson, 1999.

Vickers, Graham. *Key Monuments in Architecture: The Relationship between Man, Buildings and Urban Growth as Seen in the Metropolis through the Ages*. Cambridge, Mass.: Da Capo Press, 1999.

Watkin, David. *The Rise of Architectural History*. London: Architectural Press, 1983.

II. GENERAL INTERNET SITES

About, Inc. architecture.about.com.

Artifice, Inc. "Great Buildings Online." www.GreatBuildings.com.

III. BUILDING MATERIALS

Behling, Stefan, and Sophia Behling, eds. *Glass: Structure and Technology in Architecture*. London: Prestel, 2000.

Campbell, James W. P. *Brick: A World History*. New York: Thames and Hudson, 2003.

Cohen, Jean-Louis, and G. Martin Moeller Jr., eds. *Liquid Stone: New Architecture in Concrete*. Princeton, N.J.: Princeton University Press, 2007.

Cuyer, Annette Le. *Steel and Beyond: New Strategies for Metals in Architecture*. Basel: Birkhäuser Basel, 2003.

Pryce, Will. *Buildings in Wood: The History and Traditions of Architecture's Oldest Building Material*. New York: Rizzoli, 2005.

IV: ANCIENT ARCHITECTURE (EUROPE, NEAR EAST, NORTH AFRICA)

A. Prehistoric Architecture (Paleolithic and Neolithic)

Brantingham, P. Jeffrey, Steven L. Kuhn, and Kristopher W. Kerry, eds. *The Early Upper Paleolithic beyond Western Europe*. Berkeley: University of California Press, 2004.

Burl, Aubrey. *A Brief History of Stonehenge, One of the Most Famous Ancient Monuments in Britain*. New York: Carroll and Graf, 2007.

———. *The Stone Circles of the British Isles*. New Haven, Conn.: Yale University Press, 1976.

Chippindale, Christopher. *Stonehenge Complete*. 3rd ed. New York: Thames and Hudson, 2004.

Daniel, Glyn Edmund. *The Megalith Builders of Western Europe*. London: Hutchinson, 1963.

Gibson, Alex. *Stonehenge and Timber Circles*. Charleston, S.C.: Tempus, 2005.

Hawkins, Gerald S. *Stonehenge Decoded*. Garden City, N.J.: Doubleday, 1965.

Keeley, Lawrence H. *Experimental Determination of Stone Tool Uses*. Chicago: University of Chicago Press, 1980.

North, John. *Stonehenge: A New Interpretation of Prehistoric Man and the Cosmos*. New York: Free Press, 1996.

O'Kelly, Michael. *Newgrange: Archaeology, Art and Legend*. New York: Thames and Hudson, 1995.

Preziosi, Donald. *Architecture, Language and Meaning: The Origins of the Built World and Its Semiotic Organization*. New York: Walter De Gruyter, 1979.

B. Ancient Near Eastern Architecture (Sumerian, Mari, Babylonian, Assyrian, Persian)

Ascalone, Enrico. *Mesopotamia: Assyrians, Sumerians, Babylonians*. Berkeley: University of California Press, 2007.

Bottero, Jean. *Religion in Ancient Mesopotamia*. Chicago: University of Chicago Press, 2004.

Crawford, Harriet. *Sumer and the Sumerians*. Cambridge: Cambridge University Press, 2004.

Curtis, John, and Nigel Tallis. *Forgotten Empire: The World of Ancient Persia*. Berkeley: University of California Press, 2005.

Downey, Susan B. *Mesopotamian Religious Architecture: Alexander through the Parthians*. Princeton, N.J.: Princeton University Press, 1988.

Leick, Gwendolyn. *A Dictionary of Ancient Near Eastern Architecture*. London: Routledge, 1988.

Loud, Gordon. *Khorsabad*. 2 vols. Chicago: University of Chicago Press, 1938.

Mellaart, James. *Çatal Hüyük: A Neolithic Town in Anatolia*. New York: McGraw-Hill, 1967.

——. *Earliest Civilizations of the Near East*. New York: McGraw-Hill, 1965.

Pollock, Susan. *Ancient Mesopotamia*. Cambridge: Cambridge University Press, 1999.

Rizza, Alfredo. *The Assyrians and the Babylonians: History and Treasures of an Ancient Civilization*. Vercelli, Italy: White Star Publishers, 2007.

Russell, John Malcolm. *Writing on the Wall: The Architectural Context of Late Assyrian Palaces*. Winona Lake, Ind.: Eisenbrauns, 1999.

Van de Mieroop, Marc. *The Ancient Mesopotamian City*. Oxford: Oxford University Press, 1999.

C. Ancient Egyptian Architecture

Arnold, Dieter. *Building in Egypt: Pharaonic Stone Masonry*. Oxford: Oxford University Press, 1997.

——. *The Encyclopedia of Ancient Egyptian Architecture*. Princeton, N.J.: Princeton University Press, 2003.

Badawy, Alexander. *A History of Egyptian Architecture*. Berkeley: University of California Press, 1966.

Clark, Somers. *Ancient Egyptian Construction and Architecture*. New York: Dover, 1990.

David, A. Rosalie. *Pyramid Builders of Ancient Egypt: A Modern Investigation of Pharaoh's Workforce*. London: Routledge, 1997.

Isler, Martin. *Sticks, Stones, and Shadows: Building the Egyptian Pyramids*. Norman: University of Oklahoma Press, 2001.

Rossi, Corinna. *Architecture and Mathematics in Ancient Egypt*. Cambridge: Cambridge University Press, 2004.

Smith, Wilbur S. *The Art and Architecture of Ancient Egypt*. Baltimore: Penguin, 1958.

D. Ancient Aegean Architecture (Minoan and Mycenaean)

Evans, Arthur J. *The Palace of Minos at Knossos.* 4 vols. London: Macmillan, 1921–1935.

French, Elizabeth. *Mycenae: Agamemnon's Capital: The Site and Its Setting.* Charleston, S.C.: Tempus, 2002.

Graham, James W. *The Palaces at Crete.* Princeton, N.J.: Princeton University Press, 1962.

Hitchcock, Louise A. *Minoan Architecture: A Contextual Analysis.* Sävedalen, Sweden: Paul Aströms Förlag, 2000.

Hooker, James T. *Mycenean Greece.* London: Routledge, 1977.

Mylonas, George E. *Ancient Mycenae.* Princeton, N.J.: Princeton University Press, 1957.

Preziosi, Donald. *Aegean Art and Architecture.* Oxford: Oxford University Press, 1999.

Willetts, Ronald F. *The Civilization of Ancient Crete.* Berkeley: University of California Press, 1978.

E. Ancient Greek Architecture

Bruno, Vincent J. *The Parthenon.* New York: Norton, 1996.

Carpenter, Rhys. *The Architects of the Parthenon.* Baltimore: Penguin, 1970.

Coulton, James J. *Ancient Greek Architects at Work: Problems of Structure and Design.* Ithaca, N.Y.: Cornell University Press, 1977.

Dinsmoor, W. B. *The Architecture of Ancient Greece.* 3rd ed. New York: Norton, 1975.

Francis, Robin. *Architecture and Meaning on the Athenian Acropolis.* Cambridge: Cambridge University Press, 1995.

Fyfe, Theodore. *Hellenistic Architecture.* Cambridge: Cambridge University Press, 1936.

Lawrence, A. W. *Greek Architecture.* 5th ed. New Haven, Conn.: Yale University Press, 1996.

Robertson, Donald S. *Greek and Roman Architecture.* Cambridge: Cambridge University Press, 1969.

Tzonis, Alexander. *Classical Architecture: The Poetics of Order.* Cambridge, Mass.: MIT Press, 1986.

F. Etruscan Architecture

Boethius, Axel. *Etruscan and Early Roman Architecture.* New Haven, Conn.: Yale University Press, 1992.

Pallottino, Massimo. *The Etruscans*. Baltimore: Penguin, 1955.

Spivey, Nigel Jonathan. *Etruscan Art*. New York: Thames and Hudson, 1997.

G. Ancient Roman Architecture

Adam, Jean-Pierre. *Roman Building: Materials and Techniques*. London: Routledge, 2003.

Bianchi Bandinelli, R. *Rome: The Late Empire*. Translated by P. Green. New York: George Braziller, 1971.

Jones, Mark Wilson. *Principles of Roman Architecture*. New Haven, Conn.: Yale University Press, 2003.

MacDonald, William. *The Architecture of the Roman Empire: An Urban Appraisal*. New Haven, Conn.: Yale University Press, 1988.

———. *The Pantheon: Design, Meaning, and Progeny*. Cambridge, Mass.: Harvard University Press, 2002.

McKay, Alexander G. *Houses, Villas, and Palaces in the Roman World*. Baltimore: Johns Hopkins University Press, 1998.

Sear, Frank. *Roman Architecture*. Ithaca, N.Y.: Cornell University Press, 1983.

Stamper, John W. *The Architecture of Roman Temples: The Republic to the Middle Empire*. Cambridge: Cambridge University Press, 2005.

Stierlin, Henri, and Anne Stierlin. *The Roman Empire: From the Etruscans to the Decline of the Roman Empire*. Cologne: Benedikt Taschen, 2004.

Vitruvius. *The Ten Books on Architecture*. Translated by M. H. Morgan. New York: Dover Publications, 1960.

Ward-Perkins, John B. *Cities of Ancient Greece and Italy: Planning in Classical Antiquity*. New York: George Braziller, 1974.

———. *Roman Imperial Architecture*. New Haven, Conn.: Yale University Press, 1992.

Welch, Katherine. *The Roman Amphitheatre: From Its Origins to the Colosseum*. Cambridge: Cambridge University Press, 2007.

H. Early Semitic and Christian Architecture

Bassett, Sarah. *The Urban Image of Late Antique Constantinople*. Cambridge: Cambridge University Press, 2007.

Goldhill, Simon. *The Temple of Jerusalem*. Cambridge, Mass.: Harvard University Press, 2005.

Hamblin, William J., and David Seely. *Solomon's Temple: Myth and History*. New York: Thames and Hudson, 2007.

Krautheimer, Richard. *Early Christian and Byzantine Architecture*. New Haven, Conn.: Yale University Press, 1984.

MacDonald, William. *Early Christian and Byzantine Architecture.* New York: George Braziller, 1962.

Mathews, Thomas F. *Early Churches of Constantinople: Architecture and Liturgy.* University Park: Pennsylvania State University, 1971.

Milburn, Robert. *Early Christian Art and Architecture.* Berkeley: University of California Press, 1991.

Richardson, Peter. *Building Jewish in the Roman East.* Waco, Texas: Baylor University Press, 2004.

White, L. Michael. *The Social Origins of Christian Architecture: Building God's House in the Roman World; Architectural Adaptation among Pagans, Jews, and Christians.* Cambridge, Mass.: Harvard University Press, 1996.

V: ARCHITECTURE OF ASIA

A. Indian Architecture

Harle, James C. *The Art and Architecture of the Indian Subcontinent.* New Haven, Conn.: Yale University Press, 1994.

Koch, Ebba. *The Complete Taj Mahal.* New York: Thames and Hudson, 2006.

Kramrisch, Stella. *The Art of India: Traditions of Indian Sculpture, Painting, and Architecture.* 3rd ed. New York: Phaidon, 1965.

Mitchell, George. *The Hindu Temple: An Introduction to Its Meaning and Forms.* Chicago: University of Chicago Press, 1988.

———. *The Penguin Guide to the Monuments of India.* 2 vols. New York: Viking Press, 1989.

Moynihan, Elizabeth B., ed. *The Moonlight Garden: New Discoveries at the Taj Mahal.* Seattle: University of Washington Press, 2001.

Rowland, Benjamin. *Art and Architecture of India: Buddhist, Hindu, Jain.* Baltimore: Penguin, 1977.

Tadgell, Christopher. *The History of Architecture in India: From the Dawn of Civilization to the End of the Raj.* London: Architecture, Design and Technology Press, 1990.

B. Chinese Architecture

Dawson, Layla. *China's New Dawn: An Architectural Transformation.* London: Prestel, 2005.

Guo, Qinghua. *Chinese Architecture and Planning: Ideals, Methods and Techniques.* Fellbach, Germany: Edition Axel Menges, 2006.

———. *The Visual Dictionary of Chinese Architecture.* London: Images Publishing, 2006.

Holdsworth, Mary. *The Forbidden City.* Oxford: Oxford University Press, 1999.

Shatzman Steinhardt, Nancy. *Chinese Imperial City Planning.* Honolulu: University of Hawai'i Press, 1999.

Sickman, Lawrence, and Alexander Soper. *Art and Architecture of China.* New Haven, Conn.: Yale University Press, 1992.

Ssu-ch'eng, Liang. *Chinese Architecture: A Pictorial History.* New York: Dover, 2005.

Xinian, Fu, Guo Daiheng, Liu Xujie, Pan Guxi, Qiao Yun, and Sun Dazhang. *Chinese Architecture.* New Haven, Conn.: Yale University Press, 2002.

White, Antony. *The Forbidden City.* London: London Editions, 2006.

C. Japanese Architecture

Fisher, Robert E. *Buddhist Art and Architecture.* New York: Thames and Hudson, 1993.

Furuyama, Masao. *Tadao Ando: 1941; The Geometry of Human Space.* Cologne: Benedikt Taschen, 2006.

Mitchelhill, Jennifer. *Castles of the Samurai: Power and Beauty.* Tokyo: Kodansha International, 2004.

Naito, Akira, and Takeshi Nishikawa. *Katsura: A Princely Retreat.* Tokyo: Kodansha International, 1994.

Paine, Robert Treat, and Alexander Soper. *Art and Architecture of Japan.* 3rd ed. Baltimore: Penguin, 1981.

Turnbull, Stephen. *Japanese Castles, 1540–1640.* Oxford: Osprey Publishing, 2003.

Ueda, Atsushi. *The Inner Harmony of the Japanese House.* Tokyo: Kodansha International, 1998.

Young, David. *Art of the Japanese Garden.* Tokyo: Tuttle Publishing, 2005.

Young, Michiko. *Introduction to Japanese Architecture.* Tokyo: Periplus Editions, 2003.

D. Southeast Asian Architecture (Myanmar [Burma], Malaysia, Singapore, Indonesia, Thailand, Taiwan, Laos, Cambodia, Vietnam, etc.)

Broman, Barry. *Bagan: Temple and Monuments of Ancient Burma.* London: Paths International, 2003.

Broman, Barry, and Ma Thanegi. *Myanmar Architecture: Cities of Gold.* London: Times Editions—Marshall Cavendish, 2005.

Bunce, Fredrick W. *The Iconography of Architectural Plans: A Study of the Influence of Buddhism and Hinduism on the Plans of South and Southeast Asia.* New Delhi: D. K. Printworld, 2002.

Chihara, Daigoro. *Hindu-Buddhist Architecture in Southeast Asia.* Leiden: E. J. Brill, 1996.

Coe, Michael. *Angkor and the Khmer Civilization.* New York: Thames and Hudson, 2005.

VI: ARCHITECTURE OF THE AMERICAS

A. Mesoamerican Architecture (Olmec, Teotihuacan, Maya, Aztec)

Abrams, Elliot Marc. *How the Maya Built Their World: Energetics and Ancient Architecture.* Austin: University of Texas Press, 1994.

Adams, Richard E. W. *Prehistoric Mesoamerica.* Norman: University of Oklahoma Press, 1996.

Crouch, Dora, and June Johnson. *Traditions in Architecture: Africa, America, Asia, and Oceania.* Oxford: Oxford University Press, 2000.

Miller, Mary Ellen. *Maya Art and Architecture.* New York: Thames and Hudson, 1999.

Pasztory, Esther. *Aztec Art.* Norman: University of Oklahoma Press, 2000.

Phillips, Charles. *The Art and Architecture of the Aztec and Maya: An Illustrated Encyclopedia of the Builds, Sculptures and Art of the Peoples of Mesoamerica.* London: Southwater Books, 2008.

Pool, Christopher. *Olmec Archaeology and Early Mesoamerica.* Cambridge: Cambridge University Press, 2007.

B. Native American Architecture (North and South America)

Bingham, Hiram. *Lost City of the Incas.* Troy, Mich.: Phoenix Press, 2003.

Davies, Nigel. *The Ancient Kingdoms of Peru.* Baltimore: Penguin, 1998.

Gasparini, Graziano, and Luise Margolies. *Inca Architecture.* Bloomington: Indiana University Press, 1984.

Mink, Claudia. *Cahokia: City of the Sun; Prehistoric Urban Center in the American Bottom.* Cahokia, Ill.: Cahokia Mounds Museum Society, 1992.

Nabokov, Peter, and Robert Easton. *Native American Architecture.* Oxford: Oxford University Press, 1990.

Scully, Vincent. *Pueblo: Mountain, Village, Dance.* Chicago: University of Chicago Press, 1989.

VII: MEDIEVAL ARCHITECTURE IN EUROPE (400s–1300s)

A. Byzantine Architecture

Mainstone, Rowland J. *Hagia Sophia: Architecture, Structure, and Liturgy of Justinian's Great Church.* New York: Thames and Hudson, 1997.
Mango, Cyril. *Byzantine Architecture.* New York: Harry N. Abrams, 1976.
Mathews, Thomas F. *The Byzantine Churches of Istanbul: A Photographic Survey.* University Park: Pennsylvania State University, 1976.
Rodley, Lyn. *Byzantine Art and Architecture: An Introduction.* Cambridge: Cambridge University Press, 1996.
Swift, Emerson H. *Hagia Sophia.* New York: Columbia University Press, 1940.
Von Simson, Otto. *Sacred Fortress: Byzantine Art and Statecraft in Ravenna.* Chicago: University of Chicago Press, 1948.

B. Islamic Architecture

Barrucand, Marianne. *Moorish Architecture in Andalusia.* Cologne: Benedikt Taschen, 2007.
Behrens-Abouseif, Doris. *Islamic Architecture in Cairo.* Cairo: American University in Cairo Press, 1996.
Blair, Sheila S., and Jonathan M. Bloom. *The Art and Architecture of Islam, 1250–1800.* New Haven, Conn.: Yale University Press, 1996.
Ettinghausen, Richard, Oleg Grabar, and Marilyn Jenkins-Madina. *Islamic Art and Architecture, 650–1250.* New Haven, Conn.: Yale University Press, 2003.
Frishman, Martin, and Hasan-Uddin Khan, eds. *The Mosque: History, Architectural Development and Regional Diversity.* New York: Thames and Hudson, 2002.
Hill, Derek, and Oleg Grabar. *Islamic Architecture and Its Decoration, A.D. 80–1500.* Chicago: University of Chicago Press, 1964.
Hoag, John D. *Islamic Architecture.* New York: Harry N. Abrams, 1977.
Goodwin, Godfrey. *A History of Ottoman Architecture.* New York: Thames and Hudson, 2003.
Grabar, Oleg. "The Islamic Dome, Some Considerations." *Journal of the Society of Architectural Historians* 22, no. 4 (1963): 191–98.
Hillenbrand, Robert. *Islamic Art and Architecture.* New York: Thames and Hudson, 1998.

Irwin, Robert. *The Alhambra.* Cambridge, Mass.: Harvard University Press, 2004.

Michell, George, ed. *Architecture of the Islamic World: Its History and Social Meaning.* London: Thames and Hudson, 1978.

Necipoglu, Gulru, Arben N. Arapi, and Reha Gunay. *The Age of Sinan: Architectural Culture in the Ottoman Empire.* Princeton, N.J.: Princeton University Press, 2005.

Ruggles, D. Fairchild. *Gardens, Landscape and Vision in the Palaces of Islamic Spain.* University Park: Pennsylvania State University Press, 2003.

Stierlin, Henri. *Islamic Art and Architecture.* New York: Thames and Hudson, 2002.

Tadgell, Christo. *Islam: From Medina to the Magreb and from the Indes to Istanbul.* London: Routledge, 2008.

Williams, Caroline. *Islamic Monuments in Cairo: The Practical Guide.* Cairo: American University in Cairo Press, 2004.

C. Early Medieval, Carolingian, Ottonian Architecture

Bandmann, Günter, and Kendall Wallis. *Early Medieval Architecture as Bearer of Meaning.* New York: Columbia University Press, 2003.

Braunfels, Wolfgang. *Monasteries of Western Europe.* Translated by A. Laing. Princeton, N.J.: Princeton University Press, 1973.

Calkins, Robert G. *Medieval Architecture in Western Europe: From A.D. 300 to 1500.* Oxford: Oxford University Press, 1998.

Coldstream, Nicola. *Medieval Architecture.* Oxford: Oxford University Press, 2002.

Conant, Kenneth J. *Carolingian and Romanesque Architecture, 800-1200.* 3rd ed. Baltimore: Penguin, 1973.

Cram, Ralph. "Architecture in the Age of Charlemagne." *The Substance of Gothic: Six Lectures on the Development of Architecture from Charlemagne to Henry VIII.* Kila, Mont.: Kessinger Publishing, 2004.

Dimier, Anselme. *Stones Laid before the Lord: A History of Monastic Architecture.* Collegeville, Minn.: Cistercian Publications, 1999.

Gravett, Christopher. *The History of Castles: Fortifications around the World.* Guilford, Conn.: Lyons Press, 2001.

Krautheimer, Richard. "The Carolingian Revival of Early Christian Architecture." *Art Bulletin* 24 (1942): 1–38.

McClendon, Charles. *The Origins of Medieval Architecture: Building in Europe, A.D. 600–900.* New Haven, Conn.: Yale University Press, 2005.

Stalley, Roger. *Early Medieval Architecture.* Oxford: Oxford University Press, 1999.

D. Romanesque Architecture

Armi, C. Edson. *Design and Construction in Romanesque Architecture: First Romanesque Architecture and the Pointed Arch in Burgundy and Northern Italy*. Cambridge: Cambridge University Press, 2004.

Barral I Altet, Xavier. *Romanesque: Towns, Cathedrals and Monasteries*. Cologne: Benedikt Taschen, 1998.

Conant, Kenneth J. *Carolingian and Romanesque Architecture, 800–1200*. New Haven, Conn.: Yale University Press, 1992.

Gies, Joseph, and Frances Gies. *Life in a Medieval Castle*. 3rd ed. New York: Harper Perennial, 1979.

Nicolle, David. *Crusader Castles in the Holy Land, 1097–1192*. Oxford: Osprey Publishing, 2005.

———. *Crusader Castles in the Holy Land, 1192–1302*. Oxford: Osprey Publishing, 2005.

Radding, Charles M., and William Clark. *Medieval Architecture, Medieval Learning: Builders and Masters in the Age of Romanesque and Gothic*. New Haven, Conn.: Yale University Press, 1994.

Strafford, Peter. *Romanesque Churches of France: A Traveller's Guide*. London: Gilles de la Mare Publishers, 2005.

Toman, Rolf, and Achim Bednorz. *Romanesque: Architecture, Sculpture, Painting*. Cologne: Könemann, 1997.

Wolf, Norbert. *Romanesque*. Cologne: Benedikt Taschen, 2007.

E. Gothic Architecture

Ackerman, James. "*Ars sine scientia nihil est*: Gothic Theory of Architecture at the Cathedral of Milan." *The Art Bulletin* 31 (1949): 84–111.

Bony, Jean. *French Gothic Architecture of the Twelfth and Thirteenth Centuries*. Berkeley: University of California Press, 1985.

Branner, Robert. *Chartres Cathedral: Illustrations, Introductory Essay, Documents, Analysis, Criticism*. New York: Norton, 1996.

Clifton-Taylor, Alec. *The Cathedrals of England*. New York: Thames and Hudson, 1989.

Frankl, Paul. *Gothic Architecture*. New Haven, Conn.: Yale University Press, 2001.

Jantzen, Hans. *High Gothic and Classic Cathedrals of Chartres, Reims and Amiens*. Princeton, N.J.: Princeton University Press, 1984.

Mark, Robert. *Experiments in Gothic Structure*. Cambridge, Mass.: MIT Press, 1982.

Mâle, Émile. *Gothic Image: Religious Art in France of the Thirteenth Century*. Boulder, Colo.: Westview Press, 1983.

Nussbaum, Norbert. *German Gothic Church Architecture.* New Haven, Conn.: Yale University Press, 2000.

Panofsky, Erwin. *Gothic Architecture and Scholasticism.* Latrobe, Pa.: Archabbey Publications, 1950.

———. *Suger, Abbot of Saint-Denis, 1081–1151.* 2nd ed. Princeton, N.J.: Princeton University Press, 1979.

Saalman, Howard. *Medieval Cities.* New York: George Braziller, 1968.

Scott, Robert A. *The Gothic Enterprise: A Guide to Understanding the Medieval Cathedral.* Berkeley: University of California Press, 2006.

Stoddard, Whitney S. *Art and Architecture in Medieval France: Medieval Architecture, Sculpture, Stained Glass, Manuscripts, the Art of the Church Treasuries.* New York: Harper and Row, 1972.

Suger, Abbot. *Abbot Suger on the Abbey Church of St.-Denis and Its Art Treasures.* Edited and translated by Erwin Panofsky. 2nd ed. Edited by Gerda Panofsky-Soergel. Princeton, N.J.: Princeton University Press, 1979.

Von Simson, Otto G. *The Gothic Cathedral.* Princeton, N.J.: Princeton University Press, 1988.

Wilson, Christopher. *The Gothic Cathedral: The Architecture of the Great Church, 1130–1530.* New York: Thames and Hudson, 2005.

Worsley, Giles, and Michael Hall, eds. *Gothic Architecture and Its Meanings, 1550–1830.* London: Spire Books, 2002.

VIII: PRE-MODERN ARCHITECTURE IN EUROPE (1400s–1700s)

A. Renaissance Architecture

Ackerman, James S. "Architectural Practice in the Italian Renaissance." *Journal of the Society of Architectural Historians* 13 (1954): 3–11.

———. *The Architecture of Michelangelo.* Chicago: University of Chicago Press, 1986.

———. *Palladio.* Baltimore: Penguin, 1974.

Alberti, Leon Battista. *On the Art of Building in Ten Books.* Cambridge, Mass.: MIT Press, 1991.

Battisti, Eugenio. *Filippo Brunelleschi.* New York: Phaidon, 2002.

Blunt, Anthony. *Art and Architecture in France, 1500–1700.* Baltimore: Penguin, 1957.

Borsi, Franco. *Bramante.* Milan: Edizioni Electa, 1989.

Boucher, Bruce. *Andrea Palladio: The Architect in His Time.* New York: Abbeville Press, 2007.

Burckhardt, Jacob. *The Architecture of the Italian Renaissance.* Chicago: University of Chicago Press, 1987.

Cooper, Tracy E. *Palladio's Venice: Architecture and Society in a Renaissance Republic.* New Haven, Conn.: Yale University Press, 2006.

Droste, Thorsten, and Axel M. Mosier. *Châteaux of the Loire.* London: I. B. Tauris, 1997.

Föster, Otto. *Bramante.* Vienna: Anton Schroll, 1956.

Furnari, Michele. *Formal Design in Renaissance Architecture: From Brunelleschi to Palladio.* New York: Rizzoli International, 1995.

Giaconi, Giovanni. *The Villas of Palladio.* New York: Princeton Architectural Press, 2003.

Goldthwaite, Richard. *The Building of Renaissance Florence: An Economic and Social History.* Baltimore: Johns Hopkins University Press, 1980.

Henderson, Paula. *The Tudor House and Garden: Architecture and Landscape in the Sixteenth and Early Seventeenth Centuries.* London: Paul Mellon Center, 2005.

Heydenreich, Ludwig. *Architecture in Italy, 1400–1500.* New Haven, Conn.: Yale University Press, 1996.

Hitchcock, Henry Russell. *German Renaissance Architecture.* Princeton, N.J.: Princeton University Press, 1982.

Hopkins, Andrew. *Italian Architecture from Michelangelo to Borromini.* New York: Thames and Hudson, 2002.

Howard, Deborah. *The Architectural History of Venice.* Rev. ed. New Haven, Conn.: Yale University Press, 2004.

Hyman, Isabelle, ed. *Brunelleschi in Perspective.* Englewood Cliffs, N.J.: Prentice Hall, 1974.

Lieberman, Ralph. *Renaissance Architecture in Venice, 1450–1540.* London: Century Hutchinson (UK Random House), 1982.

Lotz, Wolfgang. *Architecture in Italy, 1500–1600.* New Haven, Conn.: Yale University Press, 1995.

Luitpold, Christoph. *The Architecture of the Italian Renaissance.* New York: Thames and Hudson, 2007.

Millon, Henry A. *The Renaissance from Brunelleschi to Michelangelo: The Representation of Architecture.* New York: Rizzoli International, 1997.

Murray, Peter. *The Architecture of the Italian Renaissance.* New York: Schocken, 1997.

O'Brien, Patrick, ed. *Urban Achievement in Early Modern Europe: Golden Ages in Antwerp, Amsterdam and London.* Cambridge: Cambridge University Press, 2001.

Palladio, Andrea. *The Four Books of Architecture.* New York: Dover, 1965.

Prager, Frank D., and Gustina Scaglia. *Brunelleschi: Studies of His Technology and Inventions.* New York: Dover, 2004.

Scott, Geoffrey. *The Architecture of Humanism*. Gloucester, Mass.: P. Smith, 1965.

Summerson, John. *The Classical Language of Architecture*. Cambridge, Mass.: MIT Press, 1966.

Tavernor, Robert. *Palladio and Palladianism*. New York: Thames and Hudson, 1991.

Wittkower, Rudolf. *Architectural Principles in the Age of Humanism*. New York: Norton, 1971.

B. Mannerist Architecture

Shearman, John. *Mannerism*. Baltimore: Penguin, 1991.

Tafuri, Manfredo. *Giulio Romano (Architecture in Early Modern Italy)*. Cambridge: Cambridge University Press, 1999.

C. Baroque Architecture

Blunt, Anthony. *Art and Architecture in France, 1500–1700*. New Haven, Conn.: Yale University Press, 1999.

———. *Borromini*. Cambridge, Mass.: Belknap Press of Harvard University Press, 2005.

———. *Guide to Baroque Rome*. New York: Harper and Row, 1982.

Hempel, Eberhard. *Baroque Art and Architecture in Central Europe*. Baltimore: Penguin, 1965.

Hibbard, Howard. *Bernini*. Baltimore: Penguin, 1965.

Kubler, George. *Art and Architecture in Spain and Portugal and Their American Dominions, 1500–1800*. Baltimore: Penguin, 1959.

Merz, Jorg M., and Anthony Blunt. *Pietro da Cortona and Roman Baroque Architecture*. New Haven, Conn.: Yale University Press, 2007.

Millon, Henry. *Baroque and Rococo Architecture*. New York: George Braziller, 1961.

Norberg-Schulz, Christian. *Baroque Architecture*. New York: Harry N. Abrams, 1971.

Pérouse de Montclos, Jean-Marie. *Versailles*. New York: Abbeville Press, 1997.

Varriano, John. *Italian Baroque and Rococo Architecture*. Oxford: Oxford University Press, 1986.

Wittkower, Rudolf. *Art and Architecture in Italy, 1600–1750*. Vol. 1, *Early Baroque*. New Haven, Conn.: Yale University Press, 1999.

Wölfflin, Heinrich. *Renaissance and Baroque*. Translated by K. Simon. London: Collins, 1964.

Worsley, Giles. *Inigo Jones and the European Classicist Tradition*. New Haven, Conn.: Yale University Press, 2007.

D. Rococo Architecture

Brumfield, William Craft. *A History of Russian Architecture*. Cambridge: Cambridge University Press, 1997.

Cracraft, James. *The Petrine Revolution in Russian Architecture*. Chicago: University of Chicago Press, 1988.

Hitchcock, Henry Russell. *Rococo Architecture in Southern Germany*. New York: Phaidon, 1969.

Otto, Christian. *Space into Light: The Churches of Balthasar Neumann*. New York: Architectural History Foundation, 1979.

Shvidkovsky, Dmitri. *St. Petersburg: Architecture of the Tsars*. New York: Abbeville Press, 1996.

E. Neo-Classical Architecture

Bergdoll, Barry. *European Architecture, 1750–1890*. Oxford: Oxford University Press, 2000.

Braham, Allan. *The Architecture of the French Enlightenment*. Berkeley: University of California Press, 1980.

Curl, James Stevens. *Classical Architecture: An Introduction to Its Vocabulary and Essentials, with a Select Glossary of Terms*. New York: Norton, 2003.

Gibbs, James. *Gibbs' Book of Architecture: An Eighteenth-Century Classic*. New York: Dover, 2008.

Honour, Hugh. *Neo-Classicism*. Baltimore: Penguin, 1991.

Kalnein, Wend G., and Michael Levey. *Art and Architecture of the Eighteenth Century in France*. Baltimore: Penguin, 1972.

Kaufmann, Emil. *Architecture in the Age of Reason*. Cambridge, Mass.: Harvard University Press, 1955.

Summerson, John. *The Architecture of the Eighteenth Century*. New York: Thames and Hudson, 1986.

Vidler, Anthony. *Claude-Nicolas Ledoux: Architecture and Utopia in the Era of the French Revolution*. Basel: Birkhäuser Basel, 2006.

IX: 19TH-CENTURY ARCHITECTURE IN EUROPE

Aldrich, Megan. *Gothic Revival*. New York: Phaidon, 1997.

Atterbury, Paul. *A. W. N. Pugin: Master of Gothic Revival*. New Haven, Conn.: Yale University Press, 1995.

Clark, Kenneth. *The Gothic Revival: An Essay in the History of Taste*. 2nd ed. London: Constable, 1950.

Crawford, Alan. *Charles Rennie Mackintosh.* New York: Thames and Hudson, 1995.

Cumming, Elizabeth. *Arts and Crafts Movement.* New York: Thames and Hudson, 1991.

Davey, Peter. *Arts and Crafts Architecture.* London: Phaidon, 1997.

Drexler, Arthur. *The Architecture of the École des Beaux-Arts.* New York: Thames and Hudson, 1978.

Gillon, Edmund V., and Henry Hope Reed. *Beaux-Arts Architecture in New York: A Photographic Guide.* New York: Dover Publications, 1988.

Greenhalgh, Paul, ed. *Art Nouveau, 1890–1914.* London: Victoria and Albert Museum, 2002.

Honour, Hugh. *Romanticism.* Boulder, Colo.: Westview, 1979.

Hourticq, Louis. *Encyclopédie des Beaux-Arts: Architecture, Sculpture, Peinture, Arts Décoratifs.* Paris: Librairie Hachette, 1925.

Lewis, Michael J. *The Gothic Revival.* New York: Thames and Hudson, 2002.

Loyer, François. *Paris Nineteenth Century: Architecture and Urbanism.* New York: Abbeville Press, 1988.

Mead, Christopher. *Charles Garnier's Paris Opéra: Architectural Empathy and the Renaissance of French Classicism.* Cambridge, Mass.: MIT Press, 1991.

Midant, Jean-Paul. *Viollet-le-Duc: The French Gothic Revival.* New York: Perseus, 2002.

Middleton, Robin, and David Watkin. *Architecture of the Nineteenth Century.* New York: Phaidon, 2003.

———. *Neoclassical and Nineteenth-Century Architecture: The Diffusion and Development of Classicism and the Gothic Revival.* Milan: Edizioni Electa, 1993.

Mignot, Claude. *Architecture of the Nineteenth Century in Europe.* New York: Rizzoli International, 1984.

Pevsner, Nikolaus. *Pioneers of Modern Design.* London: Faber and Faber, 1936.

———. *Some Architectural Writers of the Nineteenth Century.* Oxford: Clarendon Press, 1972.

Powell, Christabel. *Augustus Welby Pugin, Designer of the British House of Parliament: The Victorian Quest for a Liturgical Architecture.* Lewiston, N.Y.: Edwin Mellen Press, 2006.

Ruskin, John. *The Seven Lamps of Architecture.* London: Smith, Elder and Company, 1949.

Sembach, Klaus-Jurgen. *Art Nouveau.* Cologne: Benedikt Taschen, 2007.

Sola-Morales, Ignasi de, and Rafael Vargas. *Antoni Gaudi.* New York: Harry N. Abrams, 2003.

Summerson, John. *Victorian Architecture: Four Studies in Evaluation.* New York: Columbia University Press, 1970.

Turnor, Reginald. *Nineteenth-Century Architecture in Britain.* London: B. T. Batsford, 1950.

X: EARLY-20TH-CENTURY ARCHITECTURE (OUTSIDE THE UNITED STATES)

Andreoli, Elisabetta, and Adrian Forty, eds. *Brazil's Modern Architecture.* New York: Phaidon, 2007.

Bachmann, Wolfgang. *Icons of Architecture: The Twentieth Century.* London: Prestel Publishing, 2005.

Banham, Reyner. *Age of the Masters: A Personal View of Modern Architecture.* New York: Harper and Row, 1975.

———. *Theory and Design in the First Machine Age.* Cambridge, Mass.: MIT Press, 1980.

Benton, Tim. *The Villas of Le Corbusier and Pierre Jeanneret, 1920–1930.* Basel: Birkhäuser, 2007.

Cobbers, Arnt. *Erich Mendelsohn.* Cologne: Benedikt Taschen, 2007.

Cohen, Jean-Louis. *Ludwig Mies van der Rohe.* Basel: Birkhäuser Basel, 2007.

Collins, Peter. *Concrete: The Vision of a New Architecture; A Study of Auguste Perret and His Precursors.* 2nd ed. 1959; Montreal: McGill-Queens University Press, 2004.

Colquhoun, Alan. *Modern Architecture.* Oxford: Oxford University Press, 2002.

Conrads, Ulrich, ed. *Programs and Manifestoes on Twentieth-Century Architecture.* Cambridge, Mass.: MIT Press, 1975.

Cooper, Jackie, ed. *Mackintosh Architecture.* London: St. Martin's Press, 1984.

De Wit, Wim, ed. *The Amsterdam School: Dutch Expressionistic Architecture, 1915–30.* New York: Copper Hewitt Museum, 1983.

Dean, David. *Architecture of the 1930s.* New York: Rizzoli International, 1983.

Deckker, Zilah O. *Brazil Built: The Architecture of the Modern Movement in Brazil.* London: Taylor and Francis, 2001.

Fosso, Mario, Otakar Macel, and Maurizio Meriggi. *Konstantin S. Mel'nikov and the Construction of Moscow.* Milan: Skira Press, 2000.

Frampton, Kenneth. *Modern Architecture: A Critical History.* Oxford: Oxford University Press, 1992.

Hitchcock, Henry Russell. *Architecture: Nineteenth and Twentieth Centuries.* New Haven, Conn.: Yale University Press, 1989.

Hitchcock, Henry Russell, and Philip Johnson. *The International Style: Architecture since 1922.* New York: Norton, 1997.

Humphreys, Richard. *Futurism.* Cambridge: Cambridge University Press, 1999.

Hyman, Isabelle. *Marcel Breuer, Architect: The Career and the Buildings*. New York: Abrams, 2001.

Johnson, Philip. *Mies van der Rohe*. 3rd ed. New York: Museum of Modern Art, 1978.

Jones, Peter Blundell. *Gunnar Asplund*. London: Phaidon, 2006.

Julbez, Jose M. Buendia, and Juan Palomar. *The Life and Works of Luis Barragán*. New York: Rizzoli International, 1997.

Kirk, Terry. *The Architecture of Modern Italy: Visions of Utopia, 1900–Present*. Princeton, N.J.: Princeton University Press, 2005.

Kulterman, Udo. *Kenzo Tange, 1946–1969: Architecture and Urban Design*. New York: Praeger Publishers, 1970.

Le Corbusier. *Towards a New Architecture*. New York: Dover Publications, 1985.

Lupfer, Gilbert, Paul Sigel, and Peter Gollse. *Walter Gropius, 1883–1969: Promoter of a New Form*. Cologne: Benedikt Taschen, 2004.

McKean, John, and Colin Baxter. *Charles Rennie Mackintosh: Architect, Artist, Icon*. Osceola, Wis.: Voyageur Press, 2000.

Overy, Paul. *De Stijl*. New York: Thames and Hudson, 1991.

Pehnt, Wolfgang. *Expressionist Architecture*. Translated by J. A. Underwood. New York: Thames and Hudson, 1973.

Pevsner, Nikolaus. *Pioneers of Modern Design from William Morris to Walter Gropius*. Baltimore: Penguin, 1975.

———. *The Sources of Modern Architecture and Design*. New York: Thames and Hudson, 1985.

Rickey, George. *Constructivism: Origins and Evolution*. New York: George Braziller, 1995.

Sarnitz, August. *Adolf Loos, 1870–1933: Architect, Cultural Critic, Dandy*. Cologne: Benedikt Taschen, 2003.

———. *Hoffmann*. Cologne: Benedikt Taschen, 2007.

Sharp, Dennis. *A Visual History of Twentieth-Century Architecture*. Greenwich, Conn.: New York Graphic Society, 1972.

Stoller, Ezra. *The Chapel at Ronchamp*. New York: Princeton Architectural Press, 1999.

Underwood, David Kendrick. *Oscar Niemeyer and Brazilian Free-Form Modernism*. New York: George Braziller, 1994.

Whitford, Frank. *Bauhaus*. New York: Thames and Hudson, 1984.

XI: ARCHITECTURE IN THE UNITED STATES (1600s–1950s)

Adams, Nicholas. *Skidmore, Owings and Merrill: SOM since 1936*. London: Phaidon, 2007.

Aladdin "Built in a Day" House Catalog, 1917. New York: Dover Publications, 1995.

Alofsin, Anthony. *Prairie Skyscraper: Frank Lloyd Wright's Price Tower.* New York: Rizzoli International, 2005.

Bayer, Patricia. *Art Deco Architecture: Design, Decoration, and Detail from the Twenties and Thirties.* New York: Thames and Hudson, 1999.

Beiswanger, William L., Peter J. Hatch, Lucia Stanton, and Susan R. Stein. *Thomas Jefferson's Monticello.* Chapel Hill: University of North Carolina Press, 2001.

Breeze, Carla. *American Art Deco: Modernistic Architecture and Regionalism.* New York: Norton, 2003.

Cecil, William A. V. *Biltmore: The Vision and Reality of George W. Vanderbilt, Richard Morris Hunt, and Frederick Law Olmstead.* Asheville, N.C.: The Biltmore Company, 1975.

Condit, Carl. *The Chicago School of Architecture.* Chicago: University of Chicago Press, 1964.

Curl, James Stevens. *Victorian Architecture: Diversity and Invention.* New York: Spire Press, 2007.

DeLong, David, and Frank O. Gehry. *Bruce Goff: Toward Absolute Architecture.* Cambridge, Mass.: MIT Press, 1988.

Dixon, Roger. *Victorian Architecture.* New York: Thames and Hudson, 1985.

Downing, Andrew J. *The Architecture of Country Houses.* New York: Dover, 1969.

Drexler, Arthur. *Transformations in Modern Architecture.* New York: Museum of Modern Art, 1979.

Earls, William D. *The Harvard Five in New Canaan: Mid-Century Modern Houses by Marcel Breuer, Landis Gores, John Johansen, Philip Johnson, Eliot Noyes, and Others.* New York: Norton, 2006.

Eggener, Keith. *American Architectural History: A Contemporary Reader.* London: Routledge, 2004.

Feld, Elizabeth, Stuart R. Feld, and David B. Warren. *In Pointed Style: The Gothic Revival in America, 1800–1860.* New York: Hirschl and Adler Galleries, 2006.

Foster, Janet. *The Queen Anne House: America's Victorian Vernacular.* New York: Abrams, 2006.

Fuller, Buckminster. *Critical Path.* New York: St. Martin's Griffin, 1982.

Goff, Lee. *Tudor Style: Tudor Revival Houses in America from 1890 to the Present.* New York: Universe Publishing, 2002.

Hamlin, Talbot. *Greek Revival Architecture in America.* Oxford: Oxford University Press, 1944.

Harmon, Robert B. *Beaux-Arts Classicism in American Architecture.* Monticello, Ill.: Vance Bibliographies, 1983.

Harris, Cyril M. *American Architecture: An Illustrated Encyclopedia.* New York: Norton, 2002.

Heinz, Thomas A. *Frank Lloyd Wright Field Guide.* Evanston, Ill.: Northwestern University Press, 2005.

Hess, Alan. *Frank Lloyd Wright: The Houses.* New York: Rizzoli International, 2005.

———. *Googie Redux: Ultramodern Roadside Architecture.* San Francisco: Chronicle Books, 2004.

Hitchcock, Henry Russell. *The Architecture of H. H. Richardson and His Times.* New York: Museum of Modern Art, 1936.

Hoffmann, Donald. *Frank Lloyd Wright's Fallingwater: The House and Its History.* 2nd ed. New York: Dover, 1993.

Jones, Robert T., ed. *Authentic Small Houses of the Twenties.* New York: Dover Publications, 1987.

Lamprecht, Barbara Mac, and Peter Gossel. *Richard Neutra.* Cologne: Benedikt Taschen, 2006.

Lewis, Arnold. *American Victorian Architecture.* New York: Dover, 1975.

Lewis, Hilary, Stephen Fox, and Richard Payne. *The Architecture of Philip Johnson.* New York: Bulfinch, 2002.

Lewis, Michael J. *American Art and Architecture.* New York: Thames and Hudson, 2006.

Lowe, David. *Art Deco New York.* New York: Watson-Guptill, 2004.

Maass, John. *The Victorian Home in America.* New York: Dover Publications, 2000.

McAlester, Virginia, and Lee McAlester. *A Field Guide to American Houses.* New York: Knopf, 2000.

Morrison, Hugh. *Louis Sullivan: Prophet of Modern Architecture.* New York: Norton, 2001.

Pelkonen, Eeva-Liisa, and Donald Albrecht, eds. *Eero Saarinen: Shaping the Future.* New Haven, Conn.: Yale University Press, 2006.

Reed, Henry Hope, and Anne Day. *The United States Capitol: Its Architecture and Decoration.* New York: Norton, 2005.

Roth, Leland M. *A Concise History of American Architecture.* New York: HarperCollins, 1980.

Samon, Katherine Ann. *Ranch House Style.* New York: Clarkson Potter, 2003.

Scully, Vincent J. *American Architecture and Urbanism.* New York: Henry Holt, 1988.

———. *Frank Lloyd Wright.* New York: George Braziller, 1960.

———. *Modern Architecture.* Rev. ed. New York: George Braziller, 2003.

———. *The Shingle Style and the Stick Style: Architectural Theory and Design from Downing to the Origins of Wright.* New Haven, Conn.: Yale University Press, 1971.

Shoppell, Robert W., et al. *Turn-of-the-Century Houses, Cottages and Villas: Floor Plans and Line Illustrations of 118 Homes from Shoppell's Catalogs.* New York: Dover, 1983.

Smith, Bruce. *Greene and Greene: Masterworks.* San Francisco: Chronicle Books, 1998.

Stanton, Phoebe B. *The Gothic Revival and American Church Architecture: An Episode in Taste, 1840–1856.* Baltimore: Johns Hopkins University Press, 1997.

Stein, Susan. *The Architecture of Richard Morris Hunt.* Chicago: University of Chicago Press, 1986.

Stickley, Gustav. *Craftsman Homes: More Than 40 Plans for Building Classic Arts and Crafts-Style Cottages, Cabins, and Bungalows.* Guilford, Conn.: Lyons Press, 2002.

Stoller, Ezra. *Frank Lloyd Wright's Fallingwater.* New York: Princeton Architectural Press, 2000.

Storrer, William Allin. *The Architecture of Frank Lloyd Wright: A Complete Catalog.* Chicago: University of Chicago Press, 2002.

Stravitz, David. *The Chrysler Building: Creating a New York Icon, Day by Day.* Princeton, N.J.: Princeton Architectural Press, 2002.

Stubblebine, Ray. *Stickley's Craftsman Home.* Layton, Utah: Gibbs Smith, 2006.

Upton, Dell. *Architecture in the United States.* Oxford: Oxford University Press, 1998.

Webb, Michael. *Modernism Reborn: Mid-Century American Houses.* New York: Universe Publishing, 2001.

Wells, Matthew. *Skyscrapers: Structure and Design.* New Haven, Conn.: Yale University Press, 2005.

White, Samuel G. *The Houses of McKim, Mead and White.* New York: Rizzoli International, 1998.

Wilson, Richard Guy, and Noah Sheldon. *The Colonial Revival House.* New York: Abrams, 2004.

Winter, Robert, and Alexander Vertikoff. *Craftsman Style.* New York: Abrams, 2004.

Wiseman, Carter. *The Architecture of I. M. Pei.* New York: Thames and Hudson, 2001.

———. *Louis I. Kahn: Beyond Time and Style; A Life in Architecture.* New York: Norton, 2007.

XII: POST-MODERNISM AND BEYOND

Brown, Denise Scott. "Sexism and the Star System in Architecture." In *Reading Architectural History*, edited by Dana Arnold, 205–10. London: Routledge, 2002.

Canizares, Ana G. *Great New Buildings of the World: Works from Tadao Ando to Zaha Hadid.* New York: Collins Design, 2005.

Coleman, Debra L., Elizabeth Ann Danze, and Carol Jane Henderson. *Architecture and Feminism.* New York: Princeton Architectural Press, 1997.

Colvin, Sir Howard. "Biographical Dictionary." In *Reading Architectural History,* edited by Dana Arnold, 51–70. London: Routledge, 2002.

Fontana, Gordana Giusti. *Zaha Hadid.* New York: Rizzoli International, 2004.

Foster, Norman. *Norman Foster: Works.* London: Prestel, 2007.

Foucault, Michel. "What Is an Author?" In *Reading Architectural History,* edited by Dana Arnold, 71–81. London: Routledge, 2002.

Frampton, Kenneth. *Modern Architecture: A Critical History.* New York: Thames and Hudson, 1992.

Gehry, Frank O. *Gehry Talks: Architecture + Process.* New York: Universe Publishing, 2002.

Ghirardo, Diane. *Architecture after Modernism.* New York: Thames and Hudson, 1996.

Giedion, Siegfried. *Space, Time and Architecture: The Growth of a New Tradition.* 5th ed. Cambridge, Mass.: Harvard University Press, 2003.

Goldberger, Paul. *Up from Ground Zero: Politics, Architecture, and the Rebuilding of New York.* New York: Random House, 2005.

Guggenheim Museum. *Frank Gehry, Architect.* Exhibition catalog. New York: Guggenheim Museum, 2003.

Hays, K. Michael, ed. *Architecture Theory since 1968.* Cambridge, Mass.: MIT Press, 2000.

Jenks, Charles. *The Language of Post-Modern Architecture.* New York: Rizzoli International, 1978.

Jodidio, Philip. *Mario Botta.* Cologne: Benedikt Taschen, 2003.

———. *Renzo Piano.* Cologne: Benedikt Taschen, 2005.

———. *Tadao Ando. Complete Works.* Cologne: Benedikt Taschen, 2006.

Kahn, Louis. *Louis Kahn: Essential Texts.* Edited by Robert C. Twombly. New York: Norton, 2003.

Koolhaas, Rem. *Delirious New York: A Retrospective Manifesto for Manhattan.* Milan: Monacelli, 1997.

Kultermann, Udo. *Contemporary Architecture in the Arab States: Renaissance of a Region.* New York: McGraw-Hill, 1999.

Lefaivre, Liane, and Alexander Tzonis. *Critical Regionalism: Architecture and Identity in a Globalized World.* London: Prestel, 2003.

Libeskind, Daniel, Jeffrey Kipnis, and Anthony Vidier. *Daniel Libeskind: The Space of Encounter.* New York: Universe Publishing, 2001.

McKean, John. *Pioneering British High Tech (Architecture 3s).* London: Phaidon Press, 1999.

Nesbitt, Kate. *Theorizing a New Agenda for Architecture: An Anthology of Architectural Theory, 1965–1995.* New York: Princeton Architectural Press, 1997.

The Phaidon Atlas of Contemporary World Architecture. New York: Phaidon, 2004.

Powell, Douglas R. *Critical Regionalism: Connecting Politics and Culture in the American Landscape.* Chapel Hill: University of North Carolina Press, 2007.

Powell, Kenneth. *Richard Rogers: Architecture of the Future.* Basel: Birkhäuser Basel, 2005.

Rossi, Aldo. *The Architecture of the City.* Cambridge, Mass.: MIT Press, 1984.

Ruby, Andreas, Patrik Schumacher, Zaha Hadid, and Peter Noever. *Zaha Hadid: Architecture.* Ostfildern, Germany: Hatje Cantz Publishers, 2003.

Safdie, Moshe, and Wendy Kohn. *The City after the Automobile: An Architect's Vision.* Boulder, Colo.: Westview Press, 1998.

Slessor, Catherine, and John Linden. *Eco-Tech: Sustainable Architecture and High Technology.* New York: Norton, 2001.

Stephens, Suzanne. *Imaging Ground Zero: The Official and Unofficial Proposals for the World Trade Center Site.* New York: Rizzoli International, 2004.

Stungo, Naomi. *Herzog and de Meuron.* London: Carlton Books, 2002.

Tzonis, Alexander. *Santiago Calatrava.* New York: Rizzoli International, 2004.

Venturi, Robert, and Denise Scott Brown. *Complexity and Contradiction in Architecture.* New York: Museum of Modern Art, 2002.

———. *Learning from Las Vegas: The Forgotten Symbolism of Architectural Form.* Cambridge, Mass.: MIT Press, 1977.

Wines, James. *Green Architecture.* Cologne: Benedikt Taschen, 2000.

Wiseman, Carter. *Louis I. Kahn: Beyond Time and Style; A Life in Architecture.* New York: Norton, 2007.

About the Author

Allison Lee Palmer is an associate professor of art history in the School of Art at the University of Oklahoma. She received her PhD from Rutgers University in New Jersey with a dissertation titled "The Church of Gesù e Maria on the Via del Corso: Urban Planning in Baroque Rome." Her undergraduate degree in art history is from Mount Holyoke College in Massachusetts.

Dr. Palmer currently teaches undergraduate and graduate courses in art from the Renaissance through the 18th century, as well as several interdisciplinary humanities courses for the College of Liberal Studies at the University of Oklahoma. Her teaching awards include the School of Art Excellence in Teaching Award (2008), the College of Fine Arts Peer Recognition Award (2004), the College of Liberal Studies Superior Teaching Award (2002), and the Rufus G. Hall Faculty Award from the College of Liberal Studies (2001).

Dr. Palmer's publications focus on Italian Renaissance and Baroque art and include the following: "The Image of the Risen Christ and the Art of the Roman Baroque Tabernacle," Proceedings of the International Conference "Constructions of Death, Mourning and Memory," October 2006; "The Maternal Madonna in *Quattrocento* Florence: Social Ideals in the Family of the Patriarch," *Source—Notes in the History of Art* 21, no. 3 (Spring 2002): 7–14; "The Walters' *Madonna and Child* Plaquette and Private Devotional Art in Early Renaissance Italy," *Walters Art Journal* 59, June 2001, 73–84; "Carlo Maratti's *Triumph of Clemency* in the Altieri Palace in Rome: Papal Iconography in a Domestic Audience Hall," *Source—Notes in the History of Art* 17, no. 4 (Summer 1998): 18–25; "Bonino da Campione's Monument of Bernabò Visconti and Equestrian Sculpture in the Late Middle Ages," *Arte Lombarda* 121, no. 3 (1997): 57–66; "The First Building Campaign of the

Gesù e Maria on the Via del Corso in Rome: 1615–1636," *Architectura: Zeitschrift für Geschichte der Baukunst* 27, no. 1 (1997): 1–20; and "The Church of Gesù e Maria and Augustinian Construction during the Counter-Reformation," *Augustinian Studies* 28, no. 1 (1997): 111–40.